RELIGION AND POLITICS:
BISHOP VALERIAN TRIFA AND HIS TIMES

by
GERALD J. BOBANGO

EAST EUROPEAN MONOGRAPHS, BOULDER
DISTRIBUTED BY COLUMBIA UNIVERSITY PRESS
NEW YORK

1981

It takes two to speak the truth—
one to speak, and another to hear.

— Thoreau

TABLE OF CONTENTS

LIST OF ILLUSTRATIONS

ACKNOWLEDGMENTS

A book is the product of many minds and hands. My gratitude extends to a multiplicity of persons and institutions, but most of all to the staffs of the Romanian-Americn Heritage Center in Grass Lake, Michigan, the Archbishop's Office of the Romanian Orthodox Episcopate of America, the Horace H. Rackham Graduate Library of the University of Michigan, the Jefferson Annex of the Library of Congress, and the Baron-Forness Library of Edinboro State College.

To Stelian Stanicel, George E. Woods, William W. Swor, John J. Sibişan, Joanna Bock, Paul E. Michelson, Ştefan and Caroline Florescu, Paul A. Shapiro, Stephen Fischer-Galaţi, Preoteasa Eugeniu Uşeriu, Edward R. Kenney, Thomas A. Bobango, Julia Choilak, Rev. John Toconita, and Archbishop Valerian Trifa— your help and input in a hundred ways have determined these pages. For Janet Bobango, always the rock in the turbulent eddies of my wanderings, I am thankful every day. All these are responsible for whatever is good herein; the failings are mine.

Bishop Valerian Trifa in 1960, at the age of 46

INTRODUCTION

In a book entitled *The Never-Ending Wrong*, written in her usual gem-like fashion, Katherine Anne Porter spoke feelingly of the extreme perils faced in the legal handling and public pressures of an accused person, if he happens to have a "dubious place in society, an unpopular nationality, erroneous political beliefs, the wrong religion socially, low social standing, and poverty." In the past three-quarters of a century, millions of Eastern European immigrants came to these shores, for a variety of reasons: to find economic opportunity, freedom to worship as they chose, relief from arbitrary governments. More than one hundred thousand of these people were Romanians. They knew relatively little about America before their arrival, but in a short time one of the most impressive theories spelled out in dimly-lit citizenship classes in the shadows of factory buildings was that which taught of the American philosophy that a man is innocent until proven guilty, that justice for all must be equal under the law, that this is a government based not on the political environment of the moment but on law, and finally that evidence alone—not the inferences to be drawn from unending multiplicities of phylogenistic setpieces which plant, nurture, and harvest opinion—determines proof. Yes, the immigrants learned, this is what we came to America to enjoy. This is the story of one man who did not find it.

For thirty years the Trifa case has gone on, and the end is not yet in sight. It is an instructive story in many ways, encompassing as it does in microcosm the entire span of interwar Romanian history, and of the American ideological and ethnic-political experience since the Second World War. Popular images and stereotypes surrounding Trifa and the Romanian Legionary Movement remain today essentially as they were laid down in the days of the McCarthy era. Herein is an attempt, through what is perhaps the first critical exposition of the entire context and milieu of the celebrated case of Valerian Trifa, to place the life and times of Bishop Trifa in their proper historic perspective.

GJB
Boston College
January, 1981

[ix]

CHAPTER I
A POSTWAR PASSION PLAY

"I am the Bishop of the Roumanian Orthodox Episcopate of North and South America."

"Is there only one Bishop for North and South America?"

"Only one."

"You are Father Moldovan; is that correct?"

"Call me how you want, but I am Bishop."

"Well, when were you nominated, then, for bishop?"

"I was nominated in May sometime—April or May."

"By whom?"

"By a group of the clergy and laymen."

"Who was it? Was it the episcopate council?"

"It was a group of the priests who want to have a bishop."

"A group of priests who want to have a bishop?"

"And laymen who want to have a bishop."

"It wasn't any official organ of the Romanian Orthodox Missionary Episcopate of America that nominated you as the authority?"

"This is the answer: what is over there."

"It was no authorized church body; it was no part of the Romanian Orthodox Missionary Episcopate of America that nominated you for the office of bishop, was it?"

"No. But I mean—"

"Now, you say that election by some priests in this country but not an authorized body by the Romanian Orthodox Missionary Episcopate of America, elected you to succeed, or elected you to the vacant seat of bishop; is that right?"

"Yes."

"When did they elect you?"

"I think May 17th or 15th—I can't remember very well that date."

"Who were the priests?"

"I am not sure who they are."

"All right, then, who are they, if you know?"

"It is so many I can't remember."[1]

Nearly six thousand miles to the east, far from this scene in the crowded United States District Courtroom in Cleveland, the official bulletin of the Patriarchate of the Romanian Orthodox Church in Bucharest, capital of the newly formed "Romanian People's Republic," explained the situation this way:

> In the waters made turbulent by all kinds of passions, intrigues and personal interest, the capitalistic exploiters and the new warmongers have started to fish. They have tried to catch the Romanians of America in the nets of their nefarious propaganda and make use of them against the regime of popular democracy ruling presently in the Romanian People's Republic. They wish to make these sons of our nation mercenaries employed in the service of their imperialistic interests and maneuver them to act against the legitimate interests of the Romanian nation.
>
> But Patriarch Justinian, gifted with a brilliant intuition and the power of penetration so characteristic of him, . . . immediately saw the disastrous reality. . . threatening the religious unity and harmonious life of these far-away brothers of ours. And the solution was found by our Romanian brothers across the ocean themselves. On February 2, 1950, the Orthodox priests of America, together with the lay delegates of the parishes, resolved to renew their connections with the Romanian Orthodox Church of the Romanian People's Republic. The Church Congress, held on May 17, 1950, at Detroit, Michigan, elected the widowed archpriest Andrei Moldovan, of Akron, Ohio, to fill the vacant chair of bishop for the Autonomous Episcopate of the Orthodox Romanians of America. [2]

Yet, "the simple truth is that no Church Congress of the Romanian Orthodox Episcopate of America met on May 17, 1950 either in Detroit, Michigan or in any other place." [3]

Nineteen-fifty was an interesting year.

The post-World War II conquest of the nations of Central and Eastern Europe by Soviet-dominated Communist regimes produced often cataclysmic struggles in the United States and Canada as American churches founded by immigrants from these nations sought to break their ties with mother churches which they now saw as radically changed. For the approximately 100,000 members of a Romanian-American ethnic group spread over the North American continent and representing a variety of people ranging from Romanian-speaking original immigrants to their English-speaking second and third generation descendants, the attempt by the postwar Romanian government to impose a bishop of its choice on their American church organization was the most traumatic and divisive experience in the half-century of existence of the ancestral church which the immigrants had adapted to American conditions.

Romanian immigrants by the tens of thousands made the hard journey to the United States and Canada at the turn of the twentieth century, seeking economic, social, political—and religious—freedom in a new land, along with millions of other East European peasant folk. They came mainly from the Romanian-inhabited provinces of Banat, Transylvania, and Bukovina, territories then under the rule of the Austro-Hungarian Empire. Many of these travelers had no intention of staying in America, but wished only to earn enough money to return home and improve their status. At first they gave little thought to organizing permanent institutions such as churches.

As time went on, however, as with all Eastern European immigrants, circumstances convinced many to remain permanently.[4] The birth of children, the purchase of property or businesses, the outbreak of the First World War—all made it more difficult to leave family and friends as each year went by. Romanian colonies developed a thriving life of their own in America's industrial cities and on the prairies of western Canada. Gradually the processes of accommodation and assimilation produced a degree of Americanization, so that by the third decade of settlement a definite new type—the Romanian-American—was born.

In the meantime people felt the definite need for transplanting the strong religious life they had known back home. They did not have their own churches, so they attended other Orthodox services in Greek, Serbian, or Russian churches. The language barrier made this not very satisfactory, and the only thing left to do was to organize their own churches. Although the first Romanian Orthodox Church in North America was St. Nicholas in Regina, Saskatchewan, in 1902, it was St. Mary's in Cleveland, Ohio, which first established a regularized parish life by petitioning the chief Orthodox authority in Transylvania—the Metropolitan in Sibiu—to send them a priest. With the arrival of the pioneer missionary priest Moise Balea in 1905, other parish groups followed the example of Cleveland, several other priests arrived, and by 1912 there were enough Romanian churches that Sibiu organized them into a Deanery, a diocesan administrative unit, with Father Ioan Podea as head.

It is important to understand the character of these early churches. First, the initiative for their founding came from the immigrant people themselves. They were not set up as the result of missionary work by the Orthodox church in Romania. The immigrants in fact came from different church jurisdictions at home and so at first the American churches were under the Metropolitans of various cities such as Sibiu in Transylvania, Cernăuţi in Bukovina, or Iaşi in Moldavia. This situation meant, secondly, that attempts to establish a centralized and unitary American Diocese would be delayed by conflicts over precisely what church jurisdiction in Romania was to control the immigrant churches, a situation complicated by the fact that immigrants themselves, coming from different regions, brought provincial and regional rivalries with them to the new world, which often gave rise to intense factionalism and divisiveness within the newly-established parishes. An additional problem retarding the development of Orthodoxy in America was the constant lack of sufficient priests, and the recourse pursued by many parishes of having one of their own lay members ordained by a Russian bishop in New York led to a good deal of friction between priests sent from Romania, with proper theological training, and these "New York priests."

To bring about some order and make their parishes correctly canonical, a number of priests and laymen met in Youngstown, Ohio, in February, 1918, and requested that they be permitted to form an American Diocese under the Metropolitan of Bucharest. The complications of the First World War prevented this from materializing, and subsequent clergy conferences during the 1920s continued to try for the creation of an Episcopate.

This movement climaxed in Detroit, on April 25-28, 1929, when the first general Orthodox Church Congress of Romanian-American parishes was held. Delegates from twenty-two parishes proclaimed their desire for an autonomous Episcopate, under the canonical jurisdiction of the Patriarchate of Romania in Bucharest. The Holy Synod of the Romanian Orthodox Church was asked to approve the new diocese and send a duly consecrated bishop to head the Episcopate in the process of organizing. Already something unique was in the process of formation—the Romanian Church had no experience with missionary dioceses overseas or, indeed, outside the country. The Americans were seeking to create a self-governing diocese, tied to Bucharest only spiritually and canonically, although the men in Detroit were willing to trust the judgment of the Romanian Holy Synod in choosing their first bishop.[5] Church politics in Romania, and the world financial depression, however, meant that four years passed before final approval for the American Diocese arrived from the Holy Synod, and six years before a bishop was appointed for America, in 1935. In the meantime the Americans held another

Church Congress in Cleveland in 1932 and drew up the original Statutes for their Episcopate. These called for autonomy, the right to elect their own bishop, and canonical submission to the Romanian Patriarchate: thus the unique status envisioned in Detroit was reinforced. Although the first bishop of this Romanian Orthodox Missionary Episcopate of North and South America,[6] Policarp Moruşca, was in fact elected by the Holy Synod in Romania, the central administrative body of the American Diocese, the Episcopate Council in Cleveland led by Father John Trutza, had specifically requested Moruşca as its choice.

The bishop arrived in the United States in 1935 and on July 4 was installed at the head of his diocese amidst splendid festivities at St. George's Cathedral in Detroit. Religious life in America among Romanian Orthodox people now began to assume a more regularized pattern, as the bishop sought to create order among the many very independently-minded churches and priests. The division between the Romanian and the American-ordained clergy was settled after a fashion, churches were consecrated or re-dedicated by the bishop, and in Grass Lake, Michigan, the Episcopate bought a beautiful 200-acre estate which would become the *Vatra Românească* (the Romanian Hearth), the eventual administrative and spiritual home of American Orthodox Romanians.

Policarp, however, had been told to tie the Americans closer to the Mother Church in Romania, and here the die was cast for the turmoil to come. At the 1936 Church Congress in Youngstown the bishop presented the delegates with a revised set of Statutes which he himself had amended, and insisted on their acceptance. The major change from the 1932 By-Laws was control over appointment of the bishop for America, which was now vested in the Holy Synod in Romania. Here was the basis on which, eleven years later, Bucharest sought to impose another bishop of its choice on the American churches.

Policarp also began the weekly newspaper, *Solia* (The Herald) which first appeared in February, 1936, and the first *Solia Calendar* also came out that year under his direction. Both continue to be published today. He laid the foundation of a youth organization, and the basis for what would become a national organization of Romanian Orthodox Women. On the other hand, the bishop also upset a number of people by his militant philosophy toward other religious denominations and what many considered his overly authoritarian manner of administration. He carried on running arguments in the pages of the Romanian newspaper *America* with the leadership of the Union and League of Romanian Societies, the largest Romanian-American fraternal organization, and with Father Podea. Many priests resented him as a threat to their own local control and freedom to run their parishes as they pleased. Others disliked what they saw as Policarp's preoccupation with the Vatra and his constant requests for funds to pay its debts. When Policarp left for Romania in the summer of 1939 to attend the fall session of the Holy Synod and lobby for an increase in the Romanian government's subsidy to the Episcopate in America, there were many who were not sorry to see him leave. Indeed, he himself may have been ready to resign from the onerous burdens of trying to govern unruly Americans—people who did not render bishops and church hierarchs the homage which they enjoyed in the old country. Policarp left Father Simion Mihalţian, senior member of his Episcopate Council, as his deputy in charge of the Diocese during his absence.

The bishop's "short visit" turned into years. One month after Moruşca's arrival in Europe, Hitler's forces smashed into Poland and World War II began. Caught up in events, denounced by his opponents in America, unable to travel, by the time his situation was clarified it was too late and the new post-1945 regime in Romania soon forced him into retirement. Policarp never returned to America.[7] Here, then, began the long tragicomedy which ultimately broke the fledgling Episcopate in two, producing during the ensuing decade an internal division rooted in personality conflicts among the clergy, the alignment of American factions with Romanian political groupings, and, ultimately, an irreparable schism climaxing in 1950. For eleven years the Episcopate had no bishop, and all efforts to get Policarp released from Romania were in vain. From 1939 to 1947 the affairs of the Episcopate remained basically in the hands of Mihalţian and it was not a time of progress: with the exception of the continued juridical existence of the Diocese, and the paying off of the Vatra, the organization seriously degenerated as a central institution, wracked by political scandal, chicanery in high places, and deterioration of what unity among the parishes had existed.

Opposing Mihalţian and his Council, which included the Akron priest Andrei Moldovan as Secretary, was a group of parishes, including clergy and laymen largely in Ohio, led by Father John Trutza (1895-1954). Trutza had been instrumental in founding the Episcopate and guiding it through its early years. Accusing the Episcopate Council of bad management, the Cleveland priest and his supporters held a famous "Hallowe'en Congress" in 1943 by way of protest against Mihalṭian's policies. Labeling this assembly "illegal," the Episcopate Council suspended the insurgent priests and forbade them to attend Church Congresses for a number of years. Thus the name-calling continued as the Council and the Ohio Group arrived at a stand-off while events in Europe, of which they knew little, shaped the future of their American religious establishment.

The end of the Second World War brought the glorious "liberating" Soviet Army to Eastern Europe. On March 6, 1945, the National Democratic Front government of Dr. Petru Groza was formed in Bucharest. Eleven months later, on February 5, 1946, the United States recognized Groza's regime and re-established diplomatic relations with Romania.[8] After a seven-year absence, a royal Romanian legation returned to Washington, headed by the professor of sociology and Liberal Party veteran Mihail Ralea.[9] In the months which followed, the new communist government of Romania promulgated a series of laws giving the regime full control over the churches of the country. Persecution ranged from subtle legal maneuvers to outright imprisonment of recalcitrant priests. One major method used was to place older bishops into forced retirement, "electing" new ones more compliant with the goals of the state. Policarp was one of the first victims of the new order.[10]

In the meantime, the Episcopate Council began moving during the final weeks of 1946 towards finding a replacement for their bishop. One plan was to seek a man, to be named by the Patriarch in Bucharest, as a temporary one-year *locum tenens* bishop, to unite the organization and prepare for the transition to a new spiritual head. Specifically requested for this task was Trandafir Scorobetz, who had been a missionary priest in America forty years earlier, had presided over the 1929 Detroit Congress which established the Episcopate, and was now Bishop-Referent for the Archdiocese of Sibiu.[11] Scorobetz alone, who knew the scene in America, could produce order, most agreed. Cables were thus sent to Patriarch Nicodim Munteanu, to Metropolitan Balan in Sibiu, and to Mihail Ralea, with this message. If Scorobetz were not available, no one should be sent, the Council concluded.[12]

On February 17, 1947, the answer from the Romanian Legation showed how well Bucharest acted on the Americans' suggestion:

> We have the honor to inform you that upon the recommendation of His Grace Nicodim, the Patriarch of Romania, the Ministry of Cults has approved the appointment of Dr. Antim Nica as Bishop of the Orthodox Church of America. Please take

measures for the reception of His Grace, whose arrival will be
announced at the proper time.

> Please accept, Mr. President, the assurances of high regard.
> (signed) Pamfil Riposanu, Councilor of the Legation.[13]

Four days later in the Green Room of the Hotel Leland in Detroit,
Father Mihalţian called to order a special session of the Episcopate
Council, hurriedly convened, and welcomed two special guests—Father
John Trutza and Father John Stanila, leaders of the insurgent Ohio
priests. "Do we accept this Nica, the choice of the Legation?" a
member asked. No one answered.[14] It was adviser Nicholas Martin
who said what many were thinking: that the Council must suspend
the 1935 Statutes of the Episcopate and name a commission to revise
them, which was done. An emergency Church Congress was called
for March 28 in Detroit. Finally the gauntlet was cast down, with a
telegram composed to the Romanian Patriarch and dispatched on
February 24:

> The Council of the Episcopate, meeting in special session...
> about the coming of Bishop Antim Nica, categorically remon-
> strates against the sending of any bishop or priest unsolicited
> by us. Our decision is based upon the rights provided in the
> Statute of our Episcopate and in the consciousness of our duty
> toward the vital interests of our Church in America, and in our
> rights as American citizens. We beg you not to disregard our
> grievance, so that disastrous results and irreparable conse-
> quences will be avoided.[15]

With the sending of this cable, the Episcopate Council took the
first in a series of momentous steps to follow in the coming weeks
and months, embarked on a path leading to a complete declaration
of autonomy from the Mother Church in Romania. At the same moment, although outward signs suggested that the divisive breach which
had troubled the Episcopate for some years was on its way to healing,
in reality certain members of this selfsame Council saw the break with
Romania as a long-awaited chance to name a bishop of their own
choosing, regardless of the existence of Policarp. With the sending of
this cable, the thoughts of such men as Mihalţian, Andrei Moldovan,
Ştefan Opreanu, and the ubiquitous *eminence grise* of the Council,
Glicherie Morariu, began to turn once again in the direction of creating a bishop from their own ranks, thus not only bypassing Policarp
but solidifying for good their own dominance as the governors of the
Episcopate over Trutza and his Ohio reformers.[16] Behind the facade
of wishing for the return of Policarp and resisting Romanian communist domination over the Episcopate, this Council clique three

years later would name Andrei Moldovan as their candidate for bishop in America, urge him upon the leaderless diocese as the legitimate successor to Policarp, and then obtain Moldovan's sanction and ordination by that very Romanian government itself, in 1950. The Great Schism of the Romanian-American Church reached its inevitable climax, the creature of post-war territorial conquest and internal wrangling. The "disastrous results and irreparable consequences" would not down. And thus, too, with the sending of this cable, the strange and dramatic case of Valerian Trifa began.

CHAPTER II

THE 4M COMPANY

In the semi-organized mêlée called Romanian church history in America, somebody was always founding some kind of "new" or "independent" Episcopate which blossomed for a season and then withered on the vine. At the annual meeting of the Episcopate Council on the eve of the July, 1950 Church Congress in Philadelphia, the chartering of a new Episcopate, called "The Romanian Orthodox Autonomous Episcopate of North and South America," was noted.[1] Father John Trutza, who by now was back in control of the Episcopate Council, having emerged victorious over the Mihalţian faction in a stunning *coup* at the 1947 Congress, observed that the Articles of Association of this new "Episcopate" were dated June 5, 1950, with an address at 1799 E. State Fair, Detroit. They were signed by Father Glicherie Morariu, Nicholas N. Martin, Father Petru Moga, Paul Slobadean, and a number of other disgruntled priests and laymen, all of whom for one reason or another were inimical to Trutza's leadership.[2]

At the moment not much attention was paid to this by the Council, for since 1947 the former Council clique had tried to make a number of their supporters bishop, including Teofil Ionescu and, most recently, Father Ştefan Opreanu. The new Episcopate could have been seen merely as part of the whole affair concerning Opreanu, which was about to be settled when the Congress convened.

More puzzling was Patriarch Justinian's reference to the renewal of relations between the Episcopate and the Mother Church in Romania on February 2, for which we have no documents, but which, presumably, was another outgrowth of a whole series of meetings of Glicherie's entourage in the early months of 1950.[3] Because the situation of a bishop was intense, the Trutza Council had sent out declarations of loyalty and subjection to the jurisdiction of the Episcopate before the convening of the Congress, which the parishes had signed and returned, but other than this, scant attention was paid at the moment to the new independent diocese in the Detroit area.

More important was the resolution of the bishop issue. The Congress declared unanimously that it considered Policarp its titular head and ordered an all-out effort to obtain his return. If this were not accomplished in the course of one year, the next Congress would elect a Vicar to Policarp.[4] Most of the delegates went home from Philadelphia satisfied that the air had been cleared, the tension over the Opreanu attentat dissipated, the intransigents mollified. Before two weeks passed, Trutza got a telegram in Cleveland, from Patriarch Justinian Marina.

The Holy Synod has approved the Autonomy of the Episcopate of the Romanians of North and South America. Stop. It has approved the election of Father Archpriest Andrei Moldovan to the vacant chair of Bishop he having to present himself as soon as possible in Bucharest to be ordained into the Hierarchy. Stop. We call on all priests to unite around the new bishop, ceasing any separatism.[5]

Here was Bucharest's answer to the 1947 Declaration of Autonomy and the refusal to accept a government-imposed candidate as bishop for America. If the Patriarchate could not name a man of its own choice, the next best thing was to approve one engineered by the faction in the United States most willing to play Romania's game, i.e., the Mihalţian Council group which Trutza had ousted.

Trutza did not know that on March 17, at Morariu's house in Detroit, Glicherie, Opreanu, Moga, Martin (and three or four others possibly, we don't know) had decided to incorporate a new Episcopate and make Andrei Moldovan its bishop. This was the climax, not the beginning, of negotiations with the Romanian Church which had gone on for some time, and plans by this group to name a man of their own no doubt intensified when the Opreanu bid fell through. This meeting of six or eight people, at least one of whom did not even belong to the Episcopate founded in 1929, was the "Church Congress" which elected the Akron priest Moldovan.[6] It is hard to imagine that Moldovan himself did not know of this meeting by the time the regular Church Congress met in Philadelphia in July, which was more than three months after his "election." Yet he attended the Philadelphia Congress anyway, saw that his parish returned the loyalty declaration to the Episcopate, voted for the return of Policarp, and said nothing.[7]

Trutza now demanded that Moldovan disclaim his "election." Instead, telling his parishioners he must have a leave of absence for a health cure in Arkansas, Moldovan flew secretly to Bucharest and was consecrated as Bishop for America in the Cathedral of Sibiu, then given his official *Gramata* (title of office) at the Patriarchate in Bucharest, under the eyes of the state Minister of Cults. A letter from Policarp, "retired for reasons of health," thanked Moldovan for all of his help over the years and called on Romanians in America to rally around Bishop Andrei as Policarp's successor, and their "only canonical bishop."[8] In the meantime Moldovan's parish council members back in Akron, Ohio, were receiving postcards from Hot Springs, Arkansas, signed by their priest and reporting on how his health was improving.[9]

Meantime, the Office of the Holy Synod in Bucharest prepared Moldovan's takeover of the Episcopate in America. On November 11, 1950, the Patriarch informed Father Mihalţian that Fathers Trutza and Stanila (the president and secretary of the legitimate Episcopate Council) were suspended from their functions as priests until they turned over the Episcopate archives, along with "all mobile and immobile assets" to Moldovan.[10] Should they refuse, they were to be defrocked.[11] To his credit, Mihalţian refused to cooperate, and in an emergency session in Cleveland the Episcopate Council took concerted measures to fight such dictation by the Romanian Church and government. The archives were transferred from the Vatra at Grass Lake, Michigan, to Cleveland, along with the bank accounts of the diocese. Another resolution came forth: we refuse to recognize any bishop not elected by our Church Congress.[12] The battle-lines were drawn. On November 21 Bishop Andrei was back in America. And in the midst of this turmoil Church World Service Displaced Person No. 84, Viorel Trifa, arrived in the United States from Italy, ignorant of the maelstrom he was about to enter.

Decriers and Dissimulators

Andrei Moldovan was a simple man, and many there are who claim that if he had used different tactics upon his return to America, had remained calm and not tried to force himself upon the Episcopate, he might have succeeded, in time, in being accepted—even given the duplicity surrounding his ordination in Romania. Yet this is unlikely because, first, it was the Romanian Patriarchate which was really running things, and which dictated taking the Trutza Episcopate to court,[13] and secondly, Moldovan did not have the force of personality not to take the advice of such counsellors as Nicholas N. Martin, who was primarily responsible for the vicious smear campaign against Trutza and his fellows which followed. That this, too, had Bucharest's tacit approval was evident enough, in that the Romanian Church never made any notable efforts to temper or stop their protégés from villifying Trutza and his bishop-elect.

Thus the drama moved from the pulpits to the courtroom. On December 19, 1950, Moldovan's attorneys filed a complaint against Trutza and the Episcopate leadership in the United States District Court for Northern Ohio, Eastern Division, while Moldovan took symbolic possession of the Vatra in the presence of the tearful and frightened wife of the caretaker while Father Moga and the bishop's learned jurisconsul, Martin, looked on.[14] The hearing for a preliminary injunction was dismissed, and leave to file an amended complaint was granted the plaintiffs.[15] As the claims and counter-claims went on in the months which ensued, one thing was clear. The Trutza Episcopate chose to argue its case primarily on legal grounds, while Moldovan believed that emotion, personal attack on his enemies, and the majesty of the Romanian Church should prevail.

It is important to understand Moldovan's mentality in light of what the next few years would bring. Moldovan was a follower. Whatever his personal thoughts, none of his writings left to us show anything but complete confidence that Father Morariu, Nick Martin, and company were the salt of the earth, zealously working for the interests of the Lord. And Moldovan had that peculiar philosophical quality shared by many another Romanian priest of being able to separate his spiritualism from his politics. Christian charity and brotherly love had their place, but they might validly be suspended when it came to opposing one's detractors, and it apparently did not bother him to label his opponents every kind of villain and refuse of the earth. Calvinistically, to Moldovan opponents were not just wrong, they were evil, opposing the Lord's will, thus any tactics short of mayhem were justifiable against them.

Moreover, the pageantry, attention, and flattery he received in Romania could not help but turn his head, considering that he had spent much of his life as a relatively simple parish priest in Ohio. He was now a Bishop, at the hands of the highest hierarchs of his mother church. Something of the manner in which he conceived those who had given him this honor is revealed by his response to an attorney who asked him if Justinian were the head man of the entire Mother Church. Moldovan showed his perception of things, if not his knowledge of church organization, when he said the Patriarch was "Head man of the entire church of the whole world."[16]

This same sense of awe colored Moldovan's relationship with two of his principal collaborators and "advisers" in this mock-tragedy.

Due to the reputations which the latter projected, rather than to real accomplishment, one cannot escape the feeling that the bishop was manipulated by men whose primary concern in this whole affair was hardly justice and canonical rectitude. And in Father Glicherie (George) Morariu and "jurisconsul" Nick Martin, Bishop Andrei had two of the finest manipulators who ever sold moss from the tomb of Christ.

Glicherie Morariu (1899-1973) would have made a fortune as a private businessman, but even as an Orthodox monk he did not do so badly. Had he been in America in an earlier day, he might have been a door-to-door seller of genuine evil-eye spells against one's enemies in immigrant neighborhoods, or peddled nails from the true cross. Instead he ran a steak house and engaged in various money-making and women-chasing enterprises.[17] No one really knows how many times he was married—estimates always begin at three and range as high as five.[18] Even before he came to America late in 1928, his reputation in Romania was dubious. For some years the Metropolitan of Iasi refused to issue a canonical *gramata* (clerical license) for him, due to unanswered charges being investigated by the Central Church Council, lodged against Morariu by the Bloch Brothers firm in Bucharest. When the spiritual consistory queried Father Trutza, then in charge of the Episcopate Council, on the advisibility of sending Glicherie to America, Trutza's answer was in the negative.

Apparently Morariu was defrocked by Policarp shortly before the Bishop left the United States in 1939, and it is clear that Morariu was one of the main forces behind the effort to prevent Policarp's return from Romania. We know of at least one secret meeting on October 27, 1942, at the Palmer House Hotel in Chicago where the idea of making Morariu the bishop of an "independent" Episcopate was discussed. Although the scheme fell through as the increasingly vocal condemnation of Morariu by Trutza and his insurgents during the early 1940s began to tell, somehow Glicherie kept cropping up and acquiring titles and offices. Had he not existed in the ranks of the Episcopate, it would have been necessary to create him.

Indubitably Morariu was a charismatic personality who knew well how to ingratiate himself with individuals by flattering them and impressing them with his many contacts and Cadillacs. This was a factor which worked well with Father Mihaltian and with Andrei Moldovan, both of whom found themselves beyond their depth in the complicated Episcopate politics of a decade in which Romanian-Americans became highly politicized over the dramatic events occurring in Eastern Europe. More importantly, Father Morariu knew how to collect money when the Episcopate was in dire need of it, and he allowed everyone to think that his efforts singlehandedly brought about the paying off of the sizeable mortgage on the Vatra. These factors, and especially his close association with Father Stefan Opreanu, gave him access to the Council and account for his swift rise in the Episcopate. Opreanu dreamed of becoming a bishop, and the support of the ubiquitous Morariu seemed a likely means of attaining such a goal. By 1943 Glicherie, despite his estrangement with Policarp, was on the Episcopate Council, which was grateful for the tidy gift of $1.000 given to the Vatra fund by exiled King Carol II, then in Mexico, Morariu's leadership of a "Free Romania Committee," which he and Opreanu had organized as early as 1941 to oppose Axis domination of Romania, was deemed the reason for the ex-King's beneficence. What the Council did not know was that Morariu was carrying on correspondence with Carol in Coioacan and receiving goodly sums of money to publish pro-Carlist newspapers in Detroit and elsewhere: the ultimate goal, of course, was to restore Carol to his throne and at the same time somehow obtain possession of frozen Romanian assets in the United States.[19]

The climax of the "Free Romania" movement came on November 18, 1942, when Morariu and Opreanu were arrested as non-registered foreign agents by the Enemy Alien Board, and indicted under the Espionage Acts.[20] Yet even though released on bail, the priests continued to function on the Episcopate Council and to manage *Solia*. In January, 1945, Morariu was sentenced to five years in prison, although with the end of the war shortly afterwards, he served only a few months. In the meantime the Episcopate Council voted an oil portrait of him to be hung at the Vatra, for his successful fund-raising campaign to pay off the mortgage on the headquarters, and the man who had been defrocked by his bishop had also become "Ecclesiastical Prosecutor" for the Episcopate, no doubt to safeguard the standards of priestly conduct.

It was this kind of situation which Trutza and his Ohio group in the Episcopate opposed, and thus sought to oust him from the leadership. And it was Morariu (and those who seldom questioned his conduct) who was a prime mover behind the candidacy of Moldovan for bishop and the campaign to discredit Trutza and his followers in the Episcopate—for Trutza was the principal threat to Glicherie's power. It followed naturally that Valerian Trifa, as Trutza's personal choice for bishop, would share equally the benefits of Morariu's opposition.

Then there was Nicholas Neamţu-Martin, who grandly appeared out of nowhere at a Council meeting in January, 1943, as the "inspector-general of the Federal government."[21] It is hard to imagine what Martin told the group of his position to merit such an awesome title, but Secretary Moldovan dutifully labeled him as such in the Minutes. It is harder still to imagine what such an important individual was doing spending his time waiting on the leaders of a small and minor ethnic church, but there he was, glasses, cherubic smile and all.

He properly impressed everyone. He was named "Jurisconsul" to the Episcopate Council, whatever that meant. Martin seemed a godsend at this time of legal troubles and political turmoil. Had he not attended Columbia University, did he not know all about law and have important contacts in Washington? In fact, Martin had not even finished the 6th grade in Sibiu, and the closest he got to Columbia University was when he worked as a waiter in a New York restaurant.[22]

Martin was a type of opportunistic layman found in many ethnic communities, whose ability to project a self-designated importance matched Glicherie's fund-raising expertise. He was the living proof of the fact that a little education is a dangerous thing. Having insinuated himself into Mihalţian's Council, he acquired authority rapidly during a time of confusion by his ability to appear on intimate terms with the American power structure in the eyes of the Council, and, conversely, to dramatize his role as the representative of a significant ethnic interest group in the eyes of the non-ethnic establishment. Martin strongly reminded many oldtimers of the comparison often made between William Jennings Bryan and the Platte River of his native Nebraska.[23]

Solia had become a rather vituperative and highly contentious paper during the early 1940s, as the Council used it to assault Trutza and his Ohio group. It became even more vindictive when Martin was made, first editor, then administrator by the summer of 1945.[24] Much praise was heaped on the "Jurisconsul" for obtaining the release of Fathers Morariu and Opreanu from prison that summer. Modestly, Martin said little in the Council meeting celebrating this event, although he might have mentioned that President Truman's amnesty for those imprisoned on wartime charges had something to do with it. It was sufficient for *Solia* to describe how Martin had singlehandedly won the Second World War.[25] It is also clear that it was Martin who did much of the behind-the-scenes work in denouncing Policarp to the United States authorities and asking that the bishop be prevented from returning to America.[26] Considering that he constantly boasted of his friendship with both United States Senators from Michigan, Homer Ferguson and Arthur Vandenberg, and his connections in Washington, it is not unlikely that Martin was at least partially behind the charges of fascism levied against Policarp even from the first days of his return to Romania in 1939. It would be most revealing to document Martin's connections with Nicolae Balindu and the leftist leadership of the Union and League during these years.[27] At any rate, long before 1951, Martin had acquired large experience in labeling his opponents fascists.

Nineteen forty-six was a busy year for Martin as well, for he went off to the Paris Peace Conference as the representative for *Solia*, getting the Council's permission to do so.[28] Having a newspaper with fewer than 1,000 paid subscribers behind him, he obtained a passport from the State Department and undoubtedly took Paris by storm, calling himself the spokesman of the Romanian-American community, which meant he talked in the name of some 100,000 souls.[29] Faster than one could say Neamţu, Martin was in touch with the numerous Romanian war and political refugees thronging the French capital, and overnight he was Director of an organization called "*La Roumanie Indépendante*," and Vice-President of its National Council. The awe which such titles inspired upon his return to Detroit can only be imagined. In the midst of such world-moving, Martin neglected to register as a foreign agent, but must have managed to talk himself out of trouble.[30]

It was at the 1948 Church Congress, by which time Trutza's reform coalition once again controled the Episcopate Council, that Martin was rebuked. The jurisconsul arrived as a delegate from St. George Cathedral and was challenged by a new, no-nonsense credentials committee for "his inimical attitude and activities against the interests of the Episcopate." He was permitted to speak, but rather than defending himself read a typewritten "declaration" in a loud voice critical of the new leadership. The Congress sustained the committee's refusal to seat him by an absolute majority. Voting contrary was only Father Opreanu.[31] The Congress went on to purge other members of the pre-1947 crew, and reaffirmed the complete ecclesiastical-administrative autonomy of the American Episcopate. As for Martin, another effort to restore him as a delegate was made at the 1949 Congress, and again rejected by a vote of 31 to 13.[32] At that same gathering, Morariu, who had seceded from the jurisdiction of the Episcopate in 1947, asked to be re-admitted. The Council ignored the request when it heard that Glicherie was about to be married again.[33]

It was at this point that the ousted disgruntleds from the old cabal turned their hands toward making Opreanu a bishop. In this they had the cooperation of another anti-Trutza priest, Father Petru Moga.

A zealous and militant man, Moga had a checkered career. Early in the 1940s he was listed among the reform-minded insurgents of the Hallowe'en Congress, but two years after this event his ambition got the best of him. When Morariu was sent to prison, Moga at once left his parish in St. Paul and hastened to Dearborn, where he got himself elected pastor at Glicherie's prosperous former church, Sts. Peter and Paul. In the history of the Episcopate such precipitate moves by priests striving to improve their economic lot were not uncommon, and efforts to stop the practice had been many. For such unseemly conduct, the Council in 1945 suspended Moga and named its own commission to fill Morariu's position, although one wonders if the Mihalţian group were concerned more with preserving good order or protecting the sinecure of the mendacious monk in his absence.[34] Further consternation arose when the Spiritual Consistory met on Moga's case in February, 1946, and found that in addition to his action in moving to Dearborn, Moga had originally come to the United States with falsified priestly credentials: he'd used his brother's theological certificates.[35]

This was the beginning of Moga's disaffection with the Episcopate. In the next few years, though he worked to redeem himself with both factions (he passed a theological examination in Detroit "with an excellent performance," but, curiously, at the *Protestant* Faculty of Theology) he became one of the chief engineers of the plan to make Opreanu bishop. Moga attended a number of meetings with Andrei Moldovan, Morariu, and others in the spring of 1950 which produced the Opreanu candidacy, and went so far as to arrange Opreanu's consecration at the hands of the Romanian Metropolitan in exile, Visarion Puiu in Paris.[36] When Opreanu's bid for power was foiled by the Trutza-led Council, Moga began a very vocal campaign of calling the Episcopate uncanonical and illegal, since it lacked a bishop. Then Moga began to purge members of his own Dearborn parish who failed to support his plans.[37] Henceforth the accusation of "uncanonical" was to be a favorite leitmotif of the anti-Trutza company.

Although Opreanu availed himself of the chance to make amends with the Episcopate by renouncing his intentions at the Philadelphia Congress that summer, for Moga this was the breaking point. The priest submitted his church to the jurisdiction of Metropolitan Puiu in France, and when the Council demanded he explain himself, he did not answer. Nor would Moga sign the declaration of loyalty requested when the news of Moldovan's designs was made known. Thus he and his parish were excluded from the 1950 Congress.[38] Thus Moga's signature next appears on the Articles of Association of Martin and Morariu's "Autonomous" East State Fair Episcopate, on June 5, 1950,[39] and Moga was present at the unannounced "Congress" which met at Glicherie's house to choose Moldovan the previous March 17.[40] Indeed, the Dearborn pastor was to become one of Bishop Andrei's closest associates in the months ahead. He was with Moldovan and Martin when they "took possession" of the Vatra,[41] by then bearing the aurous title of "Secretary-Sachelar" of Andrei's Episcopate.[42]

Here, then, were the four who formed the core of the Bucharest-approved Episcopate—Moldovan, Martin, Morariu, and Moga—and who set out to vanquish the Diocese led by Trutza and whoever be--came bishop of that Diocese. Suddenly they displayed enormous concern for canonical rectitude, harping continuously on the hierarchical illegality of those who refused to accept Bishop Andrei—as though canonical correctness were something that Morariu and Moga, especially, had ever worried about in their own affairs.

The Moldovan crew represented the losers in the political and ideological maneuverings of Episcopate life during the 1940s, and none of them were morally or emotionally built to give up graciously. It was not in their interest to see Policarp return to America, so they lent their hand to discredit him with both Romanian and American authorities. It was not in their interest to see Trutza lead the Episcopate, for they could not manipulate him as they did others; thus they denounced Trutza as an insurgent troublemaker who would destroy the vital connection between Romanian-Americans and their Mother Church overseas. Above all, it was not in their interest to see a bishop elected by a legitimately called Church Congress and recognized by the faithful, for this eliminated the chance to run things through an Opreanu or a Moldovan. Their anger and chagrin at being bested by Trutza between 1947 and 1950, given the mendacity of a Morariu or the megalomania of a Martin, could not but result in an overreaction of volatility and slander, when they sensed defeat in the air.

Thus it is undoubtedly true that no matter who became bishop of the Romanian Orthodox Episcopate in 1952, he would have become the object of attack. The campaign waged against Trifa by Moldovan, Martin & Company was not necessarily created because of Trifa personally, or because the man had incidents in his own past which made him vulnerable to sensationalist allegations. The campaign was first

of all against *Trutza* and the *Episcopate* which had separated from
Romania, in which there was no room for defrocked priests and
poseur "jurisconsuls."

As for the Romanian government which supported Moldovan and
supplied his press with material against his enemies, the fundamental
fact was that the very existence of a Trifa Episcopate was an affront
and an embarrassment to the Romanian Church and the communist
regime which controlled it. It represented to the world the unwillingness of tens of thousands of Romanian-Americans to grant the legiti-
macy of the post-war Romanian government, and called to the attention of millions the loss of freedom of the Church in Romania. Destroy
the head, then, and with it the body, remained the rule of thumb on
the banks of the Dîmboviţa ever after.

Trifa himself understood this clearly at the time, noting that if
some other person had become Bishop in 1952, then that man would
be a "war criminal," or accused of heinous crimes, and he, Trifa,
would be left alone.[43] One should note in the pages of the Moldovan
press that Trifa is constantly referred to as Trutza's "stooge," or
"puppet," in the same manner as those who followed the Cleveland
priest at the Hallowe'en gathering years earlier had been labeled. Thus
it was Trutza and an independent American church being attacked
through the *symbol* of Trifa.

Had pacific and mild-mannered Father John Stanila been chosen
Bishop of an autonomous Episcopate, Bucharest would have reacted
in exactly the same fashion, and Martin would have found "documentary material" showing that Stanila had led pogroms in Youngstown, Ohio.

CHAPTER III
WAR CRIMES AND WALTER WINCHELL

At the beginning of 1951, Viorel Trifa was in Cleveland editing the Episcopate newspaper *Solia* for $30 a week, trying valiantly to build circulation and overcome an $800 deficit.[1] He spoke almost no English, but for the first time in years some kind of system seemed to be in the offing for the diocesan paper which for the fifteen years of its existence had always been hard-pressed to survive.

The stress in *Solia*'s pages during these days was naturally on the Moldovan affair, and the disastrous after-effects of the war on Romania, with efforts to collect aid for refugees and displaced persons and calls for various charity funds of Orthodox action.[2] Romania's economy was being bled white by Russian reparations demands and the era of the joint Romanian-Russian industrial and agricultural enterprises, the "SovRoms," was in full sway. Massive government expropriation of productive facilities, accompanied by two years of severe drought, meant starvation for thousands of the population, especially in Moldavia. American food supplies landing in Constanţa or Brăila were destroyed by crowds of shouting, hungry men, who were ordered to denounce the shipments as unwanted capitalist bribes, while the city administrations insisted these were spontaneous manifestations of the freedom loving population showing their devotion to the principles of Marxism-Leninism. "In the summer of 1949 the government announced a budget surplus (!) which would be used to begin construction of the Danube-Black Sea Canal."[3] Convicted priests were used as forced labor to meet the demands of the "progressive" socialist regime.[4] Such conditions, as much as Trifa's new administration, helped account for a doubling of *Solia*'s subscribers in the six months after Trifa assumed control and, of course, ensured that Trifa would also be charged in the complaint filed in Federal Court by Moldovan in December, 1950. For the first time Trifa was brought to public attention and became more widely known throughout the Episcopate.

The editor testified through an interpreter, and although there were questions regarding his personal background, such as the fact

he had come to America from Italy, who had made his travel arrangements, and so on, the focus of Trifa's cross-examination by Moldovan's attorneys was clearly to show that the anti-Moldovan campaign
waged by *Solia* was entirely Father Trutza's, that Trifa cleared everything with the Council President beforehand. Given the history of
Trutza's association with *Solia*, and Trifa's own editorial personality,
plus the fact that the majority of the paper was in the Romanian language, this was hardly the case. During November *Solia* had run a
series of articles under the headline, "Communist Plans Against Our
Episcopate!" blazoning the story of the telegrams from Bucharest to
Detroit, the post cards from Arkansas, the attempted bribing of
members of *Solia*'s staff, and the fact that Moldovan's parish in Akron
refused to accept him upon his return.[5] During December appeared
pieces on the "glories" of life in Romania under "Moldovan's masters."[6] All of this gave rise to meetings of protest in Detroit and Cleveland, as Romanian war veterans, the Romanian National Committee,
and Union and League societies denounced the communist lackeys.
Throughout the Episcopate declarations of solidarity with Trutza
and an autonomous stand poured in, and soon *America* and the Union
and League (now restored to a non-leftist leadership) joined the
fray against Moldovan. Trifa's testimony in court centered on documentary proofs of the charge of political control over the Romanian
church which he had published.[7]

Moldovan's attorneys by March sought a permanent injunction to
forbid the publication of *Solia*,[8] but as early as February 1 Moldovan began publishing an "official" newspaper of his own Episcopate,
also named *Solia*, at 141 Atkinson Street in Detroit. The Managing
Editor and Business Manager was Nicholas N. Martin.[9] Already one
of Martin's major strategies became apparent: the Trutza-Trifa *Solia*
was being used as an organ to discredit Bishop Andrei, to destroy his
credibility, and to prejudice the judicial process. This theme Martin
would return to again and again in his version of *Solia*, especially
when Moldovan lost the court case. On the surface of things, the fact
was that Martin's fundamental theme was true—the Trutza Episcopate
pulled all the stops to discredit Moldovan and expose communist
control over the Romanian church. Except that for the most part
Moldovan *had done* what *Solia* related about him, and the situation
of the Romanian people in the early years of the communist regime
was grim, to be sure.

Two additional considerations follow from the themes advanced
by Moldovan's *Solia* against its namesake in the older Episcopate.

First, Martin credited what Trutza and Trifa published with having more influence than it did—for the fact was, it was not hard to discredit Andrei and the Romanian communists at this time in American history. In the early 1950s in the United States, in the midst of the Korean War and the McCarthy era, communism was the most reviled object of all. Ideologically, the Right held the reins and persecuted the Left, and once the autonomous diocese successfully identified Andrei's Episcopate with communism, its chances for a successful transition to power were practically nil. The Moldovan counter-attack, that Trutza and his candidate for bishop were "fascists" and "Nazis," simply did not have the same impact in 1951, when the Right had been defeated in Europe and communism had swept through Eastern Europe in a burgeoning wave of "People's Democracies," and Americans were dying along the Yalu River. Thus even had the facts of the case favored Moldovan (which they did not), the times would have defeated him.

The second consideration emerges from the first, namely, that the anti-Moldovan writings in *Solia* could have little impact in prejudicing the legal process, when not only the atmosphere of the day but the facts of the case went against the Moldovan putsch. It escaped Martin that the same argument might even better be advanced against him and his cohorts. How highly ironic it was that Martin complained of damaging pre-trial publicity at the same time he was launching a campaign of slander which laid the foundation for a series of extreme accusations against Trifa which would surface again and again for the next thirty years. Seldom can a more vitiating and longevous example of prejudicial accusations designed to influence a legal outcome be found in modern American history.

Martin's misology

From the beginning Martin's journalism in the pages of the official organ of "the most canonical bishop" was on an elevated plane. "Trutzist Flunkeys Dictate to the Union and League," was the headline of the second *Solia* on March 15, 1951. For wider appeal, some features were in English, of an impeccable quality. The columns of Emil Idu rose to heights of philological and philosophic supererogation. A verbatim sampling must suffice:

> ... the most daring undemocratic journalistic assault that ever took place in recent years in any of the various Romanian newspapers .... Madness itself erupted with the furry of a volcano while it's lava of human uggliness poured firely and unchecked. ...[10]

This, of course, was aimed at *America*. When it was learned in the Martin editorial room that Trutza and the Episcopate Council had fixed on a candidate for bishop, such reportage would seem almost dulcet.

While there is sufficient evidence that Viorel Trifa never wished to become a bishop,[11] he accepted his election of 1951, hoping that he could bring the internal order and discipline which the Episcopate sorely lacked, by conditioning his candidacy on broad constitutional revisions. Between his election on July 2, 1951, and his consecration in Philadelphia on April 27, 1952, "he was the victim of the most malicious character assassination that has ever been witnessed within the experience of the people of Romanian descent in America."[12]

As Martin and Moldovan began to sense the losing nature of their cause, inevitably they became a little desperate. Bishop Andrei's activities at the Vatra resulted in a court order restricting him to use of one-half the mansion for living facilities, but his violations of this eventually earned him a citation for contempt of court. Next the eventually forbade him to publish a newspaper called *Solia*.[13] In its stead, Martin produced *Episcopia* (The Episcopate), which by September, 1951 became *Tribuna* (The Tribune), whose first headline labeled Trifa an imposter, a fake bishop. *Tribuna* sought to worry the faithful that the Vatra was soon to be sold, because Trutza was using all the money in its bank account for legal fees, which was not true.[14] Nevertheless, fighting Moldovan's legal suit cost the Episcopate what were astronomical sums at the time. A special "Defense Fund" was begun, depending on donations from church members, but this could hardly keep up with the costs of a protracted two and one-half year struggle in the courts. As of January, 1953, there was $200 in this fund to cover $14,531.46 in legal costs.[15] Twenty-seven years later Trifa's Episcopate was still being forced to raise vast sums of money to defend its bishop of Martin's charges. A conservative estimate would place the total expense between 1951 and 1980 at approximately $200,000.

Even Bucharest must have been embarrassed by the smear campaign against Trifa which followed his election. What could the Romanian Church do? It had only people of the caliber of Moldovan, Martin, and Alexander Suciu (who became the East State Fair's "official" expert on Romanian church history in America, anti-Trutza version) to act as its minions in trying to win over the American churches. Even forcing Policarp to send telegrams "condemning the rebellion led by the defrocked priest Ioan Trutza" and denying that

Trifa was his successor, which Bucharest did on the eve of the Chicago Congress, seemed mild compared to *Tribuna*'s scathing yellow journalism.[16]

In the course of the autumn of 1951, a list of accusations against Trifa appeared in the pages of *Tribuna*, a list which forms the core of the allegations against Trifa, and against which he has had to defend himself for more than a quarter of a century. Every charge was either completely false, or else a half-truth wrenched from the context of a complex period of Romanian history. A careful reader has only to compare the list of charges brought by the Justice Department against the Bishop in 1975 with the pages of *Tribuna*, or *Episcopia* or *Solia* written by Martin, Suciu, and others in 1951 and 1952, or the stories repeated year after year in the Detroit Episcopate's newspaper *Credinţa* (The Faith—begun in 1954 and still published today) to see that they are the same old Martin charges, with embellishments but now hoary with age.

Tribuna's readers learned not only that Trifa was a deserter from the Romanian army, but that he had abandoned a wife and children in Italy—or in Romania, or somewhere. It was heresy to make Trifa a Bishop; he was not even a member of the Orthodox Church; he had been excommunicated. The Chicago Congress which elected him took place in the Masonic Temple in that city; this naturally proved that Trifa was a Mason.

The worst crimes committed by the Bishop-elect, *Tribuna* wrote without reservation or qualification, were those flowing from his membership in the infamous Iron Guard Movement. Making no distinction at all between the "Iron Guard" and the Legionary Movement, the Moldovan press simply adopted the popular (and erroneous) usage of the day. Trifa was not only a member of the Iron Guard, but one of its top commanders, *Tribuna* flatly stated, as it published grainy European newspaper photographs showing someone who might have been Trifa in uniform.[17] Trifa was not only a Guardist, but the worst kind—he fomented the bloody Iron Guard rebellion against the government of General Ion Antonescu in January, 1941. Trifa was not only anti-Semitic, but a leader of pogroms. He was not only a murderer, but a mass murderer. He personally killed or ordered to be killed hundreds of Jews in Bucharest, *Tribuna* wished its readers to know, in the interest of public safety perhaps. Or perhaps he killed thousands. It was hard to know for certain. One can read stories from 1951 to 1955 to 1963 to 1978 and learn that Trifa killed either one or two Jews, or 300, or 2,000, or "thousands," or "tens of thousands," depending on how great a stir the journalist wished to get from his readers.

Editor and Publisher Nicholas N. Martin outdid himself in defending the most canonical bishop Andrei, and promoting the work of the Lord in his issue of October, 1951. Here he "exposed" Trifa by publishing three fuzzy photographs of dead bodies lying in mud and snow. Nothing in the pictures indicated the location, and the shots might have been taken anywhere in Europe from Norway to Italy or from France to Russia in the final days of the Second World War. One was simply to trust the editor's captions, that these came from Bucharest and were beyond a doubt "Victims of the Revolution Provoked by Viorel Trifa."[18] Other pictures followed in due course, especially ones of smashed and devastated synagogues.

But then, one did not have to consult only the Martin press for the facts about Trifa. September 9, 1951, brought absolute certitude, for no less a personage than the nationally-known commentator Walter Winchell, in his radio broadcast that day, named Trifa and called him a murderer, one of the "Nazi leaders who helped Hitler kill American GI's."[19] There is a curious follow-up to this Winchell broadcast. The week following the broadcast, in response to a number of letters from the Episcopate or concerned church members, American Broadcasting Company officials informed them that "copies of Mr. Winchell's scripts are not available for general distribution."[20] In reply to a letter from Vasile Haţegan, however, Paul E. Scheffels, Assistant to the ABC Vice-President for News & Special Events, told the priest, "I have checked the script of September 9 and find no mention of Mr. Viorel Trifa."[21]

Nearly two years later, when Martin was filling the ears of the commanders of the American Legion Hall in Canton, Ohio, telling them not to permit Trifa's Church to use their Legion Hall for their Congress, the Legionnaires contacted Walter Winchell's office for confirmation of what they'd been told. They learned that Winchell, when asked personally, "was not in a position to prove what he had said on the radio."[22] Martin, of course, never publicized this aspect of the matter. The rule of thumb at the Moldovan press became, after September, 1951, to include Walter Winchell at least in every third line.

Altogether, the Moldovan press was one of the most curious combinations one can find. Alongside Andrei's pastoral messages full of Christian truth and brotherhood-appeals stood columns of vilification and mayhem, with those supporting the heretic Trutza and his "stooges" labeled "suckers," "phoneys," "thugs," and so on. Meanwhile, on page two, Bishop Andrei had been received by great masses of the faithful in Ellwood City or Windsor or Cleveland, chests swelling with pride and eyes brimming with joyful tears for their only legal, canonical, hierarchical, patriarchal, valid bishop—and assuring him that a mere one or two demented parishioners were with Trutza's gang, and these had been totally ostracized. If there were any lines left, these could be used, on page three, to point out that Trutza was also a bootlegger.[23] Had it not been so tragic, it would have been ethnic comedy at its best.

The most important question is, what were Martin's sources for these charges, and were those sources objective and reliable?

We may search in vain through the pages of the Moldovan *Solia, Episcopia,* or *Tribuna* during the most intense period of their allegations against Trifa in 1951-1952, in order to find a footnote, a cited reference, or some solid piece of written research upon which the material is based. For the most part, the "story" of Trifa's activities is simply stated, to be taken at face value and assumed true because it is printed in a newspaper. Occasionally some semblance of verisimilitude is sought through phrases such as "a man who was in Bucharest in 1941 told us," or "a priest told us that he knew Trifa in Romania, and . . . ." Two observations are in order here.

First, irrespective of their contents, the above sheets were first and foremost *ethnic* newspapers. Whether favoring Moldovan's cause or anyone else's, ethnic papers are by their very nature polemical, contentious, and black-and-white in their approach to controversial topics.

Second, not only was the Martin press addressed to ethnics, but they were *special cause* newspapers, which came into being for a specific purpose, namely to convince the Romanian-American public of the rightness of Andrei Moldovan as their bishop, and the wrongness of the Trutza-Trifa side. The very manner in which they sought to pose as the legitimate continuators of the pre-1950 Episcopate by adopting the identical name for their first newspaper until a court order prevented this, suggests the intention to deceive and thereby inherit intact the relatively uninformed readership. Sufficient to say that *Tribuna* and its brethren were official organs, engaged in special pleadings.

The same criteria apply as well to the religious "Calendars" published by ethnic churches. Alexander Suciu of Chicago was a much more capable and intelligent conveyor of the printed word than Martin, and it fell to him to pen many of the lengthy, more analytical pieces "exposing" the phariseeism of Trutza. Yet neither does Suciu document his story more than meagerly. In a long offering in the 1953 *Credinţa Calendar* (Moldovan's) he actually cites a reference, using a 25th anniversary *Legionary Bulletin* in Rome, which expressed pride at the numbers of former Legionairies arriving in high places, including the Bishop of Romanian-Americans.[24] Yet, it is logical that Trifa would be mentioned by a Rome publication, having just come from five years of living in Italy.

Martin did have the possibility of obtaining certain published books and pamphlets from Romania or about Romania, which existed in the early 1950s, and these are his most likely sources. Some he may have gotten himself, others he knew of at secondhand through his contacts with Romanians in the diaspora after the war. In nearly every case, however, it is important to note that none of the jurisconsul's sources actually proved Trifa guilty of crimes or gave satisfactory evidence that he had "started" the Legionary Rebellion. From the beginning Martin's journalism used guilt by association. There *was* a rebellion in January, 1941, involving Legionnaires. Trifa *was* in Romania at that time, prominently known, and associated with the Movement. There *were* people killed, Christian and Jew alike. Therefore, Trifa was part of the criminal acts. Moreover, there were no shades of difference among Legionary followers. All were killers.

Shortly after the events of January, 1941, General Ion Antonescu caused to be published a documented study of what had taken place, and Martin may have seen material from this work. *Pe Marginea Prăpastiei* (On the Edge of the Abyss) contained the "official" statistics and viewpoints on the rebellion, and Trifa's name is discussed in reference to his earlier student activity and arrest during 1936-1937, and in connection with the student demonstration he led on January 20, the evening before the outbreak occurred. As for this latter, Antonescu's study clearly indicates that the manifestation broke up peacefully.[25] For Martin, it was sufficient merely to associate Trifa's name with such a book.

Far more useful to Trifa opponents over the years, although it does not even contain his name, was the sensational publication *Blood Bath in Rumania*, published by "The Record" News Bulletin in 1942 in New York. This was the organ of the group known as the United Rumanian Jews of America.[26] As the name suggests, this was a horrifying indictment of "Iron Guard" murders and destruction over a period of years, including the murders of Professor Iorga and of Virgil Madgearu, and climaxing with the "pogrom" of early 1941, called in the subtitle "an orgy unparalleled in modern history."

Obviously Martin used this 61 page pamphlet, for he took at least one of the gruesome photographs which he published in 1951 from it—of course changing the caption.[27] The fact that this Jewish work omitted reference to Trifa entirely did not dissuade the editor.

The same interesting omission occurs in another work which Martin may well have used, *Oraşul Măcelului* (City of Butchery) by F. Brunea-Fox, published in Bucharest in 1944, which contained a "Journal of the Rebellion and Legionary Crimes." The by-now familiar Legionary depradations are there, but the "Journal" does not even see fit to include the January 20 student demonstration; the chronology of the work begins with January 21, and Trifa is conspicuously missing from the entire booklet. One would certainly think that if the newly-elected Bishop had been a "top commander," and one of the "leaders" of the rebellion, Brunea-Fox would give Trifa a least a passing reference.

One of the first post-war works which at least merited the name of a history of the Legionary Movement was Ştefan Palaghiţa's *Garda de Fer: Spre Reînvierea României* (The Iron Guard: Toward the Resurrection of Romania). This circulated widely in the Romanian exile community, and some priests opposed to Trifa's election used it at the Chicago Congress to campaign against him.[28] Certainly Martin was familiar with its contents, which detailed Trifa's two escapes from Romania, in 1939 and 1941. The author, an Orthodox priest belonging to the second-rank leadership of the Legionary Movement, "used his book as a polemical weapon in the factional struggle for the anti-Sima group."[29] Two major items regarding Trifa are noteworthy in Palaghiţa's pages, one of which Martin seized on: at one point Sima accused Trifa of having provoked the January rebellion. Although such a statement, in the context of the entire book (which accuses Sima of terrorism and common crimes) was an obvious effort by the former Legionary chief to excuse his own failings and escape responsiblity, and flew in the face of all other known facts, the Moldovan press used it. In fact, the antagonism which developed between Trifa and Sima during 1940-1941 is overlooked, which further helps account for such a statement. The second major Palaghiţa remark concerning Trifa, Martin ignored—the flat statement that, following the demonstration of the evening of January 20, "Trifa gave not one further order and played no role in the events which followed."[30]

As of 1951, this more or less completes the list of published works Martin would have had available to him for information on Trifa's role in the Legionary Movement and the events of January, 1941.

It is true that Henry Roberts' solid work on Romania was published also in 1951, and by 1956 Alexander Cretzianu's *Captive Rumania*, but these devote only minimal space and general treatment to the rebellion, and do not mention Trifa. Martin was apparently unaware of the existence of these scholarly works.

What is more expectable is that much of Martin's information and misinformation was based on his informal contacts with Romanian émigrés in the United States, who had been involved in the Legionary Movement, or remembered Trifa in Romania, either personally or by reputation. Those on Moldovan's side in the Episcopate schism naturally remembered about Trifa what they wanted to; and, their memories were already more than a decade old.

Finally, after Martin made contact with Dr. Charles Kremer in New York, an additional source of material was available, in the form of the Yiddish daily press, such as *The Day*, and in such publications as the *United Israeli Bulletin*, the *Detroit Jewish Bulletin*, and so on. The position of these publications on the Legionary Movement needs no clarification; one hardly looks to them for dispassionate historical analysis.

Even this brief review of Martin's source material leads to the conclusion that not only did the editor practice "selective use of evidence," retaining only those items in books or pamphlets or other writings which supported his cause and ignoring contravening material within the same source, but his sources are in the main partisan and secondary, not to mention simplistic and polemical.

Dentist dementis

Despite *Tribuna*'s constant taunting, Trifa and the Episcopate never replied publicly to the questions or charges of Martin or Suciu, not wishing to dignify them with responses. When indirectly refuting them in intra-Episcopate correspondence, it was also never in kind. Basically correct was the Bishop-elect's statement in a long circular to his priests on September 13, 1951, that this was merely a more virulent form of the campaign begun against Policarp, continued against Trutza, and now aimed at him. It was Trifa's turn to bear the anti-Episcopate assault of the monks who had never gotten over being ousted in 1947. He repeated what he had told the Chicago Congress: "I have committed no crime in my life, have killed no one, not even a chicken. I was part of no criminal action. I was never married, I never converted to Catholicism, either in Italy or in Romania, and I engaged in no political action, nor have I done so here in America."[31]

In fact Trifa made it clear that he would not, as Bishop, engage in politics at all, and this did not please some of the militants in his Diocese. It was, however, ironic, that the Moldovan camp loudly proclaimed its anti-communism, while simultaneously fighting tooth and nail to remove Trifa, who would be, if anything, a strong anti-communist symbol at the head of an autonomous Episcopate.

Trifa did take steps to dispel the malicious rumors and ease the minds of his supporters before his consecration. Twice he submitted to interviews before the Immigration and Naturalization Service (in addition to the normal processing he had gone through upon arrival in New York from Europe). On May 22, 1951 he met with immigration examiner Leo M. Jaremko in the Federal Building in Cleveland. Much was made of this meeting, along with Trifa's court appearance the previous January, in Howard Blum's article in *Esquire* magazine, which stressed that the combination of these two interviews gave Trifa the chance to cover up his past "with a few glib lies."[32] Yet such was not the case at all.

What Blum does not mention, in the first place, is that Trifa at this point knew hardly any English, and the interview with Jaremko was conducted in Italian, through one Luigi Di Paolo as translator. The questions and answers were not simply conveyed from Trifa's Italian into the interviewer's English on a verbatim basis, but Di Paola explained or summarized what Trifa said. Without belaboring the point, anyone understanding the problem of linguistic barriers and nuances knows that the opportunities for misstatement are manifold. Trifa himself, at the time, was uncomfortable with the arrangement and was unsatisfied that his answers were being conveyed adequately and afraid that he mistook certain questions.[33]

Even so, there was no effort to "cover" his past. Trifa detailed for Jaremko his activities from the time he had been in the theological department at Chisinău until the moment he arrived in America—and produced the official documents and certificates of his graduation from the University of Iasi, his attendance at the graduate school of the University of Bucharest, and the documents of the International Tracing Service of the International Refugee Organization showing the times and places he had been in German prison camps. These became a matter of United States record. Statements from the Martin press that he entered the country illegally (or the constant insinuation of Kremer that somehow Trifa "snuck" into the United States) were nonsense. The Jaremko interview took note of Trifa's Alien

Registration Card No. A-7819396, with his photograph on the reverse side, showing that he had registered at the Main Post Office in Cleveland.[34]

Two questions asked by Jaremko, through Di Paolo, are central to the Trifa case. With each of them, the matter of the language/translation factor is paramount. "Was Trifa ever a member of the Iron Guard?" The answer was no, which in Trifa's thinking was the perfect truth. The organization known as the *Iron Guard* was dissolved in the early 1930s, at the time when Trifa was a university undergraduate. Hearing this name used, and knowing Romanian history, as his examiner did not, Trifa's answer in point of fact was an honest one, both subjectively and objectively. Whether he was aware at this time of America's tendency to use "Iron Guard" and "Legionary Movement" interchangeably and inaccurately (which he probably was) is beside the point, moreover, for even had the question been "Were you ever a member of the Legionary Movement?" the focus would shift to the word "member." Trifa had not been a member, nor had he belonged to any Legionary "nest." An associate of Legionnaires, a zealous supporter of Legionary goals, an activist student leader of an association which included Legionary members, yes. But not a member. This meant one who was enrolled in a "nest," had a membership card, a number, and was required to attend meetings, donate regular sums of money, and so on. The word did not fit him.

The second question lent itself to additional misconstruction. "Did you ever make any speeches or give any lectures that might be construed as being anti-Jewish or anti-Semitic?" "No, I cannot say. I don't believe so," was the answer. Ignoring for the moment the semantic problems of such terminology. Trifa's answer to these two questions-in-one was exactly half-correct. He was not anti-Semitic and never had been. He *was* anti-Jewish.

It was during the bitter campaign waged by Moldovan to block his consecration that Trifa underwent his second extended session with the U.S. Immigration Service. A barrage of letters and telegrams went out from East State Fair to every important Orthodox churchman who might be persuaded to perform the ceremony on Trifa, with the news that he was a heretic, that the Congress which elected him consisted only of laymen, and the like. Originally, the Metropolitan of the Russian Metropolia (Arch-diocese) in New York, Leonty, had agreed to consecrate Trifa, and set the date for November 22, 1951, in Youngstown. Then Leonty was telephoned and told that Trifa was to be deported in a matter of weeks and his consecration

should be stopped.[35] On November 30, having postponed the ceremony for a week, the Council of the Metropolia informed the Episcopate Council that they would have to receive "necessary government reports" before they could decide to go ahead with the consecration question.[36] At this juncture Trifa offered voluntarily to submit to an examination under oath, and this second interview, with
the New York Immigration Office, lasted for three days, December
4-6, 1951.

Father Vasile Haţegan, pastor of St. Dumitru's Romanian Orthodox Church in New York, arranged the interview, and served as interpreter for the Immigration officer at the INS building at 70 Col-
umbus Avenue. Obviously this series of sessions, which filled a 33-
page transcript, was more exhaustive and held less chance for mis-
understandings than the Jaremko interview. Trifa's questioner was
informed at least on the rudiments of Romanian history, and took
the Bishop-elect through extensive questions on his personal biography, the history of the Legionary Movement and the philosophy
of Corneliu Z. Codreanu, and Trifa's leadership of the student movement. Clarification of the matter of Trifa's membership in the Legionnaires came when Trifa noted that, although he was not what
one would term a "card-carrying member," whoever happened to be
the president of the National Union of Christian Students was considered *ex officio* a "member" or "associate" of whatever party held
power in the state at that moment. To that extent, his election as
student president in October, 1940, and his official appointment by
the King (as was customary with this position) made him part of the
Antonescu-Legionary government coalition then ruling the country.
Had Trifa held the student presidency, e.g., when the National Liberals were in power, he would have been "officially" a member of the
National Liberal government. This was quite another thing, this *pro
forma* designation, than being a regularly enrolled member who had
risen to a "top Legionary Commandant" through his work in party
cells. In any event, the importance of these three days with the Immigration and Naturalization Examiner lies in the fact that Trifa answered all questions put to him, that he offered voluntarily to be interviewed even though the INS had not called him, and not only did
Trifa not conceal his own past, he elaborated upon it even beyond
the scope of the interrogation.[37]

The conclusion reached by the Immigration Office was that there
was no reason for bringing any charges whatsoever against Trifa. The
case was closed.[38]

Here was the first of many occasions when, in response to the protracted deluge of requests from Martin, Kremer (see below), and others, the Immigration and Naturalization Service (INS) did indeed review the evidence, or call in Trifa, conducted a probe, and concluded that there was no case to be made.

There was a second, far more portentous by-product of the drive to block the consecration of Trifa. The personal appeal of Morariu and Moldovan to the New York group known as the United Rumanian Jews of America brought into the picture the persistent 55-year old dentist, Dr. Charles Kremer.[39] Hearing Glicherie describe Trifa as "a wanderer and heretic who had never so much served as an altar boy," and Moldovan expound on Trifa's "command position" during 1941 "when thousands of Jews were slaughtered," apparently triggered memories in Kremer of various rumors which he had uncritically come to accept after his postwar trips to Romania. Not necessarily because he truly believed in Moldovan's cause, nor because of any position on the schism in the Romanian-American Church, Kremer from this moment on made it his personal goal in life to "expose" and "get" Trifa.

It is largely irrelevant here to examine Kremer's personal motivations. The fact that for the next twenty-eight years, to the moment of this writing, he would bombard the Justice Department, the INS, the State Department, the Federal Courts, and anyone who would listen to him with denunciations and "proofs" about Trifa's past, speaks for itself, as does the fact that for the first twenty-three of those years, from 1952-1975, his pleas were largely ignored or—what is more important—examined and not acted upon.

What is highly relevant, however, is the fact that in the most widely read writings about Trifa, those of Howard Blum, Kremer's "material" is the primary source of information. And this "material" is so clearly self-contradictory, wrong, redundant, or misleading to anyone knowing even the bare outlines of Trifa's biography or the history of the Romanian Church in America that it cannot withstand even the most cursory scrutiny by the historian. Blum does, however, show insight into his major informant when he notes:

> Kremer had always cluttered his life with the debris from many small but intense squabbles; he could look back on nasty fights with the draft board, college fraternities, Jewish organizations, landlords. Still, he fought every argument fortified by an arrogant certitude and by a romantic compulsion to challenge what others said was impossible.[40]

Moreover, Kremer's sole biographer fails to address a number of important questions concerning the dentist's involvement in the Trifa case, not the least of which are: why, though Kremer knew of events in Bucharest in 1941, he took no overt action for at least six years to seek out those responsible, and secondly, why Kremer became so excited at Moldovan's "revelations" in 1952 (as if to say, "Aha, at last I've found what happened to Trifa!") when since at least 1947 the Romanian-language press in America was filled weekly with the polemics of the Romanian-American schism *and*, after mid-1950, Trifa's name was never absent from the voluminous accounts of the Moldovan-Trutza-Trifa case. Where had Kremer been, in other words, since 1941, that he suddenly discovered the "truth" about Trifa after eleven years?

The conclusion might be one of two reasons, or factors. That the Romanian Jewish community in New York was for the most part cut off and ignorant of the affairs of their co-nationals throughout the interior of America, is the first. Equally plausible is that Kremer never actually had any "material" against Trifa, and when put in touch with Moldovan and the Martin press, he saw a chance to use this "evidence" in another of his familiar messianic battles, and gain prestige in the Jewish community simultaneously by bringing one of the worst "Romanian Nazis" to justice. He might then say, as he so often did, and does, "Charlie Kremer did what nobody else could have done." Most likely both factors have weight. What is clear, moreover, is that Kremer largely acted on his own, finding no support among the majority of American Jews or their organizations.[41]

What the dentist did do in 1952 was to get himself elected president of the United Rumanian Jews, with a plethora of phone calls and letters. Once in command of the stationery, with its letterhead, he would command attention in official circles. An important clue to the Trifa case is contained here in Blum's (or Kremer's) own words: the letterhead

would command immediate *political* attention; elected officials would respond immediately to a vociferous Jewish-interest group (our italics).[42]

In the long run, Kremer perhaps unconsciously pointed to the heart of the matter. When the United States government, after refusing to bring any case against Trifa for twenty-five years, finally did so in 1975, it did so not because of any substantive change in the value or quantity of the allegations against the clergyman—but because it was clear that there were large political dividends to be gained. Péguy, toujours Péguy. "Everything begins in mystique and ends in politics".

CHAPTER IV

FROM THE COURTROOM TO CONGRESS
1952-1962

Moldovan lost in the United States District Court for Northern Ohio, Eastern Division, on July 8, 1952.

Moldovan lost in the United States Court of Appeals, Sixth Circuit, in Cincinnati, July 3, 1953.

Moldovan lost in the United States Supreme Court, October 10, 1953.

Moldovan lost in the United States District Court for Eastern Pennsylvania, in Philadelphia, September 28, 1954.

The story of efforts to block Trifa's consecration is an interesting one. In broad outlines, Martin and his men went to one Orthodox Bishop or Metropolitan after another with their stories against Trifa, casting doubt in the minds of the churchmen as to the canonical rightness of his ordination. Of course the Martin press made much of the Episcopate Council's frustration, as they went first from the Russian Metropolia, to the Greek Orthodox Church in America, to Visarion Puiu in France, to the Syrian-Antiochan Diocese, to the Russian Church Outside Russia. It was not only the reservations planted by Moldovan's tales which stayed the hands of these heirarchs, but the very real problem faced by all ethnic churches during the era of the communist take-over of Eastern Europe. They did not want to break relations with the Romanian Patriarchate, or get into trouble with the Ecumenical Patriarch of Constantinople, even though they may have sympathized with the plight of those in America seeking autonomy from Moscow-dominated regimes and churches. Naturally Bucharest lent all its weight with the Patriarch of Constantinople to prevent its American subordinates from cooperating with the Trifa Episcopate. All this had nothing to do with Trifa's qualifications for the office, but *Episcopia* and *Tribuna* invariably attributed it to the justice of Moldovan's canonicity and the illegality of Trifa's. Those running the press for Bishop Andrei used "canonical" so much it became almost humorous. No reference to Andrei, no speech, sermon, pastoral to the faithful, or circular but what sought indissolubly to link Andrei and "canonical," for this was his strongest feature.

Except when it came to adding "legal" master of the Episocpate, successor to Policarp, and heir to the Vatra is when the argument folded.

Nevertheless the problem of canonicity remained to plague Trifa's Diocese for the next eight years. When Trifa was finally consecrated by three hierarchs of the Ukrainian Orthodox Church (about whose canonical autonomy there was some doubt) as a last resort, the label of "samosfeat," or "self-ordained" was added to the litany of pejoratives which winked stroboscopically from Martin's pen. Here was another example of the fact that Martin did not really care about Trifa's past history, or his qualifications, or his canonicity—nor did Bucharest. The idea was to use *any* argument to eliminate the autonomous Episcopate as an entity by disrupting and confusing those who supported it. One was as good as another and, in the fashion of William James, whatever worked was truth.

So, with Trifa's ordination set for April 27, 1952, at the hands of Metropolitan John Theodorovich in the Descent of the Holy Ghost Romanian Orthodox Church in Philadelphia, Moldovan's staff was very busy. On March 18, Metropolitan John received a telegram from Father Moga advising him not to "commit this shameless act of simony to sell the Holy Spirit to a man proclaimed over the radio by Walter Wichell (*sic*) a murderer." Any Orthodox bishop ordaining Trifa would be at once "deposed and excommunicated by our Romanian Holy Synod," and all other Patriarchates would ratify the sentence. "More explanation" would follow.[1] Moga never did explain how the Romanian Church in Bucharest had any jurisdiction over the Ukrainians.

But more explanation came forth, indeed, as Trifa arrived in Philadelphia and began his spiritual preparations. The three consecrating bishops were harassed with anonymous letters and phone calls. On April 23 Kremer was contacted by "a Romanian priest" and given the news. He immediately sent a telegram of protest to the immigration service, in which the number of Jews killed in Romania in 1940 and 1941 for which Trifa was responsible jumped to "tens of thousands."[2] Kremer asked the Immigration and Naturalization Service to stop the consecration scheduled for the Ukrainian Orthodox Church, 128 Grace Road, in Bala Cynwyd.[3] They refused to interfere. Even had they wanted to, it would have been difficult, for besides his histrionic inaccuracies about Romanian history, Kremer also had the wrong church.

Friday evening, April 25, the three day series of religious services began on North Bodine Street, with Vespers. A short way into the service, federal marshalls walked into the church, accompanied by Moldovan's lawyers, interrupting the proceedings with a Federal Court restraining order, signed by Judge Alan K. Grim of the U.S. District Court for Eastern Pennsylvania. Hasty consultations followed with the lawyer retained by the Philadelphia church for its parish affairs, Maximilian J. Klinger. He tried to contact Judge Grim, who was gone for the weekend. Klinger called other colleagues and judges, and then uttered words for which his name ever after deserved honor. "Go on with the consecration: this Order is a violation of the First Amendment to the United States Constitution. It interferes with the free exercise of religion." And so they did.

The Philadelphia Story was not over, of course. On April 30, Metropolitan Theodorovich, Father Trutza, Bishop Trifa, and Father John Popovich, pastor of the Philadelphia parish, stood before Judge Grim to learn whether they would be cited for contempt of court. Attorney Klinger, upon stating that the consecration was done upon his advice, was added as a defendant. He testified that he had considered his act thoroughly and weighed his obligation as an officer of the court against his conscience. He would likely do the same thing again.[4] Maximilian Klinger was a Jew.

It took Judge Grim more than two years to ponder the case against Klinger and the churchmen. On September 28, 1954, he dismissed the charges.

History As You Like It

"Here I was beating my head against the wall and that bastard was now in bishop's clothing. Think of it! They let him become a bishop!" It was astounding to Kremer that his efforts against Trifa thus far produced no results. Kremer's concern with Trifa became total. He would cancel appointments with patients. He wrote to columnists, editors, and church officials. He called upon Detroit Jewish groups and was informed of Trifa's movements. When the Bishop traveled to a parish in Ohio or Indiana, the editor of the local newspaper would be sure to receive a letter about "mass murderer Viorel Trifa."[5] When he got only polite responses from officialdom, he made an important decision.

In 1954 Kremer abandoned his dental practice, sold his equipment, and went abroad—first to Romania, then to Israel. His friends wrongly thought he was ready to retire. Far from it. He merely wanted to be free to feed his mania. "I went abroad with only one thought-to get evidence on that bastard Trifa. I wanted to make sure that Charlie Kremer had the last laugh."[6] He stayed overseas for two full years.

Meanwhile, in Romanian-America, the campaign against Trifa continued. When Judge Emerich B. Freed rendered his decision in the case of Moldovan vs. Trutza and the Episcopate (and fined Moldovan $200 for contempt of court in the bargain) on July 8, 1952, "jurisconsul" Nick Martin came up with the interesting theory that this decision of the Federal Court in Cleveland was unconstitutional. The same applied when Moldovan lost his appeal in Cincinnati a year later. Trutza had "met secretly with the judges and gave them extra information," and so on. Moreover, the courts had committed an unpardonable error: they had ignored Walter Winchell.[7]

Two days before the Freed decision, Trifa, Trutza and a large crowd of their supporters traveled to the Vatra in Grass Lake, Michigan, and assumed control over the property, by right of a court order. In 1976, Howard Blum used this "takeover" of the Vatra as the basis for a tale whereby Trifa, at the head of a small army of trained Iron Guard commandos, stormed and took over the Episcopate headquarters. Blum's account is exciting: it reads like a raid on Dieppe. But it is primarily the product of his imagination. Blum's research was so sloppy that he even had the date wrong, and could not spell Grass Lake properly. Elsewhere, we have addressed ourselves to Blum's innumerable errors in this episode alone of Romanian church history in America.[8]

The Vatra, after nearly fifteen months of Moldovan's occupancy, was a mess, and Bishop Andrei had left a number of unpaid debts in Grass Lake and Jackson. Local creditors presented Trifa with declarations that Moldovan refused to pay them. The reputation of the Vatra and its resident was at an all-time low in the surrounding community, a factor which would take years to overcome.[9] One of the Episcopate Council's first moves was to sell the livestock to pay off these debts. "Trifa Sells Cows and Buys Himself a Car," yelled *Tribuna* in October, 1952.[10] Not exactly. Bishop Valerian (his monastic name, adopted at his consecration) made his first canonical visits to his parishes in a donated pickup truck.[11]

The first Church Congress convened under the new Bishop met in St. George Church in Canton, Ohio, on July 3, 1953. Three days before the delegates began to assemble, Nicholas Martin traveled to Canton to speak to the leaders of the American Legion Post where

the Congress was to meet. Documents were presented from Moldovan's
Credinţa, from "a Jewish newspaper in New York," and elsewhere.
Of course Walter Winchell came to Canton as well. Trifa was a Nazi,
Martin's evidence demonstrated, and the members of the Episcopate
a group of schismatic revolutionaries. What Martin did not count on
was the Legion commanders checking on his sources. It was at
this time they contacted Winchell's office,[12] as well as the FBI and
the Immigration Service, and learned that neither of these "had any
complaint against the person of Bishop Valerian. . . ."[13]

The "Official Protection" Syndrome

On May 11, 1955, Bishop Valerian Trifa gave the opening prayer
before the United States Senate, asking that the lawmakers remember
in their discussions and decisions "Romania and all the oppressed
nations" still hoping for freedom one day. It was a normal enough
thing to have taken place. Over the years many clergymen of all denominations are invited to perform this function as a courtesy, or to
help commemorate some special national or religious holiday having
to do with their country of origin. In this case, Trifa's appearance
was timed to come during the week of May 10 or Romania's traditional independence day before the coming of communism.

Howard Blum frankly states that Vice-President Richard M. Nixon
requested Trifa's presence—and then takes off into a long discussion
of Nixon's connection with and protection for the questionable Romanian industrialist Nicolae Malaxa, reputedly one of the major financial powers behind the Iron Guard. The implication is clear that just
as Nixon favored and covered up for the machinations of Malaxa
through special preference he introduced when a junior Senator from
California, so, too, he was somehow "protecting" or doing special
favors for another ex-Nazi, Trifa. However, we have no proof, only
Blum's word for it.[14]

In fact, Trifa's visit to the Senate was arranged through regular
channels, through the Senate Chaplain, Rev. Dr. Frederick Brown
Harris, in correspondence with Father Haţegan in Cleveland.[15] And
when Kremer, back in the U.S. in 1956, worked out an elaborate
theory that Malaxa was donating huge sums of money to Trifa's
Episcopate so the Bishop could bring Guardist priests to the U.S.
from South America, and that FBI Director J. Edgar Hoover was
aware of this but willing to forget Trifa's past and "make a practical
alliance with an Iron Guard commandant in the interests of anti-

communism," even his uncritical amanuensis Blum found Kremer's theory—that Malaxa bought and used U. S. officials to restore the Iron Guard in America—"incredible."[16]

Yet conspiracy theories have always done well throughout American history as an easy substitute for facts, or to provide scapegoats to explain the failing of the system. In his radio broadcast of May 29, 1955, the contentious creator of the "Washington Merry-Go-Round," Drew Pearson, asked the following:

> Attention Senators! How did it happen that Viorel Trifa, the Orthodox churchman who led a pro-Nazi, anti-Semitic student movement in Romania back in 1941 delivered the opening prayer before the United States Senate on May 11? Trifa, who claims to be a bishop but was never ordained a priest, led a Nazi demonstration before the German legation at Bucharest on January 21, 1941. He was in Nazi Germany during World War II. Yet despite his Nazi background, Trifa entered the United States July 15, 1950—of all things as a displaced person! And believe it or not gave the opening prayer before you Senators two weeks ago. Just who, Senators, picks the churchmen who lead you in prayer."[17]

Leaving aside Pearson's unsubstantiated conclusions, the broadcast was wrong even in its factual surface. The student movement led by Trifa was pro-Romanian above all, and pro-German secondly (which is not the same as pro-Nazi). Naturally Trifa was ordained as a priest prior to becoming a Bishop. He did not lead a Nazi demonstration, he led a Romanian student demonstration, which stopped at the German embassy on its way to Antonescu's Council of Ministers office. Pearson has the wrong date. It was January 20, 1941. And Trifa entered the United States on July 17, 1950. But the "official protection" theory advanced another notch.

Six days later Pearson continued on Trifa in his syndicated Associated Press column, repeating what he said over the radio, and adding that Trifa "helped instigate an armed insurrection against the Antonescu government before Pearl Harbor when Antonescu protected Jews from persecution.[18] Once again Pearson was guessing, or at any rate knew very little about Antonescu's record of "protecting" anyone in the period he mentions. For the second time Pearson expressed astonishment that Trifa was allowed to enter America under the Displaced Persons Act of 1948, with the implied suggestion that somehow he had bypassed its requirements, or an exception had been made (friends in high places again). Had the columnist who knew all and saw all bothered to check, he would have found the absolute contrary, i.e., that Trifa had been processed more thoroughly than most DP's, both in Italy and in the United States.

The furor over Trifa's Senate prayer followed a by-now established pattern of making a mountain out of a molehill. Moreover, the same obfuscation encountered in the Winchell affair seemed to be operative here. On June 23, 1955, Trifa had his lawyer Clayton E. Bigg in Jackson, Michigan, write to the American Broadcasting Company, requesting a copy of Pearson's radio text of May 29.[19] Five days later Bigg was informed that Pearson had not been associated with ABC for over two years.[20] Meanwhile the damage was done, although Pearson would return to pontificate again, with more wrong information about Trifa in his columns seven years later. And twenty-five years later, the tempest in a teapot over the Senate prayer would have a parallel with even larger ramifications, when Trifa made an address over Radio Free Europe.

In the meantime, one seeking concrete evidence of Bishop Valerian's "protection" by persons in high places would have been hard-pressed to find it. Certainly his "contacts" were not sufficiently strong to prevent his being summoned by the Federal Bureau of Investigation for a three-day examination. This took place from February 19 through 21, 1955, even before the Pearson column or broadcast. Most likely the possibility of a "leak" from the FBI as the source of Pearson's meanderings must be discounted, if only because the depth of the three-day interview went beyond the six-inch level of analysis practiced by Pearson's ilk. Moreover it is fair to say that the publication *in extenso* of *any* of the official examinations which Trifa had undergone, from the Jaremko meeting, to the 1952 New York interview, to this 1955 FBI session, would have done more to disprove the allegations against him than strengthen them.

Trifa was questioned by three FBI examiners, in the Bureau's Detroit office. By this time his command of English was adequate, and the chances for misinterpretation were minimal. In sessions which filled a 35-page transcript, Trifa and the government men discussed interwar Romanian history and the facts of Trifa's biography at greater length than ever before. Nothing relative to the Bishop's role in Romanian student life or his deeds in connection with the 1941 *émeute* in Bucharest went unmentioned. A number of major and minor points were clarified, such as the fact that there were two major student associations in the Romanian capital in 1940-41, and that Trifa's presidency of the non-Legionary National Association of Romanian Christian Students was separate and distinct from the "Legionary Students Center" commanded by Victor Dragomirescu.

Most importantly, Trifa recounted, point by point, his movements during the critical days of January 20-23, 1941. He went on record again in noting that the "Manifesto" presented by him the night of January 20 was not his own work, but had been written by Traian Borobaru over Trifa's signature, and used throughout the country as a *set piece* in the days which followed. New information regarding his refusal to work with Sima in Germany emerged, as we shall see later on.[21] The point here is that the government of the United States, through both the Immigration Service and the FBI, by the end of 1955 had investigated Trifa on his past exhaustively. There was no cover-up whatsoever. Everything was on record, and documented.

Moreover, in his interviews accompanying his application for citizenship, Trifa would go over the same ground once again, during 1956 and 1957. Charges such as Kremer's which persisted into the 1960s that there was an official conspiracy to hide or ignore Trifa's past, or a refusal to investigate him, were totally without substance. The U.S. government knew, in truth, more about Trifa than his own mother knew, and despite the pleas *ad nauseam* of his detractors, Federal authorities decided and stated openly time and again, that there was no case to be made against him, that his entry into the country was perfectly legal, and that the grounds for any deportation proceedings were lacking. The only possible justification, it would seem, for re-opening the Trifa "case" would be the discovery of fundamental, new evidence showing significant variances about Trifa's deeds from what was already in United States records. One has only to examine the records and details of the "revival" of the Bishop's case since the mid-1950s to be convinced that no qualitatively new evidence has ever been produced.

The 88 "Exhibits"

Charles Kremer returned to New York in 1956, loaded with "ammunition that would shoot down Trifa."[22] According to his biographer, he "carefully organized his evidence," but in fact, as with most of Kremer's pronunciamentos, his "exhibits" seemed more as if he had loaded a shotgun with miscellaneous scraps of Romanian newspapers and fired it at a ream of paper, then numbered the results. Of course he expected his United Rumanian Jews to be excited now, but he could not stir their interest. Acknowledging that "Charlie Kremer isn't a joiner anyway, Charlie Kremer is a founder," in the fall of 1957 he started a new group of his own, the Romanian Jewish

Federation of America, Inc. Kremer was its president and its only
member.

It was more obvious than ever that Kremer's self-appointed role
as Trifa's accuser did not represent the thought of the American Jewish population, but was for the most part a one-man crusade. It was
not possible to say how many members the dentist recruited for his
new Federation, but even allowing for the most liberal estimate, and
based on observations of those whom he was able to turn out for
street demonstrations by the 1970s, fifty would seem excessive.

On his new letterhead he mailed xeroxed copies of his exhibits to
the President and Vice-President (the latter mailing is curious, since
Nixon was supposedly deeply involved in nefarious schemes with
Malaxa and Trifa), the Cabinet, immigration officials, Romanian
Union and League societies, all the parishes of Trifa's Diocese, New
York and Michigan Congressmen, the mayors of Detroit and Grass
Lake, and any newspapers he thought ought to be interested. "Any
day now, Charlie Kremer, you'll be reading about the government
kicking that bastard out. I really had terrific stuff."[23]

The nature and content of this "terrific stuff" and how Kremer
obtained it, is curious indeed. According to Blum:

> In Romania Kremer had spent weeks searching through
> newspaper morgues. In Bucharest he found news clips that re-
> ported Trifa's speeches and there were many photographs of
> the twenty-six -year-old commandant in his Iron Guard uni-
> form.... And there were anti-Semitic publications signed by
> Trifa that had been published in the Iron Guard newspapers
> *Buna Vestine* and *Porcuna Vremei*.[24] (*sic*)

Astounding! In the period 1954-1956, with Romania under the
Stalinist rule of Gheorghiu-Dej, at a time when there existed no programs for scholarly exchange such as did not come along until the
late 1960s, when restrictions on travel and censorship and contact
with the West were at a maximum, when legitimate scholars wishing
to do research into Romanian history could not receive permission,
Charlie Kremer, dentist, can wander at will through Bucharest, visit
and comb the files of newspaper offices, make copies or take notes
on anything he wants, and do all this while focussing on the sensitive
subject of the pre-World War II Legionary movement, about which
the Romanian scholarly establishment itself was not permitted to
publish a book until 1971!

It is likely that Dr. Kremer was given this material; rather than his
having dug it out himself. In any event, the bulk of the material came
from newspapers and tendentious newspapers at that. The "terrific
stuff" included pieces from *Buna Vestire* and *Porunca Vremii*. It is

probable that Kremer spent the bulk of his two-year stay abroad in Israel, and was given his material by resettled Romanian Jews interested in opposing remnants of Legionary sentiment scattered through the Western world. It is also not impossible that Kremer maintained his original contacts with Morariu, Martin, and others opposed to Trifa. Morariu, particularly, made frequent trips to Romania during the 1950s, on one occasion delivering a Cadillac to Patriarch Justinian Marina as a gift, and he may well have been the conduit through which materials against Trifa found their way from the hands of the Romanian Patriarchate to Detroit and thence to the one-man Jewish Federation in New York.

If Kremer thought his exhibits would guarantee victory, he was wrong. Most of the officials who received them automatically forwarded them to the immigration service, and the dentist received identical responses from Detroit, Washington, and New York:

> Subsequent to Bishop Trifa's entry into the United States, charges against him were received by this service. An extensive investigation was thereafter conducted over a period of years. Although the inquiries were exhaustive in scope and nature, they failed to establish any ground upon which Bishop Trifa might be removed from the United States.[25]

At this point Kremer "realized that the immigration people were involved in one of the greatest cover-ups of all time!"[26]

Final Clearance and Naturalization

Late in July, 1955, Trifa had fulfilled the five years' residence requirement necessary to fill out his first papers for citizenship. His "Application to File Petition for Naturalization" was filed with the U.S. Naturalization Service in Detroit, Michigan, on July 27, 1955.[27] Examiner Sidney Freed was assigned to handle the proceedings which were initiated in Jackson, Michigan. The Bishop filled out the usual form N-400, and attached a supplementary sheet listing the three times in his life he had been arrested: once in 1937 in Romania in connection with a student altercation, when, as President of the Student Center of the capital, Trifa was charged and given one year's probation, although he had not been present during the incident. Then his detention by the German authorities in Bucharest in 1941, when they took him out of Romania. And finally for an Ohio traffic violation which cost him a $12 fine. Trifa also noted that he learned of his trial and conviction by Antonescu's military tribunal in 1941 only after he had arrived in the United States.

It is also vital to notice that Trifa was given a standard form to sign, which pledged that he was neither an anarchist nor a member of the communist party, nor did he believe in or advocate the violent change or overthrow of the government of the United States. This, and the basic "Application" were the only forms he was given. At no time did he receive any master list of organizations and asked to declare that he belonged to none of them. To be sure, since his initial arrival in New York in 1950, he had been given only one such "list of subversive organizations," and this was distributed on the ship on which he arrived, the *U.S.S. General Taylor*, to all passengers before debarkation. Trifa's list was in German, contained the names of 115 organizations, and *"Die Eiserne Garde"* (The "Iron Guard") was not on the list.[28] Six years later, however, throughout the whole course of his multiple interviews for naturalization, his examiner did better than provide a list. He specifically asked Trifa, time and again, in front of witnesses, if he had belonged to the "Iron Guard," and Trifa said no, for the same reasons he had given this reply to federal officials in the past. He was also asked repeatedly if he was or had been anti-Semitic, and he replied, truthfully, that he was not.[29]

In the meantime, examiner Freed as a matter of course looked into the Bishop's case file, spoke to other officials in his department and inspected the Bishop's previous transcripts with the immigration office. After more than a year had passed since Trifa's application, Freed was fully aware of the controversy surrounding the man, the more so because it was during 1956 that Kremer returned from Israel and took up his letter-writing again. It is indicative, therefore, of Freed's desire not to act hastily on the matter that, even though Trifa had submitted all the paperwork, been examined several times, and fulfilled all the requirements for naturalization, when the time came for his name to be submitted to the court for citizenship, in the autumn of 1956, Freed informed him that he intended to delay the procedure. The reason for this was likely that the FBI, confronted by Kremer's newly-arrived exhibits, had not yet finished its reopened investigation.

Trifa was told that, if he chose, he could engage a lawyer and contest the delay. He did not. He wanted that there be no doubts lingering in the government's mind which might sully his citizenship, and it was not worth it to further publicize the continuing defamations.

By the spring of 1957, nearly twenty-two months after his initial petition, Trifa was called to Federal Court in Jackson for the final ceremonies of naturalization. Freed told the Court that there was no reason whatsoever to prevent Trifa's naturalization.[30]

Whereupon he took the oath of allegiance as a United States citizen, along with twenty other persons, on May 13, 1957.

We have gone into such detail for one reason only, because ten years later, in 1967, Dr. Kremer requested a copy of Trifa's testimony at his naturalization hearing, and was told that only oral testimony was taken, there was no transcript made of the entire proceedings.[31] As Kremer immediately decided, and Blum undeviatingly copied down, the "Detroit District I.N.S. examiner had simply decided it was not necessary to follow normal practice." Therefore, "Trifa had bought the entire immigration service."[32]

In fact, Sidney Freed did follow normal procedure, perfectly normal procedure during his preliminary interviews with Trifa, and made notes on his standard forms as to the Bishop's answers to questions and his knowledge of the United States constitution and its form of government. It must be remembered that the thrust, the emphasis, of the naturalization process, was not to bare in detail every fragment of a person's past life, but to determine his suitability for citizenship at present. The examiner's task is to determine that the candidate holds no convictions antithetical to American principles, and is congenial to democratic ideals. Not only was Trifa's knowledge of U.S. civics evident, and his grasp of English becoming extraordinary for a non-native speaker, but his comportment in the United States was that of a model citizen. In short, the naturalization procedure looks to the future, rather than the past, and in light of the subsequent twenty-three years, there was no reason for the body politic to regret having made Trifa one of its own.

Yet in another sense, Freed did go beyond the call of "normal procedure" by his rigorous questioning on numerous occasions, and his decision to delay the Bishop's oath-taking for more than six months so that yet another investigation might be completed.

Persistence, the Mother of Invention

There exist a multiplicity of invented stories, half-truths, and anecdotes grounded in some half-remembered reality and embellished and repeated until fact and fiction are indistinguishable, in any large immigrant community, whose members have spent the most impressionable portions of their lives in another country. When this community hails from Eastern Europe and there is a division of philosophy among the population as to whether or not to recognize and relate to a current political regime—and when this is compounded by a vitriolic schism within the largest religious body embracing the community—there will never be a lack of individuals to come forth with their "stories" or testimony about a co-national in the opposite camp whom, for reasons of its own, the story-teller's faction seeks to discredit. Whether for prestige within his own peer group, or for some real or imagined slight or insult which he has experienced at the hands of the other faction, or simply because Romanians love to talk and place themselves at the center of the action, this phenomenon operates regardless of the length of stay in the host country or the degree of assimilation reached. Social anthropologists might explain it in terms of the transferral of the oral news network of a village peasant society to the American ethnic neighborhood. Even the dissipation of these neighborhoods into the no-longer compact ethnic communities of the 1970s does not completely extinguish this tendency, for religious and social life, based on ethnic church and secular fraternal societies, provide the social and psychological cohesion once created by sheer physical proximity.

Therefore there will never be a dearth of people to come forth and say, "Trifa? Of course, I knew him in Romania, and let me tell you . . ." whether they did or not. The number of popular stories that have circulated about the Bishop in this manner are endless, both because of his high position in the Romanian-American community, and because he has become, through no conscious effort of his own, a controversial and newsworthy figure. As with any such individual, there is a degree of vicarious excitement or psychic prestige in being able to talk about him intimately; accuracy is a secondary matter. A few examples out of many will suffice.

For a long time the story circulated, and was bandied about in the Martin press, that Trifa had converted to Catholicism before coming to America, and that he was actually a Roman Catholic priest coming in disguise to take over the Romanian Orthodox community in America—for nefarious reasons which only the wily schemers of the Vatican knew. Certain factors in Trifa's biography lent a smattering of credence to this. His uncle, Josif Trifa, was the founder of a widespread and extremely religious revival movement among the Transylvanian peasantry and had run afoul of the powerful Orthodox Metropolitan Nicolae Balan, ruler of the Transylvanian church. Balan had excommunicated Josif Trifa in the 1930s, and his nephew Viorel had a confrontation with Balan when the Metropolitan would not allow Josif Trifa to be buried in his priestly clothing.

Moreover, since the beginning of the 17th century, when the Uniate Church (Byzantine-rite Catholic) was begun in Transylvania, the Orthodox priesthood of that province had adopted a militant defensive stance toward Uniatism, which they viewed as an attempt first by the Habsburgs and then, after the 1867 *Ausgleich*, by the ruling Hungarian nobility, to Catholicize and Magyarize the indigenous Romanian population. Unquestionably this militancy and distrust of the Catholics in their midst carried over to the Orthodox immigrant population in America, the majority of which stemmed from Transylvania. The history of Romanian America since 1900 is replete with rumors and perceived threats, at one time or another, that this or that group, or faction or clergyman intended to "sell out" the Episcopate or the local parish, or whatever, to the Catholics.[33] The fact that such fears were in the main imaginary is largely irrelevant. The immigrant population of Uniates always remained small in America, with perhaps fewer than two thousand today, but the fact that the Uniate parishes submitted to the jurisdiction of the local Catholic hierarchy wherever they happened to build their churches inevitably cast a thin but definable separation between them and the majority Orthodox community.

To this, we may add two elements. Trutza, who at one time or another was accused of practically everything, was of course alleged at one point to be plotting with the Catholics. Trifa's disaffection with the Sibiu hierarchy provided the rationale for some to believe that he had turned Catholic in spite. Finally, add the element that Trifa had spent the period 1945 to 1950 in Italy, of all places, and taught at a Catholic school, and the ingredients for a fine rumor are all present. When one Father Crihalmean, a Byzantine-rite priest in Canton, Ohio, spread the story that he had met Trifa in Blaj, Romania (the administrative headquarters city of the Catholic Church in Transylvania) at the time when Trifa was there applying for reception into the Uniate Church, this was conclusive evidence of what some suspected indeed. Yet when the Bishop, on a visit to Father Traian Demian's parish in Canton, was taken to meet Crihalmean on a courtesy visit, the Catholic curate denied ever having uttered such a story about Blaj. Trifa and he had never before met each other, and the two laughed about the Orthodox Bishop's career as a Catholic, which was over before it began. Besides, such a story was not compatible with the several sets of wives and children which Trifa had abandoned in various countries.

In 1955 an article appeared in Moldovan's *Credinţa* Calendar by one George Muntean of Chicago, apparently inspired by Muntean's friendship with Alexander Suciu. Somewhat more serious was the bit of folklore to which Muntean sought to add, when he wrote that he personally knew Trifa from Romania, and had been an eyewitness to the student leader's crimes. Despite the fact that by 1974 Muntean would contradict himself flatly, and almost completely deny what he had written earlier, the damage was done, for the sanctity of print on the minds of simple people only one generation removed from a Balkan village did its work. Three, or five, or twenty years later, those seeking material against Trifa could find plenty in such articles, took them at face value and repeated the stories anew to another generation. In the pantheon of Romanian-American folklore, amidst the sometimes funny, sometimes outrageous tales of Moise Balea, Glicherie Morariu, Ioan Podea, and Policarp Moruşca, one may speculate as to the stock of stories which will surround the name of Valerian Trifa, for both good and ill, as the never-ending process of popular mythologization goes onward.

An excellent example of such folklore in the making is Dr. Kremer's ephemeral "89th Exhibit," the Romanian sculptor Constantin Antonovici and his tale of the wine-soaked non-party which he attended at the Vatra the evening after the Bishop got his citizenship in 1957. [34]

One must really credit Howard Blum for his ability to tell a good, dramatic story and give it the appearance of history. He begins the chapter on Trifa in his widely read book *Wanted!* (1976) with the scenario of Antonovici's recognition of Trifa and numerous other "ex-Iron Guardists," during a celebratory evening in Michigan at the time when Antonovici was working at Romanian church headquarters.[35] The essence of the same story is repeated in Blum's excerpt in *Esquire* magazine in October, 1976,[36] and in the ensuing four years thousands of readers among the general public have come to accept Blum's account as more or less true. In fact it is almost wholly fictitious, and even as a set-piece the narrative is marred by errors of geography, placement of persons, and dialogue so obviously contrived and patent as to be suspect from the outset. Even one with casual knowledge of Antonovici's past dealings with the Trifa Episcopate could reveal motivations of displeasure on the part of the sculptor which clearly help to explain why he would allow himself to be melded into Blum's literary theatricalism. *Au pays des aveugles les borgnes sont rois.* There remains one interesting postscript to the Antonovici fable: in an interview with *The Michigan Journalist* early in 1977, the sculptor denied ever having said anything about Trifa or any party.[37]

Bucharest Joins In

A major watershed was reached in the history of Trifa's Episcopate during 1960, when the knotty problem of its canonical status was resolved through acceptance into the jurisdiction of the Russian Metropolia in New York. Ever since 1947 the philosophy of the Episcopate had been based on the hope that the Church in Romania would again be free one day and normal relations could be re-established. This, of course, had not happened by 1960. Although the strategy of the Romanian Patriarchate in Bucharest appeared to shift from one of confrontation to negotiation as the new decade opened, the Romanian Church was no more a free agent than before.

In fact, despite a brief lull in the slander emerging from the Moldovan press, rumors were rife that Patriarch Justinian Marina planned another round in his efforts to obtain the property of the Vatra for the Romanian state, and that the Moldovan case might be re-opened in the courts. Even in February, 1960, the Episcopate engaged three lawyers to counteract this anticipated move, and sure enough by July Moldovan attorney John Vintilla petitioned the Supreme Court to review the case.[38] Yet this was no more successful than earlier.

In the meantime, searching for a hierarchical affiliation, since in the Orthodox world there could be, *de jure*, no such thing as an independent Episcopate, Trifa and his Council had made overtures both to the Syrian Orthodox hierarchy and the Patriarchate of Antioch, and the Greek Orthodox Metropolia in New York. In each case Justinian Marina intervened, denouncing Trifa to the Syrians and Greeks, and threatening a rupture of relations with the Romanian Church.

The Russian Metropolia, then, was in one sense a last resort, but nevertheless a logical choice for the autonomous diocese. Established in New York in 1917 following the Bolshevik Revolution, it had broken contacts with the mother church in Russia, while yet retaining communion with the Ecumenical Patriarchate. Moreover, early in the history of the Romanian Church in America, many of the Romanian parishes had been under the Russian Metropolia's jurisdiction, especially those in Canada. Then too, by 1960, the Russian establishment in America was moving toward the removal of all ties with Europe and Constantinople (Istanbul), looking to the future creation of an American Orthodox Church institution—a movement which reached fruition in 1970.

To laymen and non-Orthodox, all of this had little meaning. The Episcopate was hard put to explain its new affiliation, and from the opposition came the expected hue and cry: true to the legacy of Trutza, the Episcopate had been sold out, this time to the Russians, rather than to Catholics or Episcopalians.

How in the world, asked the Moldovan news organs, and the communist-backed *Românul-American*, could the Trifa organization pose in a firm anti-communist stance for thirteen years, only to end up in the lap of the Russian Church.[39] Such nostrums of course ignored the fact that the Metropolia was entirely independent of Moscow.

Equally important for Trifa personally was the question of his Holy Orders. In June, at his own request, he traveled to New York to settle the long-standing doubts as to his reception of the apostolic succession. Leonty afterwards announced that the Great Council of Bishops examined him and "through the laying-on of our hands we have confirmed his Holy Orders."[40] The *samosfeat* argument was at last laid to rest.

Yet there were important long-range implications of the link-up with the Russian Metropolia. Most of all it meant that the possibility of a reconciliation with the mother church in Romania now became more remote than ever, for Trifa's Diocese had entered what Bucharest termed "another Orthodox unity." In fact 1960 meant no sacrifice of diocesan autonomy. The Russian Church had merely assumed a "protector" status over the Romanians, in order to provide them with a valid canonical framework in which to operate and relate to other Orthodox Church hierarchies. In theory, at least, Trifa could at any time, with the Metropolia's permission, re-unite with the Romanian Patriarchate in Bucharest, although so long as the Romanian Church was controlled by a communist government, this was nearly impossible to expect.

Nevertheless Bucharest never ceased to hope that somehow the breach might be healed during the 1950s, and its advice and support to the Moldovan propaganda efforts, the attempt to discredit Trifa and sway Romanian-American support away from him, had all been aimed at winning the broad prestige and the monetary and propaganda value to be had from the demise of an autonomous Episcopate in America—whether headed by Trifa or anyone else. What 1960 meant for Bucharest was that its hopes for such a goal were dimmer than ever. It was losing the struggle. If one adds to this two other factors—the refusal of the U.S. Supreme Court in October to reopen the Moldovan case, and the death of Moldovan himself late in the winter of 1963, it is understandable why, from Bucharest's point of view, it was necessary that, despite a respite of a couple of years, Trifa once again become a notorious "war criminal."

The chief instrument for resurrecting the gore this time was Romanian Chief Rabbi Moshe Rosen. In 1950, when the process of exerting state control over every major religious establishment in Romania was well along, there were two candidates for the largely titular position of Chief Rabbi: Moshe Rosen and Rabbi David Safran, whose reputation as an anti-communist was well-known. The Communist Party named Rosen, whose office, like that of the Orthodox Patriarch, was subordinate to the state Minister of Cults. The incumbent Chief Rabbi, Alexandru Safran, was forced out of office.

In November, 1961, Rosen was sent on a trip to the West to inform his fellow Jews that the Romanian government was truly their friend. Stopping first in Paris and London to meet with Jewish groups, Rosen then arrived in New York, where he stayed three months.

The Rabbi had nothing new to say about Trifa, certainly nothing that had not been said many times before, and he offered no new substantive evidence for any of his statements. One was simply to assume that words from the Chief Rabbi of a nation of Eastern Europe bore the weight of truth—until it was remembered that official dignitaries did not receive expenses-paid trips to the West unless they had a specific task to perform for the regime. Most American Jews, knowing Rosen's background or viewing his position, saw it for what it was, and paid scant attention to him. Yet he spoke so incessantly of Trifa's war crimes and depredations that militants were blithely willing to overlook the source and concentrate on the pressure which Rosen's visit could bring to bear. They convinced Congressman Seymour Halpern of Queens to raise the issue in the United States House of Representatives and demand yet another investigation.[41]

Halpern's statement of March 1, 1962 in Congress was the by-now standard gloss for the Trifa story. After commemorating the 21st anniversary of "a grisly event in modern Jewish martyrology" he described the bloodshed and rapine which took place in Bucharest in 1941, and went on to blame most of it on Trifa. What followed was a mass of assumptions and blithe assertions, which clearly indicated Halpern's uncritical acceptance of everything he'd been told. The statement made judgmental assertions which even today have not been agreed upon in the field of Romanian history. For example, Antonescu's regime is called "reactionary but non-fascist," which is straight from the new, 1960s-style party line of official history,[42] as Romanian historiography began to rehabilitate the general slightly. Such a distinction could only have come from Rosen. The January, 1941 pogrom was conducted not only by the Iron Guard, but

also its ally, the National Union of Rumanian Christian Students."
No one had ever proved such a statement.

Halpern went on, relative to Trifa and his student society, that
"there is no doubt of their active participation in it," referring to the
three-day uprising. But there was, and there is, doubt. Halpern had
Trifa being ordained in the wrong year. He noted that his consecration was carried out despite a Federal Court injunction—but never
mentions that the case was dismissed, thus leaving the impression
somehow that, ten years later, Trifa was still in defiance of court.
Halpern demanded that the American public be made aware of Trifa's
"presence in our midst." The Congressman closed by offering to
make available to the proper authorities "the documentation which
provides the basis for my remarks today. I feel they offer more than
sufficient proof for a re-investigation of this man."[43]

Although the sources of the documentation were not revealed,
the damage was done. Trifa's opponents could now clip a page from
the Congressional Record and send it, often anonymously, to those
they sought to turn against the Bishop. The average layman in the
Episcopate, to say nothing of the non-Romanian man in the street,
now saw the prestige of the United States Congress placed against this
controversial immigrant churchman. How could they know that
Halpern was simply repeating the same tired and erroneous lines from
Tribuna now a decade old? Only one final element remained for the
irreversible process of mass persuasion to complete its involuted
cycle—to get this "stock story" on Trifa spread beyond the realm of
the esoteric foreign-language newspaper, and even the relatively
sparsely-studied Congressional Record, and into the vehicle which
could employ the techniques of thought persuasion *par excellence*—
the mass English-language press. Rosen left New York, his work begun, and moved on to bigger things.

By March, 1962, the Rabbi was in Israel, and had convinced Aryet
Tartakower, chairman of the Israeli section of the World Jewish Congress, to convene a press conference in Tel Aviv on May 3, at which
Rosen repeated his charges, to be sent out everywhere. A few days
later a postcard from Israel, insufficiently addressed simply to Bishop
"Valerian," Detroit, USA, arrived at the Detroit post office. The post-
master turned it over to the FBI, which delivered it to the Vatra on
May 8. The sender, one Karui Bariu, reminded Trifa of his slaughter
of Jews in Jassy (Iaşi) and informed him that the next day a com-
mando party was leaving Detroit, "which will catch and murder your
Eminenc (*sic*)." The message concluded:

. . . so our party will find you and kill and if this would be after one year searching: we will find you, my dear, be sure of this. And tremble, tremble, you swine, Bishop-swine we will slaughter your cadaver about kasher (*sic*) custom and hang like Mussolini cadaver, on a tree, head down, and your blood will drop down to the earth, like the corpses of the slaughtereds canins (*sic*). We have caught many culprits and you also. You will very soon see your boss Codreanu.

(*signed*) Yours truly.[44]

The Rabbi Rosen had done his work well. Where there had been for a time tolerance, he resurrected hatred. In an Episcopate which had for the most part lacked anti-Jewish sentiment, he set out to create some. And he provided the fodder for a voracious news establishment forever on the watch for sensational headlines.

"Rabbi Brands Bishop a War Criminal," blazoned the Associated Press article in the *New York Herald Tribune* the day after Mosen's Tel Aviv appearance. Two of Rosen's basic statements formed the crux of the news coverage in the weeks to follow: that Trifa was an "escaped war criminal" who was tried and convicted to life imprisonment in Romania (presumably for these war crimes, which is the clear inference the reader must make), and that Trifa "had a hand in organizing the pogrom in Bucharest in January, 1941." The *Tribune* here was moderate on the second allegation—most stories, especially if based on Kremer letters, had Trifa flatly "starting and directing" the pogrom and personally supervising the killing. Moreover the *Tribune* made up a new organization, having Trifa command the "Legionnaire Hitler Movement." No such thing ever existed.[45]

On the same day, the *Winnipeg Tribune* announced "Rabbi Lays War Crimes to Bishop," and was more specific as to how Trifa "infiltrated the Rumanian Orthodox Church in Detroit . . .with the help of former associates in the Hitler movement."[46] Whose help? Father Trutza's, who had been in America since 1922?

Paris' *Le Monde*, usually noted for its analytical coverage, saw fit to reprint what its correspondent Philippe Ben filed from New York. After observing that the American section of the World Jewish Congress demanded a new Justice Department investigation of the Bishop, and repeating the usual business that Trifa's Diocese was the illegal one which had usurped power from the original Moldovan Episcopate (which was backwards), *Le Monde* did touch on a fundamental truth. The paper suggested that with "the change of political climate in Washington," i.e., the demise of the McCarthy era, staunch anti-communism was no longer sufficient in itself to guarantee a person immunity. Did this mean somethow that U.S. court decisions and lengthy investigations against Trifa undertaken in the 1950s were now somehow to be set aside because a communist Rabbi had repeated in public the identical charges made in 1951 or 1955? Yet *Le Monde* was not above the same kind of "suggestive" and misleading writing found elsewhere.

> Non seulement il se fit élire peu de temps après chef d'une secte qu'il semble avoir créée lui-même et qui est *probablement* composée d'anciens fascists roumains, mais il avait réussi à se maintenir dans cette situation malgré un procès qui lui fut intenté par les autorités de l'Eglise orthodoxe roumaine en Amérique. Fait encore *plus stupéfiante.. .* .[47]   *(italics ours)*

The "probably" means "we don't know, but it fits the tone of the story," and "even more stupefying" suggests that it is incredible that Trifa's group won the court case, *or,* that it lost the case, but "maintains itself" somehow in defiance of the legal process.

So on it went, with the Tel Aviv, Bucharest, and New York newspapers serving as Rosen's press agents. Interestingly, the *Românul-American* printed its coverage of the "new" discoveries, in English, with the full text of Congressman Halpern's speech, and one of Martin's old photographs of corpses in Bucharest, over the caption "This and other horrible crimes were committed by Trifa's hordes on January 21 and 22, 1941."[48]

It is noteworthy that in those areas of the country where Trifa was known, or where there were sizeable concentrations of Romanian Orthodox Christians, the reporting had a different thrust and emphasis.[49] Under the rubric "A Clergyman Slandered," the *Jackson Citizen Patriot* had one of the most sensible ripostes to the new wave of insinuation:

> These charges, it should be pointed out, have not been substantiated by as much as a bit of evidence, and until there is evidence . . . it would be well to view the charges with extreme skepticism.
>
> One should consider who made the charges (a clergyman in Romania, where the church, its personnel and activities are carefully controlled by the Communist government) and the motives Red Romania might have for discrediting the bishop at Grass Lake.
>
> Unfortunately . . . many persons will tend to believe them simply because they have been publicly stated.[50]

And the *Toronto Telegram* headlined the business "Nazi Bishop Story Called Propaganda," and pointed out the chronological impossibility of Trifa having been involved in war crimes, while the *Globe and Mail* at least began its article with Trifa's statement on the issue rather than Rosen's. Nevertheless between its appearance in New

York, transferral to Detroit, and recopying in Toronto, the story underwent the inevitable subtle metamorphosis. By the time it has passed through the hands of three reporters, two separate thoughts become linked, a word is shifted here and there, and the *Globe and Mail* final version reads "Trifa had been tried in absentia by a Romanian military court and sentenced in 1941 to life in prison for pogroms against the Jewish people."[51] Rosen at least had only made the inference; now it became a declarative sentence. Trifa was never sentenced to as much as one day for any pogrom or crimes against Jews. Everybody talked about it. No one read the 1941 trial transcript.

Instead they read the Toronto *Confidential Flash*, the kind of instant supermarket-cart truth in reporting. The *Flash* reported on a "recent secret Chicago meeting of European patriots," (none are identified) who had listed plans of "action" against 16 Nazi (bold print) mass murder suspects in the United States, including "Viorel Trifa, alias Bishop Valerian." The number of murdered Jews had now risen once again, this time to 6,000.[52]

"I told you so, I told you so," chimed in Drew Pearson, back for another round. Beginning in June, 1962, and continuing through the following May, when "Nazi stories" began to reach the saturation point and no longer caused such a stir, Pearson wrote a number of articles with themes of Pro-Nazi Exiles and "Ex-Nazi Agents Still in U.S." In each case the notion that the United States was "protecting" such persons was not merely suggested, as in Pearson's 1955 pieces on Trifa, but this time frankly posited.[53] Pearson was no more accurate on Trifa's history after seven years, contenting himself with mouthing Rosen's charges, and repeating the inaccuracies of his previous columns about the Bishop's appearance in the U.S. Senate. Once again readers were told that the Antonescu government "had protected Rumanian Jews from persecution," while new items were being added by Pearson. On May 12, 1963, he wrote that Trifa's "official title" had been "Chief of Fascist Students," which was absurd, and he had Trifa giving his "rabble-rousing speech of January 20, 1941, in the Assembly Hall of the Student Union in Bucharest," which was wrong—the speech in question was given outside, in University Square. Pearson concluded by copying another paper's error, stating that "Trifa was sentenced to life imprisonment for his crimes against the Jewish people," but "managed to escape to the United States."[54]

The same day, in his "Washington Merry-Go-Round" column carried in other papers, he spoke of three men being "harbored" by the United States, one of them Trifa. This time the Bishop was identified as a high official of the "Romanian Dissident Orthodox Church." No such organization ever existed.

More interesting is Pearson's summary of the Bishop's answers when he, Pearson, interviewed or spoke to Trifa. "When I queried Trifa . . . he alibied, etc., etc. Nevertheless, the incidents in which Trifa participated helped touch off the murder of 6,000 to 10,000 Jews."[55] The number of Jews kept going up inversely to the fall of the writer's credibility, for Pearson never spoke to Trifa in his life. Fourteen years later another zealous "investigative reporter" also stated that he had interviewed the Bishop, and made him quake in his boots at the bold, informed, keen questions of his interlocutor. This was Howard Blum, who also invented a non-existent "interview" with Trifa.[56]

There was also Charles R. Allen, Jr., advertised as a free-lance journalist who had published some 250 articles in respectable outlets such as *Collier's, The Nation*, and *The New Statesman*. During the summer of 1963, members of Trifa's Episcopate began to receive in the mail an unsolicited 42-page pamphlet authored by Allen, titled "Nazi War Criminals Among Us." It was a reprint from the publication *Jewish Currents*, independently bound, with pages 18-22 devoted to "The Iron Guard and the Bishop." In what on the surface gave the appearance of a dispassionate and documented inquiry into the subject, with sources provided parenthetically in the text, Allen went over the by-now standard monologue; except he had the wrong date for the "Iron Guard" uprising. And the Bishop's age was off by two years. Dramatic, too, was Allen's interview with Bishop Trifa. His probing questions, based on wide research, almost at once aroused the Bishop's ire, who told Allen that the charges were "communist-inspired." "Did the bishop include Congressman Halpern among these?" "He is a stupid dupe," Bishop Valerian snapped. . . ." Was he innocent of these charges? "Yes!" he screamed over the long-distance wires: "The Jews were never touched!" Wasn't the bishop aware of proof of the pogrom in German and Romanian archives? "God-damn you! You Communist!" "And with that, Viorel D. Trifa, now known as Bishop Valerian, hung up."[57] Allen never talked to Trifa in his life.

CHAPTER V
WANDERERS BETWEEN TWO WORLDS

What began as a rather simple civil suit for denaturalization in United States Federal Court in Detroit in 1975 has grown over the years into a large historical debate over fascism in Romania, the relationship of the Legionary Movement to Nazi Germany, and the role played by Valerian Trifa in instigating the controversial "Legionary Rebellion" against the government of General Ion Antonescu in January, 1941, in which several hundred Jewish and Christian citizens of Bucharest were killed by "Guardists" out of control. In fact, according to Raul Hilberg in his *The Destruction of the European Jews*, 118 Jews were killed during this episode (p. 489).

In light of the importance played by the Legionary Movement in the Trifa case, some examination of its central role in the history of interwar Romania is called for. It is significant in two basic ways: first, it is Trifa's alleged misrepresentation during his naturalization process about his membership in the Legion which constitutes the government's principal claim against him; secondly, events commonly connected with the Legion led to the "war crimes" label for the Bishop, by virtue of his association with the movement.

Therefore it is vital to inquire into this unique phenomenon in Romanian history, to understand it in the context of its time and place, and seek to determine what led intelligent men and women to belong to or support it. From this it follows that sufficient evidence must be evaluated to convince reasonable men that the Legion did indeed perpetrate the crimes of which it is accused. Finally, and most importantly in this situation, does all the available evidence convince us that Valerian Trifa took part in such crimes?

Leaving aside for the moment the competency of the Justice Department to solve such thorny problems of history and interpretation, it ought to be stated at the outset that we *do not know* very much about the Legionary Movement, compared to other areas of Romanian history. Scholars, historians, and political scientists are far from agreement in their definitions and interpretations of Romania between the First and the Second World Wars.

Assumptions and Limited Access

There is little disagreement that Romania emerged from the Paris Peace Conference of 1919 with high hopes and that, as was the case with nearly all of Central and Eastern Europe (the so-called "succession states" which had dramatically gained or enlarged themselves as a result of the dismantling of the Ottoman, Austro-Hungarian, and German Empires) the country entered the 1920s with optimism.[1] In Romania's case internal land reform, long-awaited, and a new constitution in 1923 seemed to be signs of solid parliamentary life and social and economic reform to come. Yet within a few years some of the most virulent manifestations of nationalism and anti-foreign feeling in the small nation's history came into being, in the form of various parties, movements, political alignments and coalitions. Among these was the Legionary Movement.

The Movement, like its contemporary fellows on the ideological, political, and social scene, was fiercely nationalistic and violently anti-foreign. In many ways it was fascist-like, and in many ways it was completely unlike similar movements in Fascist strongholds such as Italy, Spain, and Germany. At the time a broad segment of public opinion viewed the members of the Legionary Movement as mere practitioners of demagoguery and hooliganism, and by the late 1940s a section of the popular press labeled it as merely a German Fifth Column. Yet even then, serious students of modern Romania, such as Henry Roberts, called such opinions short-sighted and simplistic, when he wrote of the movement as an indigenous and important aspect of Romanian political and social life.[2]

Ernst Nolte saw Legionarism as "one of the most original political formations in inter-war Europe," and even "the most interesting and complex fascist movement in Europe."[3] Yet popular literature in magazines and newspapers to this day, along with radio and television reportage, continues to base its treatment of the Legionary Movement (which it erroneously labels the "Iron Guard" regardless of the time-frame under discussion) on certain fundamental assumptions—notions taken for granted as requiring no challenge and thus akin to universal givens, about the Legionary Movement:

1. It was a branch or offshoot in Romania of the GermanNazi Party.
2. It was financed, organized, and directed by Germany.
3. It was a fascist party, and therefore shared all of the philosophy and goals of its counterparts in the nations of the Axis.

4. It was anti-Semitic, and therefore racist.

5. Its political thought and practical approach was fundamen-
   ally violent, and it thus attracted to its ranks the worst elements of Romanian society—thus it was made up of rabble,
   thugs, and social outcast types.

6. The names "Iron Guard" and "Legionary Movement" or
   "Legionnaire" are interchangeable.

7. The Movement was monolithic, cohesive, and united in organization and purpose.

8. There was a single Legionary Movement, from 1927 through
   1941.

9. Because some Legionnaires were guilty of crimes and violence, anyone who belonged to or was associated with the
   Movement must also have been guilty of them.

10. The Legion was the initiator and bears primary responsibil-
    ty for starting an uprising against the legally constituted
    government of Romania in January, 1941, during which
    widespread death and destruction were carried out—exclu-
    sively by Legionnaires—including a vicious pogrom in the
    Jewish quarter of Bucharest.

The list might well be extended, but it suffices to show that, if
one accepts such assumptions as true and corroborated by history,
the very linking of a person's name with such a Movement is enough
to portray him as a villainous and vicious character indeed. Yet each
of these assumptions is erroneous in part and, in some cases, totally
wrong. As for many of them, if put to historians who have spent
years studying the problem, the answer would have to be "We simply
don't know," or "We're not sure of this or that."

History and the Historians

Students of Romanian affairs, historians, political scientists, sociol-
ogists, and other professionals whose task it is to clarify, investigate,
and interpret the past are far from being unanimous about interwar
Romania in general, or the Legionary Movement in particular. In
fact, specialists in European history continue to debate, define, and
seek acceptable common ground as to what, precisely, is meant by
terms such as "fascist," "anti-Semitic," "Romanian Right," and so
on, especially within the contexts of the political, economic, and
ideological histories of individual countries. The fact is that there
was not one, but *several* "fascisms," not one but several meanings
and levels for such a thing as "anti-Semitism," and so on.

A further complication often escapes notice, given the very recent
date when Americans began to know anything about Europe east of

the Elbe. It is the very fact that we are here dealing with a historical question of *Eastern* Europe, on which scholarship in the western world is only beginning to approach the volume of works on, for example, French, German or Spanish history. For a country such as Romania, practically unknown to the American public before the Second World War, the lack of information and understanding is compounded, and the natural—and wrong—tendency to judge the facts of Romanian life by Western standards of parliamentary democracy, tolerance, due process, and all the rest of the apparatus of Western civilization leads to distortion and error.

Before 1945, then, except for a handful of works of general synthesis, such as those of David Mitrany or R.W. Seton-Watson, specialized studies on Romania were singularly non-existent outside of Romania.[4] The small number of articles and studies on the country in America rested on library shelves or in the files of doctoral dissertations in university holdings, with only minimal chances of ever being seen by the broad public.

The communist takeover of the Romanian government in 1945 raised the wall of non-contact with the West even higher, and Romanian archives and other depositories necessary for producing solid and non-involved historical works became inaccessible to Western scholars. This situation changed only in the middle 1960s, with regard to Americans. Programs such as that of the Fulbright-Hays and the New York-based International Research and Exchanges Board negotiated arrangements for the exchange of American and Romanian researchers, but problems of access to archives remained. For at least fifteen years or more after the war the documentary sources relating to local fascism counted as classified security material, and discussion of fascism appeared only in party literature and the propaganda media. Fascism was a term of abuse, applied to practically all of the interwar parties and regimes, and even today it has not lost its usage as a cant phrase for anything non-communist, much as American youth of the 1960s labeled fascist anything with which they disagreed, to the extent that the word became bereft of any real significance.

Western scholars faced with this situation enjoyed most success when they confined their study proposals in Romania to "safe" topics, those having the sanction of the state-controlled Romanian Academy or institutes of history. Articles or books stressing Romanian nationalism and the struggle for independence in the 19th century or earlier, those which glorified the nation's heroes or linked Romania to ancient Dacia and thus supported territorial and irredentist claims were welcomed. This became more than ever the case after 1965, as Romania's new self-assertive stance in foreign policy vis-à-vis the Soviet Union, and elaboration of a Titoist philosophy of construct- ing one's own path to socialism began to evolve. The Legionary Movement and interwar politics up to the mid-1960s, however, were not "safe" subjects. Zevedei Barbu, speaking of the Iron Guard, could write truthfully in 1968, "as far as primary sources are concern- ed . . . most of the studies published so far, in Rumanian or other languages, are on the whole under-documented,"[5] and eight years later one of the most informed specialists of Romanian history, Bela Vago, could repeat this statement with no fear of contradiction.[6]

In 1981 it remains the case that, apart from some excellent essays by Stephen Fischer-Galati, Emanuel Turczynski, and Paul Shapiro,[7] not a single book has been published devoted entirely to the Legion- ary Movement. The most ambitious effort thus far is Nicholas Nagy- Talavera's comparative study of the Hungarian Arrow Cross Move- ment and the Romanian Iron Guard, which is now ten years old.[8]

One must stress the paucity of literature on Romanian fascism in Western libraries first of all, because such works are the most keenly felt by their absence: there is no dearth of Marxist writings condemn- ing fascism or emigré literature extolling the Legionnaires. Bela Vago draws a useful classification of the three categories of existing litera- ture on East European fascism: 1) post World War II local (communist) literature; 2) fascist emigré literature; and 3) works written in the West by non-involved historians.[9]

Much less useful, and nearly inaccessible to the broad mass of Americans due to language barriers, are works written by Romanians on the origins and nature of the Legionary Movement. This holds true as well for the emigré literature. The difficulty here is that with the possible exception of a few Western scholars, historians or writers engaged in such works are extremely prejudiced, due to personal or political involvement, or in other ways. It cannot be stressed too often that views about interwar Romania, even on basic matters such as facts which would seem to be beyond any controversy, are widely divergent. Those uncritically seeking "proofs" about the Legionary Movement in such works are ignorant of the most basic rules of historiography.

Surveying the literature on Romanian fascism, the first post-war years begin with a work appearing in 1944 by one of Romania's most brilliant theoreticians, Lucreţiu Pătrăşcanu's *Sub trei dictaturi* ("Under Three Dictatorships"), written as early as 1941. It disappeared from the market in 1949 and only with Pătrăşcanu's rehabilitation was it reissued in 1970. To this day the book is one of the very few places one can find analysis of the social composition of the Legionary rank and file, and elite, and if one discounts Marxian formulations, Pătrăşcanu's dissection is roughly valid even today. He emphasized the strong mass basis of the Legionnaires, which was due less to importing ideas from abroad than to Codreanu's ability to adapt fascism to the "autochthonous" medium.[10] Communist though he is, Pătrăşcanu admits that the Guard was essentially made up of peasants and working class elements, though at the same time he continually reminds us of the *Lumpenproletariat* elements in the midst of the Legion in order to salvage the working class from the charge of fascism. Even this has some use in pointing up the fact that the Legion was complex and varied in its membership. To be very basic, there were all kinds of Legionnaires: moral, religious, and dedicated men interspersed with all kinds of opportunists, ranging from petty swindlers to thieves and cutthroats. At the same time the roles of young intellectuals and the Orthodox clergy were also decisive, and the incorporation of Christian Orthodoxy into political agitation does not escape Pătrăscanu's emphasis. Finally, his conclusion that the Legionary Movement was used as an instrument of "political mass maneuver at the disposal of the ruling forces," is perhaps not far from the mark, as we shall see.[11]

For more than a quarter of a century after Pătrăşcanu's study no works of Romanian authorship appeared on interwar fascism, except for the standard panegyrical pieces expounding blown-up descriptions of the dedicated anti-fascist struggles waged by the communist working masses. The turning point came only in 1971, with the holding in Bucharest of a symposium on March 4 and 5 dedicated to the "unmasking of fascism," followed by the publication of the proceedings in the form of the book *Împotriva fascismului* ("Against Fascism").[12]

Although the title suggests the militant tone of the gathering, with a purpose aimed more at condemning than analyzing, a few of the essays display clearly non-dogmatic tendencies, such as Constanţa Bogdan's *Baza Social-Economică a Fascismului in România* ("The Social-Economic Basis of Facism in Romania") and Şerban Cioculescu's *Legionarismul şi Literatura* ("Legionarism and Literature"). Despite these, the volume passes over difficult questions such as mass support for the Legion on the part of peasants and workingmen in Romania, the beloved forces whom communists consistently assume to be in the forefront of the struggles of the democratic, progressive, and patriotic forces of history, led always by the communist party—a party which, in the 1930s, never had more than 1,000 adherents by all counts, though needless to say the authors of the symposium do not elaborate on this point.

Almost simultaneously with this symposium, 1971 also produced the first book-length study in communist Romania about the Iron Guard, Mihai Fátu and Ion Spálátelu's *Garda de Fier. Organizaţie terrorista de tip fascist* ("The Iron Guard. A Fascist-type terrorist organization").[13] This had the advantage of using State and Party archival materials usually cordoned off to researchers. Bela Vago's succinct comments on the book are useful:

> . . . the selection of the archival material is obviously biased and the work suffers from some grave shortcomings. One of the main aims of the authors seems to have been the emphasis on the alleged collusion between the ruling circles (the Camarilla, the National Liberal, and the National Peasant leaders) and the Iron Guard. The authors fail to convince the reader that such collusion existed, precisely because they overplayed this aspect. The polemical tone of the work and the outspoken aim of appealing to the widest possible public detracts considerably from the scholarly value of the book.[14]

If one can expect little from officially-sponsored Romanian works, neither are the works of Romanian Legionnaire emigrés likely to provide much elucidation. In the main, those published during wartime were crudely propagandistic, while even those recent works bearing some of the apparatus of scholarship were replete with references to "anonymous forces" and "Judeo-Marxist-Capitalist-Freemason" conspiracies.[15] Horia Sima's history of the Legionary Movement is, of course, a very passionate plea on behalf of its rectitude and vehemently attacks almost every other political grouping in Romania during the 1930s.

Nevertheless, like works of communist authorship, even those strongly biased in favor of the Legion can tell us something, both in what they do and do not contain. For one thing, emigré literature devotes as much space to criticizing the authors' philosophical opponents within the Legionary Movement as to attacking Antonescu, Carol, or communism. Polemics and factionalism within the Iron Guard are clearly demonstrated, for example in one post-war work deserving of attention. The voluminous history of the Iron Guard written and published by the Orthodox priest Ştefan Palaghiţa in 1951 became a major source of material for the anti-Horia Sima group in the emigration. The author accuses Sima of terrorism, criminal behavior, and betrayal of the Legion as an agent of the King and his

Camarilla.[16] Other works in the same vein attack or defend Marshal
Ion Antonescu, either for crimes committed by the Legion during
the period of common rule (September 1940-January 1941), or for
betraying his partners in the coalition, or for doing too little to oppose
Hitlerist domination of Romania, or for doing too much. Former
Foreign Minister Michel Sturdza considered Antonescu "insane."[17]
Other emigré writings make the founder of the Legion, Codreanu,
into a semi-divinity, extolling his non-violence and humanism and
minimizing his anti-Semitism.[18] What is of most interest here is neither the truth nor falsity of such intra-group polemics, but the very
fact that the Legionary Movement was far from a monolithic entity;
on the contrary it was rife with factionalism from the beginning, factionalism which deepened and spread following Codreanu's death,
at which point one might almost say that one Legionary Movement
ended and another took form. The complicated internal situation in
Romania produced by the outbreak of World War II and the overthrow of King Carol in 1940 had the effect of further splintering
what little cohesion among the Legion remained. In any event, the
same problems in need of discussion elude the emigré authors, as
they do the Marxist researchers: the origins of Romanian fascism, its
national characteristics and individualities, its degree of indebtedness
to the Italian and German "big brothers," its links with Orthodoxy,
its anti-Semitism, and the social composition of its mass following
and its leadership.[19]

Some Western scholars have made a start in addressing such questions. The pioneer researcher was Eugen Weber during the mid-1960s,
followed by Zevedei Barbu in 1968 and Stephen Fischer-Galati,
whose insightful essays on nationalism and fascism in Romania are
probably known to the widest audience.[20] Short chapters in Ernst
Nolte's *Die Faschistischen Bewegungen*, in F. L. Carsten's *The Rise
of Fascism*, and a number of recent essays in specialized journals in
the West, have added to the corpus of work,[21] while Paul Shapiro's
learned article on the Cuza-Goga government in 1974 foreshadows
his longer forthcoming work on Romanian interwar politics which
likely will shed new light on many imponderabilia.[22]

What do such works stress in common about the Legionary phenomenon? Almost all emphasize *populism* as a characteristic feature
of the Legionaries. Hugh Seton-Watson discusses "Romanian Fascist
Populism" and the young Romanian *narodniki,*[23] while Weber discounts any bourgeois or petit-bourgeois character for the Legion,
saying instead that it was a "popular and populist movement, with a

programme which the masses (in the Romanian context of peasants and workers) recognized as radical enough for them. . . ."[24] Fischer-Galati sustains the thesis of "popular fascism" as well.[25]

A second common theme is the treatment of Codreanu's Legion as a *radical* movement rather than, as a textbook definition might have it, one of the reactionary right. In its quest for social justice, in its mysticism and revolutionary fervor for a regeneration of Romanian society, the Legion looked not to a turning back of the clock but represented, as Weber noted, "a distinctly radical social force."[26] Nagy-Talavera likewise believes that Codreanu was sincerely devoted to social justice, when he writes of the "Archangelic Socialism of the Legion" and the class struggle urged by the radical fascist movements against their own ruling classes.[27]

Thirdly, Western historians for the most part deny that communism, or the threat of it, played any significant part in the emergence of the Romanian radical right, mainly on the grounds that Romanian industrial development in the 1920s and 1930s was too insignificant to produce a working class able to threaten the state. Curiously, however, "Codreanu himself, and later Sima, in common with most of the Legionaries saw their movement as an anti-communist movement par excellence from its very inception."[28]

Finally it is worth repeating that the majority of works on interwar Romania by non-involved Western scholars dwell upon the uniqueness of the Legionary Movement on the European fascist map, and the independent development of Romanian fascism. Fischer-Galati notes that "Ideological and financial contacts between Romanian fascists and their counterparts elsewhere were surprisingly limited in the early thirties,"[29] and Weber flatly states, "While Codreanu lived, the Legion was no conscious agent of Nazism."[30]

All of the popular assumptions with which we began have not been touched on. None of the works mentioned contains an entire chapter on the anti-Semitism and the Jewish policies of the various regimes, although it is generally taken for granted even by Marxist historians that racism was not a characteristic feature of the Legionary Movement.[31] None deal adequately with delineating factions, currents, and shades of opinion within the movement, ranging from moderate to anarchic; few writers bother to correct the usage of "Iron Guard" where "Legionary Movement" is meant; no one has yet frankly stated what ought to be obvious to students of Romanian history, that "anti-Semitism" is inappropriate and should be replaced by "anti-Jewish," which really reads "anti-foreigner." Too, the outbreak of January 21, 1941, continues to be described as an attempted *putsch* on the part of the Legion rather than what in fact it appears more to be, a *coup* by Antonescu.

With this review of conflict and consensus as a foundation, we may examine anew the salient features of the complex milieu of peasant-ism, politicianism, and populism which make up the unique and ill-fated story of the men of the archangel.

A National Inferiority Complex

Not until relatively late in modern times, until the Congress of Berlin in 1878, did Romania achieve full nationhood status, and even then the conditions attached to recognition of the country's in-dependence by the powers made nationhood seem more a reluctant gift bestowed than a prize earned. While Romanians believed they had won their statehood on the battlefields of Plevna and Griviţa the loss of southern Bessarabia to Russia and the requirement that citizen-ship rights be granted to the country's Jewish minority—coupled with the overriding factor that Romania was not even admitted to the Berlin Congress as an equal in the deliberations, but allowed to appear briefly only as a supplicant—marked her as an inferior partner in the international community.[32]

As in every country arriving at nationhood in such a manner, nationalist feelings in Romania even before World War I were over-developed, as Nagy-Talavera notes, especially when combined with the particular economic and geographic circumstances applicable to much of Eastern Europe. "The absence of a Romanian middle class, almost complete foreign domination of the economy, the precarious international position of the new state between the giant Russian Empire and the formidable Dual Monarchy (with irredentas in both cases), the backwardness of the country, the people's almost Oriental indolence, and the refusal of the upper classes to have anything to do with Romanian values (which meant peasant values)—all these made certain that Romanian nationalism would manifest itself in a national inferiority complex."[33]

In the period between 1918 and 1939, this set of conditions changed only marginally, never fundamentally. The Dual Monarchy, of course, was replaced by the rise of a powerful German Reich and a truncated Hungary thirsting for revision of the Versailles Settle-ment. At times during the 1920s it seemed that Romania was making strides in reducing foreign control over the nation's resources and capi-tal, but neither political stability nor freedom from outside pressures ever lasted long enough to make this a reality. The elite classes continued to prefer to import Paris rather than identify with Romanian traditions and values, a choice which the 1940s did little to change. And the "indolence" of the population, while capable of being aroused by such movements as Cuza's or Codreanu's for brief periods, was never able to channel itself into political forms which would allow it to master its own fate in a country where parliamentary self-government remained little more than a wish.

Those few who sought to break this cycle of centuries had to have a rallying cry and a focus on which to blame the lack of progress. To be a nationalist was not enough, for everybody in Romania was a nationalist. Even the ruling classes, as Eugen Weber puts it, "loved Romania like a prey."[34] Thus the nationalists after the Great War resurrected another hallowed element of Romanian tradition to reinforce their devotion to the *patrie* and emphasize their desire to purge it of those elements which they saw responsible for its troubles. This was the "anti-foreigner" theme, the cry of Tudor Vladimirescu a century before, of "Romania for the Romanians" and only for the Romanians. It was the simplest of themes: the majority of Romania's ills stemmed from foreigners who had "invaded" the country in the past to exploit its land, wealth, and people. These must be purged from the nation's ranks or, at the very least, reduced to impotence by legislation or other means. This had little or nothing to do with race, it was a question of nationality and ethnicity. It is impossible to understand Romanians and their history without grasping this fundamental facet of the national mentality. "Romanians are decent, religious, nation-loving people, with the potential for developing their wealth and resources to produce prosperity and happiness for all. The greatest thing standing in the way of this was the non-Romanian living in their midst preventing this progress," ran the litany of the generation reaching maturity after the Great War.

In fact, the roots of such thinking were deep. The historian and economist Bogdan P. Haşdeu put it succinctly in 1871:

> Foreigners at the head of the state, foreigners in the ministries, foreigners in parliament, foreigners in the magistracy, foreigners at the bar, foreigners in medicine, foreigners in finances, foreigners in trade, foreigners in publicism, foreigners in public works, foreigners up, foreigners down . . . .[35]

Sixty-seven years later the same theme was broadcast in the bitter comments of the *Romanian Encyclopedia*:

> All manufactured articles sold in the principalities came from Austria and Prussia. . . . Our goods were taken at very low prices,

as from any other colony. Soon, French and British firms appeared to compete with the Germans, and quickly gained
ground. But this in no way changed the fact of being permanently a colony, open or disguised, of the foreigners. This cala-
mity not only keeps the whole national life in a situation of
poverty, exploitation and slavery, but also brings gradual political serfdom, stifling any attempt to conquer one's rightful
place in the world.[36]

Against such a situation one of the greatest figures of Romanian
nationalism, the poet Mihail Eminescu, railed bitterly, and became
an inspiration for the post-World War I generation. Eminescu saw the
foreign-dominated commercial middle class as the primary foe, and
urged its elimination in any way possible.

> He who takes strangers to heart
> May the dogs eat his part
> May the waste eat his home
> May ill-fame eat his name!

he wrote; to save the nation from the alien rot, even humanitarian
principles must be sacrificed. Eminescu was anti-Jewish, to be sure,
yet he attacked Greeks in Romania even more fiercely. His thinking
was elaborated and clothed in pseudo-scientific garb by Professor
Alexander C. Cuza, who became the second in the pantheon of anti-
foreign ideologists in the emerging religion of Romanianism.

Cuza was educated in French and German schools, and after a
youthful flirtation with atheism and socialism, shifted toward conservative nationalism rooted in a populist traditionalism. He emerged
from the line of nineteenth-century Romanian economic nationalists
such as Dionisie Pop Marţian, Petre Aurelian, B.P. Haşdeu, and the
prestigious historian A.D. Xenopol who saw the country's economic
problems solved only by fostering popular enterprise and expelling
the foreigners who stifled native initiative. For Cuza, who became
the dominant figure at the University of Iaşi for more than thirty
years after his appointment to the chair of political economy in
1901, "foreigner" meant primarily the heavy Jewish population surrounding him in Moldavia. Strongly influenced by the writings of
Edouard Drumont, and inspired by Charles Maurras's distrust of
liberalism, Cuza turned into a "radical conservative," (as Weber labels
him) whose doctrine was summed up by the term anti-Semitism. The
moment this is introduced, however, one must insist on the wrongness of the label. We are forced to use it as a generic term, because
every writer does; both the scholarly and popular literature on Romanian history is replete with it. By itself it is a poor thing anyway,

as Vamberto Morais has elaborated, since "Semite" applies to millions of people other than Jews and its most common application, i.e., to members of the Arab world, is thus totally illogical, since Arabs are Semitic peoples.[37] In Romania it had little or nothing to do with the racial or religious connotations to which the word commonly gives rise, and is thus additionally misleading. "Cuza's anti-Semitism was not based on the religious prejudices common in Eastern Europe, but on economic considerations."[38] Here is the heart of the matter, expressed as succinctly as possible. Romanians were, almost to a man, strongly "anti-foreigner." "Foreigner" in one of its most visible and entrenched manifestations, meant Jew. Therefore Romanians were anti-Jewish, primarily on political and economic grounds, and this had very little to do with all of the emotional and/or ideological connotations surrounding the unsatisfactory catch-all word "anti-Semitism." One should note, also, that the most rabid believers and practitioners of this Romanian variant of "anti-Semitism" were the groups directly spawned by A.C. Cuza and his followers, such as the LANC and the "Blue Shirts" organizations. Codreanu's Legionaries came only a poor *second* in their "anti-Semitism," and even Marxist historians generally take it for granted that "racism was not a characteristic feature" of the Legionary Movement.[39] One would do best to excise the usage of "anti-Semitism" from a Romanian context, if this were possible (given decades of erroneous application) and replace it with "anti-Jewish," to lie alongside "anti-Greek," "anti-Turk," "anti-Austrian," and especially "anti-Russian." In 1980, therefore, to retroactively label Trifa and his generation "anti-Semitic" is to make the same error. Trifa in the 1930s was anti-Jewish, along with most of his countrymen. More specifically, one might say he was "anti-Romanian-Jew" for Romanians were not down on Jews everywhere, only those within their own country, whom they saw, rightly or wrongly, as foreign exploiters. Too, we ought to stress, with Madame de Stael, that to explain is not to condone.

Cuza, however, was merely the synthesizer and popularizer of what in Romania had a long historic tradition—the rejection of foreigners in the public and commercial life of the nation. Since at least the sixteenth century Romanians had struggled to assert and maintain a national and state identity.[40] Throughout most of the eighteenth century, with the country ruled and administered by Phanariote Greeks appointed from Constantinople, one unacquainted with the historic past of the Romanian lands under their own rulers might assume that there had been none.

Towards the end of the eighteenth and the beginning of the nineteenth century, the Romanian boiars first began to seek the removal
of Greeks from the state administration and from the hierarchy of
the Orthodox Church, and this combined with efforts against Greek
merchants begun even earlier. Following the Russo-Turkish War of
1768-1774, a new problem emerged in the form of letters of protection and privileges granted by the Moldavian and Wallachian governments (the overbearing system of "capitulation" and extraterritoriality so familiar in the carving up of China in the late nineteenth century) to Russians and Austrians, then eventually to French and English citizens. Native craftsmen and merchants suffered as a result, so
that competition took on ethnic elements, and contributed to the
growth of an aggressive xenophobia.

During the half century which formed the second period in the
development of the Romanian national movement, from 1829 to
1881, the perceived opposition of the foreign minorities in Romania
to national goals exacerbated this trend, and produced what Emanuel
Turczynski called "prenationalistic anti-Semitism."[41] The revolutionaries of 1848, filled with the excesses of French-inspired "liberty"
and "equality" saw their hopes dashed by Turkish and Russian inva-
sions, and French-style liberalism never enjoyed more than a brief
life in the principalities. When unification finally came under Prince
Alexander Cuza in 1859, the limited autonomy permitted by the
guarantee powers and the exigencies of fundamental nation-state
building would not allow other than limited measures of social, economic or political equalization, despite the *pro forma* trappings of a
Western style parliamentarianism. More importantly here, there was
little possibility to create state-erected legal barriers to counterbalance
the increasing distrust and animosity toward foreigners. The gap between government and population, which to this day remains un-
bridged in Romania, persisted; social barriers remained standing, and
privilege, both of native boiar and foreign merchant and subject,
largely untouched.[42] The Levantine-Jewish merchant and artisan
classes, along with the Austrian and Russian subjects living in Romania, remained unreconciled to the Union of 1859 and the national
feeling it fostered, which gave rise in turn to strengthening both economic and cultural anti-foreign sentiment.

Such feeling was strongest in Moldavia. In Wallachia to the South,
the Sephardic Jews had developed a very high culture, and were often
looked on as Greeks. Moldavia, however, was full of the Ashkenazim,
who brought the lower standards, both culturally and politically, of

the life they had known in Polish and Russian ghettos. Moreover throughout these decades Jewish immigration into Moldavia never ceased to grow, as people fled from the Russian districts of Podolia or migrated en masse from the Ukraine to escape the ruthless Russian military service.

During the 1840s the Romanian assemblies tried to limit the economic expansion of these Jews, prohibiting them from buying property in certain sections of cities, and excluding them from owning food or liquor stores. Their legal position was defined similarly to that in force in Russia under Nicholas I. One effect of this was to produce a certain polycentrism, especially in Moldavia, as Jews oriented themselves to political centers outside the country in efforts to gain support for relief. This of course did not help them in their fight for equality in an era when over-sensitive nationalism was on the rise.

Both Prince Alexander Cuza and King Carol I openly promoted equal rights for Jews, but were unable to gain support for such measures in parliament.[43] When attacks on Jews broke out, requiring foreign intervention, the Jewish question in Romania became an international issue, increasing the tension.[44] It was useless to point out (even as it was pointed out by many in the 1920s and 1930s) that many of the Moldavian Jewish families had roots in the country going back to the late seventeenth century and had lived in lawfully constituted communities under the protection of the princes. The idea that all were recent "invaders" who had swarmed into the country during the decades immediately before and after the Union, was, by the twentieth century, ineradicable in the popular mind, and reinforced by savants of the stature of Nicolae Iorga himself.

Clearly, by the time of Romania's War for Independence in 1877-1878, an official state anti-Semitism was in evidence. "The victory against Turkey, paid for in blood, the humiliation meted out by Russia, and the loss of Bessarabia, accelerated the transition from a somewhat moderate national consciousness to an integral nationalism."[45] And anyone seen as opposing that national spirit, this unanimity of Romanianism, was naturally asking for trouble in Romania, or any other over-sensitive Balkan state. This took the form not only of anti-Jewish feeling and legislation—a point which cannot be stressed overmuch. It was also aimed at the Austrians in the 1870s, and most obviously at the Magyars in Transylvania during the whole of the period down to 1918. Therefore the dictation by the Congress of Berlin that Romania recognize the equal rights paragraph of the Berlin agreement, and honor article 7 of its own constitution by giving rights of

citizenship to Jews, was bound to be met with tergiversation and cir-
cumvention.

With the emergence of *Poporanism* and *Sămănatorism* in Romania,
movements at the turn of the century roughly akin to Russian *narodniki* philosophies, a new stress arose as a result of the effort to elevate
the downtrodden peasantry and bridge the vast gulf which separated
him from the intelligentsia and the governing classes. Whereas before
the orientation of Romanian literature was primarily French and German, the impact of the youthful and nationalist *Junimists* and especially the work of Nicolae Iorga in his widely influential *Neamul
Românesc* to replace foreign with Romanian culture produced new
waves of anti-foreignness which now more than ever began to penetrate the population of the Romanian countryside. The negative evalu-
ation of almost everything foreign, with the exception of France, was
highly important for the development of "anti-Semitism."

Growing Jewish influence in the national economy by the 1890s
did not help mitigate the problem, for many of the Jewish intellectuals and workers gravitated towards the Social Democratic movement. Additional impetus was thus given to the economic and cultural purists to oppose them. Not only did the newly-formed (1891)
League for the Cultural Unity of All Romanians become increasingly
anti-Semitic in its nationalism, due to the clear refusal of Jews to
assimilate into Romanian society either in speech or dress,[46] but the
conservative nationalists of the schools of A.C. Cuza and Nicolae
Iorga, stressing both economic and cultural considerations, founded
in 1885 an *Alliance Antisémitique Universelle* in Bucharest. Therefore
the national movement in Romania, aimed at a "100% Romanianism"
in culture, economy, and political life, was clearly anti-foreign, thus,
in part anti-Jewish by 1914, based on more than a century of development. It is utter historical blindness to maintain that anti-Semitism
(still we must use the word) was somehow a creation of one man, or
one movement, in the 1920s. Corneliu Codreanu and those who followed him merely partook of what, by the twentieth century, was
part of the essence of the Romanian national character, with the
added element of a virulent anti-Bolshevism and a belief in the international conspiracy theory so popular in Europe following the First
World War.

Bolshevism and Conspiracy Theory

Those who today advocate co-existence with the Soviet Union
under the ephemeral label of "detente" easily forget that the new

Europe of 1919 was born largely under the aegis of fear. Fear held by the peacemakers, especially the Big Four at Versailles, that Bolshevism was going to sweep across Europe, from East to West. To stem the "Red Menace" they adopted a number of decisions, or allowed certain conditions to prevail, such as the Romanian occupation of Budapest, which they might otherwise not have countenanced. The emergence of Bela Kun's communist regime in Hungary, of a Bavarian Marxist republic, the agitation of significant Comintern parties in France and Italy, waves of strikes in numerous countries, all coming on the heels of the Armistice, convinced those in Paris of the need for a *"cordon sanitaire"* down the middle of Europe to act as a buffer between Lenin and Trotsky's anticipated world revolution.[47] Robert Murray has described the great "Red Scare" of 1919-1920 in the United States, when fears of "radicals" and "bolsheviks" brought a wave of deportations, public hysteria, and persecution of foreigners such as had seldom been seen.[48] Indeed, public reaction against "anarchists" reached a climax only in 1926, with the disgraceful executions of Sacco and Vanzetti, at least one of whom was very likely innocent of any crimes.[49]

For Romanians, and for those in Moldavia and Bessarabia especially, the Russian revolution was a very immediate and real thing. Much of the most intense fighting of the Russian Civil War took place around Odessa and the northwestern Black Sea region, and recent Romanian historical literature is quite thorough in its documentation of Romanian proletarians who joined the ranks of the glorious Red Army, formed revolutionary support and even combat groups to join the Bolshevik cause, and so on. The danger of red revolution loomed large, then, in northern Romania after the war, and Bolshevik ideas "were rife among workers and intellectuals."[50] Codreanu's first battles were fought in Iaşi, in 1919-1920, against striking workers, when he first came to prominence as part of a short-lived strike-breaking league called the Guard of the National Conscience.

Against liberals and leftists, Codreanu and his friends took over the student movement, first at the University of Iaşi, then at other Romanian universities. Their methods were sometimes amateurish, often brutal and irreverent, but usually effective. "By 1923, student strikes could keep the universities closed for a whole semester, even against the intervention of the army. It was all in a good cause."[51] "We cause disorders, certainly, but only to prevent the great, irreparable disorder which the apprentices of Communist revolution were preparing."[52]

There was a deeper dimension, of course, to Codreanu's anti-communism. By combining his belief in the immediacy of the threat of an invasion across the Pruth, with the teachings of Professor Cuza, it was a logical step to equate communism with Jews and embrace the theory of a Jewish world conspiracy which was widespread in Europe even before 1914.[53]

The most recent work on British fascism deems the theory of a Jewish world conspiracy "the deadliest kind of anti-semitism, springing from demonological superstitions inherited from the Middle Ages."[54] As embodied in the fabricated *Protocols of the Elders of Zion*, the standard analysis stressed the political, social and economic upheaval caused by the First World War and the Russian Revolution. Those elements of society whose positions were threatened, or appeared to be in danger (the classic groups giving rise to fascist movements after 1918) adopted the conspiracy theory as a simplistic explanation for phenomena too complex to explain otherwise. George Mosse has suggested that conspiracy theories were more widespread in France than in Germany before 1914, stemming in part from the impact of French governmental financial scandals in the late nineteenth century.[55] Similar occurrences in Britain such as the Marconi Scandal and the Indian Silver affair produced a parallel effect in late Edwardian history.[56] Overriding even these was, of course, the celebrated Dreyfus case in the 1890s, which dragged on for years and clearly demonstrated the extent of Jewish control of important offices in the military and political life of France, at least to anti-Dreyfusards and those who wished to find such evidence.[57]

Compare Hillaire Belloc in 1938 with Bogdan P. Haşdeu in 1871:

> The whole of English life is interwoven with Jewry. Our leading families are intermarried with it, our universities, our legal system, our financial system of course and, most important of all, the moral tradition of our society is inseparable from the Jewish money power throughout the world.[58]

Or the columns of the *Witness*, written by a former Irish Nationalist MP, Frank Hugh O'Donnell, in July, 1914:

> Everywhere, in the United States, in England, in the British Empire, in India, in South Africa, enormous confederations of Judean promoters and directors lead and control a cosmopolitan strategy for acquiring and exploiting every possible source of wealth or prosperity throughout the world.... The new Jerusalem grows and grows by what it feeds on and what it spares not. We call the Judean victory, "Le Juif Roi de L'Epoque."[59]

Next, former Legionary stalwart and Foreign Minister of Romania under the Antonescu government, Prince Michel Sturdza, writing in 1968:

If we try to discover through the past half century of dire experiences what has been the principal auxiliary of Communism's triumph, we will find it in treacherously organized misinformation, directed and coordinated from some mysterious headquarters through many hidden or notorious channels. . . .

When the time came for the destruction of the United States Senator Joseph R. McCarthy it was not the American press alone but the free press all over the world [which carried on] a successful effort to silence a man who courageously exposed the conspiracy. . . .

The Civil War in Spain represented an apex in the fight between the Anonymous Powers, mysterious inspirers of so many statesmen and governments of the bourgeois world, and those national powers that opposed in every country Communist and pro-Communist policies. . . .[60]

Finally, Corneliu Codreanu, speaking of the situation in Iaşi in 1919:

The old students, returned now as veterans, retained the line of the traditional nationalism of student life before the war. . . these groups, small in number, were overwhelmed by the immense mass of Jewish students coming over to school from Bessarabia, all communist agents and propagandists.

. . . Thousands of students in meeting after meeting in which Bolshevism was propagated, attacked Army, Justice, Church, Crown.

. . . We, the Romanian people, would have been mercilessly exterminated, killed or deported throughout Siberia: peasants, workers, intellectuals, all pell-mell. The lands from Maramures to the Black Sea, snatched from Romanian hands, would have been colonized by Jewish masses. Here it is that they would have built up their true Palestine.[61]

Codreanu in his youthful passion went on to describe the "huge communist demonstrations on the streets of Iaşi" every few days, the starved workers "maneuvered by the Judaic criminal hand from Moscow."

If these had been victorious, would we have had at least a Romania led by a Romanian workers' regime? Would the Romanian workers have become masters of the country? No! The next day we would have become the slaves of the dirtiest tyranny: the Talmudic, Jewish tyranny."[62]

Once again, it does not matter how true or how absurd appears today the notion of the international Jewish conspiracy. Thousands in 1980 continue to believe in it, as a quick answer to unfathomable problems, the study of which is far beyond their ken. What is important herein is that Codreanu believed in it passionately, and convinced great masses of his fellow Romanians of its correctness: a Jewish conspiracy against humanity in general and Romania in particular. "His nationalism would henceforth focus on three objectives: Communism, Jews, and irreligion, all abhorrent to his profound religious and patriotic faith."[63] Nor was this all.

Souvenirs de France

One aspect of Codreanu's thought thus far neglected is the impact of the year of study which he undertook during 1926-1927 at the University of Grenoble.

This experience seems important for several considerations: Codreanu's sojourn in France not only reaffirmed his fundamental romanticism and traditionalism, but put him in touch with the thought of Charles Maurras and the ideology of the Action Française. To his anti-communism was added contempt for the heritage of the French Revolution, a legacy which in his own small country had failed to deliver on its promise of either liberty or equality; to his anti-Jewish convictions was added another bogeyman, Freemasonry, the Protestant equivalent of the international Hebraic conspiracy.[64]

Unlike Romanian youth who had gone abroad to study in France for over a hundred years and returned with liberal notions of 1789 republicanism, Codreanu did not fill his mind with Edgar Quinet and Jules Michelet, nor join Mazzinist societies—his deep emotional attachment to a semi-mythical Romanian past was, to be sure, already profound. He did, though, steep himself in that which would reinforce his own mysticism:

> I plunged into the past. And there, to the great joy of my soul, I imagined myself living in the midst of historic France, of Christian France, of nationalistic France and not in the milieu of masonic France, of atheistic and cosmopolitan France; in the France of Bayard, not the France of Léon Blum.[65]

The mausoleum of the sixteenth century French hero Bayard in the Church of Saint André held a particular fascination for Codreanu. Bayard's calm strength in the face of defeat and death impressed Codreanu immensely. While we cannot know if the future *Căpitanul* was aware of Maurice Pujo's dictum, *on ne fait rien avec les morts,* certainly his sense of the linkage between the living and their ancestors was highly developed. He described pointedly how, while at Grenoble, he often retreated to the sanctuary of the ancient Church of Saint-Laurent to spend "an hour, in total serenity, to speak to the dead."[66] Certainly, also, in confronting the teachings of the Action Française, he found others "who believed strongly in the uses of the dead as providing the traditions and firm bases of all human societies."[67] This was neither as morbid nor as impractical as appears at first glance, although some might dismiss the later Legionary cult of the dead as mere rigmarole.[68] An Italian journalist who once met Codreanu briefly refers to his movement's special *mistica dei morti*: "The rite of calling out names of the dead and answering 'Present!', taken over from Fascist practice, was used in forms some of which seemed close to magic evocation."[69] In fact, a more satisfying name for this aspect of Legionary "magic" might be an ancestor cult, a building upon the popular folk mythology and beliefs of the East European peasant, with the permanence and stability which such a linkage between traditional Romanian life and the present implies.

A second major effect flowing from Codreanu's French experience was undoubtedly his contact with the works of Charles Maurras. Maurrassian doctrine, aimed at purging the decadence from French society and restoring the classical, traditional values of his countrymen, fit neatly into the young Codreanu's *Weltanschauung*.

Reacting against the flaccid and anarchic literary trends of the *fin de siècle*, Maurras easily moved from the belief that "a decadent art was no more than a reflection of a decadent society in which it thrived."[70] France's defeat in 1870, the loss of Alsace-Lorraine, the decreasing birth-rate—all were causes and effects of the country's general decay and the accompanying moral and social upheaval. The factions Maurras saw tearing France apart in the 1890s stemmed from one certain source: the liberal and democratic misconceptions which the French Revolution had broadcast throughout the world. The Revolution, the great Evil, was responsible for the decay and corruption of the moral and political fiber of every people it had touched.[71] Even more to the point—France's corruption and disorientation could be directly tied to the growing number of foreigners to be found in public life and public affairs. These men:

> could not react to French problems in a French way because they had no roots in French tradition and carried with them none of that intuitive understanding that would belong to men who shared a common heritage. As long as these aliens were left free to colonize France and increase their influence in every walk of life, the country would be not only divided, but 'betrayed, occupied, exploited by an internal enemy.' Thus, before any attempt at synthesis or union, these foreign or ill-assimilated bodies—Freemasons, Protestants, foreigners, and Jews—must be either regulated or expelled.[72]

Maurras wished to see France return to those principles which had provided order, stability, and greatness: Monarchy, the Catholic Church, Order and Authority. In the same manner as those who pointed to the frequency of Jews among the leadership of the Russian Revolution and concluded that Bolshevism, Jews, and international conspiracy and subversion were synonymous, Maurras performed the same service for Freemasonry and the resultant debit balance of the Jacobin theorists of 1789.

Fundamental, too, for Maurras, was the absolute need for self-mastery of the individual, a belief which fit neatly into Codreanu's already firm credo of discipline, duty, and individual moral and spiritual regeneration so sorely needed in his countrymen.

> There is nothing more certain than the fact that no man is his own master, that no man rules or possesses that obscure physical realm where the tides and tumult of our blood are stirring. But one must *will* to rule it, one must *tend* to it; however insolent the claim, it is man's only guarantee against the world of darkness he carries in him. To react against one's internal sphere is a condition of an energetic and prosperous life.[73]

Purgation of the individual of the harmful humours and evil habits which an erring nation had allowed to develop in him, a restoration of the pure essence of the long line of ancestors who had struggled to make the people and the land great before dark foreigners and the forces of evil had corrupted it—to advance such a restoration, all means were good, and the end would justify them. In *Si le coup de force est possible* (1910) Maurras explicitly defined the possibility of a *coup d'état*. Codreanu would not have agreed to this, especially since Romania had a king, while France did not. More to the mark was Maurras' elaboration of who might carry out such a *coup*. The future belonged to men of action and only by action would political truth be re-established in the land. Just so, Pujo appealed to intellectuals for "French Action," to oppose the revival of *panamisme*, which he saw as a diversion to serve the interests of corrupt politicians and financiers. Equally close to home were the ideas of Paul Desjardin's *Union pour l'Action Morale*, organized to unite men of all political opinions in an effort to establish the reign of virtue and morality in the world, a goal which might in itself summarize the essence of Codreanu's message, as long as "the world" was taken to mean "among Romanians."

Moving in such a milieu, while pursuing his doctorate in economics and living on the meagre funds made by selling his wife's embroideries in local stores, making excursions into the French countryside to drink in the past, Codreanu collected ideas and impressions which ever after shaped his vision of the future he wished to bring to his people. One other formative influence must be mentioned—the fact that his closest colleague at Grenoble was Ion Moţa, visionary son and grandson of Transylvanian village priests who "had sucked his nationalism with his mother's milk."[74]

Moţa's father had been a leading figure of Transylvanian nationalism, and was the original utterer of the oft-cited statement, "everyone was a right extremist, and we could not be anything else if we wanted to keep our nationality." To the forest-inspired world of the semi-mythical *Haiduc* and the immediacy of the Bolshevik menace in the mind of the Moldavian Codreanu was thus added the militancy of the *Ardeleni*, the Transylvanian Romanian who for centuries had struggled to prevent his denationalization at the hands of Turks, Austrians, and Hungarians. Young Moţa had studied in Paris after the war, but returned to the University of Cluj where he became president of the student association and helped found the group known as *Acţiunea Românească* (Romanian Action), an organization with definite Maurrassian leanings. By 1923, the same year in which he translated the *Protocols of the Elders of Zion* into Romanian from French, Moţa brought his Romanian Action group into the newly formed League of National Christian Defense (LANC), with an antisemitic program calling for the *numerus clausus* to be applied to Jews in secondary schools, universities, and liberal professions according to their proportion of the total population.

Jews obsessed Moţa. His writings against them saw the Jewish spirit at work in everything he deplored, and he uncritically labeled as a Jew anyone he disliked, whether true or not. "Moţa's Jews were everything Romanians should have been—united, powerful, and dangerous to cross—a sort of transferred wish-fulfillment fantasy, and devious besides."[75] Moţa's reactionary romanticism, his violent wistfulness, produced a passion that was catching. When the LANC was unable to prevent the voting of the constitutional amendment of 1923 granting citizenship and political rights to resident Jews, he and Codreanu, with a few close friends, had decided to punish those who had betrayed the interests of the entire nation by voting for the law and thereby knuckling under to the demands of Romania's wartime allies. A list was drawn up of various politicians to be shot. At the last moment the conspirators were denounced by one of their own number but, although imprisoned and tried, they were acquitted and released—all except Ion Moţa, who had shot their denouncer on the very day of the trial, and had to go through a second trial later. Upon his acquittal even in this, Codreanu at once named Moţa to head his newly formed *Fraţi de Cruce* (FDC'S—Brotherhoods of the Cross) to enlist schoolboys and village youths in nationalist activity.

Moţa worked out an elaborate ritual for initiation into the Brotherhood, with mysterious, secret meetings in forests or ruins, and special
readings to be done. Comradeship, bravery, loyalty, action were the
watchwords intoned to the accompaniment of torches in twilight
clearings, songs, oaths, and the invocation of the dead. The young
man was clearly entering a world apart, he was made to feel. He would
become a person of special essence, and out of these so-called religious practices would grow mystic exaltation and the desire for re-
sounding deeds. Scoffers would call it mumbo-jumbo. But those who
have studied the role of cargo cults or themselves belonged to "secret"
societies know the sense of cohesion, of being set apart from society,
that such activities can produce. When carried on like a revivalist
church, among ignorant but self-conscious people whose sense of
common ethnicity and common cause against "foreigners" or "the
state" or whatever is perceived as the common threat, the effects in
terms of dedication and solidarity can be devastating indeed.[76]

It was Moţa, this Byronic leader who died at 34 fighting for right
order in Spain in 1937, with his romantic idealism, who formed the
perfect complement to what would become the messianism of
Codreanu, and the combination was a heady brew indeed. Moţa
spent most of the year with Codreanu at Grenoble, also enrolled at
the University, and it was often the small sums of money which he
received from home which enabled the Captain and his wife to get
by in their meagre student hostel.

France, of course, was only an interlude in their real work, but
undoubtedly the experience of the two youths at Grenoble not only
reinforced but expanded their thinking of what they must do. Somehow their homeland, threatened by communism, Jews, liberalism,
politicians and corruption and the birth pangs of a semi-industrial
order being imposed from above, must be restored to the traditional
moral rectitude of an idealized Romanian past, based on the fear of
God, purity of heart, and completely Romanian values, through the
liberating and dynamic effects of sacrifice. And this must be accomplished either legally, within the established order, or outside of it,
in the tradition of the Romanian haiduc—the Jesse James-Robin
Hood figure who descended from his mountain fastness to expel the
foreign invader, to bring justice to the poor, to right wrongs. His
methods were the only ones suitable for dealing with despoilers.

In truth, the dilemma faced by Codreanu and Moţa and thousands
of Romanian (and European) youth in the 1920s was not unfamiliar.
The alienation and dislocation produced by the First World War
throughout the Western world, the conflict between the emerging

postwar industrial-technical world and the older, slower, more secure world of traditional values fast being displaced, produced intense economic, political, and most of all psychological pressures. Confronted by new and baffling circumstances, Romanian youth, like German, Spanish, Italian, and even American youth were not alone in their desire to regain control of their own destiny in the face of the challenges of the new order.

Moṭa put it well in *Cranii de Lemn* ("Wooden Skulls") in 1937:

Our soul, still tied to another (older, better) world, wanders today in a life which is not ours. When we face the world of today, we feel alien, we find no sense in it other than the possibility of harnessing it to revive the days of old and to increase their beauty—their beauty and the right Romanian order.[77]

Here was a classic reversal of the normal generational conflict. Youth wishing to restore the goodness of a mythical Romanian past and purge the corruption of a real Romanian present. If need be they would offer their lives on the altar of the nation, these wanderers between two worlds.

CHAPTER VI
NEW MEN, NOT NEW PROGRAMS

The fluctuations of the party line over the past half-century have made Marxist historians in Romania hard put to explain the broad popular mass support enjoyed by the Iron Guard and the Legionary Movement. Usually they have dismissed this, resorting to the 1928 definition of fascism by the Comintern as appealing to "the most backward strata of the workers," or, with Pătrăşcanu, calling Codreanu's movement "a conjunction of declassés and Lumpenproletariat."[1] What this means is simply that it is embarrassing for communists to admit that great masses of the Romanian peasantry and a significant number of the working class during the late 1920s and much of the 1930s believed in, worked for, and zealously supported not the miniscule Communist Party (which had perhaps 1,000 members or so at the time of the "great anti-fascist uprising" by which it assumed power in August, 1944) but the Legionary philosophy. It was hardliner Georgi Dimitrov himself who noted in 1935 that such movements enjoyed mass support because "of their appeal to the most urgent needs of the masses."[2] Such large popular support, also, was one of the most marked features distinguishing the Romanian radical right from its Italian and German fascist counterparts. We shall use "Radical Right" for Codreanu, the Iron Guard, and the Legionary Movement, self-contradictory as this might seem, for a number of reasons.

Eugen Weber defined in 1966 the three major components of the European political Right as (a) *Reaction* against the tendencies of the present, looking back to some more or less remote golden age which it would like to recapture—certainly this fits the Codreanu ethos; (b) *Resistance* to change, or conservatism, defending the established socio-political order—here we have a problem, for while Codreanu's ultranationalism certainly marks his movement as conservative, even reactionary, he was determined to reform and eliminate completely the prevailing corrupt political order, although not in the democratic, liberal sense of the traditional bourgeois reformer, but in the sense of restoring a virtuous, semi-mythical moral order of the past, based on the Romanian peasantry; c) *Radicalism*, seeking revolutionary change usually by violent means, yet uncertain of explicit goals except the conquest of total power. Here again, the Legion does not fit the standard mold. In the early years, certainly, its militancy was pronounced, and from the Iaşi barricades of 1919-1920 to the assassination of Duca in 1933 the various organizations which were associated with Codreanu, Moţa, and their supporters did indeed resort to violence when other methods seemed closed to them. Yet as with so many outbursts of youthful excessiveness, in time the movement evolved; certainly it was far less zealous and prone to violence by 1937 than it had been in 1927 and then, it must be kept in mind, violence by the Legion for the most part was used only in response to violence on the part of its adversaries in the government, who meted out violent "justice" against the Legion at least in the measure of 10 to 1. From the beginning, Codreanu sought to use the political process and the existing scheme of things to gain power through the parliamentary system, corrupt as it was. Had he not been murdered when he was, there is a real possibility that the Legion, within a few years, would have been called to power constitutionally, like any other party formation.

Nevertheless such definitions of the Right may be a useful analytical tool, as Paul Shapiro comments, while noting that the Goga-Cuza government, although it "adopted certain outward trappings of Right-radicalism yet remained in essence an establishment party."[3] Not so with the Legionary Movement. Though it may have grown less extreme when it saw its strength growing at the ballot box, tactics should not be confused with long-range goals. The Legion was against the entire corrupt establishment of King, camarilla, and traditional parties. It would replace the current order with an aristocracy of virtue, drawn from the Romanian peasant masses and springing from the deepest wellsprings of the spiritual heritage of the people. It offered not new programs, but new men. The almost fanatical religious basis of the Legion, and its dedication to nation and tradition (along with its anti-foreignism, some would add) qualify it for the label of Right; but its dream of overturning the existing order, and its Christian Socialism, or Populist foundation, make it at the same time Radical. Romanian-style "Fascism," then, was an indigenous Right-Radicalism differing both philosophically and qualitatively from the Italian and German forms of this post-World War I phenomenon far more than it resembled them. [4]

Populism and Peasantism

Nagy-Talavera would not have a best-seller in today's Bucharest, if only for one frank statement he makes. "It is not surprising that communism never appealed to anybody of consequence among the Rumanians," referring to the pre-1914 period.[5] Most of the few Communists in Romania came from the hostile national minorities, Jews, Hungarians, and Ukrainians, who had some interest in very un-Romanian platforms such as the Third International envisioned for Romania in the 1920s. Yet there was a Socialist undercurrent not incompatible with the interests of nationalists and which centered on the fate of the majority of the country's population—the peasants. Even the N.S.D.A.P. had a bit of populism in its ideological baggage, but in Eastern Europe, where "people" and "peasantry" are one and the same thing, all Radical-Right movements had a strong Populist content.

Poporanismul ("People-ism" or Populism) in Romania was strongly similar to the *narodnichestvo* of late nineteenth century Russian intellectuals which produced the *"narodniki"* effort of "going to the people" and the Land and Liberty Party. Obviously, Russia and Romania in the years before 1914 had numerous social and economic parallels, both being countries with large latifundiary estates and recently emancipated, land-hungry peasants living in a state of what Dobrogeanu-Gherea called *Neo-iobăgia* or semi-serfdom.

The principal theme of Russian populism was that the future lay in the peasantry, in the development of communal institutions. Russia could not hope to industrialize because capitalism had arrived much too late, having barely penetrated the nation by 1900, and thus missed any chance to capture foreign markets already monopolized by the Western powers. The conclusion was that some form of agrarian socialism was the key to the future, which would avoid all the concomitant evils and social miseries of industrial capitalism.

Poporanism had its own native roots in Romania in a literary and philosophical movement at the turn of the century, part of the campaign by the Junimists, Nicolae Iorga and others to raise national consciousness and create a national language and literature. We can find a direct transfer of *narodniki* ideas, however, in the works of Constantin Stere who exercised wide influence through his populist journal *Viaţa românească* ("Romanian Life"). It is more than significant that Stere was born in Bessarabia of a Romanian boiar family, and had spent time in Siberia, banished for his activities with the *narodniki*. He was one who broke with the infant socialist movement in Romania in 1899 and collaborated with the Liberals, only because, since the prospect of revolution in Romania was dim indeed, it made sense to him to work with the more progressive of the existing parties. For some years he was regarded as the unofficial adviser of Ion I.C. Brătianu.

Shortly after the 1907 peasant uprising, Stere published a series of articles called "Social Democracy or Populism," in which he offered a new theoretical concept of the peasantry. It was neither proletarian nor bourgeois, as Marxism held, but a distinct social category.[6] Class struggle, which could exist only where the elements of production were differentiated, could not take place in a peasant society. Only cooperation would strengthen the peasant economically, this and the introduction of a true "rural Rumanian democracy."[7]

The debt owed by current Marxist latitudinarians in Bucharest to Stere is obvious when one notes his premise that different countries could evolve in different ways. Rejecting the path of industrialization after the model of Europe for the same reasons as those advanced in Russia. Stere's own idea of progress was founded on his view of Romania as a cultural and historical entity with its own "national genius," an argument widespread in the Tolstoyan milieu in which he wrote. Like most Romanian intellectuals, he was against Jews, calling them alien elements and "representatives of vagabond capital,"[8] who would disrupt the organization of the economy entirely on a peasantist foundation. Romania's hope lay in a vigorous free peasantry, master of its own land and organized in a perfected system of cooperative societies. The only industry which made sense was peasant household (cottage) industry during the winter months, which would satisfy the demands of internal consumption. Limited urban manufacturing should be maintained as well, as accessories to agriculture. But Stere was firmly anti-protectionist, and urged that existing large industries, such as petroleum, should be nationalized, not socialized, and become state monopolies.[9] The nation, in a sense, should freeze the "Golgotha of capitalist development" in its tracks, allowing it to proceed no farther.

More than one writer has shown the integral connection between the Romanian-style fascism of Codreanu and certain aspects of Stere's populism.[10] The relation of Romania to Western industrial society is closely involved here. Faced by the impact of the West, Romanians even from the early nineteenth century, very much like Russians, have been confronted with the dilemma of either adoption and imitation of Western systems, or rejection. In general, imitation

prevailed, often with very un-Western consequences, the most telling
of which was the obvious failure of Western-style parliamentarianism
in a land which had no tradition or experience of democratic government. In Stere, with his modified Romanian Slavophilism, the element of rejection was strong. In fairness to Stere, however, he did
assay a fairly rational analysis of Romanian social and economic
questions, trying to create a modified and workable system even if,
as later economists were quick to show, his paradigms were unrealistic
and his suppositions questionable. Legionarism, however, took only
what it wished to hear—denunciation of capitalism and liberalism,
the populists' organic nationalism, and the semi-deification of the
"genius" of the peasantry. Once devoid of the rational element, what
remained of populist theory was only the emotional reaction and the
negativism against the status quo. Still, Codreanu's consistent efforts
at rural self-help, peasant cooperativism and village industry, and the
system of Legionary cooperative stores he began to implement by
the mid-1930s, all show his debt to Stere and *poporanismul*, and it is
to this that much of the mass basis of his support among the Romanian peasantry may be attributed. Legionary slogans such as *Omul şi
pogonul* (the man and the plot of land) and *Hectare şi sufletul* (the
hectare and the soul) were simplified ways of expressing, not an
agrarian program, but the peasant's deep ties with mother earth. In
place of the bastard culture of the Bucharest elite with its overeager
imitations of French art, architecture, and thought, the Legion would
restore a national integrity permitting the flowering of native potential by invoking the unspoiled primitivism of peasant life—its strange,
moving music, its magnificent handwork and folk ballads, its un-
yielding attachment to God and the ancestral Romanian soil, about
which the politicians knew nothing.

Populism in combination with open, often extreme, Orthodox
Christianity, the employment of religious symbolism and mysticism
in all it did, thus formed an integral part of the Legionary ideology—
and its members were fully aware of their distinctiveness in this respect from German and Italian fascists. The peasant masses of Eastern Europe, including certainly the Romanian ploughman, remained
deeply devout, mystical, and even superstitious, which served further
to widen the gulf between rulers and ruled.[11]

The peasant philosophy of life was deeply rooted in Orthodoxy;
it was not only a form, but a way of life. This meant, however, *rural*
Orthodox Christianity, not the superficial, rather Byzantine Christianity and relationship which the Church hierarchy maintained with the
Romanian state. In fact Orthodoxy co-existed in Romania (as in

much of the Balkans) on two levels. There was the formalistic, ritualistic Orthodoxy of the Church hierarchy in Bucharest and other important regional centers such as Iaşi and Sibiu, conducted by Patriarchs and Metropolitans with Byzantine splendor and form, and having important ideological (and often political) roles in the formation of state policy, but little connection with the simple village dweller in the Transylvanian or Moldavian countryside. His Orthodoxy was of a more fundamental kind, based on the rhythms of the seasons, the agricultural cycle, and the spiritual values of the earth, family, and kinship group as promoted by the simple teachings of his small village church and a village priest who, when not at his altar, worked in the fields with the rest. It was a large part of Codreanu's mystique, of course, that he was able to identify his movement as the embodiment of this basic peasant religiosity, and collectivity.

Americans, heirs of the Catholic and Protestant traditions of Western civilization, are in the main unaware of the fundamental difference in world view between their forms of Christianity and Orthodox forms. While in the West, the state, the church, and the nation are separate entities, whose interrelations are determined by freely negotiated sets of moral and political rules (a process, of course, largely intensified by the French Revolution against which the Romanian Radical Right never ceased to avow its bitterness) in the Orthodox country, the state, church, and nation form a collective entity which has a will above that of any individual. The Orthodox Christian does not struggle, like the Protestant or Catholic, for individual salvation, and personal ethics are consequently of less importance than belonging to the Orthodox unity which includes all of his fellow men, and being carried along on the mystical tide of unity with the divine which the Church represents. One of the Legionnaire ideologues, Nichifor Crainic, considered that natural entities such as nations also participate in the hierarchical order of the Christian spirit.[12] Thus the peasant, convinced of his own role or existence as synonymous with his own folk, his own ethnicity, his own language, saw himself also as integrally linked with Orthodoxy, just as to be Irish was to be Catholic.[13]

Therefore to promote a nationalist movement, it was unthinkable that it not bear a strong Orthodox imprint. Not only did Romanian peasant Orthodoxy strongly influence the ideology of the Legion, it became one with it. And such a nationalist revival had to bring into motion, of necessity, a religious revival. Vasile Marin, Moţa's comrade in arms in Spain, explained it:

Through the national mystique is created a man stripped of
the abject materialism of the epoch. . . who passes through a
school of heroism. He becomes a man of cardinal virtues: a
hero, a priest, an ascetic, a virtuous knight. . . . Nationalism is
a knight in the service of a faith. . . his essence is the spirit of
sacrifice.[14]

Against whom was this great moral crusade directed? Foreigners,
of course, as we have seen, and the spectre of Communism, along
with the establishment philosophy of Western-style industrialization.
It remains to elaborate on that object which Codreanu and his Legion
viewed as the personification of all that was anti-Romanian, namely
the ruling classes in the form of the professional politician.

Land and Little Else

Poporanism might be said to be a natural reaction to a distinct
Romanian (and Balkan) situation, often termed *Politicianismul*. It is
best translated as "Politician-ism" or perhaps "Politician-ness," but
even in the original its obvious implication is that Romania suffered
from a surfeit of government and governors, all of them full of promises and programs, clichés and calls to action, platitudes and pledges,
old wine in new bottles with all bottles being empty. A look at Romanian politics and economics in the years after the World War will
do much to enhance our understanding of the context and atmosphere
in which Codreanu founded his movement. In broad lines the picture
is exceedingly simple. The frank truth was that the Romanian government was corrupt to the core, full of men who talked constantly of
the need to elevate the peasant and working masses and in reality
gave not a damn for either. The phanariotism and byzantine mentality
of the ruling classes was little changed from the eighteenth century,
Bacşiş (bribery) was a way of life, and Tsar Nicholas II's comment in
one of his rare *mots* that Romania "is not a nation, but a profession!"
was close to the truth. It was a regime designed by nature to provoke
outrage even in the mildest of men, much less in radically-minded
youth who sought the moral purification and regeneration of their
country.

Except for some communities of Transylvanian Saxons and some
of the German colonies in Bucovina and Bessarabia, the lot of the
peasant masses in nearly all of Romania was miserable. The tremendous irony of interwar Romanian history is that while almost all the
twists and turns of government economics were supposedly to serve
the welfare of the countryside, the peasants in their ideas, standard
of living, and level of civilization were centuries behind modern

Romanian life. From the traditional village in the Regat or Banat to the cafés of Bucharest, one passed through two hundred years.

King Ferdinand had told the troops on the embattled Romanian front in 1917, "Land will be given to you; and you will also take a larger part in public affairs." Three years later, however, in 1920, the King ousted the Transylvanian Peasant Premier Alexander Vaida-Voevod, and installed war hero General Averescu with the mission to help the landowning class avoid a truly radical agrarian reform and suppress the apparent danger from the socialists on the left.[15] Nineteen twenty-one did bring the long-awaited rural reform legislation, but implementation of the reform was so slow, and full of the usual ifs, ands, and buts of East European land programs, that peasant poverty could hardly be said to have been touched. Even though dry statistics cannot conjure up the image of the dust and dung of a Moldavian village, the daily toil, the hopes and fears of simple, superstitious people, they tell something of what reform did not accomplish. The government did expropriate great quantities of land: 6 million hectares (one hectare equals 2.47 acres), of which nearly 4 million were actually distributed to some 1,393,000 peasant families, nearly seventy per cent of those having a claim to land—which meant those with plots of 5 to 7 hectares or less. By 1930, only 7.4 per cent of the arable land was in holdings over 500 hectares, so that the big estates were indeed dealt a blow. Holdings under 100 hectares made up 85 per cent of the arable land, and those under 10 hectares, 60 per cent. But 35.8 per cent of the cultivated land consisted of holdings under 5 hectares, with 3 hectares being the median number. This last category represented 75 per cent of the holdings.[16] Using a slightly different scale, since he calculated percentages of the total agricultural area, including forest land, Roberts concluded that large properties "had not been reduced to the extent called for by the agrarian reforms, that holdings under 3 hectares still constituted the majority of the exploitations, and that medium holdings had increased in number and extent."[17]

Regardless of the validity of the Romanian census data, any set of which might be used to prove whatever one wants to prove, the matter became academic after 1929 anyway. With the onset of world-wide depression, even those medium-propertied peasants who had begun to rise a notch or two fell back to the bottom of the ladder. Land was not enough, although the "magic, misleading strength" of the slogan "land for the peasants" never lost its appeal. For the agrarian reform gave land but no farming equipment, no domestic animals, and no credit to start independent farming—nor did it touch the lack of education and the backward outlook of the village. These failings were guaranteed to worsen, rather than improve the Romanian economic situation, demonstrating once again that land reform as practiced in the Balkans was usually poor economics. The result of the 1920s "reform" was to multiply the number of uneconomic small holdings. Without equipment, newly settled peasants had to go into debt to buy or hire tools, being forced even to sell part of their new land immediately or mortgage it. While a big estate required relatively few implements, the same property when divided into thirty parcels required many more, and often former owners removed the equipment and animals before surrendering possession. This happened especially in Transylvania, where the government often colonized the confiscated lands with peasants brought from other parts of the country, which gave rise to endless complications. Naturally in accordance with traditional Romanian practice, corrupt administration of the new laws was the general rule rather than the exception. Proprietors who knew someone in the right circles could postpone land distribution indefinitely, especially by claiming a lack of surveyors.[18] As late as 1940, almost two decades after proclamation of the law, almost a million hectares of expropriated land was still not distributed, and some estates remained untouched.[19] "Land reform," actually begun during 1918, was still not complete when Romania entered the Second World War in 1941. One thing, however, the chimaera of "land to the peasants" did accomplish: it produced in the Romanian countryside that most volatile of psychological reactions which repeatedly in modern times has crystallized the wrath of the downtrodden: rising expectations, which are cut short or remain unfulfilled.

What of the second half of Ferdinand's pledge of 1917, that the peasant would have a greater share in public affairs? This promise was also unredeemed, perhaps because in Romania there was no concept of "the public." Political leaders, with one or two exceptions, were too busy following the advice of Guizot to heed that of the Steres, Mihalaches, or Codreanus.

Naturally in all countries there is a significant gap between the professionals, intellectuals, and active directors of political parties and the mass of the electorate. What made this so extreme in Romania, though, was the vast gulf which had existed for centuries between the peasant and his governors. Romanian parliamentary politics, including even the names of the parties, were simply copied from the West after 1859 by sections of the ruling groups anxious to modernize Romania, and these imported coalitions of interests had almost nothing to do with the great majority of the country's inhabitants. Thus the parties remained a field for partisan skirmishes.[20] One observer put it succinctly: "If you look at the two major parties, you see that their membership is interchangeable, with the Conservatives based on the big landowners and their clientele and the Liberals founded by young men of the same class who had been touched by western democratic and liberal ideas." So, the contenders for power changed, their labels changed, their slogans changed but, *mutatis mutandis*, the essentials remained the same and so did the opportunistic and time-serving elements of politics.[21]

The end of the First World War soon brought the end of the Conservative party, which passed out of the hands of the great landowners into neo-Conservative factions: the "Progressive Conservatives" (only in Romania could a party name itself thusly with a straight face) under Alexandru Marghiloman, and the Conservative Democrats led by Take Ionescu. With the latter's death in 1922, his followers subsequently joined Maniu, and Marghiloman's group was absorbed by other alignments. This, along with the rise of a number of new political formations, many of them very short-lived, was the most notable shift in the political pattern of the 1920s. Roberts cautions us, correctly, that too much significance should not be attributed to the disappearance of the Conservatives. It is true that the land reform and the extension of the suffrage did help to uproot the old boiar class, but the Conservatives had embraced an increasing number of non-landholding elements during its last fifteen years anyway.

> Considering the ease with which Rumanian parties were concocted from thin air and parliamentary majorities obtained, equal emphasis should be placed upon internal party weaknesses and schisms and upon the consequences of the Germanophile attitude of many Conservatives during the war. To be sure, the Conservative doctrine, if there was such, had little to offer.[22]

The point here is oblique, considering its importance. By stressing the Conservatives' internal quarreling, Roberts implies the real reason why their demise was unlikely to change much of anything: there was scarcely an iota of identification between them and the mass of the people anyway. The new conservative party of the interwar years thus became, by default, the Liberal party, recruited from the upper bourgeoisie, and also having little or no popular following. Its power lay in its economic dominance, controlling the credit flow of the country by its hold on the National Bank. Liberal governments ruled for ten of the sixteen years between 1922 and 1938, and there is no evidence during any of this time that Liberal bankers were ever effectively out of control of the seats of power.

The National Liberal Party which governed for much of the 1920s under Ion I.C. Brătianu and then Vintila Brătianu practiced almost a classical mercantilistic line. Ideas of social justice were subordinated to economic and political goals imposed from the top. The Liberals accepted reform when forced to it (the 1923 constitutional amendments on the Jews) or when it favored their interests (the foreign stabilization loan of 1928). They favored state interference when it brought contracts to the companies and corporations in which the party's members themselves were the largest shareholders. As in Russia, they were fully prepared to use the state as an instrument of Westernization, yet during their tenure of office in the '20s much fanfare was given in the official press and political organs to the slogan "by ourselves alone!" which suggested that their policy was aimed at Romanian economic autarky and the elimination of dependence on foreign capital and foreign control of the nation's resources. Much of this had to be simply window-dressing, to defuse their opponents on the left who pushed for state control and regulation, if not elimination, of foreign concessions, and on the right who continued to lament the domination of Romanian wealth by internal alien minority groups while the peasantry went begging. Paul Quinlan has shown the great extent of foreign control of the Romanian economy even on the eve of the Second World War, and if the National Liberals, who had been in power so long, were not to blame for this, who was?[23] Rather than "by ourselves alone," modernization seemed to mean colonization more than ever.

The facts and data vary in number, but not in the degree of percentages. The official *Bulletin périodique de la presse roumaine* for June 19, 1937, showed that in the textile industry 80 per cent of the engineers were Jews; in the Army Medical Corps 1,960 doctors were Jewish, 450 belonged to other minority groups, only 1,400 were Romanian; in the universities in 1934, the Jewish students made up 43 per cent of the student body, which was way out of proportion to the number of Jews in the national population. In the early days of Codreanu's movement this percentage was (in 1925) only 27 per cent, high enough at that. Weber notes that certain statistics from strongly anti-Jewish sources must be used with caution; yet considering a figure such as 14,300 employees of banks and commercial enterprises in Bucharest, which included 11,200 Jewish and only 1,964 Romanian, even were these inflated by half, the argument of the Right about foreign control of Romania would have validity.[24] One might throw in the figure for lawyers: of 10,481 in the country, nearly one-third were Jewish. For the capital city alone, the ratio was one-half. On the Bucharest stock exchange, 139 of the 142 brokers were reported to be Jewish. Of 120 pharmacies in Bessarabia, 117 of them had Jewish proprietors. The essential importance of these figures is *not* their accuracy, which may or may not be valid. The importance is that they *were* reported in official publications, and these not necessarily Legionary publications, and they *were* read by the population, and they could not fail to impress. Mass opinion is based on popular perception, not on what is or is not true. Americans, surely, should be able to sympathize with a widespread belief that foreigners indeed were taking over the country, especially in a day when Arab control of American banks and real estate, Japanese competition for the American automobile market, and the government's apparent unwillingness to do anything to the detriment of 60,000 Iranian students in American universities have become matters of real concern to the man on the street. And in the same manner, Romanians found that their government was the last place in which to find succor. Not only did the National Liberals offer no relief from foreign domination of the Romanian economy, but it was invariably to be expected in their scheme of things that industrial and commercial interests would always receive priority at the sacrifice of peasant interests. Yet even this might have been justifiable had other sectors of the Romanian economy been prosperous, which they were not. The simple truth was that National Liberal policies didn't work.

Between 1926 and 1939, per capita income in Bulgaria grew 35 per cent, and 11 per cent in Greece. For Romania the increase was 8 per cent. There was expansion of the Romanian economy, but it was anarchic, unplanned, costly, and wasteful. Industry grew according to luck, not need, and what industrial goods were produced were too high-priced for peasants to buy. Peasant poverty meant that an expanding internal market simply could not occur. Nor did the profits from industrial growth accrue to a healthy and growing middle bureaucratic and white collar class, for, as we have seen, a restricted minority controlled the capital and monetary flow, in combination with foreign companies (especially British, French, and American) which owned at least two-thirds of the oil industry, banks, and insurance companies of Romania.[25] The upper classes lived in luxury with gambling palaces, American cars, and Paris fashions; in the salons of Bucharest, the "Paris of the East," one could enjoy the *douceur* of the best of European food, wines, and women. In the countryside one child in five died before it was one year old.

The peasant in his bucolic mountain village, full of droning monotonous work and proverbs, saw the state as representing two things
to him: paying taxes and giving up his son as a soldier. Peasants ate
enough, if without any variety, but the quality of diet showed in the
high infant mortality and the prevalence of pellagra and other nutri-
tional diseases. Industrial workers in many cases were even worse off,
for the peasant outside of the city could at least grow his own food.
Although food prices in the urban markets were cheap, they had to
be, since industrial wages were so pitiful. Colin Clark estimated Romanian working class income to be the lowest in Eastern Europe,
even below the 1914 level.[26] This in a country with one of the greatest economic potentials in Europe, with great and widespread natural
resources. As the Moţi sang wryly:

> Gold lies in our mountains' core
> But we beg from door to door.

Small wonder that Western political theory, with its identification of
government and people (at least in the abstract) had no meaning in
Romania. As Charles and Barbara Jelavich have put it, the political
attitude of the population in general was "distrust toward authority
and indifference to the concept of civil responsibility," acceptance
of corruption and deception in political life as normal and natural.[27]
Ion Mihalache characterized the government well, in his description
of the Liberal Party:

> . . . [it] has had the tactic of bringing to its bosom the most
> advanced elements and of uniting them with the most conser-
> vative and reactionary elements. For the advanced elements it
> has one task: to write principles into the program; for the re-
> actionary elements it has another: not to carry them out.[28]

How to break such a cycle? Through democratic elections, based
on an informed citizenry? Of course, but such things were not part
of Romanian tradition either. Extending the suffrage after the First
World War did not lead to political democracy, and elections were
simply another *pro forma* exercise stemming from the grafted-on
Western system which could not transcend the basic phanariotism
in which politics was the art of formulating new clichés to use on the
amorphous mass of peasants. Roberts' succinct phrasing would be
disputed by no serious student of Romanian history:

> Romanian elections were notorious for their corruption,
> ballot stuffing, and general unreliability as measures of public
> sentiment. Perhaps only two elections in the entire period
> [1922-1945] were at all free and fair. . . . Many governments
> were in power through no popular mandate whatsoever but
> merely through political arrangements; dismissals were equally
> arbitrary and only occasionally resulted from the loss of popu-
> lar confidence. It would be futile and misleading to explain the
> course of Romanian politics by an analysis of the elections.[29]

Nor should it be forgotten in all this that in practical terms Romania was a police state. While the army did not play as prominent a role in politics as in other Balkan states, it was always present in the background to preserve law and order. More useful to the regime in power was the *Siguranţa*, the secret police under the control of the Ministry of the Interior. These were used to keep people from the polls in districts where an anti-government vote might be expected, or to herd people to the polls, or to arrest demonstrators, or to create demonstrations, depending on the needs of the day. Cracked heads and violence were no more uncommon on election day than at other critical times in a country which had yet to learn the concept of a loyal opposition.

As for the quality of the electorate or its ability to articulate its needs and translate them into political action, this, too, was lacking. At the beginning of the twentieth century, over three-quarters of the country's population was illiterate, and until after World War II less than 1 per cent of peasant youths pursued any studies beyond elementary school, as until 1920 at least, many of them still owed villein labor to landowners. Education was of and for the cities, not the countryside. Fischer-Galati estimates there were eight city boys to every rural youth, in secondary schools, few of them going on to universities, especially with the onset of the depression. Between 1929-1938 some 283,583 students in all attended institutions of higher learning and less than 10 per cent completed a degree.[30] When they did, there were no jobs for them, for the bureaucracy could not absorb them, nor could the teaching profession. This explains partially, perhaps, the seemingly vast number of "journalists," who used such a phrase to stress their membership in the intelligentsia although their work might consist of an occasional article in a home-made broadside or sporadic pamphleteering.

What did happen, however, in Romania was important to the growth of Right-wing parties between the wars. One government measure was the inauguration of numerous scholarship programs to rural students in an attempt to create the skilled basis of people for modernization and industrialization. Although far from successful in this goal, since industrial growth lagged far behind population growth and the infra-structure of a technical-industrial society grew only haphazardly, not as the result of any conscious planning of what to do with new graduates, the new educational outpouring did have a vitally important effect on Romanian society. It produced one of the classic situations conducive to radical movements, the growth of an educated class in an undereducated society which could not absorb more than a tiny portion of students and graduates.

What took place was fundamental to the growth of Legionary support, and that of other right-wing movements. For the first time in Romanian history, a generation of peasant sons had left the village and emerged from the ranks of the provincial ignorance of centuries. Deeply religious from their home lives, and seeing for the first time the promise of raising their status by joining the ranks of the educated, they were all the more frustrated by the realization that in such a system as Romania's the promised land was not to be. Joining a party machine meant openly foreswearing whatever principles one had; maintaining one's principles meant abandoning the idea of a career.

Research into revolutions and the nature of mass movements is clear on this point: it is not the miserably poor who rebel, but those who have tasted better things. A grievance is most poignant when almost redressed, Eric Hoffer tells us.[31] In both France and Russia the land-hungry peasants owned nearly one-third of the agricultural land at the outbreak of revolution, and most of this had been acquired during the generation or two preceding the outbreak of revolution.[32] Not only had the agrarian reform of the early 1920s, even with its defects, created a sizeable new class of middle-level or petit-bourgeois landowners for the first time, but these could now combine with spirited and ambitious, and newly cosmopolitanized (read, intellectualized) peasant youth to form a revolutionary body of socially dissatisfied, disgruntled people, ready to express ambient frustrations in word and action. As even a superficial observer will note, the student classes in Romania between the wars were in the vanguard of every radical and nationalist movement. We are much more dissatisfied when we have something and want more, than when we have nothing and want some. Then, too, to the specifics of the Romanian phenomena were wedded the peculiar *Zeitgeist* of the post-1914 generation throughout Europe.

Truly historical generations are not born: they are made. The dashed hopes of the war to end all wars, the disillusionment of the young in all the nations of Europe after 1918, with the implications of this for the future, still remains a topic for research which will offer new insights into the psychology of the mass movements of the post-Versailles decades. For the moment, compare Codreanu's thinking and preachments with:

> They waited for the moment when their generation would rise again and take its rightful place. In the meantime, they suffered from the mediocrity of everyday life that fell on their "warm enthusiasm" like a "perfidious, little grey rain." It had

taken no more to master them and quench their ardor. . . than the signing of the peace and the return of the "bad doctors" who governed France.

But what a sudden desire sometimes comes over us to unbend, to strike the air with our now impotent fists, to spit in disgust. And before the clouds that pass in the sky, what nostalgia rises in our troubled hearts.[33]

The writer was Henri de Montherlant, who spoke of the need to "subject oneself to an iron discipline, without end and without profit, to search for a solution, knowing that the problem is insoluble." Farther to the East were the German *Jugend*, the very term itself an innovation in linguistic usage which denoted something distinct from the past, a generation which "represented not merely an age-group (as before the war) but a new and radically different category of human beings."[34] German youth, too, sought to flee from the unpleasant realities and dilemmas of Wilhelmine Germany into a "knightly and rural world of youth where they could dream, untroubled, of cultural renewal."

As they hiked through the unspoiled countryside, danced around flaring bonfires, sang folk songs, strummed their guitars, and declaimed Nietzsche's *Zarathustra* and Stefan George's poetry, they could forget the asphalt and the grey working masses of the cities and congratulate themselves on having achieved a true national community or *Volksgemeinschaft* within their marching groups.

They believed that they had escaped from the lies and hypocrisy of the adult world, and they fancied that they were laying the foundation for a new and better Germany. Ethical purity and spiritual growth were their objectives. . . .[35]

From another corner of the continent:

We are going to flood with our curiosity and our enthusiasm the most remote corners of Spain: we are going to get to know Spain and to sow it with our love and indignation. We are going to travel the fields like crusading apostles, to live in the villages, to listen to the desperate complaints . . . . We are going to create among them strong bonds of sociability—cooperatives, circles of mutual education; centers of observation and protest.[36]

Of course this was José Ortega y Gasset, for whom the crisis of his homeland could be solved only by "Regenerationists" who would raise the level of Spanish civilization. "European man is beginning a new exodus toward another historic ambit, toward another mode of existence," he prophesied in 1933.

Someone once remarked that Codreanu's speeches and writings describe every effort or step undertaken by the Legion as a "struggle"— the "struggle" for education, the "struggle" for votes, and so on. It was part of the image of righteous, sword-bearing youth, cutting a swath of fiery purity through the cancer of state corruption:

> Every article has the thunder and the sound of a proclama-
> tion; every polemical thrust and witty remark is written in the
> style of a bulletin announcing a victory; every conversation
> takes on the air of a Cataline conspiracy or a club of sanscul-
> lottes; every title is a program; every criticism is a taking of the
> Bastille; every book is a gospel; and even private letters have
> the panting and gallop of apostolic warnings.[37]

Here was Giovanni Papini, burning with the fever to transform others
and become their moral guide which characterized so many Italian
youth. He could have been describing the emissaries of the Archangel
in Romania. "With the older generation one era ends, with us another
one begins. We are the pioneers that head the column of the future,"
wrote Codreanu of his "struggle" to reshape the nation. The "Captain"
was a perfect manifestation of the charismatic leader, whose "new
men" partook fervently of the ideas in the air of Young Europe of
his day.

He directed his appeals to the young in the high schools, normal
schools, trade and commercial academies, theological seminaries, and
villages which city intellectuals and politicians ignored. Interestingly,
Codreanu's movement departed from typical right-wing configura-
tions in that war veterans did not form more than a nominal part of
his organization, nor did he attract the important hierarchs of the
Orthodox Church as much as he did village priests. In effect, at least
in the early years, his movement was a crusade of adolescents, and
even in the late 1930s unformed youths made up a large proportion
of his cadres. This may well have been a reason for the continuing
failure to develop the all-encompassing discipline which the Legion
so often lacked, and in addition explains why the movement never
quite ceased to attract young people of the type more interested in
marching and fighting than sacrificing and purging their souls to regenerate society. The socio-psychological history of Legionary support continues to await its researcher.

Besides youth and the peasantry in general (as we have seen) by
the 1930s industrial workers too came to support the Legion in significant numbers. This is a phenomenon which never ceased to baffle
interpreters of the Romanian scene at the time, who insisted that
communists had infiltrated the movement and made up a significant
part of its ranks. The fact that one of the largest sources of support
for the Legionary Workers' Corps led by Dumitru Groza during
1940-1941 consisted of the men of the Grivița railroad shops, the
scene of one of the greatest socialist-style proletarian uprisings of
1933, seemed irreconcilable. Communist writers, naturally, are embarrassed by such facts, and must resort to emphasizing the "lumpen"

nature of these misguided proletarians. In fact, worker support for the Legionary movement is not that much of an enigma, if one remembers the briefness of the Romanian industrial experience. Large numbers of urban factory workers in the 1930s were ex-peasants who had abandoned village life only a few years previously. More to the point is the fact that moving into town did not mean a severing of all ties with the village, nor with its mentality. While many workers undoubtedly commuted daily or every few days by train between their rural homes and their work in town, others surely made the village and relatives the center of their holidays and weekends. This is true for large numbers of peasants even today in Romania, for whom the passage of many years as factory laborers or semi-skilled craftsmen has not changed their essentially peasant personalities.

Thus five years or a decade into the post-war world, the ex-peasant "enlisted in the service of modernization" in railroads, gas works, factories, port facilities continued to view such new things as alien forces. He did not identify with the factory owners and their interests, certainly, nor, as in the West, did he share in the goals and ideology of the industrialization process. The peasant remained the manipulated, never the participant, in the new society. He punched his time-card and continued to hang garlic over his door. And he remained susceptible to evangelical calls to nation, church, and folk.

Legionary Beginnings

Between the World Wars, fascist and radical-rightist movements in Romania took a large number of forms, and developed in two phases. Fascism appeared as an element in larger political parties, and often led to a schism after a short time, such as the case of Octavian Goga and Vaida Voevod's defection from the National Peasant Party. There was also "borrowed fascism," which followed the traditional Romanian practice of imitating more developed European states. An interesting example of this type was the short-lived *Fascia Naţională Română*, which began as a student organization in Bucharest in 1923 and was then absorbed into Professor Cuza's League of Christian Defense. The group was explicitly modeled after Mussolini's brand of Italian fascism, with all the trappings and the promise of a two-year dictatorship to eliminate rotten politicians. Its program was populist, anti-Semitic, anti-Communist, and anti-parliamentarian, but it never went beyond a rather jejune schoolboy exercise and remained far too academic to appeal to wide levels of the population.[38]

The Legion of the Archangel Michael was, as we have already seen in part, something else, an authentic Romanian movement of the Radical-Right. It had certain fascist traits and copied some Italian and German features, but here the similarity stopped. In its origins, it existed well before Hitler's N.S.D.A.P. came onto the national scene in Germany. Having looked into some of the Legion's intellectual underpinnings, it remains to review the steps in its path to glory.

Corneliu Zelea Codreanu was born in Iaşi in 1899 and grew to be extremely tall, handsome, and impressive, with powerful and compelling features. Interestingly, he was not of peasant stock; his father taught in a provincial high school and brought his children up in the cult of his adopted Romanian fatherland.[39] One of Codreanu's brothers was named Decebal, another Horia, and a sister was Iredenta. Between his eleventh and his sixteenth year, the boy went to the famous Manastirea Dealului Military Academy, and this training had a permanent impact not only on his thought, but on his soul. He emerged firmly devoted to order and discipline, the fear of God and only God, and the benefits of physical hardship, marching, the outdoor life. His teachers convinced him that the future belonged to the elite, and the elite meant men of character. It also meant sacrifice, poverty, and a hard and severe way of life. When Romania entered the Great War in 1916, Codreanu was still too young to enlist, but he followed after his father's regiment and observed the battlefield for several weeks. He was eventually admitted to officers' school, but the war was over by the time he graduated.

Codreanu began his career in the spring of 1919 when he entered the law school of the University of Iaşi. His father was an active politician and a colleague of Professor Cuza's, and by 1920 Codreanu seemed to spend more time fomenting student riots against Jews and Communists, or organizing his companions in the forests near Huşi, on the border, to fight Bolshevism, than he did studying. Even then, such activities were carried on amidst the background of secret nighttime oaths in forest clearings, as the strong streak of ritualism in the future leader never left him. During 1922 he studied at the University of Berlin and later, as we have discussed, he spent a year at Grenoble.

During 1923 he became one of the organizers of Cuza's League of National Christian Defense, which emerged primarily to oppose the pressures which in that year culminated in the granting of citizenship to Jews resident in Romania. This was one of the most vexatious conditions imposed on Romania by the Paris Peace Conference. The Brătianu government had resigned in protest over its inclusion in the settlement, and only after the powers in Paris sent an ultimatum, which suggested to Romanians the possible loss of her territorial gains, did Vaida Voevod sign the treaty. In Bucovina, for example, 40,000 Jews were threatened with remaining stateless, on the grounds that they were refugees who had only recently entered the country. This theory of the "Jewish invasion," although only partly true, died hard, and although the Jews of the Old Kingdom (about 75% of them, at least) had been naturalized by decrees of 1918 and 1919, the acquisition of Bessarabia, Bucovina, and Transylvania added approximately 563,000 Jews to the population, and minority rights for these existed only in the peace treaty and not in the Romanian constitution.[40]

The amendment of 1923 was not nearly so all-encompassing or devastating as all the anti-Jewish uproar would lead one to believe. Minority rights were granted, but only grudgingly, and obliquely. Article 133 of the Constitution of 1923 simply ratified the decree laws of December 28, 1918, and May 22, 1919 applicable to the Old Kingdom. The law now read:

Only naturalization shall place a foreigner on an equal footing with a Roumanian as concerns the exercising of political rights. Naturalization shall be granted individually by the Council of Ministers.[41]

This was not ascribed citizenship, therefore. The burden of acquiring naturalization was left up to the individual. A Jew seeking citizenship had to declare before a law court that he had been born in the country and that his parents had never been under the protection of a foreign power. It is impossible to tell how many of the country's minority residents took advantage of this clause, but certainly some, perhaps as many as 25% did not, and thus remained technically stateless persons. What many Romanians complained of, however, is that at the same time this latter group managed to avoid the censuses (and taxes) they continued to hold real estate and exert practical monopolies over business enterprises, especially in Bessarabia and the northern border regions. On this the constitution was also explicit:

Only Roumanians and naturalized Roumanians may acquire title to and own rural real estate in Roumania. Foreigners shall have only the right to the revenues from such real estate.[42]

Here was a devilish clause, designed to settle nothing.

It was from the agitation over Jewish citizenship that Codreanu emerged onto the national scene. In many ways he and his fellow Moldavians were less incensed over such limited concessions to minorities than at the politicians whom they saw as once more kowtowing to foreign pressures and spoiling the fruits of the creation of Greater Romania, by voting for such measures. It was at this point, when lists of political leaders to be shot were discovered, that Codreanu, Moţa, and their fellow conspirators were arrested and imprisoned for five months. After a trial in which the court was obviously sympathetic to their youthful, if misguided, nationalist zeal, all were acquitted. "Codreanu returned to Iaşi and apparently gave up any further thought of murders."[43] In his Legionary manual he later described his experience while awaiting trial in the prison church, when he daily meditated before an icon of the Archangel Michael, the warrior saint.[44] It was in this traumatic period, somewhere during these anxious days, that he decided violence was not the way, but faith and labor was. Once released from prison he set up in Iaşi the first of his Brotherhoods of the Cross, with Moţa to head them. And almost at once Codreanu forgot, or was forced to forget, depending on one's point of view, his new vow.

The first project of the Brotherhood was building its own student center near Iaşi with homemade bricks and money earned by working in market gardens. Singing and marching as they carried materials, they had barely begun when the prefect of Iaşi himself led squads of police and gendarmes to break them up. Arrested for no apparent reason, they were tied up with ropes, dragged through the streets, spat on, beaten, humiliated, and released only when Professor Cuza and other citizens intervened. It was Codreanu's first experience with naked injustice, and such an occurrence was not unusual in Romania. What was worse was that an "official inquiry" brought a decoration for Prefect Manciu. Codreanu brought suit in court, and the case was dismissed. So he openly shot Manciu in front of the Iaşi city hall.

Americans have only to reflect on the code of our ante-bellum South or of the Western frontier to understand that public opinion was completely on the young man's side. The authorities decided to hold the trial in another Moldavian town, while citizens and school-children took to the streets and demonstrated outside the prison yard for Codreanu's release. Then they moved him all the way to the other end of the country, to Turnu-Severin. Thousands of tracts alerted the citizenry to support the accused. Trainloads of sympathizers poured into the city, so that the court had to adjourn to the local theatre to hold the crowds. The jury stayed out a few minutes and returned wearing the red, yellow, and blue emblem of the LANC on their lapels, having voted unanimously for acquittal. On his way back to Iaşi people came to the train stations to see him as he passed, priests blessed him, and his homecoming was celebrated by crowds with flowers and songs.[45] It was not the first time he realized his power to inspire or, better said, the power of that which he represented to move men. In the elections of 1926 the LANC won 120,000 votes and elected ten deputies, including Codreanu's father. Yet the preliminary phase of searching for a permanent vehicle for national regeneration was not yet over. Temporary victories could not solve the internal divisions in the LANC, and the first of several factional divisions took place between 1925 and 1927.

In the first place, Cuza and many older nationalists were worried over the tendency of the angry young prophets to take matters into their own hands. Codreanu and Moţa, on the other hand, were fast moving toward a disciplined movement along paramilitary lines, based on the experience of their successful student agitation and with the Brotherhoods now available as recruiting and training organizations. It was partly to avoid an open break with Cuza that the two youths went off to Grenoble for a year. Cuza remained tied to parliamentary politics and, as his young protegés had predicted, the LANC disintegrated into internal struggles. Its parliamentary delegation split into rival groups, and its vote in the 1927 elections dropped to 52,481, or a mere 1.9% of the total, and it won no seats.[46] In the following year's balloting, the LANC dropped to 32,273 votes, for a 1.14 percentage.[47] Anti-Jewish platforms alone were not sufficient.

On November 8, 1927, the Day of St. Michael, the Legion of the Archangel Michael was organized with the administering of an oath to a small group of followers, by Codreanu, Moţa, and four others who had drawn up their guidelines earlier that year. The newly-sworn were then sent to take small quantities of earth from Romanian battlefields, to be worn in pouches around their necks—the *pamântul strămoşesc*, which was also the title of the paper placed at their disposal by Ion Moţa's father.[48] Beginnings of the Legion were modest, and financial problems great. The arrival of the National Peasant Party to power during 1928 had much to do with this, for it attracted large peasant support which would otherwise have likely gone to the several new right-wing parties. Iuliu Maniu, National Peasant Leader, did not have the magnetism of a Codreanu, but nearly alone among Romanian political leaders of his day he represented a man of personal morality and some measure of political rectitude. The early years of the Legion were thus inauspicious, and by the time it was two years old, only forty members might show up when Codreanu called a regional meeting in Iaşi.[49] Enthusiasm, however, compensated for the lack of numbers. The Legion marched and sang, and preached "bread and justice" slogans reminiscent of another charismatic leader a decade earlier. By the end of 1929, after marches in the area of Galaţi, Focşani, and even into the Moţi region of Transylvania, Codreanu decided on a full-scale program of going to the people.

The upsurge of the Legionary movement during 1930 and 1931 had its basis in two major phenomena: the worsening economic crisis of the country with the onset of world economic depression, and the essential failure of the National Peasant regime to redeem its promises. Henry Roberts has cogently analyzed the policies of Maniu and the National Peasant Party during their first eighteen months in power, and concluded that the government "was not very 'peasantist' either in its composition or in its activities."[50] This does not mean that it did not have an agrarian program, or that it was indifferent to the peasant. Indeed, there was some homogeneity of economic, agrarian, and administrative policy, in such measures as the laws for mines and state enterprises, in the cooperative reorganization legislation, and reform of the National Bank and the state accounting system which the National Peasants enacted. Yet the chief concern when the party came to power was for greater political democracy and more economic liberty. Their problem thus became one of timing.

The National Peasants sought to reverse the economic nationalism and semiautarky of the National Liberals just at the time when the European economy, spurred by the depression, the drying up of foreign trade and international credit, was moving into a new phase of economic nationalism. And in their preoccupation with such large affairs, as so often happens, the peasant was lost sight of. We cannot blame Maniu and his group for not seeing the full consequences of the world collapse of the 1930s; but the fact that they were committed to a pattern fast becoming anachronistic wrought havoc with their internal position. Finally, faced with the political crisis of the renunciation of the throne by Carol II in 1928, followed by Carol's dramatic return in 1930, and the rising anti-democratic forces and anti-parliamentary movements generally besetting Europe as the new decade opened, the National Peasants, bereft of the fervent peasant support of the early 1920s, had few defenses. They had lost touch with the masses, with the primordial qualities which they had embraced earlier, as they became institutionalized and professionalized. The contrast with what the Legion did was enough to demonstrate the difference starkly.

"The Legion does not make electoral promises" said Codreanu at the end of 1929 as, beginning in Bereşti, his Legionaries marched through the valley of the Pruth, from village to village, on horseback. Ignoring the protests of local authorities, the young militants addressed peasants in churchyards and were met as they went with crowds holding candles. The momentum grew as young men from each place joined them, and their numbers mounted. Wearing turkey feathers on their fur caps in the fashion of the legendary *haiducs*, Codreanu's marchers were met in the Moldavian custom by peasants pouring water in their path for good luck. In torchlit circles amidst the weathered headstones of their forefathers, the peasants heard the awesome young man dressed in their traditional white linen costume tell them that the politicians in Bucharest cared nothing for them, that the King and his camarilla were a grafting lot allied with Jewish banking interests, and that only a rebirth of peasant honesty, virtue, and the values of their ancestors would allow them to control their own destinies. His eyes shone with the light that one finds in paintings of fifteenth century madonnas, and he penetrated to undefined depths of their souls.

In January, 1930 came the first great march into "Jewish-Communist" Bessarabia. The Legionaires wore white crosses on green shirts as they passed into the region of Cahul. "We looked like Crusaders, and we wanted to be Crusaders who in the name of the cross entered the struggle against godless Jewish might in order to liberate Romania," Codreanu said.[51] For a time he had official support for his venture across the Pruth, when Vaida Voevod, as Minister of the Interior, granted him permission in July for a second, larger demonstration into the region.[52] Already, however, the authorities were growing more and more nervous over such large numbers of earnest and organized columns of young men in the north. There was also the concern not to antagonize Russia with demonstrations and potential outbursts so close to the border. Major disturbances broke out in Maramureş that month of July, 1930, in which a heavily-populated Jewish town was set on fire, many said by members of the Legion. Certainly Codreanu expected at any time that his men might be assaulted, either by the Romanian gendarmerie, or some kind of real or fictitious fighting forces put together by the Bessarabian aliens and communists. Thus the second march into Bessarabia was preceded by the formation of a combat organization within the Legion, called the Iron Guard: "an organization of militant youth to combat Jewish communism," he called it. Although the move into Bessarabia went off peacefully enough, political changes in this highly unstable period were occurring rapidly. At the end of the year, Mihalache replaced Vaida at the Ministry of the Interior. When a Legionnaire took a point-blank shot at a Bucharest journalist who had criticized the Movement, and some Aromani students made an attempt on the life of the Minister of Agriculture, Mihalache in January, 1931, ordered the dissolution of both the Legion and the Iron Guard. Searches and arrests followed, and when it was shown that none of these incidents had been initiated by Codreanu or the governing Legionary collegium (executive committee, in a sense) the usual acquittal followed. Yet a concerted campaign of denunciation of the Legion accompanied the trials for "conspiracy to overthrow the public order," in which arrests without warrants, raids on Legionary houses, and detention "on suspicion" were much in evidence. The National Peasants, no less than the Liberals, knew how to use the police apparatus.

For the next eighteen months, violence was rife between the Legion and the forces of government, as the former sought to fight fire with fire and organize politically, and the latter strove to keep them away from the villages during elections. Codreanu was practical enough to know that gaining political strength was one way to oppose (and expose) the politicians and at the same time remove some of the stigma of radicalism from his movement and attract followers disgusted with the major parties. Nineteen thirty and nineteen thirty-one were crucial years, therefore; the first, or organizational phase of the Legionary Movement may be said to have ended, and the second phase, that of the mass movement, began, with the decision to offer candidates for parliament. Yet for a time things remained very fluid. New parties, groupings, fronts, and alignments were constantly appearing—at least three separate small organizations imitative of the German Nazis sprang up in the first years of the decade, separate from Codreanu's movement, such as the obviously unoriginal *Svastika de Foc* ("Swastika of Fire"), and it is very likely that violence provoked by such extremists was blamed on the Legionaries. The government could not always discriminate which among numerous opposition organizations were responsible for specific disorders, thus it lashed out indiscriminately.[53] Political life in Bucharest itself remained extremely unstable, and not until the end of 1933 with the coming of the Tătărescu administration did any semblance of order or continuity prevail as alignments shifted, formed, dissolved, and re-formed, under the manipulations of the King. There is some evidence that Carol cooperated, or at least maintained a "wait and see" attitude toward the Legion during the early 1930s, in the event that it might prove useful to him.[54] Historians have yet to firmly sort out the shifting sands of this confused period. What is certain is that as each month went by after his return from exile, Carol steadily moved to assume more personal control of the government, and by the mid-1930s there were few who did not recognize that the King was a master of the see-saw of parliamentary politics and of playing off one party or clique against the other.[55] Moreover his Jewish mistress and later wife Magda (Wolff) Lupescu became the very incarnation of the corrupt alien influence-peddling and wholesale plunder of the country by the king and the politicians against which the Legionaries and thousands of others railed. One could buy at *duduja*'s house practically any state position, for the right kind of money placed in the proper hands. The "international Jewish conspiracy" seemed fully confirmed with Carol-Lupescu in power and parliamentary puppets to do their bidding. This was the view, at least, from the village. Added to economic times harder than ever before and the onerousness of the police state atmosphere, it made for a highly paranoic, volatile situation, one which would undulate in intensity throughout the decade, but never really disappear.[56]

The results became very apparent in the 1931 elections. From its miniscule showing of 32,000 votes the previous year, the LANC more than tripled its support, garnering 113,863 ballots and 8 parliamentary seats. At the same time the "Labour and Peasant Group," actually a communist front coalition, received 73,000 votes and 5 seats, which showed not only that the elections represented an *anti* vote against the Iorga-Argetoianu government, but that the talk of alien impact was not all idle. Most of the Labour-Peasant Group's strength came from Hungarian industrial workers in Banat and Transylvania.[57]

Running under the rubric "Zelea Codreanu Group," the Legion picked up 30,783 votes, or 1% of the total, which was not insignificant, considering the government's recent concerted efforts to frighten the populace out of supporting the movement, and supposing that the surprising comeback of the LANC drew votes away from Codreanu. No mandates went with such a showing, but chance intervened. A by-election was held in Neamț in August, and Codreanu was elected to the chamber. He would take the crusade directly into the "cave of the lion," he told his people.

Codreanu was obviously not the typical parliamentary agent for his constituents, concerned only with securing sinecures and winning debating points. He proceeded to launch into a denunciation of political plundering and the private finances of leading politicians. He demanded the death penalty for misuse of state funds (a measure which, if enacted, might well have wiped out the entire governmental establishment of the country) and climaxed his assault by exposing a loan of 19 million lei made to Foreign Minister Nicolae Titulescu by the Marmaroş-Blanc Bank, and scathingly accused deputy Ion G. Duca and other high officials of erratic financial manipulations.[58] Certainly, at this point, if not earlier, the decision in the Bucharest establishment that this young man had to be checked had been made.

A year after Mihalache's purge, the regime went after the Legionaries again. When Codreanu's group tried to run in a by-election in Tutova in the spring of 1932, all repression possible was brought to bear. Reinforced platoons of gendarmes assembled to keep campaigning Legionaries out of the villages. It was clear that two new elements were now introduced into Romanian politics, however: the Legion was disciplined enough to hold out in the face of force, and use hit-and-run tactics. Most importantly, "the Legion answered violence with unbridled counterviolence. When captured Legionaries were mistreated, their comrades in a regular streetfight captured the gendarme outpost and liberated the prisoners."[59] The government party presses, led by *Viitorul* and *Dimineaţa*, accused the Guard of "anarchist attempts to overthrow the government."[60] When the Legion won the by-election, with Codreanu père joining his son in parliament, the Iorga-Argetoianu ministry again order the Guard dissolved.

Persecution, as so often happens, only stiffened resolve and brought wider support. The July, 1932, elections produced 70,674 votes for the Legion, and five seats in the chamber, thus more than doubling its vote of a year earlier.[61]

Now running candidates in 36 electoral districts, the Legion appeared on its way to concerted parliamentary strength. Noteworthy were the sources of its votes: mainly the dissatisfied regions of Bessarabia, and the Transylvanian Moţi districts. Yet Guardist and police clashes continued until Vaida Voevod, who again took over the government at the end of May, sought to defuse things and silence his critics who called him weak and unable to maintain order. In a meeting with Codreanu he suggested some "positive, constructive work," to remove the image of disorder surrounding the movement.[62]

The response was a dam construction project in the village of Vişani, where annual floods washed away peasant squatter homes. Two hundred Legionaries were mobilized for the enterprise, which was barely begun when several companies of gendarmes attacked them, some of the workers being trampled to the ground. In charge of this defense of the public order was Armand Călinescu, one of

Romania's "strong men," as the press described him, who not only hated the Legion but saw in its persecution a means of political reputation.[63] When in the fall of 1933 Carol once again called the Liberal Party to power under Ion G. Duca, the stage was set for full confrontation.

During the last weeks of the National Peasant government, Duca visited Paris, thus confirming what the Legion and others had said: that "Romania had to have France's permission to form its own government." Regardless of the truth or falsity of this, it was apparent that Duca was openly hostile to the Legion and the Guard and had more than once declared his intention to move strongly against it. On the other hand, one must remember first and foremost that Duca was a politician, and a Romanian politician at that, in the midst of a very unstable period of Romanian politics between 1930-1933, and was doing all he could to bring his Liberal Party back into power and discredit the regime of the National Peasants. He used political rhetoric as freely as the next man, and said what had to be said to please his listeners. The problem is that historians, too, can forget context and environment and thus perpetuate what is only that—rhetoric— far beyond its lifetime. Thus the hearsay of nearly fifty years ago continues to ride this morning's headlines. Duca's visit to Paris centered on two major items: internal finances and foreign policy. It was the failure to obtain substantial foreign loans to stabilize the foundering Romanian economy that had helped produce the fall of the Liberal Party earlier, and the forced resignation of Iorga's government in June, 1932. Duca was in France to obtain money; he would have hotly denied "conspiring with the Judeo-Masonic bankers," but such was the oratory from the Right back in Romania.

French political and financial circles naturally wanted guarantees of future Romanian stability. What better thing for Duca to say than that the Legionary Movement was an "anarchistic, subversive movement in the pay of Hitler," and promise that he would render it impotent?[64]

The second purpose of the visit dovetailed with the first. The French were busy in the early 1930s consolidating their anti-German alliance system to bolster the chimeric Maginot philosophy. In January, 1932, the Poles, with French urging, had signed a treaty of friendship and non-aggression with the Soviet Union, and now both Poland and France were urging Romania to do the same. The influential Foreign Minister, Titulescu, who represented the Versailles system and the French-oriented Little Entente, was concerned over the

possible impact of such a step on Bessarabia, and as of Duca's trip to
Paris, Romania and the U.S.S.R. had still not resumed diplomatic relations, a step which was two years in the future. Disagreement between Titulescu and Vaida Voevod on the Soviet question had helped
prompt Vaida's resignation from the government in October, 1932,
and even though he returned in January, 1933 to head one of the final,
brief National Peasant alignments, the Soviet problem remained a tense
question. Titulescu himself was anti-Legion primarily because the
movement's vociferous anti-communism, its continued agitation over
and within Bessarabia, and its role as a cause of internal instability (one
might point out that this view was a two-edged argument, since the government made full use of violence against anyone when it saw fit) interfered with his conduct of foreign policy.[65] Therefore the Foreign Minister seconded Duca's efforts in Paris, and Titulescu's influence in the
West, far more so than the potential prime minister's, was considerable.[66] One thing was clear: Duca needed French sympathy at a time
when the rise of a strong Germany once more seemed to be in the offing, and Duca said what was needed to calm French anxieties that Eastern Europe might be drifting into the Nazi camp. It is *just* possible that,
had Duca been negotiating for loans and moral support from *German*
bankers for some reason, he would have denounced back home the
"godless communists" who formed an "anarchistic, subversive movement in the pay of Stalin."

There were other complicating factors. The year 1933 had produced some of the worst internal violence in Romania from the left.
On February 1, oil workers at Ploieşti struck over a wage decision,
and a prolonged fight ensued between strikers and government troops.
At the same time in Bucharest some 7,000 workers in the state railway shops, centered on Calei Griviţa, went on strike. The government hurriedly proclaimed martial law in Bucharest, Cernăuţi, Iaşi,
Galaţi, Timişoara, Ploieşti, and the oil fields. The Communist Party
and its affiliates were dissolved again, as they had been in the '20s,
and the regime passed laws against "antisocial and antistate organizations." These produced protest demonstrations from the railway
workers, troops appeared, and vicious street fights followed, with
arrests and broken heads galore. Tension persisted for the rest of the
year, and such events made it hard to ignore the Legion's preachings,
along with those of other groups on the right, that the leftists and
communists were far from an idle threat. But it was not politically
or diplomatically expedient in Paris for Duca to speak of communist
agitation at a time of Franco-Russian rapprochement. It was fine to
speak of "Nazi agitation," for this put him alongside the French.

Still, it was over-obvious and should have been transparent, how
Duca sought to maneuver in the morass of shifting alliances and
chaotic unrest on all sides. The fact was that Duca had no solid
proof whatsoever that Codreanu and his movement were in "Hitler's
pay" or, for that matter, even in Hitler's camp. He just *said* it, for
effect, and thus repeated what anti-Legionary politicians at home
circulated as hearsay. Hitler, after all, had taken power in Germany
only a little more than eight months prior to Duca's coming into office on November 14, 1933; the German chancellor had hardly had
time to build a coordinated and well-financed fifth column movement abroad, when his own domestic policies were barely underway
in the autumn of 1933. Nagy-Talavera in his work on the Green
Shirts also overlooks the chronology of 1933, and thus his argument
that French officialdom at the time of Duca's visit was severely worried about a Nazi sweep of the Balkans is premature. This fear was
real in 1936 or 1938, certainly, but not when the Führer had been in
power less than a year.

Having said all this, we return to the central fact: the hearsay
charge that Codreanu was financed by the N.S.D.A.P. naturally
found its way to the press. Few speculated that the charge was much
more logical if lodged against the outright imitation fascist groups
such as the Swastika of Fire, or the members of the LANC, about
whom it is easy to show that they had received party advice, para-
phernalia, and monetary donations from the German Nazi Party in
the past.[67] In the West, looking at the bewildering Romanian political scene, it was all too easy to confuse Blue Shirts, Green Shirts,
Brown Shirts and No-Shirts. It was all "more or less the same." Hearsay charges made against *anyone* in 1933 Romania should be taken
cum magnum grano salis and treated for what they were worth: part
of the polemical morass. Yet history has its own convoluted course
and does not always obey the puny logic of men. Instead Duca's
hearsay nearly half a century ago will be repeated and offered as unchallenged truth in a Detroit courtroom to "prove" that a man was a
Nazi, and Justice Department lawyers with a command of perhaps
two words of the Romanian language will use the highly political
newspapers of a volatile period, no less, in *Eastern Europe*, no less,
as objective source material to make their case. It would be almost
ludicrous, were it not so tragic.

And so Duca returned to Bucharest, stating that he had to "chan-
nelize" the energies of the Iron Guard, an interesting phrase which
meant: the entire police machine of the country was let loose on the

Legion, to keep them from the polls in the coming elections. Not surprisingly, the Legion resisted. Thus ten days before the balloting, on the night of December 9, 1933, another, final dissolution of the Legion was announced; and in a massive pre-dawn roundup, some 18,000 Legionaries were arrested, chained, and thrown into jail. In the resistance, eight Legionaries died.[68] And since Romanian elections "are always won by the government that makes them,"[69] Duca's Liberals got 50.99 per cent of the votes. This gave them 300 seats in the chamber, once they had barred the Legion from taking any part in the democratic process.[70]

Nine days later, on December 29, Duca was shot dead on the railroad station platform in Sinaia by three Legionaries, who at once gave themselves up to the authorities (some reported in a type of trance) to expiate their deed. These three, the *Nicadori*, a word made up of the initials of their names, became the first Legionary legend.

Opinions differ as to whether Codreanu himself had prior knowledge of this assassination, and whether, indeed, he might have ordered it. We do not know. What is certain is that he shed no tears for Duca. This raises what Roberts calls a "problem inherent in the judgment of every extremist movement, and particularly important in this one." The "politics of civility" were as unknown in Romania as in Algeria, Viet Nam, or Afghanistan. Between 1924 and 1939, even a superficial count demonstrates that eleven murders or attempted murders were carried out by Legionaries—while 501 Legionaries were killed in various ways by Romanian state authorities. One of General Antonescu's special commissions itself shows 292 Legionaries killed with no trial in the period of only eleven months from November, 1938, to October, 1939.[71] The official German news agency, DNB, moreover, reported in 1940 that the number from April to December, 1938, alone was 1,221 Legionaries eliminated by the regime.[72] Both at first and second glance, there is little doubt that the establishment defended itself far more ruthlessly and bloodily than its assailants did, and used every means at its disposal, legal or illegal: army, police, gendarmerie, the military and civil courts, the entire administrative apparatus with all its possibilities of intimidation, chicanery, and control. Every election left in its wake the detritus of killed, wounded, and arrested. A mere glance at the literature on Romania written by Westerners in the 1920s and 1930s convinces us that "Balkanization" was synonymous with violence and corruption and Romania was called "the most Balkanized country in Europe."[73]

It is thus simply not enough to write in an American newspaper—thousands of miles and a thousand political light years away from interwar Romania—that "Look, the Legion was a Fascist-Nazi bunch of murderers; in 1933 they assassinated the Prime Minister himself in cold blood." What must be somehow included, and somehow portrayed, is the *context* of the story, the background against which the Legion operated, "its violent methods reflecting the encompassing violence of the society in which it moved, the brutality of its methods reflecting the brutality with which the men in power sought to meet its calls for change."[74] We do not have to sympathize with Legionary ideas or motives fulfilled by bloodshed, but it is imperative in history, and in simple fairness, to understand the circumstances which drove them to it. The Nicadori, rightly or wrongly, believed they were saving the nation by their deed, and saw all other forms of redress closed to them. It is curious to many, but perfectly understandable if one grasps the essence of moralism implicit in Legionary doctrine, that the trio who killed Duca gave themselves up. Though the Christian laws of brotherliness and forgiveness had to give way to a higher law of national preservation in this case, this did not mean that their act was any less the sin of murder, which had to be atoned for and repented on a personal level. Thus they willingly accepted to be punished, and went off to life sentences in prison.

Meanwhile Codreanu went into hiding in the following weeks to escape the fury of the oligarchy, and his whereabouts during this time are still a mystery. When the atmosphere finally calmed, he was sent before a sympathetic military tribunal, and acquitted—but not before one of his close friends was tortured to death by the police for refusing to disclose "the Captain's" whereabouts.[75] By 1934, Duca's place was taken by Gheorghe Tătărescu, who dutifully ruled the country until December, 1937, "carrying out the will of his master the king."[76] The Iron Guard, and the first phase of the Legionary Movement, came to an end.

Totul Pentru Ţară

The neo-Liberal policy of the Tătărescu years, characterized by increasing corporatism and forcible industrialization, came down harder than ever on the ranks of the peasantry. Depending on what area of the country one surveyed, the general standard of living in 1940 was anywhere from 33 to 64 per cent lower than that of 1916.[77] The repressive apparatus was used not only to quash opposition groups (the law "for the protection of the order of the state") but to

collect taxes and arrears from the hard-pressed populace with a ruthlessness unsurpassed since Phanariote days. Many of the poor had
their last belongings sold at public auction. Sometime early in 1934
Codreanu decided that he could win power by constitutional means,
and was pragmatic enough, in light of all that had happened since
1927, to form a political party. Such a party, however, was to be no
more an electoral machine in the traditional sense than Codreanu
had been a traditional deputy in the chamber.

The *Totul Pentru Ţară*, or "All For the Fatherland" Party was presided over by General Gheorghe Cantacuzino, "a fierce, bemonocled,
hirsute old soldier, much decorated for his war service commanding
the Frontier Guards Brigade, for which he had been given the appela-
tion *Granicerul*. In the 1936 London-published manual, *Politics and
Political Parties in Romania*, in which each Romanian party was allowed to write its own brief statement of beliefs and positions, the
"All For the Country" Party, as it labeled itself, admitted that in
some respects it resembled Fascism and Hitlerism, but rightfully
noted that it had "its own origin and is profoundly Romanian." Its
principles, in truth, antedated Mussolini-style fascism, going back to
1922. "Apart from admiration, therefore, we have no sort of contact whatever either with Mussolini or with Hitler." The main emphasis was on the "educational sphere," which was the same old idea
of making "new men," Christian, nationalistic, and able to regenerate
Romania.[78] The *Totul Pentru Ţară* became a combination Civilian
Conservation Corps and League for Social Justice.

The next three years were years of success from this standpoint.
Scores of work camps sprang up on land lent or donated by wealthy
supporters, one of them the king's own brother, or friendly communes
or villages. Voluntary labor forces dotted the map of Romania, re-
pairing roads and village bridges, building churches and dams, digging
wells and working for "the collective and national solidarity."[79]
Boiar sons worked side by side with sons of laborers and peasants.
Legionary cooperatives, stores, and restaurants were founded. Such
commerce was a new field for Romanians. Codreanu wanted to
prove that not only Jews could be successful in this area. Although
the T.P.Ţ. concentrated on the countryside, the Corps of Legionary
Workers was formed in 1936 in addition to the dozens of labor camps.
This, combined with the "Battalion of Legionary Commerce" which
covered Bucharest and the major provincial towns with shops, helped
finance vacations for underprivileged children and brought funds to
the movement.[80] There was also a Legionary Welfare Organization,
and a Legionary Sanatorium was opened at Predeal with payment

fixed according to one's ability to pay and "according to his conscience." The poor received treatment free.

Unquestionably such adjustments of the Legionary program to the new situation of the middle 1930s did much to win ever broader support for the movement, and allowed it to arrive, for a time, at a watchful *modus vivendi* with the state regime. Such a retrenchment did not mean any abandonment of Codreanu's anti-Jewish position, nor change his insistence that no negotiation on such national issues as the pretensions of Hungary to Transylvanian territory, or a potential rapprochement with the Soviet Union was possible. It is worth stressing that at least until the end of 1936, the Legion continued to vigorously uphold the Versailles-Trianon Settlement of 1919, and oppose all attempts at revision. Here was another argument against those interpreters who saw Codreanu and his group as irrevocably aligned with Germany. It was only *after* it became clear, as a result of Hitler's move into the Rhineland, that the West had no real intent to enforce the Versailles pact, that Codreanu, along with a vast majority of other Romanian leaders, was forced to reverse his position and choose a pro-German line as the only feasible alternative to the looming menace of the Russian giant.

Discussion of this crucial 1934-1936 period also brings up the pivotal question of the source of Legionary financing. For more than four decades now we have heard constant noisy accusations against the Legion for "being in German pay." Like a worn-out record, this same leitmotif runs throughout the thousands of pages of U.S. government material against Valerian Trifa, most of it based on the spurious Kremer material. It is time to state frankly that not a single, non-involved serious historian has been able to demonstrate to this day that Codreanu received any significant financial support from Germany or from Nazi sources. Moreover, lest it be said that mere inability to disprove is not in itself proof-positive, it should be added that neither has any accepted authority on Eastern European history seen fit even to raise the issue other than as merely another aspect of the confusion which prevailed (and continues to prevail) in popular Western sources when dealing with the plethora of groupings on the Romanian Right in the interwar era.

First, to raise funds Codreanu during these years established the "Friends of the Legion," made up of both domestic and foreign sympathizers who, "because they were government employees or had business interests" could not join the Legion openly.[81] Nagy-Talavera believes that the main contributions probably came from industrialists like Nicolae Malaxa, "from some rich aristocratic sympathizers, and also from *Jewish* (our italics) industrialists and financiers such as Auşnit, Kaufman, and Şapiro, as a kind of reinsurance."[82] Although King Carol made a number of presentations to the German ambassador about Nazi help to the Legion, Professor Hillgruber, one of the most learned students of Romanian history in our country, could not establish any concrete data about Nazi financial support to the Legion.[83]

Eugen Weber confirms such thinking when he states that "until 1938, the Legion seems to have derived the bulk of its funds from the contributions of members, dignitaries, and deputies, from donations, and at times from subsidies provided by sympathetic government officials."[84] Roberts also considers it logical that certain Jewish businessmen gave Codreanu what amounted to protection money, just as they contributed to Franco, and in his well-informed treatise, *Destin de la Roumanie* in 1954, Henri Prost affirms Legionary subsidies through Spanish channels, though the Legion always denied this. One can, in addition, search through the thousands of pages of the official *Documents on German Foreign Policy* and come away convinced that, if Nazi funds flowed to Codreanu in any manner other than occasionally and perfunctorily, it was a secret even to the highest members of German officialdom.[85]

Once again we must return to the confusion and indiscriminate lumping together of the various elements in the Romanian political spectrum of these years to understand the very real possibilities of perpetuating half-truths and mistaken notions. In the 1930s all the Romanian Right sought German support, some to a far greater extent than others. No one, least of all American officials in the Department of Justice, seems bothered by the enormous paradox, however, of the intensely nationalistic Legionaries taking money from and (presumably) thus serving the ends of alien nations, especially when it became clear that Germany was bound to court both Hungary and Russia, not to mention Bulgaria, by catering to revisionist politicians in those states. It must be urged above all that it was the movement led by Octavian Goga and Professor Cuza which above all displayed Nazi trappings and most completely imitated the German scene with its Blue Shirt squadrons. Cuza and Goga were both invited to Germany, where they met with Hitler and Goering. So had the Neo-Liberal leader Gheorghe Brătianu made the pilgrimage to Berlin. Yet it was the Legionary leaders, who refused the German invitations, who were called Nazi tools. Roberts concludes:

All the evidence leads one to believe that serious German support went largely to Goga and Cuza, whose coalition itself seems to have been spurred by German intervention.[86]

Confusion in the public mind, and an inability to distinguish between groups which persists to the present, is revealed when one considers the words of the *Bulletin périodique* for September 9, 1936, referring to "the Iron Guards of Mr. Cuza," and the Hitlerite subventions they received.[87] Sir Reginald Hoare, however, still declared that in 1937 the "Iron Guard was not directed by Germany and remained a pre-Nazi formation."[88] Nor should we ignore Hoare's popular, and incorrect, usage of "Iron Guard" as a title, indicative as this is of the loose and fast manner in which terminology, names, parties, and alignments were thrown about interchangeably, in the constantly shifting political dunes of Carolist Romania.

Logic, in fact, supports the case against German financial backing, at least during Codreanu's lifetime. After 1932, and especially with the new emphasis on concrete economic programs developed by Codreanu by1936, the Legion's popular base of support was growing vastly. Over half the country's four-score counties had been organized, seventeen legionary publications turned out some 35,000 copies a month, and membership may have stood at about 15,000.[89] There were 4,200 Legionary nests in 1935; by January, 1937 there were 12,000 and by the end of the year, 34,000![90] Such a mass movement hardly had to plead for funds from a foreign country.[91]

Weber suggests that the Legion did receive "support" from Germany "at least in 1937 and early 1938, although probably not nearly as much as did Goga."[92] But this is another story, for by this time Carol's government had launched all-out warfare on the Legion. With Codreanu's death and the movement in disarray, deprived of its popular base of support, the surviving leaders during 1938-1939 did indeed fall back on certain German support, and paid for it by allowing themselves, even if often unconsciously, to be used to further Nazi policy goals. Their having been driven to this by necessity does not alter the fact that while Codreanu lived the Legion was run by and for Romanians alone. With the death of the Captain, the Legionary Movement, as it had existed, came to an end, and something rather different replaced it.

To all this must be added the general Legionary distrust of the Romanian German minorities, of which the largest were the 237,000 Saxons of Transylvania and the 223,000 Swabians of the Banat. There were also 70,000 Germans in Bukovina, and a colony of 80,000 in Bessarabia before the summer of 1940.[93] As early as 1930 a Saxon named Fabritius started an *Erneuerungsbewegung* based on the principles of National Socialism, which was then not yet even in power in the Reich. Shortly afterwards Fabritius along with a Saxon Nazi named Gust founded a Nazi Party of Germans in Romania, which enjoyed support among Swabians as well. In 1934 the Bucharest government dissolved this party, but it reappeared under another name. By and large, the spread of Nazi sympathies among all Romanian Germans, especially the young, was significant and is well-documented. And as early as 1933 Legionary leaders made it clear that they regarded extra-national loyalties or proclivities as unsound. Moţa in 1933 remarked seriously that "the Germans must remain loyal to Rumania. Rumania will feed only loyal nationalities, but enemies will not be tolerated."[94] Another ideologist for the movement noted: "minorities can have rights only in proportion to their loyalty to the Rumanian state."[95] As Romania's Germans evolved growing support for a full-blown *Volksdeutschpartei* under Andreas Schmitt by the end of the decade, the Legion opposed such tendencies of political estrangement as vigorously as it did all other "alien" movements and loyalties. There is in fact much testimony to the effect that while Germany truly wished to keep all its irons hot in Romania, and passed out its largesse to every group which it believed might prove useful to German ends, the Legion was apparently assigned one of the lowest priorities on the scale. Turczynski frankly notes, "on the contrary, the Guardists were shunned by Berlin, which preferred orderly action through the King to working through illegal and untested ideological sympathizers."[96]

Finally, one or two questions should conclude our pondering of this theme—minor ones, such as: if Codreanu was "in the pay" of Hitler, or in the Reich's "employ" or "subsidized" to any real extent, why did the Führer allow King Carol to murder him in 1938? And why, in the most critical moment of all in January, 1941, did the Germans not move to support the Legion against Antonescu, rather than allowing their "protegés" to be drowned in blood? Clearly, it requires rather dramatic logical convolutions, along with a sensational misunderstanding of the implications of Legionary thought and its relation to the dictates of *Lebensraum*, to continue to believe unqualifiedly in the shopworn "in German pay" theory of Legionary finances.[97]

National Christians and Carlists

All of this is not to downplay the very real and constantly increasing economic and political penetration of Germany into Romania as the final half of the 1930s began. In Romania the shift in the international political balance most of all, led to the growing economic influence of the Reich. King Carol found himself in an ever narrowing *cul de sac* as the appeasement-minded West displayed its inability to produce little more than febrile rhetorical reactions to the series of moves that spread from the remilitarized Rhineland to the Austrian *Anschluss* to the surrender at Munich. In the process, the Little Entente and the Balkan Entente, along with the whole post-Versailles system which had since 1919 formed the fundament of Romanian policy, fell by the wayside. Titulescu, the very symbol of the League and the Versailles settlement, was removed from the Foreign Office in August, 1936. His fall marked the turning point of the country's international orientation. Carol personally undoubtedly wished to stay clear of German influence, since only attachment to the West guaranteed the retention of the territories won in 1918. Yet with a weak Britain and France, and a burgeoning, militant Germany—a Germany which might well come to an understanding with revisionist Horthy Hungary and with the Russians who had never accepted the loss of Bessarabia—what could Carol do?[98] As a result, Romania in the course of the next few years came to be identified in the West with pro-German policies. Parliamentary government came to an end in 1938 and a German-style dictatorship replaced it. Finally, of course, Romania found herself on the Axis side during the Second World War. By implication, then, if we apply the creative backthinking so fondly indulged in once wars are fought—and lost-by somebody, any prudent Romanian who lived in the country during all or part of the war, or at least down to August, 1944, must have been if not a Nazi, at least pro-Hitler. We are still fond of blaming the simple German peasant hoeing his potatoes in a field alongside which runs the railroad track carrying Jews to extermination camps, for the Holocaust. So, as Romania became Germanized in the period 1938-1944, we in the West, forgetting that parliamentary government as we know it is an alien concept east of the Ringstrasse, assume that such was the will of the people.

What was most important after 1936, as Roberts notes, is that the extreme Right became more and more blatant; anti-government activities became, if possible, more widespread and violent.[99] And the King grew frightened. It was one thing earlier in the decade to play one group off against the other through a combination of force, bribery, and political shifts, when the opposition numbered only a few thousand in each alignment, and groups continued to splinter, coalesce, factionalize, and disappear from month to month. By 1936 those which had survived—the Cuza-Gogists and the Legion particularly, had taken on the characteristics of true mass movements, so much so that in the normal course of things Carol might be forced in the foreseeable future to grant them power. With some 34,000 Legionary nests throughout the country by the end of 1937, Codreanu spoke truly when he said that the Legion would "never resort to a conspiracy or a *coup d'état*." When the astounding news came that Iuliu Maniu and Codreanu, along with Gheorghe Brătianu, had come to a non-aggression pact or understanding in November, 1937, to insure free elections following the resignation of the Liberal government, one can imagine the scenario which flashed through the mind of Carol II: 1) Maniu, given his intense personal opposition to Carol's relationship with Lupescu, was planning somehow a repeat of 1928 when he had managed to depose Carol and replace him with a Regency; 2) the Legion, with the increased strength and prestige which it would indubitably gain through a linkage with the National Peasants, would be in a position to force Carol's hand on a pact with Germany, or force some strong anti-Soviet posture—in any event, the King's freedom of action would be severely circumscribed; 3) fixing the election might for the first time become difficult for the regime. These, and many other factors weighed on Carol II, not the least of which was the fear that the immensely popular Codreanu wished eventually to take Carol's place, not merely to serve him. A number of analysts of the Romanian scene, moreover, would argue that by 1937 Carol had already decided to establish his own personal dictatorship, and this combination of two of the most powerful leaders in the nation made such a goal more difficult than ever. Unquestionably the Maniu-Codreanu understanding foiled the king's plans for a gradual rapprochement with Germany and an increasingly strong royal control over the nation, and the December 20, 1937 election results showed just what a dilemma was produced for the monarch indeed. Tătărescu's "Government Bloc" won only 35.92 per cent of the ballots, for 152 parliamentary seats; the 1926 election law required a party to receive at least 40 per cent for a legislative majority.[100] Equally portentous was the National Peasant garnering of over 626,000 votes for 20.40 per cent and 86 seats. But what more than anything indicated both the mood and the political drift of the country was the vote for *Totul pentru Ţară*: 478,368 votes, 15.58 per cent of the whole, carrying 66 seats in the chamber—from a party which had been outlawed a mere four years before. From 70,674 votes (2.37 per cent) and five seats in 1932, its electoral strength had increased sevenfold, and amounted to nearly twice that of the Cuza-Goga Blue Shirts represented by the National Christian Party, which had garnered only 9.15 per cent and 39 seats.[101] Such election results pushed the king to an extraordinary decision, and at the same time revealed much about the merely *pro forma* manner in which "parliamentary government" had always worked in Romania. The King proceeded to act, at least in part, as though the people's judgment had not been rendered. He did not call upon the Liberal Party to form a government, but neither did he follow the *vox populi*. Bypassing both Maniu and Codreanu for obvious reasons, he called upon Goga and his National Christian Party on December 28 to form a cabinet. In combination with the 80-year old Professor Cuza, Goga put together a heterogeneous coalition which had a life of 44 days. The brief and hectic career of the National Christian Party government had a significance, however, far beyond its lack of longevity: it was the prelude to dictatorship in Romania, it was notable chiefly for arousing foreign protests because of its fearsome anti-Jewish measures, and its documented role as Germany's principal Romanian client since at least 1934 had the effect of identifying the nation irretrievably with Hitlerism in the eyes of the West. And, even more germane to our discussion, the accession of Goga to power produced a situation which it is vitally important to bear in mind: 1) The "National Christians" launched an unprecedented, bloody, anti-Semitic terror, both through legislation and by giving free rein to their armed, swastika-wearing blue-shirted *Lăncieri* squadrons; 2) at the same time, the Goga-Cuza forces waged full-scale warfare on Codreanu's Legion, whom they saw as their chief rivals to power in the state. In the devastation of the years which followed, as accounts of massacres of Jews, confiscations of property, beatings and rapes and arson came out of Romania, common sense tells us that distinctions between *Lăncieri* and Legionaries were more often than not unclear, hazy, or ignored altogether. This was all the more true since, with Carol's seizure of complete personal power by the end of the year and the ruthless campaign of annihilation of the Legion pursued by the state throughout these months, the Legion was in no condition to defend itself or clarify its image or position. Put as simply as possible: during 1938-1939 Codreanu's Legion was on the run everywhere, and as a coherent organization ceased to exist. It was the simplest of things for the establishment to blame the Legion for every evil and every persecution that took place in the country. Thus the crimes of the *Lăncieri* were automatically blamed on the Legion, certainly while the Cuzisti were in power, and afterwards the Legion was the natural whipping boy and scapegoat for whatever went wrong in the country or whatever crimes the monarchy wished to cover. The testimony is clear, from manifold sources if one bothers to seek it, that Carol's practice more than ever was to manipulate one group against the other: to use the fear of the Legion, for example, to justify his suspension of the constitution and seizure of absolute power in the name of "preserving the nation from anarchy"—or from Nazis, or from Communism, or from whomever was handy to receive blame. It was a familiar political game of the twentieth century era of dictators, not only in Romania, but in many a country.

One has only to consider that the worst anti-Semitic terror of modern times in Romania was launched not by the Legion, but under Goga and Cuza, at a time when Legionaries were being arrested and murdered by the government as zealously as were Jews, to realize how distorted historical assumptions can continue to rule the public consciousness decades after the events.

The National Christian Party was formed on July 16, 1935, through the merger of Cuza's League of National Christian Defense (LANC) and Goga's nationalistic, anti "Judeo-Magyar" National Agrarian Party. It called for the application of *numerus clausus* in all areas of national activity, and urged the expulsion of Jews from the country if they or their ancestors had entered Romania "by fraud" or at any time "after the signing of the peace treaty."[102] Those Jews who remained were to be excluded from all public offices and restricted by a *numerus clausus* in other areas.[103] From the very beginning Goga and Cuza associated the PNC with international fascist causes, and their close links to Hitler were secret to no one. Cuza commanded his blue-shirted elite para-military units, and the elite party militia called the *Lăncieri* which between 1935 and 1937 "were responsible for Jew-bating and brutality" which should be contrasted with the commercial enterprises and constructive work camps of the Legion. The PNC openly imitated Hitler and Mussolini by organizing massive displays of disciplined manpower. In November, 1936 they managed to have 200,000 uniformed men assembled in Bucharest for a PNC congress.[104] Goga told Francisco Franco's delegate in Bucharest that, at a word from the *Caudillo*, "I will send you immediately 100,000 men . . . volunteers to fight in Spain."[105]

Philosophically and spiritually, the Blue Shirted throngs were completely unlike Legionaries. The Cuzisti were essentially conservatives, intended to appeal to the developing Romanian middle class. They were not interested in revolutionary transformation of the existing system, or any radical changes in the pseudo-parliamentary structure; they simply sought to replace National Peasant and Liberal Party rule with their own. Codreanu correctly termed them as simply "another face of the government." The PNC had no real quarrel with the monarchy or the ruling oligarchy, as did the Legion, nor did the PNC worry about spiritual regeneration or the making of new men. They wished to eliminate Jewish domination from middle class life, and enjoy the benefits of power, no more nor less. One found little talk of spiritual or moral crusades, and even less practice of Orthodox Christianity among its ranks, which were basically composed of anyone who wished to join, simply by giving money and donning a uniform. In this manner Cuzisti ranks were filled with drifters, the unemployed, and the dissatisfied—here was the repository of the true *Lumproletariat* element—who contrasted strongly with the idealistic Legion member who, in theory at least, had to go through a probationary period of three years before being admitted to a nest and was then faced by the dictum of Codreanu that "out of 100 prospective candidates, there might be one or two with the potential to be called true Legionaries. Choose them and send the rest home."

Shapiro demonstrates unequivocally that the PNC, not the Legion, was the primary agency of German/Nazi support and the main recipient of German financial aid and favors in Romania.[106] "Both the *Auswärtiges Amt* and the *Aussenpolitisches Amt* of the NSDAP passed over the Iron Guard as a prospective primary recipient of German favors . . . . The Germans wanted a subservient, stable, and anti-Semitic government in Romania much more than the unpredictability and internal upheaval certain to accompany the accession to power of a group of nationalist and mystic social revolutionaries."[107] Admitting that the *Auslandsorganization* of Bohle and the SS had some ties with the Legion, Shapiro continues, "these were not significant enough to worry the Romanian government. In contrast, the PNC's ties with German officials provoked repeated Romanian diplomatic protests against German intervention in Romania's domestic affairs." And finally, "from 1934 on, Goga was their (Rosenberg and Schickedanz of the *Aussenpolitisches Amt*) principal Romanian client, and they provided him with all the material and advisory help they could muster."[108]

Thus early in 1938 the new government deprived Jews of their citizenship by the hundreds of thousands, closed their businesses, and dismissed them from the professions. The ruffians of the *Lăncieri* increased their numbers to tens of thousands in a short time. "The most unrestrained anti-Semites filled the administrative posts of towns like Cernauţi, Iaşi and others with the heaviest Jewish populations. In the realm of the arts, the century-old "classic" play, *Bloodsucker of the Village*, blatant in its excoriating portrayal of Jews' depravity, was dusted off for the cultural enlightenment of the public."[109] Jews responded with an impressive passive resistance, closing their shops and factories, warehouses and stores, and bringing the already shaky economy nearly to a standstill. Their leaders appealed in London and Paris for League of Nations intervention. When the Minister of the United States, Franklin Mott Gunther, handed Goga a protest from Jewish organizations in America, Goga retorted that "these (American Jews) are merely impudent!"[110] The U.S.S.R. broke diplomatic relations. Goga could afford to ignore such soundings from abroad: the king could not.

Carol had to find a government which would suit the popular will and yet be under his own control and acquiescent to the whims of the camarilla surrounding the palace, perhaps one of the few (and last) genuine indications of the monarch's sincere efforts to retain some semblance of the parliamentary system. He proposed to Codreanu, through General Ion Antonescu, a coalition government of Goga, Vaida, and Codreanu. Unwilling to have anyone believe he had become a tool of the king, Codreanu, given his principles, had little choice but to refuse. Besides, he truly believed that time was on his side; another one or two elections might well see his party receive a majority. Nor could he very well join in a coalition with Goga immediately after the previous weeks had witnessed a full-fledged war between Legionaries and Cuzists in which two Legionaries were murdered, fifty-two gravely wounded, and 450 arrested.[111]

Yet another consideration should be advanced with regard to Carol's proposal. His willingness to bring the Legion into the government indicated, besides his recognition of its electoral strength in the recent balloting, the fact that the king considered the Legion *less* extreme, and *more* representative of the broad mass of peasant and worker opinion than the Goga-Cuza alignment. For Carol's intent was to *modify* the regime and reduce tension, not increase agitation in the country or abroad. Even if one argues that, indeed, Carol's primary concern was his own power and position and that such an offer for what could amount to at best merely another shaky coalition was only another kingly ploy to advance Carol's purpose of seizing complete authority, which may well be the case; nevertheless the king's perception of the Legion as an acceptable alternative is what matters here. With Codreanu's refusal to be manipulated, of course, the history of Romania was forever altered. Once more Carol's fear rose to the surface. "The versatile, resourceful King had to destroy the (Legion) by any means at his disposal." On February 12, 1838, he dismissed Goga peremptorily. New elections were ordered for March, but Codreanu ordered the Legion to withdraw from any campaigning, because even before Goga's departure Carol's voice over the radio informed his people that he was suspending the constitution, dissolving all political parties, and promulgating a new, "frankly Fascist, corporatist constitution, with greatly increased royal prerogatives."[112] The traditional Romanian referendum followed, with 99% of the voters approving the king's actions. The logical capstone of the Liberals' economic and political thought for a generation was thus actualized: a corporatist Fascist state led by an industrial clique, with a virtually dictatorial king. All that remained for Carol was to eliminate the one leader who was much more popular, appealing, and charismatic than he, thus in the spring he moved against the Legion. Even in February, a plan to assassinate Codreanu had been foiled. Now Professor Iorga in his resurrected *Neamul Românesc* began a series of violent verbal attacks on the Legion. When Codreanu replied, he was arrested on April 17 and given six months' imprisonment on the charge of libeling a member of the government, even though the letter to Iorga was of a private nature.[113]

Now the entire force of the regime fell upon the heads of the Legion, in the person of Minister of the Interior Armand Călinescu at the head of the army, the gendarmerie, the police, and the border militia. Simultaneously with the arrest of the Captain, 30,000 Legionary homes were searched and countless goods confiscated. Thousands of Legionaries were arrested. Gheorghe Clime, designated as temporary leader by Codreanu during his imprisonment, along with almost the entire Legionary leadership, was imprisoned in the concentration camps and prisons of Jilava, Miercurea-Ciucului, Rămnicul-Sărăt and Vaslui. Rumor was that thousands of Legionaries would be transported to the lonely Island of Serpents in the Danube Delta as a prison colony. The rank and file fled to the forests of the Transylvanian Alps and Carpathians and hid. Refugees fanned out everywhere. The universities were closed, since students were a major source of

Legionary sympathy. For a time the system of nests continued to exist, but these grew isolated and ineffective once the central command structure was knocked out by Călinescu. As the formerly strong and cohesive organization grew more fragmented, persecuted, and completely disrupted, only a small corps of second-rate leaders remained. Eventually they would form another "Legion," but never would it be the same. And in fighting back against Călinescu and the regime, the remnants of the Legion invited swift and merciless retribution. On November 30, the military attorney's office attached to the Second Army Corps reported that the night before, Codreanu and thirteen other Legionaries had all been "shot while trying to escape" from prison.[114] In reality they were loaded into a truck, bound hand and foot with ropes, and driven to a deserted road. When the vehicle stopped they were garroted to death from behind, then shot methodically in the back of the head. The bodies were brought back to the military prison in Jilava near Bucharest, where acid was poured over them before their burial in an unmarked common grave surmounted by a large stone slab. What vivid testimony to the fact that "Codreanu was Hitler's man in Romania" as many have mouthed it for so many years since. The death truck returned to Jilava less than forty-eight hours after King Carol left his meeting with the Führer at Berchtesgaden.[115]

Legionaries everywhere learned the news with outrage, tears, and despair, for "the Captain" was more than a mere organizational head, he was the very symbol of their hopes for the future of the nation. The body of the Legion might be reactivated eventually, but the soul was gone. One group of refugees, who had managed to escape the Călinescu-Carol terror by fleeing into Poland and Germany, held long discussions during the dark winter nights which followed, but spirit was so low that little agreement was reached. A few urged immediate efforts toward a *coup d'état*, but most realized the futility of such talk so long as the position of the murderous king, now enjoying more or less complete German support, remained impregnable. One of the latter was the twenty-four year old student leader Viorel Trifa, who remained in Germany until the final collapse of Carol's regime.

Plate I.
*Trifa in 1931, on his graduation from the
Gheorghe Lazar Lyceum in Sibiu*

Plate II.

Corneliu Zelea Codreanu
Founder of the Legionary Movement in Romania

Plate III.
Viorel Trifa in 1950, as editor of Solia

Plate IV
The Reverend John Trutza (1895-1954)
who led the struggle to separate the Romanian-American Church
from the Romanian Patriarchate

A church dinner in Akron, Ohio, 1951. At far left is Trifa. Father John Trutza is fourth from the right, next to Akron parishioner Dumitru Szilagy, who received Andrei Moldovan's fabricated post-cards from Hot Springs, Arkansas

Trifa in St. Paul, Minnesota, in 1955, at the installation of a new pastor of the Romanian church

Plate VI

The Bishop inducts new altar boys at Cleveland's St. Mary Church in 1979. At left is the Reverend Vasile Haţegan; far right is the Reverend Nathaniel Popp, who in 1980 became auxiliary Bishop for Trifa's diocese

Valerian Trifa presides at the Church Congress which elected the ROEA's third bishop, in September, 1980, in Cleveland

Plate VII

The press reports the Trifa case

Plate VIII

Bishop Trifa – a winter scene
(photograph by Lawrence Mureşan)

CHAPTER VII
FROM CÂMPENI TO CALEA VICTORIEI

The land is of stone, and life is ruled by the stormy conditions of rugged mountains with ragged crests rising high in the wind which sweeps eastward from the plain of Pannonia and batters the Western Carpathians ringing the Transylvanian plateau. It is the land of the Motzi. Here there are only fir-trees, people, axes, and rocks, and the human inhabitants over countless generations have absorbed the virtues and faults of the hard land in which they dwell: grim, craggy, silent and enduring. They invented the *tulnic* and the shepherd's pipe to express their sorrow without words. Even today, amidst the grimy bustling industrialization being imposed on the regions around them, life consists of a few essentials and ways of doing things recall the patterns of earlier times, other centuries. Cottages perching on the hillsides and nestling in the valleys belong to the days of Horea and Avram Iancu more than to the atomic world of the twentieth century.

The town of Câmpeni forms the western point of a triangle drawn from the very center of the Transylvanian Plateau some eighty-eight miles northeast to Turda and about the same distance southeast to Alba Julia. Today it belongs to Alba County. In 1914 the area formed the county of Turda and was part of the Austro-Hungarian Empire. Here, five kilometers outside of Câmpeni on the very day that the Great War began, Viorel Trifa was born, to Dionisie and Macinica Motora Trifa.[1]

The family was not wealthy, but owned livestock and made a decent living from a few hectares of land, which classified them as *fruntaşi*, or independent peasants of the first class. Viorel was the eldest of seven children who helped their father farm and cut wood which was then hauled to town in wagons and sold. When not busy with his modest lumber business, Dionisie Trifa taught the local one-room grammar school in the canton of Dealul Capsei, thus his sons had their father both in school and at home for the first four years of elementary education. Viorel's job, when he was not at his desk, was taking the sheep herd to graze on the slopes of the hills, within sight of the legendary Mt. Găina, and to cut hay in season.

There was no high school near the home, so in 1924, at age ten, Viorel was sent to the Horea Gymnasium in Câmpeni proper. Since money for boarding school in the town was not to be had, the boy walked to school about five miles away every day except in wintertime. Then in the fall of 1927 came a determining move in his young life. He entered the Gheorghe Lazăr Lyceum in Sibiu, and began to live in the ancient Saxon city with his uncles, Constantin and Iosif Trifa. Not only was he in one of the best high schools in the country, but Viorel's uncle Iosif was a priest of high reputation and unique personality. Under the sponsorship of the Orthodox Archdiocese of Sibiu, Father Trifa edited and published two weekly newspapers, *Lumina Satelor* ("The Light of the Villages") and *Oastea Domnului* ("The Army of the Lord"). The latter was the organ of a movement of religious revival founded by Iosif Trifa after the First World War, a movement which by the middle twenties had thousands of devotees throughout the nation.

At a most impressionable age, then, Viorel Trifa found himself in a most stimulating atmosphere, both spiritually and intellectually. He had originally come to Sibiu thinking to study agriculture and return home to improve the family holdings. His sojourn in the tradition-laden walled city changed all that. With a large library at his disposal and the chance to meet religious figures from all over the country at his uncle's home, his goals turned to theology. Bible seminars, community singing, and the absence of smoking and drinking as he worked through his high school years, indeed, made him a serious young man, intense, even something of an ascetic.

Iosif Trifa, like many Orthodox clergymen in Transylvania, inherited from his nineteenth century forebears a certain militancy in his practical theology. One of the purposes of *Oastea Domnului* as a movement, other than spiritual elevation of the peasantry, was to combat the competing religious proselytization and inroads being made by Protestants and various sectarian churches in this era. To be sure, Orthodoxy in Transylvania since 1699 had been much more of a fighting church than its counterpart in Moldavia or the Old Kingdom, as a means of survival against Habsburg-imposed Uniatism and the Reformed faith extending its influence from Hungary.[2] Inevitable as it was that Viorel Trifa would be drawn into the orbit of his uncle's interests, by the time he graduated from high school in the spring of 1931, it was decided by mutual agreement between uncle and nephew that the boy would pursue higher studies and assist Iosif Trifa in the future, especially in the journalism of the movement. Viorel's talent for writing was already apparent, and he had picked up much of the technical side of printing and newspaper publishing over the years. His ability to relate to simple country people in his personal contacts, and his speaking ability, seemed to stamp him as an ideal lay missionary, to take the message of religious regeneration to the countryside.

In assessing young Trifa's personality as he left the confines of family and set out in the world at age seventeen, one notices first of all his intelligence which combined with an intensity of purpose shared by his generation, the first to emerge from the Romanian village and pursue education in any sizeable numbers. As such, Trifa saw himself as a visible link between the old and the new generations, the conduit for easing the transition from the centuries of rural isolation and stagnation to the modern world. At the same time, however, the traditional virtues of the Transylvanian peasantry were deep-rooted in him: family, devotion to the land and people, a conscious populist strain. If he were not yet fully aware of the miseries foisted upon the Romanian peasantry by the regime of *politicianismul*, at least he was conversant after his apprenticeship in Sibiu, with the fact that Romanian society suffered from many ills, among them a rampant materialism and perhaps an over-docile ecclesiastical establishment which had allowed the old ways and old virtues to slide and be obscured in the pursuit of worldly goals. Thus in the spirit of *Oastea Domnului*, Trifa left Sibiu intent on working toward the betterment of Romanian society through individual moral and spiritual regeneration.

Other than through newspapers, however, and contacts made in his uncle's circle, he had no direct contact with the political and ideological currents then sweeping through the country. Certainly he read about the turbulent events of the late twenties and early thirties, knew of such things as the anti-communist upsurges in Moldavia, the Legion of the Archangel Michael, the tremendous emotion surrounding the arrest and trial of Codreanu in the Manciu case. There is no way of knowing how the philosophy of the postwar generation of outraged youth meshed with the prism of Trifa's own perceptions. What is evident, however, is that talk of rejecting bourgeois materialism, regenerating the nation by creating new men—Christian, spiritual,

moral rebirth of the people—matched his own background and mind
set. Such was the *Zeitgeist*, the spirit of the times, the ideas in the air
of those in their teens and twenties, as was happening all over Europe.
And, like American youth in the 1960s who sought a return to fundamental things, to Mother Earth, to the natural environment, to self-
expression and a turning away from bourgeois values, there were all
types of currents and degrees and methods of participation in striving
toward that goal, ranging from joining political activist groups and
disrupting political conventions to retiring from it all to live in a des-
ert commune. For the most part, Trifa was not moved toward political activism, at this point in his life at least, but saw the best means
as writing and preaching a restoration of native Romanian rural values,
rooted in the village and the Orthodox Church. One final element of
his personality is almost too obvious to mention: his unrelenting Romanian nationalism, a devotion to the nation which Romanian boys
inhaled with their first breath. Trifa's aunt herself was a niece of
Avram Iancu, and the same heady brew of 1848 flowed in the veins
of this first generation of young men to see the creation of Greater
Romania become more than a poet's dream.[3]

Theology Student

Where should Viorel study? The famous Andreana Theological
Seminary was right next door in Sibiu, but several factors militated
against Trifa's enrollment there. His uncle knew most of the professors
personally: charges of favoritism might be raised, for Viorel knew
them also, from Iosif Trifa's home. Moreover the school's strict regime for students led to a good deal of rule-breaking and circumven-
tion, while total conformity with it might well stifle one's personality
completely. Just at this time, however, a new Theological Faculty
was opened in Bessarabia, at Chişinău, as a branch of the University
of Iaşi.[4] Two important factors made the school highly recommend-
able. It contained some of the best professors in Romania, not only
in theology, but in other areas,[5] men of the stature of the Archimandrite Iuliu Scriban, Valeriu and Cicerone Iordachescu, Father Vasile
Radu, Nichifor Crainic, I. Popescu-Prahova, Constantin Tomescu,
Toma Bulat, Gala Galaction, and others. Equally important, too, for
the far from wealthy Trifa family was the availabilty of scholarships,
of which none were offered at the Sibiu Academy.

Trifa applied for one of the twenty Chişinău scholarships open to
forty candidates, and came in sixteenth on the list. He was off to
Bessarabia, where not only his formal training in theological studies
would continue, but another kind of education would begin.

In the next four years, from 1931 to 1935, as a university student, Trifa distinguished himself both in his formal studies and in university activities. He pursued Orthodox theology, liturgics, apologetics, and church history, along with iconography and Byzantine art. He read widely in philosophy, political theory, Romanian and European history, and acquired what was for his time and place, a relatively broad grasp of Western religious tradition and the role played by Orthodoxy in the universal scheme of things.[6] When he graduated in 1935, it was *Cum Laude*.[7] He had many friends, but was not a party-goer or a socialite; yet he was an activist student leader, as he had been since high school. At age fourteen he was president of a student literary society which sponsored public evening programs in Câmpeni. At the lyceum he had been president of the "St. George" Society, which coordinated religious extracurricular activities. Thus almost from the time he entered Chişinău Theological School Trifa became president of the theology students' association; and by his final year, 1934-1935, he was chosen president of the city-wide University Students' Society. Certainly his connection with the notable *Oastea Domnului* movement played its part in all this, but so did his scholastic record, and his outspoken personality.

Life in Chişinău, however, was not all confined to university classrooms, and it might be said that an entirely second learning process took place for Trifa and many other students during holidays and summer vacations, when they often worked on farms or boarded locally in the towns and villages outside of Chişinău and observed the misery of life in what numerous authorities have called "the most misgoverned province in Europe,"[8] or at the very least, in Romania. Nagy-Talavera refers plainly to "the tormented and many times shamefully castigated peasantry of this region," who listened to the message of Codreanu in 1930 "with bared heads,"[9]

The history of Bessarabia's incorporation into Romania in 1918 is still bitterly controversial. It is not our concern to delve into Romania's rights, or lack of them, to this region. What is important here is that following its union with Greater Romania, not a single impartial observer (and this, of course, excludes any Romanian writer) failed to point out that the province went to rack and ruin. One of the most respected interwar historians of Romania described it thus:

> Formerly the vineyard of the great Russian Empire, and one of its richest grain-bearing districts . . .[Bessarabia] simply went to rack and ruin. Trade with Russia came to an end. Romania itself is a wine-producing country, and could not provide a market for Bessarabian wine. No interest was taken in the

magnificent fruit of the Dniestr valley. No roads were built. The Romanians, whose nationalists spoke with such indignation of the backward condition in which St. Petersburg had kept the country, did nothing to improve communications—on the ground that it was a frontier province, and an enemy invasion would be assisted by good roads.

The land reform gave the peasants the land, but Bucarest immediately disinterested itself in the peasants after the execution of the reform. The peasants of Bessarabia were the most primitive and the worst equipped of Romania. They did not know what to do with their land. Production was disorganized. This natural granary suffered from grain shortages. People died of starvation, and food had to be rushed in from Wallachia.

The birthrate was enormously high, and the subdivision of holdings proceeded rapidly. Relative overpopulation was more severe than would appear from the statistics of density of population, as agricultural methods were so much more backward than anywhere else in Romania. A rural proletariat formed as elsewhere in Eastern Europe, with a standard of life lower than anywhere else except perhaps Polesia. Political conditions were terrible. Officials came from the Old Kingdom simply to plunder the province. It was a colony to be exploited. Anyone who complained of the outrages of the officials was a 'Bolshevik' and treated as such. He was lucky if he got off with a mere beating.[10]

Henry Roberts seconded the theme of exploitation in Bessarabia, in describing how the national unification measures of the 1920s served primarily the Old Kingdom at the expense of the extremities. "Bessarabia suffered wretchedly from the administrative centralization, [and] seems ... to have been a place of exile for unsuccessful administrators and political black sheep."[11]

Even allowing for exaggeration, such portraits of the region contrast sharply with present-day Romanian historiography (including the literature of the emigration in America) which always pictures the Bessarabians burning with zeal to join their southern brethren. Nevertheless, Seton-Watson perhaps dismisses too lightly the reality of the impact of the Bolshevik revolution on Bessarabia and Moldavia, which, as we have seen, was certainly perceived as real enough by the inhabitants of Iași and the area after the war. On the other hand, such conditions went far to reinforce the hatred of the Bucharest political establishment which grew among the reform-minded generation of the interwar years. Thus the profound influence on Trifa and his fellows of living and moving in the environment of Bessarabia during the early 1930s is paramount in understanding the formation of their sense of mission, of outrage, of crusading zeal for the betterment of their countrymen.

It has been held by many that Bessarabia "provided a revolutionary leaven for the rest of Romania. To a degree this is true. Even before the First World War both socialist and populist theories were transmitted from Russia to Romania through Bessarabia."[12] Whether Trifa was affected by this revolutionary leaven directly is difficult to say. What is clear is that the years at Chişinău politicized the young man to the extent that he became an ardent life-long opponent of socialist and communist ideas. Moreover, one could hardly be a university student in Bessarabia, with a traditional Romanian upbringing combined with a strong Christian Orthodox background, and not share in the general distrust of aliens which was part of the very spirit of the era among Romanians, as we have discussed at length. The large number of Jews (250,000) in Bessarabia, the type from the classical Pale of Settlement, were naturally most unhappy with the post-1918 mixture of Romanian anti-Jewish feeling, misrule, and government corruption. The Jewish masses in Bessarabia, even more so than in other parts of the country, were staunchly "Jewish nationalists" and "unassimilated." In seeking ideas the Jews of Bessarabia "certainly preferred communism or Zionism to Romanian nationalism—let alone to Romanian romantic nationalism—a position utterly inconceivable to the Pale of Settlement Jews."[13] So, too, in nearby Bukovina, the culture of the heavy Jewish population, concentrated mainly in Cernăuţi, was German, held over from two centuries of Habsburg rule, while at home in Transylvania Trifa had had ample opportunity to learn that the culture and language of Transylvanian Jews was Hungarian—a factor all the more sensitive in the minds of Romanians due to the *Kulturkampf* which they had waged against the Hungarian kingdom in Transylvania for countless generations. New to Trifa then, during his university years, was this encounter with Bessarabian Jews whose culture was Jewish or Yiddish—anything but Romanian, and who had never even gone to the lengths of learning some degree of functional Romanian in order to achieve a measure of accommodation, as had happened at least in Transylvania. Enough has been said, then, to insist that it was natural for Trifa to share in the anti-foreign, anti-"non-Romanian" outlook of his generation, the more so as we observe him spending his formative college years in the province where such beliefs were heightened by one's daily surroundings. Once more, and not too often can it be stressed: such beliefs were not only anti-Jewish; they were anti-Hungarian, anti-German, and anything else, for such was the general Romanian mindset. Bessarabia was the very embodiment of the reasons for being both anti-Jewish, and anti-Bucharest establishment, and anti-communist, and populist, and dedicated to restoring traditional Romanian Christian values, real or imagined. Again, there is no evidence whatsoever of any direct contact by Trifa with Codreanu during his university years. Certainly he followed with keen interest the marches into Bessarabia of this period and the turmoil surrounding the dissolution of the Iron Guard during 1933-1934. Whether Trifa subscribed fully to all of the mystical and romanticized cargo cult philosophy of the zealously reincarnated *haiducs* is hard to say: youth, even serious youth, has a penchant for the dramatic, the sensational, the adventurous. Yet given the background and personality of the theology student leader, even given the fact that the Orthodox priesthood in many respects was in the forefront of those supporting Codreanu, one suspects that Trifa's sympathies were more intellectualized than physically overt, expressed more often verbally in the endless night-long discussions of student days than through acts of passing out pamphlets or taking part in street marches. His subsequent actions bear this out. It was his obvious intent to contribute his share toward national regeneration as a lay missionary spreading the gospel of *Oastea Domnului.*

From Student to Activist

Even before his graduation, Trifa and his family discussed his ordination into the priesthood, once he had his theology degree. He could easily have been given any parish he wanted in his home area, or even one in Sibiu, but he never abandoned his intention to join his uncle in his religious movement. He did not wish to be tied to a parish, which might well limit his mobility. Besides, he owed his uncle something for all the time and money this worthy had invested in him. Trifa thus returned in the spring of 1935 to Sibiu to work as assistant manager of the movement's newspaper, and business manager of the printing shop. At the same time he traveled widely throughout the country for the first time, preaching in villages, visiting local chapters of *Oastea Domnului*, and starting new ones. It was what he did best: reading, writing, organizing, urging, guiding. More than ever, such travel brought the destitute condition of tens of thousands of his countrymen home to him, and destroyed whatever optimism might have lingered in his mind that the "parliamentary system" under the benevolence of Carol II could offer any salvation. The impressions gained in Lapuşna and Soroca were expanded by those in the country at large, after one full intense year of working for the Army of the Lord.

His lay missionary work accomplished two things on a personal plane: it acquainted him with a wide circle of young professional men and students, all of whom were becoming actively or passively involved in one or another aspect of the multiplicity of philosophical/political movements of the day. Regardless of ideology or orientation, all had one thing in common—opposition to the status quo and a desire to change it. Still, Trifa joined no movements or organizations. Instead, he realized that he needed more study. He had a growing reputation as a writer and orator, and in his messages to his readers and listeners he combined appeals to a renewal of religious faith with criticism of the multifarious ills of the country. Many there are (including especially members of the Romanian emigration in the West today) who reminisce dreamily about the "good old days" in Romania before the Second World War and the halcyon life-style enjoyed by all. They are akin to Americans who long for the "Gay '90s" and are oblivious of or ignore the fact that most of that vaunted decade was laced by one long economic depression. Any gains registered in the general economic picture of Romania during the 1920s were wiped out by the world economic crisis which followed 1929. The briefest of glances at Romanian histories amply document the poverty of the countryside and the exploitation of the many by the few. One child in five died in peasant families before the age of one year. Foreign business interests owned the majority of Romanian industry, minerals, and oil production. And anything was for sale for a price. If for no other reason than that academic credentials remained a source of status in Romanian society, where upward mobility for village boys was such a limited phenomenon, and would thus assure him of a more receptive attention from the lower-level officialdom which directly affected the lives of the countryside, Trifa decided to enroll at the Faculty of Theology at the University of Bucharest in the fall of 1936, to begin work on a doctoral degree in theology. Simultaneously he audited lectures at the School of Letters and Philosophy.

For a time he commuted between Sibiu and Bucharest, but this was not only expensive, but impractical. At the beginning of 1937 he moved to Bucharest and took rented lodgings while he continued to study philosophy and began to prepare his thesis. His reputation preceded him. Even in December, 1936, he had been elected vice-president of the students in Letters and Philosophy. Soon after his move from Sibiu, he became president of the University Students' Center of Bucharest. The Center had its own building, separate from the university, and represented all students, regardless of their fields or faculties, in one central organization. Trifa was thus responsible, along with administering the daily correspondence and projects of the Center, for representing the student body of the capital in its dealings with both the university administration and with public officials of the capital over such matters as student housing, food, tuition, scholarships, and so on.

Also during 1935 and 1936, even while still working full-time for *Oastea Domnului*, he attended the traditional national student congresses held in various cities. While a member of the students' society of Chişinău, and later president, he had attended Congresses at Sibiu, Braşov, and Craiova in his official capacity, and these gatherings gave him familiarity with other student leaders and personalities throughout the country. In this manner he came to know Ion Moţa, who was president of the students at the University of Cluj.[14] Certainly through Moţa and others who were directly involved in the Legionary Movement, Trifa was confronted directly for the first time with the chiliastic evangelicalism of the Codreanu crusade. Much of his background and inclination naturally drew him to sympathize with such millenarianism, in many of its broad principles. The Legion, likewise, realized that it could make use of bright young men like Trifa, especially with his speaking ability and his student contacts. Whether it was a mutually decided thing, or whether Trifa felt he could be of more use in promoting the reform aspects of the Legionary program by remaining aloof from the trappings and mechanism of the organization is hard to say. What is clear is that Trifa never applied for formal membership in the Legionary Movement; never became a member of a nest, nor went through the mechanics of joining. It was sufficient that he believed in and helped to proselytize selective portions of its creed—for as in all things he did, Trifa's participation was selective. He believed, as he himself has said repeatedly since, "heart and soul" in the Legion's message of moral regeneration, an end to political corruption, an end to control of the nation by foreigners and a grafting camarilla surrounding the monarchy. This was sufficient to create a reciprocal relationship of cooperation and purpose.[15] It was most likely sometime during the fall of 1936, during his first semester at the University of Bucharest, that Trifa was introduced to Codreanu, whose interest in student problems was always strong. Codreanu did not attend student congresses, but had perhaps heard about Trifa's speech at Craiova on religious sects. Trifa was one of the ideal persons to assist Codreanu in the promulgation and carrying out of a most important goal. It was at this period that the Legion was in the midst of creating its program of voluntary work camps, business enterprises, and cooperatives. Why did Romanians not elect to go into business; why did Romanians allow "foreigners" to monopolize trade and commerce, from the level of the village store right up to that of the great industrial enterprises? One answer was that for generations Romanian students studied almost exclusively to be lawyers, doctors, or professors. Only such callings, which placed one in the ranks of the "intelligentsia" or "intellectual class" were considered respectable for those with university degrees or higher education of any quality. Commerce was not only demeaning, but was the exclusive province of Jews and other foreigners. Such a philosophy became a self-fulfilling prophecy, for if Romanians did not enter business or the trades, *ipso facto* such endeavors became all the more monopolized by non-Romanian elements. It was precisely this attitude (not recent by any means, but one which antedated the very creation of Romania in the nineteenth century) which Codreanu sought to break down, and Trifa, with his influence on large numbers of students, could help modify this thinking by encouraging young Romanians to compete with the aliens and "beat them at their own game," so to speak. Such was the tenor of Trifa's first contacts with Codreanu, and probably as much to Trifa's surprise as anyone, early 1937 found the lay missionary, theology graduate, editor and preacher, suddenly running a grocery business, as he was placed in charge of the *Obor Consumul Legionar* (Legionary Consumers' Market) on Soşeaua Colentina, which by the end of the year was combined with a restaurant. Actually Trifa shared the directors' duties with Petrică Bolintineanu, whose family owned a large flour milling enterprise in Bucharest, but the missionary-cum-manager went on to organize another Legionary cooperative in the heart of the Jewish business district in Bacău. Here he arranged for and oversaw a fleet of trucks for bringing in flour from Galaţi. Interestingly, while overcoming the initial difficulties of such a large-scale project, Trifa was offered assistance by one of the most prominent Jewish merchants in the city. There is sufficient testimony to the effect that in many quarters Jewish businessmen welcomed the appearance of such Legionary business enterprises—no longer could they be accused of monopoly or price carteling—while Legionary members striving to run successful shops and restaurants and work camps used energy that might otherwise be expended in overzealous political directions. For Trifa himself, although the half-dozen projects which he helped to begin proved fruitful, the realization that his talents (and interests) were not primarily those of merchant or restaurateur was not long in coming. He was willing to contribute to the success of the Legionary cooperative effort, however, and even delivered "The Lecture of a Grocery Boy," at a weekly Bacǎu discussion series, which he still recalls with unconcealed amusement.

Confrontation

Despite the fundamentally non-political nature of his activities to this time, during 1936 and 1937 began Trifa's involvement in conflict with the power of the state. Although neither episode was the result of any illegal behavior on his part, both had the effect of identifying him with the anti-establishment opposition to the regime. Here again, caution in assigning labels must be used. In Romania under the arbitrary regime which called itself a government, what was "illegal" was whatever displeased the regime, in this government of men, not of laws.

The April, 1936 student congress at Târgu-Mureş has been notorious for decades as the meeting at which Legionary "death squads" were formed to assassinate specific government officials and politicians whom the Legion hated or feared. There are two problems, however, with the pall which has long stood over the Târgu-Mureş Congress. First, all of the discussion of the "death squads" is contained only in literature which is anti-Legionaire, either in the official press of the day, in communist publications, or among those who, seeing the Legion as a threat to their own power sought to discredit it by conjuring up memories of similar "assassination lists" supposedly drawn up by Codreanu and his colleagues in the 1920s during the early days of the LANC movement. Secondly, no one who actually took part in the Congress and is living today in fact saw or heard of the famous "death squads," or if they did, what took place was rather less extreme, although easily misconstrued far out of proportion to reality.

In fact, in many ways the Târgu-Mureş gathering was one of the best organized congresses put on under the sponsorship of the National Union of Romanian Christian Students, the umbrella organization encompassing all of the various Student Centers and associations of students in individual university departments ("faculties" in the Romanian usage) throughout the country. The city was chosen as the site for the Congress well in advance, and a steering committee traveled there to discuss arrangements with Târgu-Mureş officials who agreed to make available part of the local military barracks for sleeping quarters. Townspeople also offered rooms in their homes, and schools were closed to allow their auditoriums to be used for sessions of the Congress which, like any such convention, brought a certain amount of fame and money into the city. Some trouble began, however, even before the Congress, when the free student trains bringing the delegates from all over were interrupted.

By 1936 such special trains had become traditional. In the 1920s penniless students wishing to travel to congresses made a habit of crowding into train cars without tickets and refusing en masse to be put off. After a few incidents of this kind it was decided that to avoid trouble the government henceforth would provide special free trains, with assigned quotas for each school or university, since students were going to maneuver free transportation anyway. Thus a school would send its names to the Ministry of the Interior, which would then issue authorizations for so many free passes to the chief of the railroads.[16] This had worked well for some years. Towns along the route would even provide free lunches as the student trainloads passed through and, except for the normal boisterousness and exuberance expected from young men on a holiday, trouble was minimal. For some unexplained reason, in the spring of 1936 as the train from Bucharest (which carried naturally a fair share of delegates) was leaving for Târgu-Mureş, Minister of the Interior Ion Inculeţ ordered the train halted in mid-journey. One explanation was that the delegation from Bucharest was composed largely of Legionary members or sympathizers intent on provoking trouble at the Congress. It is true that Green Shirts were much in evidence, but many wore them who were not and never would be members of the movement. In any event, hours went by, and along came the train from Cernauţi; so hundreds of students jumped off the Bucharest train and caught the other. With no official explanation forthcoming on the Bucharest train, the Congress began with many of the students in a bad mood, for the story was that the government had tried to prevent the Congress and the tight police security in the town confirmed such stories.

Trifa was in Sibiu in April, 1936, and decided to attend the Congress on his own initiative, for he had at this time no official student position. He took a train to Târgu-Mureş and arrived to be greeted by Gheorghe Furdui, who was president of the National Union of Romanian Christian Students (NURCS). Would Trifa, given his reputation and speaking ability, lend his support to the Congress by making a speech? Trifa agreed and after some hasty preparation delivered the following day a strongly-worded presentation on the corrupt influence of the camarilla surrounding the royal court on the nation's political life. "Who dominates this country? Foreigners! Are they honest and loyal to the nation? No!" And so on, the usual stuff of convention rhetoric, and the message of Romanian youth for many years. Other orators spoke out against corrupt politicians. A major theme was the adoption of the *numerus clausus* principle in higher education. Titus Radu and Vasile Haţegan, also in Green Shirts, spoke in the name of Romanian-American students, for both were studying in the country for the Orthodox priesthood. Again, the Green Shirt was not necessarily a specific badge of membership in the Codreanu movement. One could buy them in any shop, and those who sympathized with the ideas and goals of the Legion's religious-ascetic creed by the middle 1930s often donned such garb for special occasions, to display their solidarity. The Green Shirt in fact became for many a badge of youth, a sign of identification with a set of ideals.

John J. Sibişan, today an attorney in Cleveland, Ohio, was present at the Târgu-Mureş Congress in 1936. His memory is one of relative calm prevailing, as the students policed their own ranks. "The Congress, like all such meetings, was a gripe session, but factionalism among the students (who hailed from all parts of the country) made for a general lack of coherence, and few specific decisions were taken," Sibişan recalls, while noting that many young men spent much of their time in the cathedral at religious services and drifted in and out of the sessions as they learned of one speaker or another whom they wished to hear. The two fundamental themes were corruption in government and Jewish economic control of the country. Even so, incidents of anti-Jewish harrassment were few. Sibişan heard of no such thing as death squads or assassination units.[17] Nor did Trifa.

What did happen in the heat of denunciations of those whom the delegates saw as opposed to their interests and those of the nation, is that various students in the excitement of the moment stood up and vowed that they would "fight to the death" for their principles and goals. Others formed groups of volunteers to keep an eye on specified public officials and report to student groups and Legionary groups of police or army activity which might be aimed at them. These "monitoring committees" were appointed, and included both Legionaries and non-Legionaries. One must keep in mind the tension in Romania, the state of siege mentality of opposition groups. The incident of the train was seen by many as a sign of close police surveillance. In effect, the Legionary members of the Congress—and others, too—were issuing their own warning to the state that they would forcefully fight for their demands, if need be: this was the meaning of Târgu-Mureş. It was the politicians, growing more afraid of the Legion and its large following among the student masses, who after the Congress made up the label of "death squads," called all the speakers pro-Nazi, and thus used the usual devices to discredit opposition and distract public attention from the truth of what many of the students had underscored about the rottenness of the Romanian regime. Also ignored was the fact that, in a town with an approximately 75% non-Romanian population in 1936, Târgu-Mureş was the scene of no more disturbances than were attendant upon any other gathering of this kind.

Nevertheless the government could hardly allow such an open and manifest display of the disaffection of between ten and fifteen thousand students to go unchallenged. It had to be blamed on "fascists," "communists," Legionaries, Cuzists, or someone. First the Procurator (District Attorney) in Târgu-Mureş called in a dozen of the leaders or well-known individuals at the Congress, and sought to indict them, probably for crimes against state security, the usual handy catchphrase. The local magistrates, however, found "no cause" and released them. Here it might have rested, had tension between the Legion and the King not increased as a result of the Moţa-Marin funeral early in 1937. Following this, investigations into the Târgu-Mureş charges were reopened: it was as good a reason as any to harrass and break up Legionary students and their friends. This time the case was moved to Braşov, and indictments against Gheorghe Furdui, Alexandru Cantacuzino, Paul Craja, Ştefan Georgescu, Toader Ioraş, Nicolae Crudu, and others resulted in their sentencing to one to one-and-a-half years in prison. Trifa was also called by the police and given a hearing but was soon separated out, along with Iosif Bozantan, as "not a student leader."[18] He was convicted of *lèse majesté* for his denunciatory speech against the camarilla. He at once appealed the sentence, while two lawyers in both Braşov and Bucharest offered to defend him free of charge. The case was dismissed in the appeals court or, at least, Trifa returned to Bucharest and heard no more of it.

One thing this, Trifa's first direct confrontation with the legalized persecution of the regime, demonstrated. The state admitted, albeit unwillingly, that Târgu-Mureş was a student congress, not a Legionary one, and it was valid to discriminate among formal members and those who merely preached the same ideas. Of course the government was correct in assuming that some who had been Iron Guardists years before were now counted in the ranks of the Legion, and that there was a certain degree of continuity among those who had folowed Codreanu for ten or even fourteen years by this time. To say otherwise would be delusory. But the point remains that not everyone who donned a green shirt or made a speech was planning mayhem and assassinations, and as in any large mass movement there were purists, fanatics, liberals, extremists, and moderates—all seeking, by their own lights, a more perfect Romanian society. Should the regime at any point wish to extirpate all those who opposed it, it would have been necessary to jail all but one-half per cent of the entire population of the country. For the moment, since it was easier to leave someone free for the exploiters to exploit, the government threatened only. Not until 1938-1939 would it resort to mass murder to remove the Legionary thorns in the establishment rose garden.

Pursuit and Flight

It was not only the tension held over from Târgu-Mureş which stepped up the government's persecution of Romanian students, but the fantastic outpouring of public sympathy surrounding the return to Romania of the bodies of Vasile Marin and Ion Moţa, in February, 1937, which helped determine the regime that it must defuse the student movement. "With unerring showmanship, their funeral in Bucharest was turned into a Legionary triumph." The deaths of the two youths at Majadahonda fighting for the Franco cause in Spain became a symbol not only of the struggle against communism, but of the willingness of Legionary youth to give their very lives in what they conceived as a struggle against reactionary monarchy and the forces of darkness. The rightness or wrongness of the Spanish hostilities is not the issue, but the perception of Romanians that Moţa and Marin embodied.

Trifa was directly involved in the ceremonies. As president of the University Students' Center by that time, he met the funeral train at the frontier near Cernăuţi, and formed part of the official escort as the train wound its way to Bucharest, between rows of peasants kneeling along the railway tracks over which passed the car bearing the caskets. In the capital the funeral cortege was attended by the Ministers of Germany, Italy, and Franco Spain, representatives of Portugal and Japan, delegates of the Polish Patriotic Youth, and tens of thousands of others. Such a fantastic manifestation of veneration and admiration could not but upset Carol immensely. Should such masses—and the sea of green shirts must have given them serious pause to reflect on just where the people's loyalty lay—managed to exert unified strength there would be no stopping them. The Moţa-Marin funeral, then, added measurably to bringing on the final crisis between Carol and Codreanu and, as a natural by-product of this, for the Romanian student cohorts.

Even before the Braşov trial of the Târgu-Mureş group, Trifa and half a dozen others were arrested as a result of a disturbance involving a Liberal Party student who was beaten up by several of his fellows at a student's home. Though Trifa had not even been present, he was also charged, as the government proceeded to turn the incident into a *cause célèbre* to defuse student solidarity. Interpellations were even made in parliament, given that the fellow attacked had high connections, and Trifa and his colleagues accused of "crimes endangering the security of the state," a nice tag when the authorities really had nothing specific on anyone. The accused were given a one year suspended sentence after the expected guilty verdict was pronounced. Trifa, after all, could be innocent of any part in a public brawl: but one "crime" was as good as another, and had he not been in the great funeral train escort?

This episode, and that which followed in Braşov in May, were the sum total of Trifa's "arrests" and career of "lawlessness" prior to Carol's organized purges and mass murders of 1938. In both cases the affairs sprang from the political motivations of a government which was running more scared as each month went by and sought ways and means to stymie one of the most vocal of the groups opposed to it: the students. In no instance was Trifa ever charged with any substantive crime. The contrived phraseology of the charges meant in plain language, "He made speeches we didn't like, he wore a green shirt sometimes, and he openly sympathized with the ideals of the dreaded Legionaries." In a free society, he would not have been detained for one day for any such "offenses," and those who point to the "long criminal record of arrests and such" held by Trifa prior to his coming to America show an utter lack of comprehension not only of Romanian, but of any society in a state of revolutionary tension and flux.

But Trifa's odyssey had barely begun. The University of Bucharest was closed at different times during 1937, and what with legal harrassments and handling manifold student problems, Trifa found it increasingly difficult to concentrate on his graduate studies. For a few months, also, he took over the management of Moţa's newspaper, *Libertatea*, in Bucharest. Finally early on a dark morning in April, 1938, the sky fell in. Trifa was sleeping at the house of a friend in Bucharest. About 3:30 a.m. came a pounding at the door, and within minutes the police had taken the owner of the house off with them. He was wanted for questioning at the "commissariat." The man's wife awakened Trifa. "They've taken Petrică."

"They've taken Petrică. Did you hear?"

"Yes. Did they ask about me?"

"No. They said nothing. They did not know you were here."

Trifa dressed and began to make telephone calls. Every house held the same message. The police had come during the small hours and dozens of students, journalists, professors, workers, were arrested and taken. A few hours later he cautiously went out to find the morning newspapers. LEGIONARY PLOT UNCOVERED! LEGION PLANS REVOLUTION AND MURDER OF GOVERNMENT! POLICE DESTROY CONSPIRATORS' PLANS! CACHES OF ARMS SEIZED! screamed the headlines.

For a while Trifa stayed with one or another friend who would hide him in Bucharest. Within a few days all those who had escaped the first dragnet were called for in the newspapers. "The following are invited to present themselves at the prefecture of police for questioning"—and Trifa saw his own name. By the summer he left the capital and crossed into Transylvania, camping in the mountains, moving from village to village where he was sheltered by those who were loyal to the young missionary from *Oastea Domnului*. Friends from Bucharest came from time to time, with news and food. He was told of the murder of Codreanu and the thirteen. Hundreds of Legionary leaders, or those suspected of favoring the Legion, lay in concentration camps or were dead. By the end of the year the authorities not only began to intimidate anyone they thought might be sheltering fugitives from the law, but now their houses and property were confiscated. At some point Trifa, like many others, decided he could no longer endanger his friends. When news came that contacts had been arranged for those wishing to get across the border, he made his way to Cernăuţi in Bukovina. With the help of some friendly army officers, one group of refugees had already crossed the border into Poland on December 15. A short time later Trifa, along with Nicolae Pătrăşcu, Lt. Anghel Dragomir, and Titu Cristescu, arrived at Slobodka, in Poland.[19]

The four were detained for some time by the Polish officials, who did not, however, prevent them from traveling west. Earlier groups of refugees from Romania began to assemble in Berlin, finding work and housing under assumed names. By the 1st of April there were about thirty prominent Legionaires, or their supporters at nearby Amalienhof, including Elena Codreanu, the Captain's wife, and the would-be leader of the dissembled movement, Horia Sima. Trifa arrived on April 30, 1939.[20]

Why Germany? Primarily because it seemed the safest place. Codre-anu had made no secret of his preference for Germany in the East-West confrontation which he predicted was bound to come between Germany and Russia. Exile in Russia was unthinkable, and to stay in Poland, or Yugoslavia or Bulgaria would be dangerous, for these states, growing less able by the day to resist the demands of their stronger neighbors, might well give in to a request by Carol's govern-ment that they surrender political escapees, if only to court favor with Romania and win moral support or buy time—for Romania every day passed more under German influence. Germany alone was strong enough to do as it pleased, and had little need to heed any re-quests for extradition. Once convinced that Germany above all wish-ed internal stability and quiet in Romania, in order to allow nothing to threaten their projected sphere for raw materials, the Romanian exiles decided, correctly, that this was the best place to be until the white terror at home subsided.

Almost at once, however, disagreements began among the little band of refugees as to the future course of action. Some, such as Sima and Constantin Papanace thought of immediate reformation and revenge. Yet it took immense oracular powers at that dark mo-ment to know that in less than a year and a half the Legion would be anything more than a memory, much less in partial control of Ro-mania. Trifa, who had heard of Horia Sima only vaguely, was one who believed not only in the wisdom of waiting to see the evolution of European events, but in making fruitful use of the fate which had placed him unexpectedly in Germany. The record is clear that Sima and Trifa disagreed from the beginning on matters of philosophy and the practicality of any immediate return to the country. The best testimony is that of Sima himself. It was obvious that Trifa was al-ready making plans to establish himself in Berlin, seeking a work per-mit, and trying to get admitted to the University to continue his in-terrupted studies. Since the previous April, he had been on the run for more than an entire year. It was also evident that Trifa was only marginally connected with the group at Amalienhof. He had never been a member, nor a part of the inner councils of the Legion. He had taken advantage of the underground escape network which the movement had worked out through its nests in the north of the country—that was all. During the first weeks of May, apparently, as the Legionary group set to forming a new command structure, Trifa was asked to allow his lodgings to be used for meetings, at least one of which he attended. The talk centered on a *coup d.état*, which news "from the country" suggested was being arranged. The Berlin group should be ready to sneak back across the Romanian border and be ready to assume power. Trifa ordinarily spoke little at these sessions, but he could not forbear to remark on the feasibility of such grandiose schemes. "What, you are going to make a revolution with one second lieutenant in the palace guard who promises to help you? Be realistic!" Instead, Trifa let it be known that he planned to study in Berlin; only by preparing patiently for the future would they be up to the task of governing or leading a national revival some day. Sima's reaction to this sarcasm was to reply in kind:

"Should we expect that Carol was going to surrender power to us because of degrees we had acquired at Berlin? Or, being in possession of these titles, we could better penetrate into the midst of events and combat them with superior arms? I was forced to believe that this was the thought of Trifa, who left the life of the group and our preoccupations and devoted himself exclusively to his studies."[21]

Trifa in fact did just that, and for the rest of the time he remained in Germany, during this first period of exile, had little to do with the plans or assignments of his co-nationals. For a time he hoped to obtain a scholarship to the University of Berlin through the Lutheran Church, as some friends back home had given him a name or two to contact; this proved fruitless. In September, 1939, he registered at the University on his own, and once his German improved he managed to remain there by tutoring and doing odd jobs. For nearly a year he studied history and journalism.[22]

His eyes were also opened regarding the philosophy of the Third Reich. He was a frequent visitor at the Von Humboldt Club for foreign students, where discussions of politics were, as in any student house, everlasting and passionate. It was Hitler's policy on the Ukraine which revealed to Trifa directly, if he had not suspected as much before, the grandiose plans of the *Lebensraum* empire of the East. He met Ukrainian students brought to Germany specifically to be prepared ("trained" is Trifa's word) to return home and lead an autonomous Ukraine: and this well after the signing of the German-Soviet non-aggression pact of August, 1939.

Trifa read Rosenberg and Eichsted on craniology as well, and learned in a humiliating confrontation with a German girl that, although Romanians might be tolerated in the Aryan atmosphere of the Reich, their heads were shaped all wrong to expect more than condescending acceptance. Trifa reports that he "asked a hypothetical question to a German girl from Stettin as to a friend of hers (one suspects that the "friend" may have been Trifa himself), whether she would marry him should he ask her. "Never!" was the reply. "Just because we're polite doesn't mean we'd ever marry people like you."[23]

Down with Carol, Up with Sima

To intelligently assess the complexities of Romania's history between 1938 and 1941 in a few pages is an impossibility, and it will not be our task here. The organization and enforcement of Carol II's state order, the purges waged by the Călinescu government, the forces which produced Carol's abdication in September, 1940, and the course and final outcome of the ill-fated National Legionary State, are subjects on which the veil of history has only begun to be removed. Until western scholars have complete and non-selective access to Romanian archives for these years, much will remain unknown.

In terms of the case of Valerian Trifa, however, several broad themes are relevant, all of which serve to undercut certain fundamental assumptions which the United States Justice Department, along with scores of Trifa's denouncers and detractors over the years, have continued to take for granted.

Assumption one: Horia Sima was the natural successor to Codreanu, and continued to lead the same essential "Legionary Movement" which existed upon the death of the "Captain." This is quite wrong. The Legionary Movement as such went through at least three distinct phases, the first ending in 1933 as we have seen, the second ending with the stone slab at Jilava. One might well argue that it ended completely on November 30, 1938, and another Legionary Movement replaced it.

Assumption two: The "Legion" having remained essentially the same after its regrouping in 1940, with the return of the exiles from Germany and the power-sharing coalition with Antonescu having been created, it thus retained its monolithic and hierarchic structure. Splintering, factionalism, and lack of solidarity—thus any separation of its supporters into radicals, moderates, and conservatives—did not take place. This, too, is quite wrong—demonstrably, obviously wrong, if we are to give any credence to the historical documents which we do have, from British, German, Romanian, and American sources.

Assumption three: Because the Legion was anti-Jewish, i.e., anti-foreigners, any violence or killing of Jews in Romania during this period must automatically be the work of the Legion: no other party or group could possibly be the culprits. This is even more fallacious than the first two givens. Romania was, throughout the 'thirties and especially by the time the Second World War approached in 1941, an incredible maze of parties, insurgents from parties, Carlists and anti-Carlists, Cuzists, communists, and Legionaries of at least three or four varieties. All Romanian parties were to some extent anti-foreign, anti-Semitic, or anti-Jewish, and all parties, including the regime, had no compunctions whatsoever about resorting to violence to gain their ends. Once this is understood, and combined with the confusion that invariably accompanies cataclysmic changes and revolutionary situations among a people who even in times of peace are volatile in their dispositions anyway, common sense dictates that, while indeed men who called themselves Legionaries did kill people in Romania in 1941, and especially in January, 1941, so did Cuzists, *Lăncieri*, and a lot of other men who used the moments of anarchy which arose to settle old debts, to relieve years of pent-up frustrations, to strike out blindly against those who, rightly or wrongly, they believed were their oppressors. Can we comprehend the situation from today's Main Street, U.S.A., of a land five thousand miles and two hundred historical light years away from our society, values, customs, and political mores, in a capital city in which the Countess Waldeck recorded "the abandon with which every racial group and political and court faction was busy hating every other racial group and political and court faction?"[24] Allowing even for the potential of understanding such a situation, what are our sources of information? Assumption three falls miserably when we recall that both the official state press and the news released to foreign correspondents originated with Carol's government before his fall, and that the reports of January, 1941 were provided by the officials controlled by the victor in the power struggle, i.e., General Antonescu. History is written by the victors, it is said truly—or in the case of 1941 Romania, it is written by historians who are told what to say by those who have wiped out all opposition. The conclusion must be, that specific responsibility for Legionary crimes can be assigned no more nor less absolutely in the course of a civil war situation with all its attendant outrages than can the onus for crimes fall on other, non-Legionary groups. The whole confused maelstrom falls into one vast historian's *non liquet*, for one thing only is certain: things are seldom as they seem, and almost never as reported.

Horia Sima came from Făgăraş in the Transylvanian Alps, where he taught secondary school. He had been the student of the Legionary ideologue Nae Ionescu and the regional Legionary chief of the Banat, and was thirty years old at the time of Codreanu's death in 1938. Nagy-Talavera states openly that Sima "never had the integrity or the vision of Codreanu."[25] Sima was a young man in a hurry, an opportunist who became adept at playing the Bucharest game of musical alliances, jumping from Carlist to Antonescu to Germans and back again as he struggled to grasp power. The net effect of his work was the politicization of the former Legionary movement in order to turn it into a ruling party. On the way to this he succeeded in antagonizing numerous elements of the "old guard" or those who had been with Codreanu since the early days of the movement, and acquired, among large segments of the Legionary movement in exile after 1941, the title of usurper.[26]

Some there are who lay the blame for Codreanu's death on Sima's wrongly-timed militancy and refusal to adhere to the Captain's advice from prison. Codreanu had dissolved the *Totul Pentru Ţara* party shortly after Carol proclaimed his new constitution in February.[27] Even after his fraudulent trial he insisted from prison on keeping within the bounds of legality and avoiding provocation.[28] Through his wife and friends who were permitted to visit him, he sent out messages concealed on scraps of paper, with simply "Silence, silence," written on them.[29] Some of his "followers" however, did not respect this advice, and unquestionably Sima was one of these. Sima had appeared in Bucharest only a year or two before and worked as a contact man coordinating activities and messages between various Legionary nests. His disposition was toward action, and his anti-Jewish feelings strongly developed. His patience ran out when he observed the organized persecutions of the regime during 1938, and he did not agree that resignation and calm were the way to respond. Gathering others of like mind around him, he saw the Captain's imprisonment as a chance to advance himself within the movement, and in a few months his underground teams were distributing incendiary letters and flysheets, then went on to shootings, sacking of Jewish taverns and shops, throwing bombs in synagogues, and setting fires in timber yards. The leadership "having been taken over by provincial militants,"[30] and with his designated leader, Gheorghe Clime, also in jail, Codreanu knew that such acts were endangering his life and that of other imprisoned Legionaries. At least one writer suggests clearly that a student attack on the rector of the University of Cluj and the killing of the policeman who accompanied him on November 24 were the final straws which sealed Codreanu's fate.[31]

Codreanu pretty clearly did not wish to see Sima at the head of the movement, should anything happen to the Captain. Even at the time of the Moţa-Marin funeral, he had discussed with his closest lieutenants the arrangements for the succession, stating that those of the "highest grade" in the Legion, i.e., those who belonged to the governing body or the "Forum," should meet to name someone, and had made them swear an oath at the time to do so. Sima was not a member of the Forum, nor did he have the rank at that time which would entitle him to participate. Specifically naming the Banat leader, Codreanu went on: "The improvizations of Sima, encouraged by such (self)interests, can produce only the unhappiness of the Legion and the misery of the country."[32] Instead, Codreanu named people such as Clime, Al. Cantacuzino, Ion Banea, or Ilie Gârneaţă as possible "Captains."[33] His warnings to Sima from prison were apparently ignored.[34] One might elaborate much further on this situation, but suffice it to say that there existed at the time, and continues to be heard today, the theory that Sima's acts were the major factor in Carol's decision to do away with Codreanu; more, that Sima was in contact with Carol's police at certain points and that he may have been, consciously or unwittingly, an instrument used by Carol while under the impression that he, Sima, was manipulating things.[35]

What is clear is that during the first exile in Germany in 1939, Sima was evidently not looked upon as the leader of the Legion, either. In May, the month after their arrival, the Legionaries met for the "organization of the Legionary Command in Berlin." The priest Dumitrescu-Borşa was chosen as chief of the group, while Sima was assigned to handle "connections with the country" (i.e., Romania).[36] Constantin Papanace was chosen as Borşa's assistant, and from this point on Papanace clearly grew suspicious of Sima's ability constantly to escape the clutches of the police on his numerous trips back into Romania, while those he was scheduled to meet, or everyone around him, was arrested.[37] Whatever the truth, it seems plain from the sense of the various Legionary writings, that a schism opened and continued to widen between Sima and the Papanace group in Berlin as time went on. While the former worked to spread his name throughout the country and ensure that all the underground Legionary nests came to see him as the vital spark keeping the movement alive, the latter tried in vain to make its authority felt from Berlin through official "delegations" which arrived to receive advice and bring messages from the country. Moreover a splinter group surrounding Codreanu's father continued to act on its own within Romania, and rejected any "successor" to the slain hero except Codreanu *père* or the Captain's widow. Not one "new" Legion, then, but three distinct Legionary offshoots emerged between the end of 1938 and September, 1940.[38] In the end, Sima's work within the country paid off for him during 1939, for he became known as the man who organized the bloody opposition to the Călinescu terror, and thus exerted a strong appeal to those elements who were by now eager to put on a green shirt and be done with prayer, restraint, the path of gradualism, and seize what they could from the chaos of the moment. Ex-Cuzists, unemployed peasants in from the countryside, city proletarians, gypsies, and the adventurous hangers-on who flock to the scene of any action now began to join Sima and, incidentally, the "Legion," once the standards were relaxed.[39] There is no absence of historical parallels to what Sima managed to accomplish. He presented himself and his immediate followers as "doers," in the face of unrestrained persecution from the regime. Carol's abolition of even the parliamentary forms had sealed off the last outlet for popular discontent and frustration. By implication the gradualist, legalistic path advocated by Codreanu earlier no longer applied, was futile in the face of the no-holds-barred approach of Carol and Călinescu. Sima thus placed himself in the forefront of the fast-quickening revolutionary tide from below, and carefully managed his own apotheosis. By the time the Papanace group returned to the country from Berlin, Sima had already consolidated his power over a fundamentally new Legion.[40] Whether he did so with the secret help of Carol, as a means for the king to control the Legion, probably cannot be proven. But certainly some of his former comrades continue to think so.[41]

All of this was carried on against the background of outright warfare between the Legion and the government which intensified throughout 1939. "Captured Legionaries were tortured, murdered, and their mutilated bodies quietly and efficiently cremated."[42] According to police accounts, during February alone, during the brief government of Patriarch Miron Cristea, the number of Legionaries arrested ran into the thousands. In some cases the death penalty was pronounced, in others, prison sentences ranging from six months to twelve years.[43] When the aged Patriarch died on March 7, the real power in the government, Armand Călinescu, became the new premier. Here was a positive indication that Carol's determination to wipe out the guard was uncompromising. Călinescu's hatred of the Legion predated his premiership by many years. As a minister in the cabinet of Vaida-Voevod, he had urged stern measures against Codreanu.[44] As Minister of Justice under Goga and Cristea as well, he was impatient with Carol's efforts at mediation, however modest, and it was well known that he had long desired a free hand against those he called "the terrorists."

No one expected that the Legion would not retaliate, and on September 21, 1939 it managed the feat which proved its undoing. Călinescu left home for the royal palace about 2 p.m. on the road leading to Cotroceni (today Blvd. Dr. Petru Groza), and where it intersected with Ştirbei Vodă his car found itself suddenly blocked by a hay cart thrown across the street. Six young men jumped out of the car behind Călinescu's, shot his bodyguard, then Călinescu at close range; he died on the spot. One assassin was captured at once, the other five raced to the headquarters of *Radio România*, broke into the studio and announced in trembling, triumphant tones that they had killed Călinescu, and "the murder of the Captain has been avenged!" Then, in true Legionary tradition, they quietly waited and surrendered to the police.[45] Carol had the five returned to the spot of the deed that very day, where they were shot and their bullet-torn corpses left there for days inside a roped-off area to rot as an example.

Carol appointed General Gheorghe Argeşanu as ad-interim premier to organize the bloodbath which followed. In every county a certain number of Legionaries had to be executed or hung from telegraph poles or lamp posts, and their bodies displayed for days for the edification of the citizenry. While the average number per county was supposed to be three (this is the figure used in a number of sources) some prefects handed over convicted criminals to satisfy the blood quota instead, while in other places the local authorities had long awaited such a carte blanche to kill local opponents and surpassed their quotas enthusiastically. It is impossible to tell how many Legionaries perished, but the lists in a Legionary album total 76 for September 21, the day of the Călinescu act, alone. And the government sought not only quantity: when the official terror squads arrived at the concentration camps of Râmnicul-Sărât, Vaslui, Miercurea-Ciucului and the prison hospital at Braşov, they shot Clime, the T.P.T. leader; Polihroniade, the Legionary foreign policy expert; the attorney Tell; the Transylvanian Ion Banea. Murdered peremptorily were the poets V. Cardu and C. Goga, the professor of engineering, Ionică; the student leaders Furdui, Cotigă, Antoniu, and V. Rădulescu, the youth leader Istrati, and the list could be extended. Altogether the government disposed of at least 300 lives within one week.[46] The state radio read letters demanding the extermination of all the relatives and lineage—the entire families, old and young—of those who killed Călinescu. Such was the state of mind during the terror. One would expect, of course, that the Germans (whom we have been told constantly not only financed the Legion but supported it in all things) would move to intervene against such massacres. They never even lodged so much as a protest, as the retribution for Călinescu was exacted two and three hundredfold.[47]

As suddenly as it began, Carol's persecution ended, for the world was moving too fast, and the King had to keep pace if he were to survive. Already Poland had surrendered, the victim of German and Russian promises of non-aggression. Romania's declaration of neutrality, as in 1916, sought to buy time and see which side in the vast war now beginning was most likely to prevail. For the next few months calm prevailed and Romanians confidently awaited the expected victory of France, mighty France, while the press in Bucharest published pro-French editorials. The spring of 1940 brought the stark reality home, and the court grew progressively uneasy. It was time for a reconciliation with the opposition; with Hitler's *panzer divisionen* massed on Carol's northwestern border, ready to crash through by way of Nazi-enslaved Hungary, with troop trains carrying assault divisions through Czechoslovakia to the Romanian frontier, the "nerve war" was in full blast against Romania and the result was the desired state of panic, aided and abetted by thousands of Nazi "tourists" who, "with portmanteaus bulging with the uniforms and weapons of the German army and air force, had swarmed into Bucharest and invaded the Romanian countryside."[48]

Carol scurried. He renounced Great Britain's "guarantee," and offered Hitler one concession after another. Abandoned was the new constitution so pompously inaugurated a year earlier. Most of all, he sought to unify the nation by offering reconciliation with the suborned and lacerated Legionaries. The slayers of Călinescu were allowed reburial according to the rites of the Orthodox Church. Lower-ranking Legionary leaders were released from prison. In November, Tătărescu had returned to head the government, and was told to work earnestly on a reconciliation between "the Guard" (the old nickname was so engrained in popular, common usage that it would not down) and the King. The former "Front of National Rebirth" which since 1938 had covered the King's absolute rule was now transformed into another totalitarian party, the Partidul Naţiunei, the "Party of the Nation," and Carol invited the Legionaries and other groups to join, telling them that the officials who had been guilty of killing their members in recent years would be punished. So fast did the regime change its attitude, however, that in March, 1940, Carol announced that the Legion had pledged allegiance to his national front program, but this was mere window-dressing. Sima, Papanace, and other leading Legionaries were not even in the country, but in Berlin. Some newly-freed members of the movement, such as Radu Mironovici and Constantin Stoicănescu, arrived in Germany late in the month, apparently having worked out a *modus vivendi* with the government and acting as delegates to see what could be worked out with the main Legionary group. Yet when Sima and others re-entered

the country in May, they were arrested and detained nearly a month.[49]
Carol's announcement appears more as a trial balloon, which produced
no results until the summer, when Sima suddenly found himself *per-
sona grata* at the palace. An audience with the King produced by
June 23 an announcement that Legionaries henceforth formally subscribed to the King's Party of the Nation. Sima was correct when he
noted at the time, "The whole world is going topsy-turvy."[50] He
and the Legion had gone from hunted fugitives to courted supporters
in the space of nine months, so fast did the pressure of international
events force the King to reconsolidate his posture internally. But not
all Legionaries, and especially not all the old Codreanists, agreed
with Sima's rapprochement with the monarchy. The Legion in the
old days, too, had been invited to the palace, had been promised
positions and powers by the king, and had refused to compromise its
anti-court, anti-politicianismul, anti-Lupescu stand. Codreanu had always believed that by biding its time and maintaining steady growth,
the Legion would come to power on its own through constitutional
means, without having to surrender any of its ideals. Sima's apparent
"bargain" with Carol could easily be seen in some Legionary quarters
as a sell-out for the sake of political power—besides, Sima was not
even the acknowledged leader of the entire movement. What must
some have thought when on June 28, 1940, Sima was named Under-
secretary of State in the Ministry of Education? As for Carol, his
position is easier to comprehend. Three days before he had been presented with a 24-hour ultimatum by the Russians, demanding the
outright cession of Bessarabia, and by the 28th Russian troops were
already entering the province amidst scenes of humiliation and chaos.
Sima argued strongly in Legion councils that internal feuds had to be
suspended for the time being, while others (called "Maximalists" by
some) refused to cooperate unless the King's abdication were demanded. It is worth noting that the leading Legionaries in Berlin still
did not return to the country, despite the presence of a few of their
number in the government, and would not do so until September 15,
more than a week after Carol's resignation.[51]

   During the two hot, tense months which followed, Carol continued
to retrench. At the beginning of July Tătărescu's government gave
way to that of the pro-German Ion Giugurtu, who named Mihail
Manoilescu, a friend of the Legion, as foreign minister. Horia Sima
became Minister of Cults and the Arts. Anti-Semitic legislation was
introduced in great haste to court German favor. The Germans showed their appreciation of this trend in their direction by imposing on

Romania the Vienna Award, whereby a huge section of northern Transylvania was arbitrarily given to Hungary.

Michel Sturdza claims that Sima's resignation from the government after serving only a few days was due to his seeing these territorial losses on the horizon, and that he had agreed to cooperate originally only because Carol agreed that not one inch of the nation's territory would be abandoned.[52] In reality, Sima continued to have difficulty retaining his position vis-à-vis the Legion. A group of Legionary leaders met in Bucharest on July 14, as one handbook puts it, "to obtain the rejection (*dezavuarea*) of Horia Sima. The manoeuvre failed. After explanations given by Sima . . . they approved his position, etc."[53] This merely illustrates what has been said as to lack of unanimity in the Legionary position. In fact, during July Sima was resisting demands that he establish a new Legionary Forum, as Codreanu had recommended before his death, to run the movement. Sima finally gave in on this, but it was not until the afternoon of September 6, with the King's abdication message several hours old, that the Legionaries group in Bucharest officially gathered at the house of Colonel Zăvoianu and proclaimed Horia Sima the successor to the Captain.[54] When the final crisis came on August 30 with the spread of the news of the partitioning of Transylvania, Sima's people were set. The revolution which toppled Carol II represented not only the victory of all those forces which had opposed him for so long, but the end of Horia Sima's nearly two-year campaign to place himself at the head of the Legionary forces. Even so, his control was never to be complete, nor were all factions in the movement ever reconciled to the fact that anyone could take the place of Codreanu. As it turned out, Sima fell short of the Legionary ideal in ways certain to produce disaster.

By the end of August, then, the system that abandoned one-third of the nation's territory without firing a shot, thus surrendering millions of Romanians to a foreign yoke—that system had to go. One is hard pressed to assign the greater weight for Carol's downfall to Sima's Legionaries or the King's own avarice. It was not an unusual sight to see people weeping publicly in the streets upon hearing of the loss of the "Ardeal." After a great demonstration around the statue of Michael the Brave in University Plaza, with people calling for Maniu and shouting "Let us fight!" other crowds filled the streets with green shirts and marched down Elisabeta Boulevard toward the palace. Meanwhile Legionary leaflets were being distributed in the military barracks demanding that the King and Lupescu go. Efforts were made to seize public buildings in Bucharest, and the telephone exchange and other installations in Braşov and Constanţa were in the hands of the Legion by September 3. Close attention should be paid to the theme of the Legion-inspired revolution of September, 1940, at a time when German armies had already smashed their way through Poland, France, Belgium, Holland, and were gearing up to rule the entire continent: in Romania the cry was "Not one more acre!" and to the King, "Fight, or go!" The Legion continues to be viewed by some as simply a regional branch of National Socialism. Yet it was in the forefront of Romanian political groups to demand resistance to the Vienna Diktat with all the armed force the nation could muster— and this meant war not only with Hungary, but with Germany.

It was a brief and nearly bloodless revolution. A few warning shots were fired in the Palace Square, more symbolic than anything else. Carol asked General Coroama, Commander of the Bucharest Army Corps, if he were prepared to order troops to fire on the rioters. The General said no. On September 4 Carol called in General Ion Anton-escu in an eleventh hour effort to save himself. Instead Antonescu asked for dictatorial powers, and got them. Two days later, with the agreement of Maniu and Constantin Brǎtianu, the General demanded the King's abdication, and after a lengthy discussion as to precisely how much gold and how many jewels and how many Rubens and El Grecos he could take with him, Carol of Hohenzollern left Romania.

September to January

Viorel Trifa had no part and little information as to all that had transpired in Romania during 1939 and 1940, other than what he heard from occasional visits to friends in Legionary circles in Berlin, or read in the German papers. He remained at the University, and his name is absent from any of the literature describing the activities of the Legionary group in Germany during this period, after the initial escape from Romania and settlement in Berlin. He was chosen to no offices, given no assignments. He had nothing to do with any of the negotiations setting up the new system of power shared in Romania between the Legion and Antonescu which governed the country until January, 1941. Trifa was in Berlin at least until September 11, 1940.[55] When the news of the fall of Carol reached him he was, like many other Romanians abroad, excited at the prospect that at last he could go home again, to see friends and family. He arrived at Bucharest's North Station on September 15, the same day with Papanace, the Captain's widow Elena Codreanu, and the Queen Mother of Romania, Elena, returning from exile in Italy. A huge

crowd of Legionaries, soldiers, officials of all kinds met the trains bringing back hundreds of those finally safe from Carlist persecution.[56]

The word came to the returnees that the honorable Horia Sima,
"commandant" of the Legionary Movement, invited everyone to visit
him as soon as possible—presumably to be organized, given positions,
and so on. Sima was busy mending his fences.[57] But Trifa did not go
to see Sima at all. Like many others, he was aware that the situation
remained unsettled and confused, and that he, Trifa, was no longer
even marginally in touch with whatever leadership existed. And he
had other things he wished to do first. Meeting him at the train was
his old friend Petrică Bolintineanu, at whose home Trifa had been
the night of the mass arrests in April, 1938. They went off to the
Obor to do the one thing Trifa had on his mind during all the hundreds of miles of his journey: eat *ciorbă de burtă*.

In the meantime another friend found him with a message: Mrs.
Iridenta Moţa, widow of Trifa's friend Ion Moţa, dead in Spain, wanted to see Viorel at her house as soon as possible after his arrival. First
Trifa spent one or two days visiting those people who had hidden
him during his underground months of 1938, and included a stop at
the home of the widow of that soldier who had led him across the
Polish border. Mrs. Moţa's request was not entirely unexpected. Would
Trifa resume the editorship of Ion Moţa's newspaper, *Libertatea*? He
was the best qualified person to do this, was Iridenta Moţa's argument,
since he had managed the paper for some months. More importunate
was the need to fulfill her husband's earnest desire that the paper's
voice, and the spiritual message of the Reverend Ion Moţa, not be
subsumed in the militant rhetoric which was to be expected now that
the Sima group was in control. Interesting it was that Sima had indeed
been in touch with Mrs. Moţa on the question of the paper. The
commandant's wish was also to see *Libertatea* reappear—under the
editorship of a capable hand which should be that of anyone (in
Sima's words) but Trifa.[58] This may be precisely why Iridenta Moţa
asked him, first of all. One of Trifa's undeniable qualities always was
a sense of loyalty to his friends and those who had helped and sheltered him, often at their personal risk. Such a presentment therefore
he could not refuse. In addition, he truly believed in the spiritual
and ideological message which *Libertatea* represented, and this would
be one way to reinvigorate some measure of the earlier philosophy
of the movement. He agreed to edit *Libertatea*. And still he did not
go to see Sima.

Trifa's work on *Libertatea* between October, 1940, and January, 1941, has formed part of the official package of Justice Department allegations against him. Parts have been mistranslated.[59]

As one should expect, *Libertatea* under Trifa's guidance was aimed at the peasantry, and written in simple language for circulation in the villages. It reflected Trifa's style, developed over many years of work on *Oastea Domnului, Lumina Satelor*, and other moral-spiritually oriented papers for the countrymen, of simple, direct appeals to moral conduct, faith in God and the nation, and in the creed of Moţa, Marin, and Codreanu. The language was direct, mildly militant, didactic, but neither unctuous nor thrasonic. The paper appeared once each week, therefore its straight news reportage took the form of simple resumés of the week's events, thus most space was devoted to basic expositions of Legionary positions, Romanian foreign policy, and appeals for right conduct. The first issue, containing what the Romanian press calls the "program-article," appeared October 13, 1940, in which Trifa evoked memories of the Captain and Moţa, and offered a straightforward statement explaining perhaps more than a hundred learned volumes exactly *why* Romania must join with the Axis in the war—"By the time England arrives to help us, we'll be totally annihilated."[60] In speaking before the great student demonstration held on the traditional December 10 holiday, he carried this theme further, as well as in his description of the great Legionary march in Bucharest on October 6 at which General Antonescu appeared in a green shirt. "Romania is not alone; we have strong friends in the world," was the theme which needed constant reinforcement when one considers the fact that *without* an understanding with Germany in 1940, Romania was indeed alone in the most perilous spot on the earth.[61]

Equally relevant was Trifa's long article entitled "Sign Me Up in the Legion." "Who does not believe in God does not believe in the Legion," is the stress. Putting on a green shirt doesn't make a Legionary, but being a "clean man," (*omul curat*), one who neither smokes nor drinks nor blasphemes his neighbor, who works for the common good without coveting possessions, position, or honors. If one wants to join the Legion in order to put himself in a position to become mayor of his village, or a notary, or gain a sinecure as a forester, or the like, then the Legion does not want him. Devotion to God, to people, and to country (*Dumnezeu, neam, şi ţară*) make a Legionary.[62] It was the message of *Oastea Domnului*, as expected, and hardly the words of an extremist fanatic calling for blood. Indeed, one finds few remarks attributable to the Legionary zealot; the usual and by-now nationally common phraseology about Judeo-Masons in Paris are scattered here and there, and one article applauds the new law passed prohibiting non-Romanians from owning rural property. Yet, for every reference to Sima, there were ten to Codreanu. One may, to be sure, detect a conscious effort to restore Legionary standards somewhat to the higher plane of the pre-1938 Legion. In any event, Trifa's career at *Libertatea* must be seen in the context of Romanian journalism. Those who in 1980 America have missed the pleasure of wading through thousands of pages of communist historical books, articles, and magazines will fail to understand the use of stock catchphrases referring to anti-communists as "retrograde fascist bourgeois elements" who are automatically and eternally "reactionary." Just so, Trifa employed the cant of his day to denounce the opposition, as "Judeo-communist-Masonic conspirators." Revolutions are, after all, little more than games of language, for language is all we have. Given *that* time, and *that* place, Trifa's journalism was mild, and to judge it by the standards of any other day is to misread the past.

No sooner had Trifa returned and it became known that he was available for service in the new Romania being built, than he was again drafted as a student leader. On September 27 at the Student Center gathered the Supreme Council of the National Union of Romanian Christian Students, with delegates from the entire country present to reorganize student life. This included both Legionary and non-Legionary students, as it had years earlier. Trifa's election as President of the NURCS on that day has been seen by some as deliberately staged by the Legionary regime to bring the student body under its control. Hundreds of official U.S. documents repeat the flat statement that the National Union was merely "the student branch of the Iron Guard." This was impossible, since the Iron Guard did not exist in 1940, having been dissolved at least seven years before. In fact, Trifa encountered opposition to his election from within the Union, specifically from Legion members who saw his election as a missed opportunity to politicize the entire membership.[63]

What happened after, however, gives rise to the associational *cul de sac* of ascribed guilt devoid of fact. Sima, in pursuing his own efforts to centralize power in Legionary hands, requested the Ministry of Education to draw up new legislation requiring that the president of the National Union of Students had to be nominated by the government and confirmed by royal decree, thus tying the Union closer to the regime and serving to legitimize and elevate its status in the eyes of the non-Legionary students who, hopefully, would better support the state. As a result of this, although Trifa's election was in no way influenced by government action, he became, *ex officio*, a designated government appointee with King Michael's order of November 4, 1940, appointing him President of the NURCS.[64] This did not mean that he was given an office, or government powers or prerogatives. He continued to divide his time between the *Casa Studenţilor* and Strada Popa Savu Nr. 56, the address of Iridenta Moţa, which held the administrative offices of *Libertatea*. He made speeches at student celebrations, sang and cheered and marched with his student friends, and drummed up enthusiasm for the "new order," the "new Romania," free of corrupt politicians, foreigners, and godless men. He predicted that his country, and her ally, Germany, would win the war. Would we expect him to say otherwise? He pledged the youth of the land to total support of the government, to the Conducător Antonescu and his partner Sima. Would we expect him to do anything else? He won growing recognition throughout the capital for his speeches, always well-organized, strong, full of vitality. He spent much of his time at the Ministry of Education, working with Minister Traian Brăileanu on the serious problem of thousands of student refugees now adrift in the country as a result of the losses of Bessarabia, northern Transylvania, and Bukovina. This naturally meant as well the loss of the universities at Chişinău, Cernăuţi, and Cluj and the displacement of entire student populations who had to be resettled. Many of these were arriving in Bucharest, and problems of housing, feeding, and re-registering them were manifold. This had been the fundamental reason for the decree attaching the National Union to the government in an official capacity, and Trifa had helped to work out the measure in conference with Sima and the Ministry of Education. In this manner, money for student refugees could be appropriated and funneled through the Education ministry. Trifa often worked 18-hour days requisitioning and disbursing these funds and solving a thousand problems in a city flooded with displaced persons. On top of this, on November 10, Bucharest was devastated by an earthquake, adding additional problems of housing and medical care to everyone's duties.

Yet Trifa had no command; he was a part of the National Legionary State, yet not one of its officers. He bore the title of "Assistant Commander" proudly, for it had been given to him by Codreanu years before this, as an honorary badge in recognition of his important contributions to student life and Legionary philosophy and goals. At the same time, both during his chairmanship of the Bucharest Student Center in 1937-1938, and now in 1940, he was never "Commander of the Legionary Students." The "Legionary Students' Center" was a separate and distinct body, with its own headquarters and its own "commander," who in 1940 was Vasile Andrei. Its offices, so to speak, were at Nr. 3 Strada Gutenberg, or at Legionary headquarters in Bucharest, not at the University. Some students who belonged to the National Union of Romanian Christian Students, Trifa's organization, were Legionaries, for one could belong to both groups, just as there were in the National Union students who belonged to the Liberal Party, the *Tineretul Naţional Ţărănesc* (National Peasant Party Youth), the Socialist Party, and indeed to the outlawed communist party. Legionary students in the National Union in fact were a minority, and many would not have voted for Trifa's election as President since it was a well-known fact that he was not close to Sima.[65] Trifa's position was therefore unique vis-à-vis the National Legionary State; a separate but parallel association based on a mutuality of interest.

The Short-Lived Marriage

No seasoned observer of the Romanian scene would have predicted that the coalition between Ion Antonescu and Sima's Legion could last, even as long as it did. For the nearly five months in which the pair "governed" Romania, the alliance was obviously a marriage of convenience, shaky and troubled from the outset, and it was only a matter of time, given the nature of Sima's incomplete control over the undisciplined extremist wing of his organization, and Antonescu's unbending personality which allowed little room for compromise. The determining factor in the divorce, however, was that Antonescu had the law, the courts, the lawyers, and the ultimate judge on his side, which is to say, the backing of Germany; the Legion did not. For forty years one of the fictions of Romanian history has been that between January 21-25, 1941, the Legion staged a rebellion against Antonescu in an attempt to seize full power. Nearly everyone since has accepted and perpetuated the story that the Legion rose up against the legitimate government and the resultant bloodbath, coupled with a vicious pogrom in the Jewish quarter of Bucharest, was the Legion's responsibility. It should surprise no one by now when we say that the truth is more like the reverse; that logic, evidence, and common sense all point to an interpretation of January, 1941, as a *coup d'état* launched by Ion Antonescu to drive the Legion out of the government, an attentat which the Legion met with armed resistance. Those who adhere to the "standard" account have never been able to explain two basic things: why, when such intense efforts have always been made to prove the close linkage and support of Hitler's Germany for the Legionary Movement, did the Germans support not the Legion, but Antonescu, at the most critical moment of the Legion's existence? And why—how—can we assume that the entire truth of the January uprising is before us when all the major, and most of the minor, accounts of events are those supplied by Antonescu or other less-than-objective sources?

Ion Antonescu was a short, lean officer with a high forehead topped by red hair. He was known to all as the *Câinele Roşu*, the "Red Dog," which said something about his uncompromising disposition. He was widely known as a political general. One unfriendly witness describes his most notable qualities as "arrogance, ambition, and a high capacity for grumbling his way to promotion . . . which gained him general dislike in the army."[66] He was known during the 1930s to be a surface sympathizer with the public policies of the Legionary Movement, while at the same time he professed an unalloyed loyalty to the King and openly showed it. Once made Chief of the General Staff, though, he evidenced such an openly hostile attitude toward the Minister of War that Carol had to dismiss him. At that time, Antonescu had been heard to say that someday he would make those responsible for his removal pay for it, especially since "I am the only one qualified to occupy" the position.[67]

The friction which developed between Antonescu and his Legionary partners was well known to all principal parties—including the Germans and the leading Romanian Jews—from the beginning. Antonescu's establishment of a commission to investigate alleged Legionary crimes did not endear him to his co-governors, especially when he took his time punishing those still being held for murders or crimes against Legionaries under the old regime. Two incidents particularly exacerbated the tension.

Even from September the policy of reburying the bodies of Legionary victims of the Călinescu purges had been carried on. One of the few trips which Trifa made outside of Bucharest during this time was for the reburial of Predeal Legionaries who had been thrown in unmarked graves. The government order of November that the bodies of Codreanu and his fellows which lay in Jilava Prison were to be exhumed and reinterred with appropriate honors might have been expected to cause tension. In that same prison were 64 men arrested in September for crimes against the Legion under Carol, and who, rumor had it, were not going to be punished. Thus far in three months the Justice Ministry had delayed any movement on their case. They were guarded by a special unit of Legionary militia, alongside the regular gendarmes at the prison. In the suspicion that characterized the relationship from both sides in the Antonescu-Sima ambience, the continued holding of the Carlists produced a volatile situation. The evening of November 27, 1940, hundreds of people gathered to witness the removal of the stone slab covering the Captain and thirteen others. The sight of the horribly disfigured and decomposed bodies produced a psychological shock that led to tragic consequences. After several hours consumed in the grim duty of identification and transferral of the separated remains to the hearses stolidly sitting in the glare of the floodlights, with people sobbing and men muttering to themselves at the sight of their Captain, some began hollering, shouting that someone must pay. Before anyone knew what was happening, a group of men, of which it is impossible to name specific persons, ran to the cellblock and in ten minutes of frenzy, with the crowd urging them on, murdered all 64 prisoners in an outburst of surrogate vengeance. Even though most of the population may have felt the dead "had it coming," Romania was horrified at the brutality of the deed. Yet revolutions, like it or not, carry with them the inevitable possibility of mob action and blood sacrifice against the *ancien régime*. The only surprising thing is that in the six months of Legionary rule there were not more Jilavas. Then on the following day came something worse, which could not even be mitigated by the element of psychological shock and spontaneity of the prison affair. The Legion proceeded to wipe the slate clean by murdering the venerable Nicolae Iorga and the respected economist Virgil Madgearu. More might have died but for Antonescu's intervention and that of the horrified and embarrassed Sima. During the violent Cabinet meeting which followed, Antonescu demanded the leadership of the Legion for himself, and an open break between the co-leaders was avoided only by the intervention of Dr. Hermann Neubacher, the German economic adviser. Sima made categorical promises that such violence would stop, and Antonescu withdrew his demand. Nevertheless "Antonescu would have liked to crush the Legion then, but it was impossible because of his uncertainty concerning the German attitude."[68]

Even more disquieting to Antonescu, however, were the "reforming glances the Legion cast toward the army."[69] In the recital of various Legionary depredations during these months, the large picture which shows a full-scale anti-bourgeois revolution in progress throughout Romania is often overlooked. The Legion aimed at a leveling of society. As it gained momentum and became more radicalized in the classic pattern day by day, every institution in the country felt the hand of the new philosophy—schools and universities, teachers and students, the army, the church, all were to be purged of the damning influence of the Legion's foremost enemy: bourgeois individualism. Antonescu saw all this as Bolshevization, and when he read in a Legionary publication, "The officer must no longer belong to a separate caste . . . he must be elected by the soldiers under his command . . . the army must belong to the people," he worried indeed.

In the meantime, despite his pledges, Sima could not keep order, and with the influx of hundreds of thousands of new members, many of the worst kind and variety, order and discipline broke down at times completely. It is not possible to tell how many new members joined the Legion during these months. Sima says about 500,000, which might be too high. The important thing to note is that this represented quantity, but hardly quality. And it certainly did not represent the Legion·of Codreanu: the Legion of spiritual sacrifice, work, devotion to discipline and duty. It represented instead the new Legion, the post-1938 Legion of opportunists, whom even the old Legionaries referred to contemptuously as "Septembrists."[70] It should not be forgotten that only a few hundred of the Legion's old members were still alive.[71] Also worth noting is that, since the 1940 Legionary persecution fell particularly hard on its old political opponents such as the Cuzists and *Lăncieri*, many of these hastened to change the color of their shirt and join the bandwagon in order to be on the side of the "ins."[72] Finally the years of being hounded, murdered, and persecuted from every side were over, and the Legion was in the saddle. It does not require much imagination to understand why they now went to excess, or why every drifter, malingerer, gypsy, ex-Cuzist, and Bucharest pimp now hastened to put on a green shirt and do as he pleased, with order in the state having almost completely broken down. Nevertheless, this did not mean all Legionaries. Codreanu's father hated Sima and embarrassed him every chance he got.[73] There were armed clashes between different Legionary factions around the Green House, Codreanu's old headquarters, in Bucharest. On November 8, Codreanu *père* made a violent outburst against Sima in Iaşi and three days later he and his son Decebal were fired upon by would-be assassins.[74] And lest it be forgotten, Trifa himself was identified with the Moţa-Codreanu faction, not with the hordes who clamored for revenge and quick enrichment.

Antonescu could not live with anarchy, and Sima refused, or was unable, to put a stop to it. The advice of the German Minister in Romania, Wilhelm Fabricius, was that the *Conducător* must see the

Fuehrer. In the middle of November Antonescu made his first trip to Berlin. It was here, and not in Bucharest, not in the mind of Sima or the Legion, and certainly not in the mind of Trifa, a student leader who had no command of any kind and was not privy to the deliberations of high authorities, that the ouster of the Legion was decided. Germany was the decisive factor, and in jockeying for German support, the Legion was hopelessly outmatched. It is clear that even before the Jilava killings, at his first encounter with Hitler, Antonescu sought to undercut the one ultimate plank in the Legionary program which gave them mass support: their opposition to the cession of Transylvania. The Red Dog began with a sharp attack on the Vienna arbitration. Hitler told him that the last chapter in the history of Transylvania had not yet been written, and even hinted that something might be done after the war to rectify the Bessarabian situation. There was no outright pledge of German support against the Legion at this meeting, but the impression made on Hitler that Antonescu was the best man to ensure peace and stability for Germany's plans in Romania was inescapable. Again and again it is made clear that Germany's interest in Romania is dictated by one thing and one thing only: oil.[75] Hitler for certain was completely uninterested in the working out of any Legionary "new world." For Hitler, Antonescu's visit came at a crucial moment, as well. Molotov had left Berlin only days before, and the decision to invade Russia had already been made. A little sense of perspective suffices to convince even the most hardy advocate of the German-Legionary alliance theory that Hitler did not intend to allow a bunch of fanatics in Bucharest to spoil his grand designs for the conquest of a continent.

Early in December, Sima went on a tour of the country, meeting with Legionary commanders in numerous cities. This was interpreted naturally by Antonescu's people that a rebellion was preparing. If this was indeed the case, Sima seems to have kept it a secret even from his top commanders. When the "outbreak" came in Bucharest in January, the Legionary leaders in Iaşi knew nothing about it.[76] Yet when Nicolae Pătraşcu made statements such as "The divorce between us and the general is irremediable . . . . A great abyss is opening between us . . . we are many and he is alone,"[77] one cannot discount the opinion held by many that the Legion was planning something. Yet, in the end, Antonescu beat them to it; and he was not alone.

The Germans grew more and more agitated over the potentially disruptive influence on their *Südostraum*. There was much talk in Berlin and Bucharest of imminent English air attacks on the oil fields at Craiova and Ploieşti.[78] The Wehrmacht High Command made it plain even in September that although the roughly 200,000 German troops in Romania were ostensibly there to "instruct our friend Romania in organizing and training her armed forces... their real tasks... are to protect the oil fields."[79] In light of both coming operations in the Balkans, and Operation Barbarossa, any disorder or chaos created in the rear of German armies by the Legion was intolerable. Even on November 19, Neubacher wrote from Bucharest to Foreign Ministry Economic Director Carl Clodius,

> My main pedagogical task consists in making it clear to the Guardists that there is no place in the new Europe for an isolated revolutionary laboratory. . . .
>
> The Guard must at the moment be protected from itself; otherwise it will soon lose its already severely impaired credit.[80]

Antonescu's second visit to Hitler was the final confirmation needed for the *Conducător* to make definite his plans. Meeting with the *Fuehrer* on January 14, 1941, it was not hard to convince the Germans that he could no longer work with the Legion, and Sima and his cohorts had to go. That month had already produced an intensification of the Legionary campaign to discredit Antonescu, and the extremist press wildly attacked the bourgeoisie, the British, and the Masons in Antonescu's government. The Legionary police, with Sima's blessing, raided the central Masonic Lodge in Bucharest, and supposedly found a cache of documents outlining a secret plan to eliminate the Legionaires from the government, and implicating some of Antonescu's ministers in the fabled and detested "Judeo-Masonic Ring."[81] Gheorghe Barbul, along with Hillgruber, relates that when Antonescu asked Hitler what to do about the fanatics, Hitler curtly replied, "One must get rid of them," and gave Antonescu one of his famous lectures on the salutary effects of a machine gun.[82] Hitler apparently gave Antonescu a free hand, especially when he reminded the General how Hitler had had to "discipline" Roehm and his people in 1934, and saying that whatever Antonescu did, he would not endanger the support of the Reich for his regime.[83] An indication of the trust placed in Antonescu was the fact that at this meeting Hitler told him of the Russian invasion and the part Romanian soldiers were to play in it. This was more than six months before the first assault.[84]

No sooner did Antonescu return to Bucharest than he took the first of three steps in a concerted move to execute a coup against the Legion. He signed a decree abolishing the Romanianization Commissioners, the Legionary-controlled committees which had wrought havoc with the national economy. This destroyed the Legion's revenue apparatus, and was a direct blow at its prestige. The following day, January 18, came another of those intervening acts which shaped the developing drama. The Chief of Railway Transport of the German Army in Romania, Major Doehring, was murdered on the streets of the capital by a Greek, one Demetrios Sarantopulos, whom some evidence suggests worked for British intelligence.[85] Each side pounced on the event to use for its own purposes. Antonescu at once fired the Legionary Minister of the Interior, General Ion Petrovicescu, on the pretext that he was incapable of protecting the lives of German allies. Again, prior to January 20 and certainly after his return from Salzburg and Hitler, Antonescu had already taken the decision to get rid of the Legionary Director of Police Operations, Alexandru Ghika, when he learned that Sima had told Ghika to follow only his orders, and not Antonescu's.[86] The General also prepared orders for the removal of Bucharest Legionary Prefect of Police Radu Mironovici, and the Legionary chief of security, Constantin Maimuca. They were to be replaced with trustworthy army men. Once the lower level prefects were then removed throughout the *judeţe*, the fundamental police power of the country would be in Antonescu's hands. Antonescu's account of the "rebellion" afterwards sought to make it appear that these replacements followed "hostile demonstrations" throughout the country in the two days preceding January 21, but this is demonstrably false. His new men, designated to replace the Legionary prefects, showed up to assume their offices the morning of the 21st, which they would hardly have done unless they knew in advance what was expected to happen. As for hostile demonstrations, Elie Sturdza, who commanded all Legionary forces in Iaşi, a city of some 200,000, a man whom it would seem logical of Sima to inform if indeed the Legionary leader were finalizing his plans for a concerted rebellion, never even heard that there was a demonstration on the Petrovicescu matter until January 22nd.[87] This and other testimony makes Antonescu's claim that "final instructions went out by courier (from Sima) the night of January 20," rather suspect, especially when at another point the General said it was the night of the 19th.[88]

In fact, the essential source of information on the events of January, 1941, for a host of somewhat non-discerning people ever since, was Antonescu's own official version, which he ordered written and published later in the year. *Pe Marginea Prăpastiei* (On the Edge of the Abyss) became the standard explanation of events, which were labeled pure and simply a "Legionary Rebellion." He described how the Legion planned its uprising carefully, and gave the signal in the series of nation-wide speeches on the previous Sunday. In fact, a standard speech had been given by numerous orators in various cities, once again urging Romanian support for her German and Italian allies. Trifa had given one at the Student Center in Bucharest. Sima had ordered the country-wide demonstrations to offset what he saw as the Legion's growing disability to retain German confidence. Clearly, Sima knew that he was losing in the struggle against Antonescu. Clearly, he knew that the General's sessions with Hitler had been to his (Sima's) disadvantage, and clearly, it is entirely possible that had he had the control, and more time to act Sima would have produced some attempt to oust Antonescu. But this remains speculation only, because on January 21, 1941, Sima did not have anything ready, and instead Antonescu made a coup against the Legion. If it was otherwise, other factors make no sense.

1. At least twice, Antonescu was gone from the country, in November, and in January for a matter of days. If Sima had a coup planned, was that not the time to launch it? Yet nothing happened.

2. During the days from January 21 to 25, 1941, all accounts, including Antonescu's own report, state clearly that Sima was nowhere to be found, and we are still speculating as to who hid him, and where. If one produces a rebellion, does he not stay around to direct it?

3. Logic dictates that a carefully planned (or even casually planned) rebellion requires that some word be passed to the people who are to carry it out—that orders be given, units moved into place, and so on. But the police and security forces of the Legion moved nowhere. Not a single word or order of any kind is on record anywhere showing that Sima issued a directive to anyone telling him to do anything in terms of moving against Antonescu, his army, or any section or individual of Antonescu's government. And yet the Legionaries had the Legionary Police; they had the City Police Prefecture; they had the police in the whole country under Ghika; and they had all the county prefects. Did the whole country, the whole capital city at least, rise up against Antonescu? Not even a part of it.

4. Except for one letter of Sima to Hitler earlier in January, no body of evidence sustains the thesis that Sima or other leading Legionaries actively solicited or tried to line up German support for their "rebellion." When the violence did break out, German assistance was on Antonescu's side, a fact which is common knowledge. The obviousness of this fact alone, and the violence it does to those who continually invoke the close linkage between the Germans and the Legion, seems to escape many.

5. Antonescu's own office was in the same building, on the same floor, next door to Legionary offices in the Council of Ministers. With the Legion's vaunted reputation for ruthlessness and violence, does it not defy reason to suppose that they would have hesitated to seize Antonescu at once at the very start of their "rebellion," to kill him or at least take him prisoner? Does revolution ignore the head of the state when he's in the next room? But no attempt of this kind was made by anyone.

6. The Jewish murders and devastations, which are invariably attached to the makers of the rebellion, whomever that might have been—what were the bulk of Legionary forces doing wreaking vengeance on Jews in the Dudeşti and Văcăreşti Street areas, or in the Jilava Forest outside the city? What purpose would be served in a Legionary coup by wasting time, effort, and manpower rampaging through the Jewish sections, when this would contribute nothing to the defeat of Antonescu? Even if we accept the Antonescu-initiated theory of the rebellion, the same question stands. At the most critical moment, when it is fighting for its life against being surrounded and eliminated by Antonescu's army, what sense does an attack on non-government, non-Antonescu civilians and synagogues in another part of the city add up to?

7. Over the radio, Antonescu blamed the uprising on "British secret agents, Jews, university students, professors, radicals, out-of-work union members, Communists and professional troublemakers." What did the Legionaries in fact do? Their various officials arrived at their offices that Tuesday morning and were suddenly informed by telephone or messenger that they had been replaced. Here were new appointees, Antonescu men, demanding that they surrender their positions. They refused until official orders signed by both Antonescu and Sima were received. That was the agreement of September, 1940, and only legally would they be ousted. The only places occupied by Legionaries on January 21 and after were those places and buildings where they had already been located.

We must conclude, with Weber, that the "Legion's 'rebellion' was actually its resistance to a coup by its governmental partner to eliminate it from power."[89]

8. Once again, for those who still insist that the Legion was merely a branch of the Nazis in Romania, let it be noted which side the Germans immediately responded to, with help and advice—Antonescu's. Ribbentrop himself told the German Minister in Bucharest telegraphically on January 22, "there is no longer any room for half measures . . .

Antonescu should proclaim the seditious Legionnaires to be rebels. . . .
he must secure his rule in the capital and in the country by all means
available to him . . . General Antonescu should immediately proclaim
himself the leader of the Legion . . . . Oral addition: Marxists to be
executed. Idealists to be exiled to Germany on condition that they
must refrain from all political activity, otherwise they will be extra-
dited."[90] Moreover, the Halder Diary (cf. German archival volumes)
for the evening of January 21 noted that the military mission had instructions "in case of necessity to support Antonescu with military
power. . . ."[91] Can we remain in doubt as to whether the Legion was
Hitler's protected protegé in Romania? Weber sums up the whole
most succinctly when he says, "At no time does Hitler, who thought
well of Codreanu, seem to have given a damn for the Legion. Those
who were smuggled out, probably in German uniforms, owed their
escape to the private enterprise of the secret services and a few German friends."[92]

9. The "pogrom" in Bucharest? It was not a pogrom in the sense
that it was a concerted and organized plan of attack on Jews and
Jewish homes, businesses and temples. It was a spontaneous, disorganized case of what happens when anarchy prevails in a large urban
setting; with all law and order having broken down for three days,
looting and drunkenness were rampant, and every criminal type,
gypsy, *Lăncieri*, Cuzist, Legionary, thief and cutthroat came out of
hiding to burn, rob, smash, kill, and destroy. Some were Legionary
"Septembrists," no doubt. None were given any orders by anyone
to murder Jews or Christians. When it was all over, a most carefully
researched Jewish publication appeared in Romania at the end of the
Second World War, written by Matatias Carp, a prominent leader in
the Bucharest Jewish community. This was the famous *Cartea Neagră:
Suferinţele Evreilor din România, 1940-1944* or the *Black Book:
the Sufferings of the Jews in România.* This was specifically com-
missioned by Jewish organizations to document Jewish deaths and
property losses, and to serve as a basis for war reparations at the
Nuremberg trials. Similar studies were done for other European
countries. It comprises three large volumes of material, volume I
alone running to 373 pages. At the end of this first volume, Carp
lists the names and locations of Jews killed during the "rebellion,"
including even those whose bodies could not be identified. The list
contains 120 names or entries.[93] Nowhere does Carp gloss over
events, for he documents every instance of brutality and destruction
during these January days in Bucharest, right down to the graphic

blood-curdling details, complete with photographs. Therefore he has not taken short-cuts nor ignored any effort to be complete. Thus one hundred twenty Jews died during the uprising.[94] Weber reports that "official figures" for January 21-23 show 370 dead and 44 wounded in Bucharest, and 46 dead and 78 wounded in other parts of the country.[95] This exceeds the combined total of the Carp and Woods figures for the capital city alone. One should then add that most responsible accounts state that 68 of the Jews murdered were found in the Jilava Forest, leaving at most 52 souls slain in town,[96] which is where the majority of the Legionaries were reported by witnesses to be. Those who speak of 6,000 slaughtered in Bucharest alone, or 10,000 or more, are repeating fiction.[97]

To return to the *Black Book*. One should note Carp's statement on page 74 that it was in the interest of the Jewish community in Romania to keep alive the distrust and ill-will between Antonescu and Sima. Truly, neither one approved of Jews[98] but forcing the Legion out of power was the best solution to a bad dilemma for Jewish interests. Even more interesting is Carp's declaration that the Legionaries were not responsible for the "revolution." Although the Legion is certainly accused of complicity in the murders, not once does Carp accuse any specific ranking Legionary or supporters of having performed any specified deed of violence. In fact he notes that boys of twelve and all kinds of quasi-Legionary types were involved in looting buildings and property.

Before leaving this extensive bit of source material for anyone wishing to reconstruct a portrait of what happened in Bucharest in January, 1941, it would be logical, in light of the countless stories, accusations, allegations, and insinuations over the course of forty years aimed at showing beyond doubt that Viorel Trifa not only "caused" or "ignited" the Legionary "rebellion," but actively took part in a murderous pogrom, to expect that Trifa and information about him would play a substantial role in the *Black Book*. He is not even mentioned anywhere.

Just Another Demonstration

The weekend of January 19, 1941, was a busy one for Trifa. On Sunday he took part in the hastily-organized national demonstration of support for the Axis allies, where he delivered a standard speech given by various prominent speakers in a number of cities. On that same Sunday was the opening of a long-awaited student project, in which Trifa had invested much time: a student medical dispensary at

the Faculty of Law building near Strada Plevnei. Among the hundreds
of students and dignitaries was Mrs. Antonescu. Apparently the Major
Doehring shooting had not served to inspire much response in student circles or otherwise, for no attention was given to it at either of
these affairs. Monday, January 20, was a normal day and Trifa went
about his business until mid-afternoon when he got word that he
should report to Horia Sima. When he arrived, he was informed that
Sima wished to have a large student and workers' demonstration
held that evening, at about 7 p.m. or so in front of the University.
Trifa's immediate response was that it was already too late in the
day: there wasn't enough time to organize such a thing in a mere
three or four hours and have it be successful. Sima's answer was simple
and direct: "It is all taken care of," was the essence of the Vice-
President's response. The orders and arrangements had already been
made or given out. Dumitru Groza would be there with his Legionary
Workers' Corps, Andrei would bring people along from the Legionary Student Center, announcements had been sent to the National
Union headquarters, and so on. All Trifa had to do was make one of
his well-known speeches. And Sima handed him a "manifesto" of
some 300 words which had Trifa's name on the bottom and had already been sent to the printing office to be reproduced. It had been
written by Traian Borobaru. Seeing the pattern of the previous Sunday repeated, Trifa left, slightly dismayed that lately his public speaking seemed to be required almost daily, and this interfered with his
student work.

He next went by the National Union offices, to see if anyone had
been informed about the demonstration, and from there he proceeded to the University where a crowd was already gathering. Presumably, besides messages sent by courier or telephone, Sima had also
had the manifestation announced over the radio. Darknesss comes
early on winter afternoons in Bucharest. By 7 p.m. or thereabouts,
some 5,000 persons—a great many of them students, some of them
Legionary members of Groza's workers' corps, many from the Legionary Students' Center, and the usual number of curious citizens
who happened to be in the streets and joined the throng to see what
was going on, had gathered in the University Plaza, at that time at the
intersections of Boulevard Elisabeta and Boulevard Brătianu. Trifa
stood upon the base of the pedestal of the statue of Michael the
Brave facing the main University building and in a loud voice delivered the prepared "manifesto," all of which took perhaps less than five
minutes. Except for those in the very front ranks, the dim light would

have made it impossible to see his features or how he was dressed—
neither of which really matter, since no one has ever contended that
he did not give the speech that night. Whether he wore a green shirt
under his winter overcoat, really seems irrelevant also. Most likely he
did.

What is contentious is the testimony of people who will swear that
Trifa advocated a pogrom that night, or used phrases such as "Get
the Jews," or "Kill the Jews," or openly called for revolution against
Antonescu, because only if he did, and such things immediately followed, could one reasonably accuse this man at this demonstration
of being the direct causal factor which set in motion events of the
so-called "rebellion," and its accompanying crimes.

Leaving aside the fact that it is hard to imagine, if Trifa was calling
for Jewish blood, how more than a few people heard him, despite
the good acoustical setting of the particular site of the speech, if one
were a Jew, at that moment would he have stayed on the scene, much
less pushed up closer to the front to hear and see all? What is more likely as a factor influencing the "memories" of so-called "eye-witnesses"
is the fact that in the days which followed, Sima's group, which had
control of the radio station in the capital city, had Trifa's speech
broadcast again and again over the radio on January 21 and 22. But
Trifa was not doing the broadcasting, it was merely his speech being
read by someone else "in a nervous voice," and we have no less a
testimony to this than a Jewish source itself, or at least a highly non-
Legionary report.[99] How many people in the entire city of Bucharest
containing several hundred thousand souls, had ever actually heard
Trifa's voice, unless they were students or in the habit of attending
student affairs or rallies? It is not only likely, it is definitely less than
mere speculation to allow that many people who heard this message
on the radio and heard it identified as "the words of comrade Viorel
Trifa," thought that Trifa himself was uttering it, or, with the passage
of twenty, thirty, or forty years, remember only the name and mentally link it to the January events.

What was in the "manifesto?" Actually, very little more than the
generalities and platitudes one would expect, given the time and place.
Romanian students will not stand for the gunning down of a German
officer in the streets by agents of the British and Freemasons, Trifa
said. The brave General Petrovicescu, who would have prevented such
things, had been dismissed from office, also at the behest of the British
and masons. The government must be purged of those in the employ
of Greeks and Jews. Specifically, Eugen Cristescu (an old Călinescu
man) and Alexandru Roşianu at the Interior Ministry, were named as

worthy of being ousted. "We want a Legionary government!" Trifa concluded, which is as close as he ever came to fomenting any specific action or deeds. In fact, the speech was nothing new at all, but a continuation of the rhetoric which Sima had already used on several occasions that month when he promised "an imminent disclosure of material about masonic machinations against the interests of Romania plotted with the help of British intelligence."[100]

What happened next was also old hat to Romanians by now, for parades, marches, speeches, and manifestos were the normal stuff of life in Bucharest these days, and the night of the 20th of January was no different. The crowd marched off in the direction of Calea Victoria, toward the headquarters of the Council of Ministers, where Antonescu's office was located. On the way they paused in front of the Italian and German Legations to cheer and express their support for their allies. It took several hours for the throng to regather in orderly fashion in front of the Council building, nearly a kilometer away from the site of Trifa's speech. Again they cheered and shouted their loyalty to Antonescu, to Romania, to their allies, to Sima, to Petrovicescu, and so on. The *Conducător* was in his office, and sent one Colonel Elefterescu down to see what the crowd wanted. Marin Preda in his fictional work *Delirul* recreated the scene when Elefterescu returned to the General and was asked who was leading the demonstration.

"Viorel Trifa and Dumitru Groza."

"Hmm, hmm, Dumitru Groza, that communist?"[101]

Antonescu may well have confused Dumitru Groza with the well-known communist leader Petru Groza, later prime minister of Romania's first post-war regime. It may be that Antonescu was once more trying to paint the Legionary movement with communist stripes, to further convince the Germans of the necessity of supporting him and not Sima. And it is true that talk of communist infiltration of the Legionary movement was another aspect of the rumor-factory that characterized official Bucharest at any given moment in those days.. Yet it is also likely that the exchange between Antonescu and his officer never took place; it was thrown in by Preda as something that the General was *likely* to have said. Nor must we forget that, writing in 1971, it is in Preda's interest in socialist Romania today to show communists in the forefront of dramatic confrontations in the 1940s, when in fact their numbers at the time were miniscule.

Be all this as it may, the main point is that although the Trifa-Groza demonstration may have angered Antonescu, he was well aware that it would have little or no effect on the machinery he had already set in motion, as we have seen. The orders for the replacement of Legionary prefects and police and ministers were already prepared; all the General had to do was sit it out until the following day, when the army had its orders to occupy the public buildings.[102] Whatever Sima hoped to accomplish by having Trifa speak, the manifestation had no impact on Antonescu, surely, and thus was "just another" bit of Legionary gamesmanship; the *Conducător* proceeded with his plans. If Trifa's speech was so inflammatory, as we are constantly reminded today, if he himself was such a rabid inciter to riot and pillage, then the great question remains: why did the so-called "rebellion" not start that evening? Even testimony which has no reason to be friendly to Trifa agrees that the demonstration the evening of January 20 broke up peacefully. When they had informed the General of their demands, and cheered, and sung a song or two, Trifa told everyone to go home. And they did. By 11 p.m. the crowd had dispersed peaceably, and Trifa himself went home to bed. Antonescu's own account of the January days confirms this, for all references in *The Edge of the Abyss* to January 20 testify that nothing happened that evening. Search through one after another book or article of Western historical authorship on the 1940s in Romania and we find that none of them view the January 20 demonstration as the starting point of the outbreak of the following days, but in fact all concur on January 21 for the outburst, when Antonescu's army moved against offices held by Legionary ministers. Added to this, we find numerous accounts in books and articles written by eyewitnesses and participants specifically disavowing any activity or role in events played by Trifa after the evening of the 20th.[103] A recently discovered work published in 1944 and containing a "Journal of the Rebellion and Crimes of the Legion," begins its "journal" narrative with January 21, and never mentions the student demonstration of the previous day.[104] Surely, if Trifa was so instrumental in "sparking" the "rebellion," if he was such an important man in this whole chain of events, one would expect to find much more about him in the historical record. Instead he is missing. He went home and went to bed. The next day he went about his regular routine until he heard what was taking place. Then he went and hid. Hardly the behavior of the "leader" of a planned uprising. It is so obvious that the allegations of Trifa's cause-and-effect relationship to the outbreak of January 21-23 are simply a *post hoc ergo propter hoc* argument, that to discuss it at greater length almost seems superfluous. Yet, we may ask further: where *was* Trifa after the action began on the 21st? With Sima? He was nowhere to be found, either. Some persons claim Trifa was in the Jewish section, leading attacks. If he "led" the whole rebellion, or even a part of it, why was he not in the Prefecture building, or in Strada Roma with some of the Legionary forces, or in some other besieged headquarters command post, giving orders? No historical record places him in any of these spots. Instead he took the time to ride in a side car to Văcărești Street, in the midst of a time when the Legion was fighting for its very life, and direct that a synagogue be burned down? Would such actions advance the cause of defeating the forces of Antonescu one iota? Hardly. Was Trifa among those taken prisoner by the army when the Legionaries finally surrendered the buildings they had fortified? He was not. We do not have to take Trifa's word for anything relative to his movements that day of the 21st. The fact that the historical record speaks for itself is sufficient, especially if reinforced by fundamental logic.

In fact, on that Tuesday morning Trifa set out on his normal round of activities, which included appointments with Alexander Cretzianu, the Finance Minister, and with Education Minister Traian Brăileanu. When he arrived for the meeting with Brăileanu and found the Minister absent, he inquired as to his whereabouts, for he had student business to discuss. Instead Professor Traian Herseni, one of Trifa's former teachers, appeared, and asked if Trifa had not heard what was going on. "What?" "Antonescu has dismissed all Legionary prefects; they've been told to surrender their offices. Their replacements have been coming in all morning. The Legionary prefects refuse to move. They are trying to force us all out of the government, even though we are half the government, by law." And Trifa left the Ministry. He went to the University. On Calea Victoria and Boulevard Elisabeta he saw armored cars and a crowd gathered in the vicinity of the Prefecture of Police. A few shots rang through the air. He tried to telephone the Prefecture, but there was no answer. Trifa went to his rented room on Calimachi Street (off Şoseaua Colentina today) and packed his bag. He changed his lodgings and hid, and as the days went by and the daughter of a pharmacist friend with whom he stayed brought him newspapers, the full import of it all became clear.

For Trifa, whose surprise at Antonescu's *putsch* was as great as anyone's, the events of January 21 brought the start of a long and harrowing nine-year exodus. It was April, 1939, all over again. He was on the run.

CHAPTER VIII

DACHAU: ECONOMY CLASS

Romania entered the Second World War as a belligerent on June 12, 1941. It has always seemed slightly ludicrous to label any of Valerian Trifa's activities in Romania as "war crimes" when his country was not at war in January, 1941, and he left Romania for Germany nearly three months to the day before Marshal Antonescu brought the nation into the conflict. This, all the more so as he was in Germany not by choice but by circumstance, and he spent nearly three years as a prisoner, held in German concentration camps. This is the historic fact, easily proven by the copious records of the International Tracing Service of the United States Army after the war, and repeated in the extensive investigation files of the Army Intelligence Corps (CIC) headquarters in Munich, two other CIC unit reports, a U.S. Embassy clearance report in Rome, a file in the Interior Ministry office in Italy, and three files in the U.S. Document Center in Berlin, all of these generated during the period 1945-1950 when Trifa was in Italy and had applied for permission to emigrate to the United States. Anyone caring to search will find that Trifa was Prisoner No. 44559 and was assigned Certificate of Incarceration No. 0718/T33710 by the International Tracing Service, along with the dates of his detention in Dachau and Buchenwald.[1]

Trifa hid out in a variety of places in Bucharest after January 20, 1941, while the authorities hunted for Antonescu's enemies and hundreds were jailed as the government arrested everyone in sight. Trifa's first thought was to attain political asylum in Yugoslavia. There he had student associates and friends who might shelter him. About two weeks later he boldly entrained at the North Station in Bucharest on the departing train for Timişoara, in the West of the country and close to the Yugoslav border. A few hours out of the station the train was stopped, and on the platform of the small Oltenian town Trifa saw German and Romanian soldiers preparing to search the train. He left the car quickly, on the side opposite the platform, and hurried across the tracks—directly into the arms of a German soldier. He asked to see the man's commanding officer. An hour later he was on the German troop train, heading back to Bucharest. The orders had gone out to the German army to round up Legionary members and prominent supporters and hold them. By the end of the first week of February Trifa found himself, along with nearly fifteen others, in the basement of the German Economic Mission in Bucharest, where they were held and hidden for over a month, denied all contact with the outside.

All this was partly explainable by the fact that for some time the Germans simply could not decide what to do with all the anti-Antonescu fugitives they had rounded up. Some were kept at the German Cultural Attaché's house, some at the Economic Mission, some in spots which could claim extraterritoriality, and others which could not. Adding to the complexus was German irritation with Antonescu. One thread generally agreed upon in the contradictory accounts of the Antonescu *putsch* is that the German officials, especially Neubacher and von Neurath, had mediated the truce of January 24 between the government and the Legionnaires, and done so "in good faith" that Antonescu would keep his word that there would be no mass reprisals. To this end, "saving" or protecting some of the Legionaries was a means for the Germans to bring some modicum of psychological calm—and at the same time exert a certain leverage on Antonescu to guarantee his continued cooperation. When the *Conducător* began his roundup of enemies, many of the Germans in the capital were furious and saw this as a violation of his pledge. Hardly were they going to hand over their detainees at that point.

Moreover in Germany itself there was divided opinion, as Schellenberg and others make clear.[2] Hitler and Ribbentrop by now were strengthened in their earlier opinions that the Legionaries were an immature band of troublemakers who threatened Germany's plans for Romanian obeisance and compliance in creating the *Völksraum*. Himmler, on the other hand, along with Neubacher and his circle, saw the practical advantage to be gained by having the threat of a released Legionnaire corps to hold over the head of Antonescu, and thus did not share the *Fuehrer*'s attitude of the "Legionaries be damned," after January, 1941. We do not know all the maneuvering which went on in the weeks which followed the *Walpurgisnacht* of the Legion, a topic which would repay close scrutiny by a promising graduate student. What is clear is that Himmler's position won out. By March 13 Trifa and the others were on a train for Germany, hostages for the good behavior of the Romanian regime in Hitler's war.

The issue of Trifa's whereabouts during the next four years, then, can hardly be viewed as the result of his conscious decision to spend the war in Germany because of Nazi proclivities. He had little choice in the matter. Even assuming that he did, for the sake of the argument, where else was a Romanian fugitive to run to in March, 1941? It is easy to forget the obvious fact that by the end of that year practically all of Europe was under Axis domination.

There is no good reason to describe here all of Trifa's movements once he arrived as a prisoner in Germany, and in the slender historical record of the Legionaries during the second (and for many, their final) exile; Trifa is encountered merely as part of the general group. This time, unlike 1939 and 1940, he was not able to go his own way, and thus the appearance of his name on documents or in connection with activities carried on at the direction of German authorities should not be construed as necessarily self-initiated. Once again, when one is in a foreign land and in conditions of captivity, it is natural to stay with and support one's own fellows from home. Nevertheless it is clear from the exile literature bearing on this period that the Sima-Papanace dichotomy among the Legionary ranks continued to exist, and was intensified when Sima managed to escape from captivity. Those who remained, lodged in a type of outdoor SS camp at Berkenbrueck (including Trifa) were plainly told that if Sima were not found and returned they would be shot, so outraged was Himmler at the Sima flight. Fortunately for them, Sima was caught, but for many of the exile group, including Trifa, the ill will engendered against Sima for endangering their lives, and violating the declaration against engaging in any political activity on German territory which all had been required to sign, lasted for years.[3]

Trifa was moved from detention in Vienna to the Berkenbrueck camp on April 19. Here he was supposed to be put to work cutting firewood in nearby woods, but this did not materialize.[4] On May 5, along with Dumitru Groza, Trifa was called to the office of the Gestapo in Berlin for interrogation.[5] In the meantime, back in Romania, an Antonescu-ordered Military Tribunal of Cassation and Justice was busy pronouncing verdicts on Legionary leaders and followers. On June 15, 1941, the court sentenced Trifa to forced labor for life for "crimes against the state," and assisting in an "uprising against the order of the government." In other words, Trifa supported the forces resisting Antonescu, and was on the losing side. There is no mention whatsoever of "war crimes," or of "murders," of Trifa's having killed anyone or of crimes against individuals. The sentence is exactly what one would expect from a politically dictated tribunal in the aftermath of a revolutionary period.

Trifa himself was unaware of the court action in Bucharest, and did not learn of it until years later when he was in Italy. He had more immediate concerns. On Christmas Day, 1942, he was transferred from the relatively tolerable atmosphere of Berkenbrueck to the concentration camp at Buchenwald, where he remained for two months. On March 1, 1943, he went to Dachau and was confined there in a cell for one day short of eighteen months.

At Buchenwald Trifa and other transferees among the Romanian prisoners were kept in an isolated unit, surrounded by a barrier surmounted by barbed wire and glass. In Eugen Kogon's 1950 book, *Der SS Staat*, one may locate the area of Trifa's captivity on the site-plan of the Buchenwald camp just to the east of the SS troop barracks in the area marked 14.[6]

In Dachau, where he spent the longest time, Trifa was classified, as at the former camp, as a *Schutzhaft*, or political prisoner being held in "protective detention." These were kept in the SS section of the camp, the *Schutzhaftlager*. The latest comprehensive study of the Dachau system speaks specifically of the category in which Trifa was included, that of a number of prisoners termed *Ehrenhäftlinge*, or so-called privileged prisoners who lived in the *Ehrenbunker* in individual cells. These included "German and foreign politicians, members of the higher clergy and of the aristocracy, towards whom the regime, in spite of everything, wished to prove its capacity for a certain amount of consideration."[7] These prisoners were also of different nationalities. Trifa's immediate neighbor in the next cell was the famous German dissenting pastor Martin Niemöller, and the anti-regime Monseignor, John Neuhäusler was for a time also in Trifa's *Stube*.[8]

Trifa was in fact downright lucky on two counts. At Dachau it was the "politicals" who were preponderant, in contrast to camps like Auschwitz and Mauthausen where corruption was rampant, prisoners had their food and clothes stolen and were maltreated in the bargain by other prisoners in the most odious manner. Secondly, if one had to be sent to Dachau, the spring of 1943 was a relatively favorable moment, for it was just at this time that a somewhat new regime was initiated and conditions were not quite so grim as earlier. When German industry began to slow down due to lack of workers, the regime turned to the use of slave-labor from the concentration camps. Improvements were thus made in living conditions to increase output, the food improved slightly, and so on. Officially the SS could no longer maltreat the prisoners. Yet this did not mean that the disciplinary regime was any the less harsh.[9] Moreover the commandant at Dachau from September, 1942, to November, 1943, was SS Sturmbahnführer Martin Weiss, whose administration on the whole was considered slightly more humane than his predecessor's, even if his motivation aimed more at higher work outputs than humaneness for its own sake.[10] Weiss' successor, Wilhelm Weiter, remained in charge until Trifa's release. He was said to take his duties "very lightly" and made no basic changes in the camp.[11]

Trifa's living conditions in the *Schutzhaftlager* cell were then, physically, better than those in other parts of the camp, to the extent that he was not forced to do long and hard daily manual labor on little food. He wore his own clothing instead of the rough prison uniform, and occasionally one prisoner in the block could collect small sums of money from each cell and purchase small personal items such as soap or toothpaste from the camp commissary—when these were available. He was let out of his cell to visit the laundry room and for brief daily exercise periods in the yard. This was the good part. The rest of the time, day after day for one and a half years, he was confined to a room about ten feet by eight feet wide, with one window high in the wall through which one could see only part of the sky, due to a shelf extending outward from the window ledge. The food was plain, heavy, and monotonous, consisting of soup and potatoes and potatoes and soup. Trifa spent a good deal of time undergoing medical treatment for intestinal problems, a condition which developed at Berkenbrueck and was exacerbated by the Dachau dampness and prison fare. Above all there was the psychological trauma, the monotony and boredom and morale-breaking ignorance of one's fate, the crawling slowness of time when one is in the control of others under lock and key. Paul Berben, the official historian of Dachau, reports on the prison psychology so quick to develop:

> Many prisoners lived in a constant state of worry. They were afraid of going hungry, of being hit, of falling ill, of being sent away in a trainload to the unknown. Above all, they were afraid of dying, and death was always present with the sight of corpses and the smoke (and smell) from the crematorium always present in the air. Uncertainty undermined morale. When he arrived in the camp no one knew how long he was to stay there, since there had been no conviction to determine the length of sentence. No one was in a position to forecast what would happen to him from one minute to the next. Only those with inner strength and resources could survive.[12]

Trifa, to be sure, had strong inner resources, but this does not make the loss of one's freedom any more acceptable. To an educated man, in fact, deprivation of liberty is perhaps even more onerous than for one with more limited horizons and aspirations. We know that during 1943 it became Gestapo policy to break up groups of prisoners and scatter them throughout various camps, if they contained men from the same region, or of the same nationality or political leanings. It is likely this which explains Trifa's being sent to Dachau in the first place.[13] Thus he saw few of his fellow Romanians during this time, was never told exactly why he had been imprisoned nor how long he was to stay. He received no mail, was unable to learn of his family back in Romania or inform them of his whereabouts. Of the progress of the war the prisoners were told nothing, and overriding all as 1943 turned into 1944 was the thought that one day the entire camp would erupt in a vast explosion from the increasingly frequent Allied bombers passing overhead. If not that, then the Germans, should they be forced to evacuate hastily and destroy the evidence of what took place at Dachau and other camps, would blow up the camp themselves and massacre the inhabitants. Commandant Martin Weiss as Inspector of Camps is said to have refused to obey Hitler's order to do exactly this at Dachau on April 28-29, 1945.[14] It is unlikely that being a "political" would have carried much weight by that time.

The very fact of Trifa's release on August 30, 1944, is testimony not to his favorable record of supporting German policy, but to the relationship between the holding of the Romanian Legionary group and Romania's cooperation in Hitler's war. Trifa and his fellows were released almost at once following the capitulation of Romania under the invasion of Russian armies. Holding the Romanians as a guarantee of Antonescu's behavior was now passé; instead the Germans thought to establish some kind of Romanian government-in-exile, with the country now under Russian occupation. Trifa was assigned residence in Vienna. But the theology student, lay missionary, reformer, dramatic orator, had had enough. He could hardly bring himself to cooperate with a German government which had for three and a half years held him a prisoner. Besides, there was his feeling of distaste for Sima and his past and future policies, which had contributed so largely to the disastrous dénouement of the once-inspired Legionary Movement.

The testimony of many contemporaries, including Palaghiţa. Papanace, and Sima himself, is clear: Trifa refused to take part in any new Romanian political grouping in exile. "It would be easy to put you back in the camps," he was told. But he was adamant. The international situation worked in his favor. With the Red Army racing toward the West, and the Allies approaching the Rhine, the rapid breakdown of the German machine allowed for manipulations and evasions of authority. Just at this time the Metropolitan Visarion Puiu arrived in Vienna, seeking to establish a Romanian Orthodox Diocese outside of Romania. Puiu had been a high-ranking member of the Holy Synod of Romania, the former Metropolitan of Bukovina, and during the war Exarch of Transnistria. In August, 1944, he found himself in Croatia just at the moment when Romania turned from the German camp to the Allies, with Russian troops penetrating deeply into its territory. Puiu decided not to return to the country, and removed to Vienna, from whence he began a somewhat futile effort which lasted the rest of his life to create around himself a Romanian Orthodox diocese which would encompass all Romanians throughout the world outside of Romania. For Trifa, however, Visarion came on the scene at a critical moment. He was able to convince the Germans that he could be more useful by assisting the Metropolitan in an exile church establishment. He thus became Puiu's secretary. Most importantly for his own safety, Trifa bought time and was able to stay in Austria a few more months and remain aloof from German plans involving Sima's group. He incurred the wrath of some of his old Legionary acquaintances. By March, 1945, he was receiving letters threatening him with death.[15] Yet he had gained the time he needed. As the Allies closed in on the Third Reich, Trifa had no desire to remain for the *Götterdammerung* certain to come. In April he stole across the border and made his way to Italy, finding temporary shelter in a Roman Catholic monastery. For the first time in years he found some measure of peace.

Soon he filled out papers at the International Red Cross to migrate to the West, but a new disappointment confronted him. People with practical professions were wanted—not theologians or student leaders, regardless of their organizational and administrative abilities. So Trifa was bypassed in the quotas. Fate ordained that he would remain in Italy for the next five years.

January, 1946, found him learning Italian and substituting as a teacher in the Catholic Missionary College of San Giuseppe, lecturing in ancient history, geography, and foreign languages. The school was pleased with his work, and the relative calm and beauty of Italy, even war-torn Italy, was profoundly welcome, given the hectic days and sleepless nights behind him.

Yet destiny, while it may leave us at rest for a moment, is only waiting for its appointed time to move us on. For Trifa, this came one morning when his mail brought him a copy of the Romanian-American Episcopate's official newspaper, *Solia*, sent him by a friend who had managed to get to the United States. In fact, Trifa's intention was, if possible, to migrate to Canada first; his second choice was South America, and only thirdly did he select to go to the United States. Now he saw the name and address of a certain priest named Trutza in Cleveland, Ohio. It would do no harm to write and ask this man if he knew anything of the whereabouts of certain of Trifa's relatives who lived somewhere in Ohio. Thus Trifa wrote a fateful letter, addressing his request to Father Trutza. "Ohio is a big state," the priest responded, and at once wanted to know if the young man were related to the famous Father Iosif Trifa. Thus a correspondence was begun, whose consequences are well-known.

A few months afterwards, when the newspaper *America* was seeking an editor, Trutza mentioned to manager Iosif Drugociu and others the young Romanian theologian in Italy with much experience working on newspapers. The Church World Service, not so burdened with refugees now as earlier, began to process the papers.

The Immigration and Naturalization Service file no. A7819396 for a Displaced Person quota immigrant had its inception here, in Italy. Trifa's past was investigated intensively by official agencies of the United States government for the first time—and this in a period when documents were fresh and available and witnesses still living who were parties to the events—and he was subjected to the exhaustive system of clearances listed earlier. These included at least six separate investigations through the channels of U.S. Army Intelligence, the last report coming through the CIC office in Trieste on January 16, 1950. All this was in addition to the ordinary Displaced Persons processing when Trifa first arrived at the DP Camp in Italy in 1945.[16] Finally in May, 1950, Trifa was notified by the International Refugee Organization to report to the United States Processing Center in Bagnoli for formalities connected with a U.S. visa. Here he spent some three weeks with all the prescribed stages of interviews, Consular Service reports, and the like. By this time he had been subjected to nearly a whole year of investigation. If the United States had the slightest reservation at that moment, one would expect to learn of it. Instead, Trifa was granted his visa and called to Bremerhaven for embarkation, in July.

It would appear at this point that, for Trifa, the dawn was finally breaking as he boarded the *USS General Harry Taylor* on his thirty-sixth birthday and followed the path covered by thousands of his countrymen over the decades in search of a new life. He sailed for the United States of America. In less than two years he was in the midst of the *Sturm und Drang* of the divaricated American Episcopate; FBI reports on him were filed as early as September, two months after his arrival, and again in December, 1951; 263 individuals and 130 other leads provided on him were pursued and 56 were interviewed by INS or Justice Department officials; and he was subjected to a barrage of calumny and denigration which made even interwar Romanian rhetoric seem mild.[17]

Many a second thought must have passed through the mind of the newly-arrived, as he wondered why he had not remained with his original intention to go to Canada or somewhere else; for the new day in the West seemed to disclose only that the path of Sisyphus which seemed to characterize his life had merely taken another turn.

CHAPTER IX

ERRARE HUMANUM EST

"This picture of Valerian D. Trifa being ordained a bishop was taken by a parishioner in 1958," wrote the *Philadelphia Inquirer*.[1] The only thing the paper did not explain was how the parishioner took a picture six years after the event happened. Trifa was ordained on April 27, 1952.

"The 72-year old bishop," narrated the *Detroit Free Press* in an issue of November, 1976.[2] Trifa in that month was 62 years old, but what is a decade or two?

"The Ukranian *(sic)* Orthodox hierarchy finally accepted, and in April, 1952, Trifa was anointed *(sic)* in Chicago," misspelled the *Detroit Magazine*.[3] This was not bad reporting, except that the proper word is "consecrated," not "anointed." Oh, yes, it took place in Philadelphia, not Chicago, but the writer was only a few hundred miles off.

"John Trutza, a Cleveland priest who had studied with Trifa in Romania in 1940..." wrote Howard Blum.[4] Trutza came to America in 1922, when Trifa was eight years old; he returned to Romania for short trips during the 1930s, but never exchanged a word with Trifa until 1950. Certainly he never studied with him.[5]

This was perhaps not as noticeable as the map printed in the *Milwaukee Sentinel* during 1977 and labeled "Shaded parts of map locate areas occupied by Israel since 1967." The map was of the United States, and shaded in was most of the Mississippi Valley.[6]

At one time in October, 1977, Ottawa editors could not seem to make up their minds as to just how many days Marion was in danger. The *Ottawa Journal* headlined "Marion freed after 81-day ordeal," while the *Ottawa Citizen* blazoned the news, "82-day ordeal over," and readers of the *Ottawa Today* noted that "After 83 days, Marion safe."[7]

A United Press International wire service item of June, 1975 revealed astoundingly that Prime Minister Harold Wilson recently announced that "the British people had voted overwhelmingly to stay in Europe."[8]

Then there were the Milwaukee headline, "Man Eating Piranha Mistakenly Sold as Pet Fish," which suggests for want of a hyphen the horse was lost,[9] the Peoria, Illinois headline, "Argentina's Junta Picks Obscure Army Man As President," set flush beside a photograph of Hubert Humphrey,[10] and the intelligent composition and placement of headlines and captions which have resulted in such interesting news stories as "Louisiana Governor Defends His Wife, Gift From Korean,"[11] a photograph underscored by the line "Sen. Weicker With New Bribe, Camille DiLorenzo Butler,"[12] "Sophia, Audrey Hepburn Expecting," immediately following the rubric *It Happened Last Night*, along with two photographs of smiling mothers in hospital rooms holding bouncing new babies under the section masthead *Night Sports Final*, not to be outdone by the succinct *Contra Costa Times* observation of May 31, 1977, in its headline "Greeks Fine Hookers,"[13] and Alamogordo's eye-catching column labeled "Pastor Aghast at First Lady Sex Position."[14]

There is the "DNR Hunt Survey to Question Dogs," the "Stiff opposition expected to casketless funeral plan," and the guilt by association resulting from the inadvertent juxtaposition or composition of picture and caption, such as the picture of the newly-elected president of the United Way of Westchester, "only the second woman in the nation to hold a similar post." The picture has the lady in front of her home, with one hand resting on a lamp post in her yard."[15]

The *Wall Street Journal* on March 2, 1967, announced "The late Henry Luce, founder of *Time* (who had died that week) won't appear on the magazine's cover next week."[16] He did.

A bit of history from the *Washington Post*:

> The AFSC began by reconstruction work in World War I and fed the needy of all views after the Russian Revolution, headed by future President Herbert Hoover.[17]

Also from the *Washington Post*:

> Former Rep. Gray said last night: "Nobody's investigating me. Nobody's called me. I never had anything to do with selecting an architect. How can you investigate somebody for something he's never done? I've never received a nickel or any kind of favor from anybody associated with the building industry or an architectural firm in my 20 years in Congress."

> Former Rep. Gray could not be reached for comment.[18]

Such clear-cut sources and reportage, more than anything, point up the truth of the January 3, 1977 headline in the *Indianapolis Star*, to wit: "Newspaper is America's Most Valuable *Educationl* Agency." Yes, that's how they spelled it. Later, one would suppose, the *Star* might print, as did the Yellville, Arkansas *Mountain Echo*, a line entitled, "*Corection.*"[19] And so on.

Not only placement, countless factual errors, page layout and positioning of photographs and captions, and headline composition help to determine what the public is led to believe by newspapers and other products of the print medium, but when one adds emotional climate, years of psychological conditioning by a press establishment which is, after all, composed of human beings with their own intents and purposes, the press may be used even to convince people that they behaved not as they did, but as they *thought* they did, or should have. Consider the National Opinion Research Center's findings on the support given by the American electorate to John F. Kennedy, who in 1960 was elected President by 49.7 per cent of the popular vote. In June, 1963, 59 per cent of the respondents in a NORC survey claimed to have voted for Kennedy in 1960. Immediately after Kennedy's assassination, this posthumous landslide swelled to 65 per cent. Thus in November, 1960, one out of every two voters had chosen Kennedy; three years later, two out of every three believed they had.[20] It is superfluous, almost, to mention the famous poll predicting Alfred M. Landon's overwhelming election in 1936, or what the Chicago papers foresaw as the inevitable outcome of the 1948 Truman-Dewey struggle.

One does not blame the press entirely, for its information is only as good as the source of the news. In the 1790s Thomas Jefferson clearly stated that one absolutely could not trust newspapers.[21] He wrote at a time when newspapers had only appeared on the national scene as specific instruments and mouthpieces of party factions and political interest groups. The situation is less extreme in this respect, today, to be sure. But this was not the case in Europe, however, and especially in Romania between the two world wars was it not the case.

No informed person in the West today needs to be convinced of the power of the communications media for good, or for bad, purposes, or of its ability to shape, modify, heighten, or stimulate public attitudes and receptivity. *Repetitio est mater studiorum* runs the time-honored phrase, and nowhere is this more evident than in the bombardment of people's minds a thousand times a year from a score of directions. It may mean the automatous linking of the Mafia and men of Italian ancestry, of the quality of inscrutability with the Chinese, of Prussian characteristics with Germans, money-grubbing and haggling with Jews, and thus "advertising" and deliberate repetition of associations serve to reinforce stereotypical thinking. In the same way, the media can produce a reflex action creating the belief that one man's name and "Nazi" are synonymous.

"Rabbi Brands Bishop a War Criminal" (16 point type)
"Bishop Declares Charge is False" (10 point type)
"Rabbi Lays War Crimes to Bishop" (1962)
"Says Detroit Bishop Was Nazi" (1962)
"N.Y. Congressman Demands US Government Investigate 'Bishop Valerian' Trifa" (1962)
"Call Bishop in U.S. War Criminal" (1962)
" 'Nazi Bishop' Story Called Propaganda" (1962)
"Rumanian Bishop Who Served Nazis, Now in U.S." (1962)
"Bishop Admits Past Pro-Fascist Ties" (1972)
" 'Rumanian Bishop Admits He Directed Pro-Hitler Group" (1972)
"Witnesses Recount Iron Guard Bestialities: Trifa's Admission of Fascist Ties Provides Missing Link" (1972)
"Bishop Under Inquiry on Atrocity Link" (1973)
"Bishop in U.S. Is Under Investigation on Possible Tie to Fascist Atrocities" (1973)
"Prelate Denies Connection With Pogroms of 40's" (1973)
"Atrocity Charges Leveled at Bishop" (1973)
"Bishop Fights Deportation to Romania" (1973)
"Bishop in U.S. is Identified as Young Fascist in Romania" (1973)
"U.S. Reviews Romanian Bishop's Citizenship After Atrocity Charge" (1973)
"Anti-Semitism charges denied by Romanian Bishop" (1973)
"U.S. Reviews Naturalization of Rumanian pogrom suspect" (1973)
"Bishop Denies War Crimes Fights" (1973)
"Nazi Criminals in U.S. Probed" (followed by one picture: that of Trifa) (1973)
"Bishop Trifa's Link to Iron Guard Atrocities Studied" (1974)
"Trifa's Citizenship in Jeopardy: Rabbi Rosen calls for Justice" (1974)
"Bishop Due Here is Facing Charges in War Atrocities" (1975)
"United States Bishop Tied to 1941 War Crimes" (1975)
"Trifa was Killer of Jews, Rabbi Rosen Tells Investigator" (1975)
"Visiting Bishop Called Ex-Nazi" (1975)
"Romanian Bishop Faces Deportation in Slaying of Jews" (1976)

"National Church Panel to Weigh Membership of Suspected For-
mer Nazi" (1976)
"Bishop Censored on Nazi Charges" (1976)
"Michigan Bishop Censored as Nazi Killer" (1976)
"Searching for Jew-Baiting Trifa" (1977)
"Trifa's Terrors Jolted Sculptor's Memory" (1977)

The list could easily be extended through the fall of 1980, but this
should suffice. It is a mere sampling out of literally thousands of similar headlines, captions, or lead-ins published in the Western press in
two decades. We have ignored, even, the more sensationalist material
which sprang from Nicholas Martin's pen for years in the early 1950s.
The above appeared, furthermore, not merely in the yellow press of
the supermarket racks, but in respected papers of general circulation
and subscription entering every American home from New York
City to Winnipeg, from Detroit to Toronto, Jackson, Chicago, Regina,
Akron, Los Angeles, Indianapolis, Easton, Washington, Cleveland,
Miami, Lansing, Philadelphia, Rochester, St. Louis, San Jose, to Paris
and Tel Aviv. It has been what is termed "saturation coverage." If
there is any chance that regular readers of the nation's press failed to
have it planted in their minds that "Trifa" and "Nazi" were somehow
connected, it was not for want of effort. And whether intended or
incidental, the effect is the same.

To this must be added the electronic media. During 1976 and
1977 Howard Blum was catapulted onto every possible talk show on
radio and television throughout the United States and Canada. In all
his appearances Blum gave prominence most of all to Trifa's case. In
a majority of cases, Trifa was the only "Nazi War Criminal" Blum
talked about. He blasted the Bishop with epithets such as "Nazi,
guilty of Pogroms in Which Thousands of Jews Died." In Chicago,
Blum mentioned the number of victims as at least 30,000. Audiences
at his personal appearance tours rose as the number of victims rose,
Dr. Kremer followed in Blum's footsteps. During 1977 he was all
over the country for special interviews on radio and television, while
in March, 1976, Simon Wiesenthal toured the United States, lecturing in a dozen cities, and giving repeated attention to the name of
Trifa in the questioning periods following his speech on the work of
his Vienna documentation center. Interestingly, however, Wiesenthal
prior to 1973 at a luncheon in New York at which he met with David
Horowitz and the American Zionist Federation, Wiesenthal had never
before mentioned Trifa as a war criminal. In his own bulletin for
January 31, 1977, Wiesenthal writes that his information on Trifa

came primarily from Dr. Kremer.[22] However, appearing on the NBC Today Show with Barbara Walters and on NBC's Tomorrow program in the spring of 1976, Wiesenthal again mentioned Trifa as "co-responsible for a pogrom in Romania." Visiting Montreal, he told a press conference that "Iron Guard Commander" Trifa was planning to move to Canada. This triggered headlines in Canadian newspapers and Jewish protests to the Immigration Department in Ottawa.[23] Such involvement by perhaps the most prominent "Nazi-hunter" in the world was, of course, devastating in terms of the public association of Trifa and war criminals. Yet again it should be stressed that, were Trifa truly the prominent "Nazi" portrayed by the deluge of print and talk shows, why did the chief of the Vienna Documentation Center get into the case only in 1973?

One tally of the number of broadcasts during 1976-1977 alone dealing with Nazis in America or directly referring to Trifa on public television, interview programs, news broadcasts, spot announcements and the like counted at least fifty widely heard or viewed transmissions. A vital question is, who was telling the other side of the story, trying to establish a bit of perspective? For the most part, no one. Trifa by and large refused to give interviews, for obvious reasons. Either the lead-ins or the background material would be the occasion to frame the interview against the background of pogroms, war crimes, and atrocities, or the headline would sing of "Bishop Says He's Not a Nazi," and the same cause would be served. The efforts of his church organizations, such as the Orthodox Brotherhood, the *Arfora* (National Organization of Romanian Ladies' Auxiliaries), or AROY (American Romanian Orthodox Youth) were useful as far as they went, but their publications and protests could not command national network time nor more than limited space in letters-to-the-editor columns here and there. Even elementary students of mass persuasion techniques know that a major factor in its success is that there has been no counter-propaganda.[24]

The Encoders

It is not our task here to repeat the ample stock of research over the past decades centered on message distortion by communicators, whether they be newspaper reporters, advertising copywriters, or broadcasters. The number of articles, books, graduate school theses, and columns devoted to communicator accuracy, the cognitive stress which bears upon it, and the biases and predispositions which determine what encoders do to messages would fill a library. In the same manner, studies investigating audience consumption, message exaggeration (seldom message minimization) and the fundamental role of the mass media in the very socialization process itself are replete with data sufficiently copious to convince even the most skeptical that mind management by the mass media in the advanced industrial age is not only a very real phenomenon, but that its dangers are the more real because the public at large is so blithely unaware of it.[25] Few of those who read and seek to understand their world systematically or dare to call themselves members of the intellectual community would argue that the content of the majority of popular media programs or articles are "light, superficial, trivial, and in some cases vulgar and even harmful."[26] There is little chance that the majority of the American public will read this, or any other book of serious import. Somewhere it is written, "God preserve us from the man who forms his fundamental ideas from the pages of the daily newspaper." Yet this is indeed the case in our society, and represents a far more threatening situation to our future as free people than a few dozen aging Nazi war criminals, real or imagined. The Trifa case, indeed, is the living example of it.

When one hears the familiar cliche', "I only know what I read in the newspapers," it is revelatory of the essence of the problem. Even when various polls are not being used for mind management, the fact that the average individual has neither the time nor the disposition to pursue information on his own works against anyone accused in the public press. Joseph Klapper, director of social research for the Columbia Broadcasting System, observed in 1967:

> . . . There is another area in which mass communication is extremely effective, and *that is in the creation of opinion on new issues*. By "new issues" I mean issues on which the individual has no opinion and on which his friends and fellow group members have no opinion. The reason for the effectiveness of mass communication in creating opinions on new issues is pretty obvious: The *individual has no predisposition to defend, and so the communication falls, as it were, on defenseless soil*. And once the opinion is created, then it is this new opinion which becomes easy to reinforce and hard to change. This process of opinion-creation is strongest, by the way, when the person has no other source of information on the topic to use as a touchstone. He is therefore the more wholly dependent on the communication in question.[27]

One might ask, from where does the average American reader or auditor gain his information about Romania in the 1930s, about the meaning and definition of fascism, about the truths of this or that person's politics and past in another time and another world. How

does Mr. Brown or Jones form an opinion, in other words, objective
and unbiased about Valerian Trifa? He doesn't. He is one of those
termed by Charles R. Wright as "the susceptibles." The socialization
process to which he has been subjected most of his life by everything
he has read and heard and been taught has predisposed him to three
fundamental notions: 1) "Nazi," means, automatically, bad; 2) Jewish
groups, seeking to exact justice for crimes of the past, are morally
and ethically justified in pursuing individuals identified as Nazis; 3)
the constant repetition of one man's name in the media, linked with
the term "Nazi" must prove an association between him and "bad."
One might add a fourth assumption, basic to legions of Americans:
"If it's printed, it must be so; they couldn't put it in the paper if it
weren't true, could they?" Because most readers are not at all source-
conscious of what they peruse, and they dissociate content and
source in their own mind, arguments repeated often enough change
their opinions, or, more likely, provide them from the outset. Mr.
Jones is saved the effort of thought and interpretation. It is packaged,
canned, and doled out to him in easily digestible bits.[28]

F. Lee Bailey has demonstrated effectively the impact of pre-trial
publicity on the judicial process, both from the positive and negative
side.[29] The trier of fact in a courtroom must reach his conclusions as
to a defendant's guilt only on the basis of evidence presented in
open court, and not on any outside influence. If a judge or jury
members are exposed to material beforehand, and this material is
not eventually admitted as evidence, then the defendant's right to a
fair trial is violated. Carolyn Jaffe cites the Supreme Court in *Marshall
v. United States*:

> The prejudice to the defendant is almost certain to be as
> great when that evidence reaches the jury through news ac-
> counts as when it is a part of the prosecution's evidence.[30]

How many jurors might one find who have not, in some shape,
manner, or form, heard media accounts of the case of Valerian Trifa?
They have had thirty years to do so. Moreover, evidence of "a defendant's alleged criminal activities unrelated to the crime for which he is
being tried is ordinarily inadmissible in court."[31] How easy it is to forget that Trifa's legal case centers around one issue: lies told at a
naturalization hearing. It has nothing to do with war crimes, murders
of Jews, or Nazi activities. The legal issue centers on one item. It is
the press which insists the case is a judgment on Trifa's whole life,
and the entire scope and intent of Romanian history for thirty years
prior to 1941. What is called "miscellaneous inflammatory material"

in the standard categorization of evidentiary matter which is prejudicial to the right to a fair trial, has been, in the Trifa case, the standard fare of millions of readers for years. "Surely only a perverted form of justice would permit jurors (or a judge) to be aware via news media of information which that same justice forbids those jurors to take cognizance of in open court."[32] Justice Frankfurter put it well:

> In securing freedom of speech, the Constitution hardly meant to create the right to influence judges and juries. That is no more freedom of speech than stuffing a ballot box is an exercise of the right to vote.[33]

Again, advances in sociological analysis and the scientific study of the manufacturing of public opinion(s) made since the Second World War are replete with examples of the impact of media coverage on trials and courtroom determinations. Joseph T. Klapper and Charles Y. Glock have shown by a content analysis of nine New York newspapers which covered the celebrated "Condon case" how "the background material for use in the running news stories had the effect of building up the case against Dr. Condon, but did not build up his defense to anywhere near the same degree."[34] Martin Millspaugh's widely circulated article on "Trial by Mass Media?" illustrates clearly that the stimulus of four Baltimore newspapers covering the murder trial of a black man was clearly not calculated "to bring an impartial public opinion to bear on the trial" in the facts presented to potential white jurors. In this case also, the Baltimore Supreme Bench convicted three radio stations of contempt in obstructing justice for the "indelible effect on the public mind" which they created prior to the trial.[35] The situation has not fundamentally changed since the days of the above cases. From the trial of Dr. Sam Sheppard to press coverage of the 1967 Detroit Riot to that of the 1968 Democratic Convention to the handling by the press of the Jack Ruby case, no end of examples exist to bring home to Americans what Richard B. Morris calls "the failure of the judicial process to bar from the courtroom outside pressures that preclude a dispassionate administration of justice." The distinguished American historian might be addressing the Trifa case itself when he writes in 1967:

> The supercharged emotional atmosphere in which trials with political overtones are too often conducted had in earlier years also hung over courtrooms hearing labor cases and still too often infects trials where the accused is from a minority group.[36]

Indeed, we need not return to the New Orleans lynching trial of the 1890s, or the Hall-Mills or Sacco and Vanzetti era to find trials which assume the character of a sporting event or a circus performance. We have only to listen to one of Dr. Kremer's emotional tapes or see strutting storm troopers moving across our TV screens against the air of *Horst Wessel Lied* with a picture of a Michigan bishop superimposed, fade-in, fade-out, then gaze at piles of bodies being buried by tractored bulldozers at Auschwitz.

Nazi-Mania and Holocaustism

One Romanian Orthodox parish declaration put it concisely: "Telling Frightening Nazi Stories is Big Business These Days."[37] Since 1945, or at least since the Nuremberg trials with their revelations of inhuman atrocities, the subject of Nazis and the Third Reich, for whatever reasons, has never failed to exert a fascination on the Western mind. In literature, film, radio, television, and the daily paper, both fiction and non-fiction, critical, satirical, romantic, even propagandistic, accounts of Germans and Germany have never lacked for an audience. This is part of the very socialization process itself for what now makes up at least three generations of Americans born either during or after the war. For at least forty years, since our entry into the conflict against the Axis powers, the social, emotional, and intellectual environment of America has conditioned people to hold a negative, pejorative, even disgusted image of Hitler's Germany and all its works. This may well be as it should. The point here is simply that "Nazi" is one of the codewords guaranteed to produce an attitude of revulsion in the minds of the public. More "susceptibles"— indeed, an entire population, is a ready-made market for information which is sensationalistic, exciting, and phlogenetic. Although this general "anti-Nazism" which became one of the givens of the Western mentality tended to subside during the McCarthy years, when fear of communism and bolshevik subversion replaced it for a time, it has always been easily resurrected and, as with most "popular" subjects, is subject to recurrent trends and cycles. Furthermore, aversion to communism and a mind-set producing instant mental repugnance against the persecutions and mass murders carried on by communist regimes never has seemed to take root as deeply as the anti-Nazi syndrome, perhaps because most Americans never had any direct contact with communist regimes, whereas many thousands had the occasion to be part of the Allied armies in Germany at the end of the war. Yet the Cuban missile crisis, the Berlin Wall, the new awareness of an active-aggressive America combatting communism around the globe which the administration of John F. Kennedy produced did much to heighten public consciousness of a common American mentality in this regard, and the 1960s saw the active "anti-Nazism" of the immediate postwar years subside.[38] As domestic concerns replaced international ones among the priorities of the American public, however, in the 1970s, as Vietnam ended, "detente" began, China was suddenly America's friend, and Israel fought two "preventive wars" against her neighbors, once again the focus shifted. The 70s brought, in the penny press, the supermarket and department store newsstands, and on the flickering indoctrination box before which millions of Huxley's brave new men spent their days and nights, the upsurge of Nazi-mania in all its paralgesic splendor.

To be sure, though, the proliferation of Nazi-oriented material, at least in the area of popular literature, contained a new emphasis. In addition to the plethora of serious studies of the Hitlerian era and events in Europe themselves, a rash of books emerged focusing on the Nazi emigration, the ex-Nazi chieftains in exile, hiding out in the cities and jungles of South America, posing, with new identities, in innocuous civil service jobs in postwar Germany, or enjoying the good life as respectable Westphalian bankers or prosperous owners of Paraguayan *estancias* with the profits of secret caches of Nazi gold and investments carefully planned by Martin Bormann and the resources of the *Kameradschaft*, which smuggled thousands of Hitler's minions out of the devastated Reich. Most popular were stories with the theme of Nazis hiding out in America.

So many works of this kind, differing only in names and plot convolutions, have appeared in the past decade that merely to name them all would require many pages of print. They have taken on the character of a literary *genre*, akin to the murder-mystery of Agatha Christie, the western of Louis Lamour, or the insipid Harlequin romance. Consider the dust jacket content description from the September, 1980 Pocket Books edition of Harold King's *Closing Ceremonies*, and let it stand for all:

Opening Ceremonies: Berlin, 1936
Adolf Hitler's Olympics commence, and a young athlete—Eduard Reichmann—dedicates his life to his Fuehrer.

Paraguay, 1976
In a daring raid on a secret Nazi shrine, three invaders die. One—Aaron Miller—escapes with an awesome relic: the urn containing Hitler's ashes.

Now the last terrified Nazi chieftains have set loose *Das Kettenhund* to retrieve it—Hitler's "Chain Dog," Eduard Reichmann.

But Reichmann has a plan of his own—a plan that requires the death of a world leader . . . a plan that will pit him against the secret agents of several nations . . . against his fellow Nazis. . . against his own long-thwarted needs. . . against a beautiful, tormented Nazi-hunter. . . and against a vengeance-obsessed American named Aaron Miller.

Soon they will meet, in an unscheduled Olympic contest-to the death. In the final seconds of the Closing Ceremonies.[39]

Browse through the paperback shelves of any bookstore, drugstore, supermarket, or publishers' overrun catalogues in America, and one may find with no effort, at any given moment, half a dozen titles belonging to the Nazi-mania *genre*; they are easily identified, for almost invariably there will be a *swastika* somehow embodied in the cover design. The following list is a random sampling, gathered over a period of a few weeks, and resulting from no particular search. A concerted effort to produce a comprehensive list would result, undoubtedly, in a hundred titles.

Ladislas Farago, *The Game of the Foxes*	(1971)
Robert Ludlum, *The Scarlatti Inheritance*	(1971)
Frederick Forsyth, *The Odessa File*	(1972)
Aldo Lucchesi, *Feast of the Jackals*	(1972)
Ross Macdonald, *The Dark Tunnel*	(1972)
Charles Whiting, *The Hunt for Martin Bormann*	(1973)
William Goldman, *Marathon Man*	(1974)
Ladislas Farago, *Aftermath: Martin Bormann and the Fourth Reich*	(1974)
Robert Ludlum, *The Rhinemann Exchange*	(1974)
Thomas Gifford, *The Wind Chill Factor*	(1975)
Isser Harel, *The House on Garibaldi Street*	(1975)
Howard Blum, *Wanted! The Search for Nazis in America*	(1976)
Len Deighton, *Funeral in Berlin*	(1976)
Al Dempsey and Robin Moore, *The Red Falcons*	(1976)
Ira Levin, *The Boys from Brazil*	(1976)
Jack Higgins, *Storm Warning*	(1976)
Madelaine Duke, *The Bormann Receipt*	(1977)
Erich Erdstein, *Inside the Fourth Reich*	(1977)
Robert Ludlum, *The Chancellor Manuscript*	(1977)
Trevanian, *The Loo Sanction*	(1977)
Michael Barak, *The Enigma*	(1978)
Oliver Crawford, *The Execution*	(1978)
Len Deighton, *SS-GB*	(1978)
Robert L. Fish, *Pursuit*	(1978)
Jack Higgins, *The Eagle Has Landed*	(1978)
Hans Hellmut Kirst, *The Affair of the Generals*	(1978)
John Lee, *The Thirteenth Hour*	(1978)
Herbert Lieberman, *The Climate of Hell*	(1978)

Robert Ludlum, *The Holcroft Covenant*	(1978)
Ben Stein, *The Croesus Conspiracy*	(1978)
Craig Thomas, *Wolfsbane*	(1978)
Joseph Borkin, *The Crime and Punishment of I.G. Farben*	(1979)
Louis Charbonneau, *The Lair*	(1979)
Gillian Freeman, *Diary of a Nazi Lady*	(1979)
Ken Follett, *The Eye of the Needle*	(1979)
John Lee, *The Ninth Man*	(1979)
Joseph E. Persico, *Piercing the Reich*	(1979)
Harry Patterson, *To Catch a King*	(1979)
James and Suzanne Pool, *Who Financed Hitler?*	(1979)
Steve Shagan, *The Formula*	(1979)
Paul Spike, *The Night Letter*	(1979)
James Herbert, *The Spear*	(1980)
Robert Holles, *Spawn*	(1980)
Thomas Horstman, *The Kessler Alliance*	(1980)
Stephen Hunter, *The Master Sniper*	(1980)
Eugen Kogon, *The Theory and Practice of Hell*	(1980)
Max Lamb and Harry Sanford, *The Last Nazi*	(1980)
Ib Melchior, *The Watchdogs of Abaddan*	(1980)
Boris T. Pash, *The Alsos Mission*	(1980)
Mike Pettit, *The Axmann Agenda*	(1980)
Philippe Van Rjndt, *The Trial of Adolf Hitler*	(1980)

The given dates are those for the original appearance of the books. In addition to selling in the millions of copies, they have gone into second and third editions, are printed and reprinted. While most are fiction or semi-fiction, even those offered as serious studies contain enough of the atmosphere of the Nazi spy *genre* to qualify for such a list. Besides this, there is the uncountable number of Sunday supplement features, yellow press exposés, and titillating or sensationary little pieces in a thousand places throughout America, bought and read with avid interest by an untold number of people each day during the same ten years.

In addition to the excoriating headlines and news articles centering on Trifa listed earlier, there has been no dearth of journalistic pieces of a broader nature, calling attention to the Nazi-in-hiding theme. Such is the tone of:

"Nazi War Criminal Hunt Pressed in United States"—the *Los Angeles Examiner*, December 31, 1973.

"Nazi Criminals in the United States Probed"—*Chicago Sun Times*, December 31, 1973.

"Ghosts of the Past are Haunting Suspected Nazis in United States"—*Washington Star*

"The Nazis Next Door"—*New York Daily News*, July 14, 1974.

"Nazi Fugitives in the United States," *Police Gazette*, January, 1975.

"War Criminals," *Washington Star*, May 25, 1975.

"Israel Sifts Nazi Data for United States," *New York Post*, June 15, 1975.

"Nazi Hunting in America," *The Times of Israel and World Jewish Review*, October, 1975.

"The Hunt for an American Nazi," *Esquire Magazine*, October, 1976. (A reprint of the chapter "The Bishop and the Dentist" from Blum's *Wanted!*)

One of the best-timed "studies" appeared in the summer of 1980, in the *Monthly Detroit* magazine. Handed out in the various packets to thousands of delegates to the Republican National Convention was this timely publication, which on pages 62-70 contained Victor Livingston's damning article, led off by letters three-fourths of an inch tall: BISHOP TRIFA: PRELATE OR PERSECTOR?

In addition to the usual numerous errors in the historical discussion of the Legionary Movement, the thrust of this article, more than most, sought to convince the reader that the "Iron Guard" was not merely a historical epiphenomenon of interwar Carlist Romania, but that it was alive and well today in the United States. Using a twelve-year old picture of young boys saluting at a Codreanu memorial service in Detroit, dwelling on interviews with ex-Guardists in their apartments full of Sima-Codreanu memorabilia, and failing to distinguish between the expectable reminiscences of old men with a natural tendency toward a certain thrasonical and jaded pre-war nationalism in their conversation, Livingston's assemblage of facts and quotations, given without context or qualifications, amount to a more than usually vivid installment of Nazi-mania. One sample will suffice. On page 66 is the line: "Trifa appears repeatedly in Horia Sima's *History of the Legionnaire Movement*." It is not explained that in most places, Sima is critical of Trifa for not cooperating with him better.

Students of mass psychology and the audience perception of media messages would have little difficulty categorizing this sub-species of Nazi-mania article, i.e., the type which not only *identifies* "Nazis" in the midst of the population but adds the element that they are actively working *today* to resurrect their old organizations, build up a network of power, and thus, by implication, launch some action which threatens the United States—or selected portions of the population. It is little more than the stock conspiracy story given additional reality by placing it in the immediate present and dwelling on living persons, rather than couching it in terms of something now over and done with, in the past. Taken as a national phenomenality, the sum total of Nazi-mania outpourings over a period of years serve to create *social anxiety* in the population. A sense of urgency is generated when the mass media insistently hammers away at people with dramatic accounts of the worsening and seemingly insoluble social problems of crime, juvenile delinquency, drugs, moral turpitude of public officials, or, the actively plotting Nazis in our midst. The result is to make people

> impatient with a slow, objective, and dispassionate scientific orientation toward the problems and encourage a search for immediate opinions and social remedies.[40]

Such controlled presentation falls into the *repertorium* of the well-known study by Janis and Feshbach on the effects of fear-arousing communications.[41] While not highly personalized in their audience appeal (with the exception, perhaps, of the heightened sensibilities of Jewish readers) still to the general population there is a sufficiency of personalized threat-references explicitly directed at the audience, i.e., implications that "this can happen to you." So we glance at the picture of the suspicious bishop.[42] Equally if not even more devastating to a man facing a lengthy court ordeal was the sheer bad luck of having his case come to trial just at the apogee of one of the strongest revivals of Holocaust-ism in recent decades in America.

During 1978, the "Holocaust" was commercially wrapped, packaged, and sold like a laundry detergent. For four days in April, as Henry Feingold accurately noted:

> One could not avoid the Holocaust even if one wanted to. It was everywhere. In New York City the newspaper of largest circulation, the *Daily News*, serialized Gerald Green's book version of the screenplay. Throughout the nation newspapers featured Holocaust supplements. Jewish and non-Jewish agencies printed thousands of brochures to help "teach" the Holocaust in tandem with the TV production . . . .

> The professionals knew how to break through to the public. A major TV network had after all set aside nine hours of expensive prime viewing time on four consecutive days to tell the TV viewing public about what befell European Jewry during the war. Everything from the pre-showing saturation promotional campaign to the idea of a daily sequence in prime time (called a mini-series by the pros) was designed for maximum impact.[43]

There was no intended or intrinsic connection between the Trifa case or the Nazi cases and incredible flurry to promote Holocaust memories that year. Nevertheless the result was obvious enough. Nazis and alleged Nazis would get even more of a battering from the press than ever, and public sensitivity to the whole issue would be heightened more than in years. Social anger, if not social anxiety, was again aroused by the hawkers of demonic Nazis and innocent Jewish victims. In fact, even before the airing of the famed NBC program on April 16 through 19, numerous Jewish individuals and agencies were disturbed over the lack of authenticity of the script, and expressed distress at the promotional campaign which they saw as not only tending to fictionalize, but trivialize a crucial event in Jewish history.

We know that a consortium of fifteen Jewish agencies headed by the Jewish Welfare Board was given no input into the production, despite their remonstrations, and was presented with a *fait accompli* by the time the previews were ready. Henry Feingold's review is so to the mark that it deserves repeating *in extenso*:

> For the millions of dollars NBC spent . . . it has received. . . a slick professional package which misses few tricks in the manipulative art of tugging at the public heart strings. What has happened is that commercial television has discovered a technique and a theme for exploitation. There is a story line which is promoted as being based on "true" facts but is actually a skillful veiling of the line between truth and fiction to produce a plot that might have happened that way, something that is factual in its parts yet completely fictional in its essence. That technique is then applied to an ethnic grievance for commercial exploitation. Undoubtedly something about the saga of the American Indian, the Irish potato famine and the "troubles" or perhaps the suffering of Japanese Americans interned during the war is already on the drawing boards. . . .
>
> To find a plot connection between [various isolated events] and also between the personalities involved. . . Green is compelled to become a contortionist. Thus, while it may be true that the individual incidents are based on fact, the story in its entirety is the most improbable fiction.

Addressing the question of whether or not it is at least better to have had this type of program than none at all, Feingold might well be writing not of the Holocaust, but of the entire subject of our study here, the Trifa case:

> The problem with such priorities is that they are based on a rather narrow view of how the public can be taught an historical event. Direct telling of everything with no heed to meaning leads to dreadful over-simplification of complex issues until one begins to wonder if fictionalized history is not worse than no history at all.[44]

Indeed. And moreover, such "history" may well *inure* the public to a lack of any true understanding of such an important and complex event. Any teacher of American history who has ever tried to give to his sophomore students a serious and scholarly picture of the settlement of the American West knows exactly the problem. He is fighting the awesome impact of untold miles of cinema footage which has little concern for the Turner thesis.

Nevertheless, bad history or not, the spring of 1978 produced for militant American Jews what could not have been an undesired effect. Although awareness of the Holocaust as a distinct subject of study, lectures, literature, and popular media programming had been growing during the decade, proliferation of Holocaust-related activities in the United States and the Western world literally snowballed.[45] Suddenly there were Holocaust newsletters, funded by the National Endowment for the Humanities. The first issue of *Shoah* announced an "Annual Scholars' Conference" on the Holocaust in New York, and Regional Conferences in Tulsa, Dallas, and San Jose. The Jewish Media Service reported evaluative material to lend on hundreds of films dealing with the Holocaust. Editorial boards for input into such newsletters and anticipated journals were composed of persons from a dozen different colleges. Specific new courses for credit in American colleges and universities, centering on the Holocaust, were added to those previously offered at institutions such as Temple and Boston University.[46] Learning packets were developed for elementary and secondary schools.

Then came July 3, 1979. Following ten hours of intense debate, the West German Bundestag voted 255-222 to abolish the statute of limitations on the prosecution of individuals sought for or accused of war crimes. Only a few months earlier public opinion polls showed an overwhelming majority of Germans opposed to any law extending or abolishing the time limit for Nazi criminals. One writer at least gave direct credit to "the immediacy of the NBC series" in changing German opinion, although this may be somewhat of an overstatement. The same piece referred to "Cardinal Treifa (U.S.)."[47] Yet such a thoughtful decision in Bonn was symptomatic of the far-flung success of those spreading the Holocaust message, after a mere couple of years. Neo-Nazi groups in Munich or in Skokie, Illinois could also be counted

on periodically to stir up passions with requests for parade or demonstration permits.

If one had no choice in the matter, as Trifa did not, and was forced
to confront a denaturalization suit with overtones of Nazism and
Holocaustism, all this was hardly the emotional, psychological-societal
climate conducive to assuring a fair hearing. Along with this general
environment, intensified by untold specific linking of the bishop's
name with "Nazi" there were other occasions when popular literature
and television did more than imply that Trifa was what the allegations
said he was; it was frankly stated as fact. A sampling of the 1979-
1980 material will be more than enough.

For the sensation-hungry there was the *Star*, which on March 13,
1980, on page 21, under the heading "Decent U.S. Citizens—or Nazi
Butchers?" splashed a leadline, "Devout churchman named as 'Ivan
the Terrible' who gassed 500,000 people." Underneath was Trifa's
picture, captioned "Thousands killed." In fact, the article centered
on John Demjanjuk, said to have been a guard at Treblinka, who is
now an officer of the Ukrainian Orthodox Church. Demjanjuk is pic-
tured in normal clothing, while Trifa's picture has him in clerical garb.
Who is to know at whom the headline is aimed?[48]

For the slightly more literate devourer of the spy/terrorist international agent and plot novel, the summer of 1980 had much to offer,
including a paperback book which asked, on page one:

> But what of the many former Nazis now living in America?
> Estimates of their number range from thirty-eight to several
> hundred, depending on their reported Nazi rank. Their Ameri-
> can identities run the gamut; from retired "businessmen," car-
> penters and housekeepers to one man who holds a high position
> in a religious order.[49]

If this were not plain enough, as the novel develops and the Soviet
assassination team working to "sanction" the "top Nazis in the U.S.A."
begins to close in on its prey, the bad guys, scurrying around to find
new hideouts, keep making telephone calls to a never-seen churchman
in Michigan to get new orders.

For the even more literate, but sometimes gullible, consumers of
the products of so-called investigative reporting, there was Jack
Anderson. On December 6, 1979, in a nation-wide broadcast over
ABC's "Good Morning America," Anderson stated

> First, let me tell you about the war criminal. His name is
> Valerian Treifa (*sic*). . . . He was a leader of the Romanian Iron
> Guard which was aligned with the Nazis. He was sentenced to
> life in prison for his war crimes. . . . Today this mass murderer
> is a bishop in Detroit. . . .[50]

Blithely ignoring the fact that he had made wrong statements of fact, Anderson went on to state that on the previous evening a telephone interview with Trifa had been broadcast over Radio Free Europe, dealing with church matters and Romanian ethnic affairs. A White House aide, Paul Hents, had sanctioned the program, which was interpreted as official sanction of Trifa's presence. The "Good Morning America" segment closed with the news that Congresswoman Elizabeth Holtzman was now demanding that President Carter fire Hents. "In other words, the war criminal is now a church leader with a following, so the White House doesn't want to offend him."[51]

This was not the first time, however, that Anderson made statements of this kind. Seven months earlier on a May 17, 1979 morning show hosted by David Hartman, he made what one protester to the Federal Communications Commission called "vitriolic and libelous" statements about Trifa.[52] In response to one parishioner who asked why Trifa or someone in his diocese could not demand equal time for rebuttal, the FCC replied that equal time and the personal attack rule under Section 326 of the Communications Act do not apply to "bona fide news interviews."[53]

The high point of Trifa's trial in a public medium came the evening of January 13, 1980, with an ABC "News Closeup" Documentary entitled "Escape from Justice: Nazi War Criminals in the United States." During the hour long program, Trifa's picture was flashed on the screen several times, interspersed with qualifying remarks and pictures of piles of cadavers from German death camps.[54]

The newspaper promotion and reviews of the program were equally wrong-headed. "An ABC documentary tonight reports on war criminals who slipped into this country," announced the *Akron Beacon Journal.*[55] John J. O'Connor of the *New York Times* set the special theme in his preview article of "protection" enjoyed by the war criminals in the U.S., resurrecting old canards about Project Paperclip in the late 1940s whereby the U.S. brought German scientists to America after the war, which was hardly relevant to Trifa.[56]

Of course there were outraged protests from members of Trifa's church, and from Romanian-Americans unaffiliated with his diocese. These appeared with every major media revival of the case. Sometimes they were even printed.

To err is human indeed. To err repeatedly suggests either lack of competence or malevolence.

CHAPTER X

LARGE POLITICAL DIVIDENDS

Ralph B. Guy, Jr., United States Attorney, received the usual letter from Dr. Kremer early in 1973, offering his help and asking that denaturalization proceedings against Bishop Trifa be initiated.[1] Kremer somehow always assumed that whatever the government had on Trifa was superfluous, and if only it would look at *his* evidence, it would be convinced. Guy passed the message on to the Detroit office of the Immigration and Naturalization Service. On April 16, 1973, A.J. Salturelli, District Director of the INS, Detroit, answered Guy:

> Subsequent to Bishop Trifa's entry into the United States, charges against him were received by this Service. An extensive investigation on all such charges was thereafter conducted over a period of years. Although the inquiries were exhaustive in scope and nature, they failed to establish grounds upon which Bishop Trifa might be removed from the United States. . . .
>
> Bishop Trifa subsequently applied for naturalization and, in the course of the proceedings, all avenues of inquiry into the charges brought against him were again thoroughly explored. . . . The Court found him qualified for naturalization.
>
> After. . . Trifa's naturalization this Service again considered every scrap of information and evidence in his case, and concluded that there was insufficient evidence on which to base the institution of denaturalization proceedings. . . Dr. Kremer has been notified on numerous occasions. . . .[2]

Earlier, on March 2, James F. Greene, Associate Commissioner in charge of Operations and sometime Acting Commissioner of the Immigration and Naturalization Service in Washington, had used almost the same words in writing to Kremer—"all charges, accusations, and adverse information were presented . . . and there was insufficient evidence," to proceed against anyone.[3]

In the meantime, David Horowitz, of the World Union Press Syndicate in New York had also been corresponding with Salturelli and other officials. On April 5, 1973, Salturelli made it plain that only new testimony, witnesses who actually saw Trifa commit crimes, would justify reopening any case against him. The year before, Greene tried to satisfy Kremer by having the New York INS District Director interview him and receive copies of Kremer's "exhibits."[4] When Kremer finally put together all 88 of them and their receipt was acknowledged by the Justice Department, it was November, 1973.[5] Kremer had also contacted Senator Jacob Javits to put pressure on the INS, but as of mid-year Greene informed the Senator there had been "no developments in the interim" to alter things.[6] Kremer wrote to President Nixon and Attorney General Elliot Richardson anyway, because, as he told them, it was rumored that Trifa had "many friends" in the FBI and INS, who likely were covering for him.[7] Horowitz suggested to Salturelli that "maybe some of the investigators have erred *and possibly more than that.*"[8]

For Kremer and his correspondents, this series of round-robins had gone on for years, and might have continued to do so, but a number of factors began to coalesce in the early 1970s to produce a turning point. Crucial was the publication in the *New York Times* on December 26, 1973 of a wire service story that the Immigration Service was considering a review of Trifa's naturalization, even though judgmental documents by persons in high government positions abounded to the effect that there was no case to be made. What is important is that almost at once five hundred pages of material against Trifa was compiled by the Romanian Jewish Federation of America, the Anti-Defamation League of B'nai B'rith, Wiesenthal's center in Vienna, the *United Israeli Bulletin*, and unofficially, the Romanian government, and sent to Charles Gordon, general counsel of the INS.[9] This was not a cache of virgin material. When the government finally turned over the bulk of its material to Trifa's defense counsel, the INS files alone filled eight volumes. But even a cursory reading of these makes it plain that they contribute nothing new and different from what the INS and FBI had been hearing for the past 25 or 30 years. In fact it was plain that, given these eight volumes, in addition to the certified record of the government's case, that just about all of the material was given or brought or sent to the government agencies involved, and very few items bore evidence of having been the result of any active investigation or "thoroughgoing search."

Unbelievable as it may seem, even after the filing of the suit in 1975, the first time that the U.S. government apparently made the slightest overt effort in requesting information on the Trifa affair from the government of Romania was in January, 1978. Nearly three years went by before the country where Trifa's "crimes" supposedly took place was asked to cooperate and lend its resources. The simple fact seems to be that the INS, the FBI, and other agencies for some reason finally decided to bring suit in 1975. But aside from additional superfluous copies of 1950 documents which they already had, nothing new came forth. The "new" material and the "new" witnesses, after four years of the ongoing suit, were few indeed. By the summer of 1979, it was reported to the Romanian Church Congress in Michigan that thus far the government had deposed a grand total of three witnesses.[10] Who were the three? They were Sidney Freed, Rabbi Rosen, and Louis Varichione (who was in charge of the CIC clearance office in Italy). Their testimony was all on the books long before 1975. Even if we advance the theory that someone, somewhere, in the INS or Justice Department did truly believe they had a case to be made in 1975, without the necessity of any additional "discovery" period, the passage of three years *ipso facto* is highly suggestive that they were mistaken.

We must ask exactly why, after rejecting the pleas of Kremer and others for so many years, and after a decade of relative calm over Trifa and his past, was 1975 seen as the appropriate time to actually bring a suit which by rights should have been filed in 1955 or 1957, if it was to be filed at all?There is no one answer, but the key lies in the combination of circumstances—psychological, political, and diplomatic which began to coalesce in the early 1970s. For the sake of brevity, the ingredients may be labeled improved Romanian-American relations, the Yom Kippur War, Watergate, Constantin Antonovici, and Elizabeth Holtzman.

A new departure in relations between the United States and the Socialist Republic of Romania came about with the exchange of visits between Richard Nixon and Nicolae Ceauşescu during 1969-1970. In the years which followed programs of trade and cultural exchange grew rapidly. In 1972 the creation of the *Asociaţia România* (Romania Association), with its offices today at No. 35 Bulevard Dacia, was the occasion for much fanfare and publicity about the new improved relationship. The specific task of the Association was to promote tourism and travel from the United States for the ever-expanding tourist industry, and to facilitate arrangements for scholarly exchanges, joint symposia, and the like. Romania's concerted drive to acquire Western currencies for industrial expansion and to bolster her decade-old policy of growing economic differentiation from the Soviet bloc by 1975 found her seeking the coveted status of most-favored-nation trading partner with the United States—a desideratum which the visit to

Romania of Gerald Ford and the passage of the Trade Act of 1974 helped to bring closer. Thus by the middle of the decade the Romanian regime had more reason than ever before to appear amenable and cooperative in the eyes of the United States Congress.

At the same time, as always, any Romanian policy reorientation had its counterpart in the dealings of the Romanian Patriarchate with the Romanian-American churches headed by Trifa. The Romanian Church, completely under state control, was expected to follow the new line and warm up to the Americans. One can almost sympathize with the Patriarchate's dilemma in the early '70s. On the one hand, the firm alignment with the Orthodox Church in America to which Trifa had brought the Vatra Episcopate precluded, perhaps forever, any re-establishment of relations, canonically or otherwise, with the mother church in Romania. The Romanian Holy Synod, like the hierarchy of the Greek Orthodox Church in Europe, refused to recognize the existence of the OCA or its right to enroll ethnic denominations in America, thus cutting them off from their European connections. Trifa's entire career as a churchman had produced an autocephalous, self-governed American-Romanian church establishment, whose very existence was an embarrassment and an affront to the Bucharest regime. His uncompromising anti-communism remained as firm in 1970 as in 1950.[11] On the other hand, there was the new climate of relations. The Holy Synod's solution, as always, was a type of farraginous carrot-and-stick diplomacy which, at least from Trifa's standpoint, had the advantage of being nearly completely transparent.

One major move by 1974 was the recall to Romania of the Archimandrite Bartolemeu Anania, a political churchman who had spent some years in Detroit editing the official newspaper of the Romanian Orthodox Missionary Archdiocese, the small Romanian-American Episcopate which had remained canonically tied to Bucharest and was now led by Archbishop Victorin Ursache, successor to Andrei Moldovan. Anania seldom missed a chance to villify Trifa in the pages of *Credinţa*, and his removal signaled a new approach from Romania.

At a theological conference in Bucharest that year, Father John Meyendorff of St. Vladimir's Seminary in New York was told to urge Trifa to initiate correspondence with Patriarch Justinian Marina, who supposedly was now disposed toward "full freedom" for the Romanian-American churches if the "canonical obstacles" could be obviated.[12] But this was hardly new. Removing such obstacles meant that Trifa should withdraw from the OCA, which he would never do.

In July, 1974, Trifa talked with the Patriarchate's representative to the World Council of Churches at the Vatra. Recognize the OCA, Trifa argued, and advise all Romanian parishes under Bucharest's control to join it.[13] In September, while on a visit to Romania, Attorney John Sibişan delivered a letter from Trifa to Justinian to this effect.[14] But here matters stalled, for it was the usual ploy from Patriarch hill.

While apparently engaged in amicable discussions of the gulf between it and the majority of the Romanian-American faithful, Bucharest lent overt support to Father Mihail Iancu in Detroit who was actively seeking to break his parish away from Trifa's jurisdiction by resorting to court action and a public relations campaign designed to alienate hundreds of parishioners.[15] During 1975, in Los Angeles, efforts of the Missionary Archdiocese to disrupt another of Trifa's churches and form a splinter congregation elsewhere were also partially success-ful.[16] Meanwhile Trifa was not idle. In a widely-circulated "Open Letter" to the new Romanian Association he raised embarrassing questions as to why Romanian citizens did not enjoy freedom of travel and movement, while noting that the vaunted "Romanian-ness" preached by the Association depended on the degree of eco-nomic gain which the state sought from those nations where Roman-ians lived.[17] Moreover during 1972 in Paris the staff of the Roman-ian Embassy walked into the Romanian Chapel and tried to install a priest of its own under less than pacific circumstances; following this the Patriarchate set up a new Romanian Orthodox Diocese of France, with its own hand-picked bishop.[18] At the end of 1972 Trifa informed the Romanian Church that the "entire strategy of the Patriarch's representatives here in America was and is to break par-ishes, to create disorder and to attack me personally in all things and by all means," which if it were not the absolute truth, remained not far off the mark.[19] Thus after a series of overtures which amounted to no essential change of policy during 1972-1975, the Romanian regime had gotten nowhere in weakening Trifa's Episcopate. It con-tinued to support Mihail Iancu, even when he lost his case to the Vatra Episcopate in the Supreme Court of Michigan, and as late as the autumn of 1977 when Nicolae Corneanu, Bishop of the Banat, visited Trifa in Grass Lake, his message was that Bucharest was now willing to recognize the Orthodox Church in America if Valerian would return his diocese to the jurisdiction of the Romanian Patriarchate.

Unable to garner the submission or financial control (there was the heart of the matter) of Trifa's diocese, Bucharest saw another avenue of approach. There continued to be agitation in America over the Nazi business. The state wished to gain good will in Washington. What better way to support the move to denaturalize Trifa, as Romania had done in the days of Moldovan, than to discredit and, hopefully, remove the Bishop. The agent for this, as in the previous decade, was Rabbi Rosen, who began once more holding press conferences and traveling to New York. Let the American government think we have material evidence to help its case against Trifa, seemed to be Bucharest's idea—no matter that they had nothing which had not been seen many times before—and the campaign for most-favored-nation status will be helped along.

The Romanian establishment therefore became an active ally in the new round of Nazi-hunting by 1974. Someone got to Constantin Antonovici, but for some reason the sculptor decided to break his years of silence. Suddenly Antonovici found the courage to come forth and give a statement to investigators of the Immigration Service. One wonders, after some seventeen years had passed since his previous involvement with Trifa, just what the sculptor was told or promised by the professional Trifa-hunters—perhaps his picture with the Patriarch on a postcard.[20]

Quickly other Romanian "immigrants" were produced for the INS in New York by the Romanian Jewish community, including Velvel Sapsa, Jean David, and George Muntean. Each reported that they had seen or heard Trifa in Romania, which was hardly astounding news.[21]

Against this background, 1973 was the year of another crucial war for Israel in the Middle East. Awareness of American support for Israel as a *sine qua non* of U.S. foreign policy grew as it had not since 1967. Combined with the Nazi-mania and Holocaust whirlwind of the popular media, anyone alleged to have been at any time anti-Jewish was going to be hard-pressed—Trifa or anyone else.

Finally, in 1972, Elizabeth Holtzman was elected to Congress, the youngest woman (at age 31) ever sent to the House of Representatives. Her 16th district, encompassing Queens and other parts of the New York City area, contains one of the largest and most self-conscious Jewish populations in the country. Holtzman's rise in Washington was rapid. *Newsweek Magazine* reports she "made a splash with her tough-minded performance during the impeachment debate in the House Judiciary Committee," and calls her "a favorite of last-ditch liberals," who has almost never voted for a defense-spending bill. She is quoted aptly:

Government follows Newton's law of physics. Objects stay at rest until they're pushed.[22]

Holtzman began to push the Trifa case, indeed.[23]

On March 19, 1979, the Hollywood, Florida *Sun-Tattler* carried a Scripps-Howard release detailing Representative Holtzman's criticism of the work of the federal task force known as the Nazi War Crime Litigation Unit, which was established in part by her efforts in July, 1977. Holtzman was upset because the task force, operating under the aegis of the INS, was spending less than half the money allocated to it by Congress to pursue Nazis in the United States. The Immigration Service immediately promised to spend another $300,000 during the fiscal year. The piece concluded by quoting an aide to the Congresswoman: "It seems to me it would pay large political dividends to the administration pursue (*sic*) this program. After all, it's a big issue in the Jewish community and among a lot of World War II veterans too."[24]

Under Holtzman's continued prodding, by late 1979 the Special Litigation Unit had its budget raised to five million dollars. When the Congresswoman succeeded to the chairmanship of the House Committee on Immigration, Naturalization, and International Law upon the retirement of Pennsylvania Congressman Joshua Eilberg (who himself had done much to push the Nazi-hunt), she was in a position to exert powerful leverage. It is noteworthy that when Romanian-American groups supportive of Trifa sent memoranda or declarations to government officials, or asked for interviews with regard to Trifa's case, the answers were invariably that they "could not comment" upon a case then before the courts.[25] Yet clearly Holtzman, like her predecessor, used at least part of her staff for working specifically on the Trifa and other "Nazi" cases, and her Congressional immunity gave her freedom from any reservations as to public statements prejudicing the issue. She not only elaborated on the activities of "one of the most infamous of the alleged war criminals living in the United States," referring to Trifa, before Congressional committees, on repeated occasions, but made it clear as well that the cooperation of Romanian authorities was an essential *quid pro quo* for the most-favored-nation status which Romania sought so eagerly. In a statement before the House Ways and Means Committee's Subcommittee on Trade, June 22, 1979, Holtzman outlined recent unsuccessful efforts to obtain material from Bucharest, and pointedly stated:

> While at this time I would not advocate passage of a disapproval resolution on the Romanian MFN waiver, I would urge the Subcommittee to take no action which would indicate approval of the waiver until the Romanian government has fully cooperated in the prosecution of the Trifa case.[26]

As most-favored-nation status, moreover, is granted only for one-year periods, and is thus regularly up for renewal, it became a viable club. On June 10, 1980, Ms. Holtzman again testified to the same subcommittee, and repeated her warning to the Romanians, practically in the same words.[27]

The same evidence was evident in the U.S. State Department. As the case wound on and mountains of documents were not forthcoming from Romania, the State Department, like Holtzman, concluded this was due solely to a refusal of Bucharest to cooperate. Deputy Secretary of State Warren Christopher's communication to the American Embassy in Bucharest in January, 1978, confirmed the linkage between U.S.-Romanian political goals and Trifa. Noting that the Department of Justice was "extremely disappointed" by the Romanians' failure to provide useful information on Trifa, Christopher advised the Ambassador:

> Trifa case will undoubtedly come to attention of Congress and could become the subject of unfavorable publicity. Romanian Government may wish to take that into account in deciding whether to admit Asst. U.S. Attorney from Detroit.

And again, before closing, Christopher stressed:

> Since case will go forward in any event and GOR non-cooperation is likely to result in adverse publicity, GOR [Government of Romania] may wish to reconsider its decision not to supply further evidence.[28]

We should bear in mind that this message was sent more than thirty-two months after the initial filing of the suit against Trifa.

Trial without end

The Trifa court case began officially on May 16, 1975, when Assistant United States Attorney Michael Gladstone caused a summons and complaint to issue in the United States District Court in Detroit. A denaturalization suit began against Trifa on the grounds that he had obtained naturalization "by the concealment of material fact."[29]

The bishop's first response was to contact Cleveland Attorney John J. Sibişan, for many years one of the two main legal counsels of Trifa's Episcopate. Sibişan's first thought was the need for a lawyer specializing in Immigration Law, but as the newspaper buildup made it obvious that this was to be more than a one-man lawsuit, Sibişan and Episcopate counsel John Regule from Sharon, Pennsylvania, began to search for assistance, even as Sibişan filed the first entry of appearance as Trifa's lawyer in the case, on June 12. A month later, following a suggestion of Father John Badeen of the Antiochan Orthodox

Church in Detroit, the two contacted William W. Swor, of the Detroit firm of Metry, Metry, and Sanom. At that time only twenty-seven years old, Swor had already built an impressive record as a defense attorney in First Amendment and other constitutional law cases. He agreed to handle the case, and on October 21 filed the defense's Answer to the Complaint. The Answer accepted all of the government's statements of fact relative to Trifa's citizenship procedure, while categorically denying any persecutions or killing of anyone, and urging that the Affidavit showed no good cause for the action.[30]

This was further developed in Swor's Motion to Dismiss which appeared on December 11. Basically, the defense argued, the complaint did not claim that the government relied on the supposed misrepresentations during the naturalization process. The matter of "reliance," i.e., whether or not the government would have denied Trifa his citizenship had it known the truth of his misrepresentations, was to become crucial in the debates. For the first time, as well, Swor raised the question of delay, arguing that by not bringing the action until eighteen years after the granting of citizenship, Trifa was denied due process of law. Indeed, witnesses who might have assisted either side had died by that time, and more were to expire in the coming five years, or become incapable of trustworthy testimony. Memories of events in the 1940s, already dim in 1957, would be more beclouded by 1980. Finally the Motion to Dismiss went to the core of the matter. The government's right to a "do-over." The action was improper where the government fully investigated the charges which it now sought to use to revoke citizenship, prior to the time it was granted. [31]

U.S. District Judge Cornelia G. Kennedy denied the motion to dismiss. The defense of Laches, i.e., negligence or carelessness on the part of the government in not acting sooner, was not available against the government, she ruled, although it was a viable defense in proceedings between private individuals. Interestingly, though, Kennedy did not say that there had not been palpable inaction or negligence on the part of the INS or Justice Department, only that they did not exist in the court record thus far, which was another thing.[32] And on the vital question as to whether the government had all of its present "evidence" long before 1975, the judge noted that if this proved to be so, "then, of course, we would have a different situation. . . ."[33] One year later, when a total of 1521 pages of material was turned over to defense counsel for their study, hardly a page of it was material which, as one attorney put it, "the government had not been hit over the head with" on a regular basis since 1950."[34] Yet the "different situation" foreseen in Kennedy's pronouncement never seemed to materialize. As 1976 appeared, it was plain that the case dealt not with absolutes of truth, but with political necessities."[35]

Meanwhile William Swor continued to seek additional wisdom for the defense, and by July 30, 1976, Trifa accepted his advice to hire George E. Woods of Detroit as Chief Counsel for the Defense. Woods, at age 53, had more than twenty-five years experience as a successful and highly-paid trial lawyer. If William Swor's initial reaction to the Trifa case was to be struck "by the fundamental unfairness" of giving the government endless chances to try and retry one man, Woods was eventually to call it one of the "greatest debasements of due process and constitutional law ever."[36]

In the next four years Woods became as knowledgeable on the history of interwar Romania as a non-specialist is ever likely to be, in the English language materials. He assembled what amounted to a small library in his office. He and Trifa began a never-ending research project, gathering testimony and documents from around the world, spending countless hours in consultation in the bishop's office before multiple jammed filing cabinets and paper-strewn desks, or high in the air above the streets of Detroit in Woods' Citibank office. The amount of paperwork was absolutely phenomenal and the documentary piles grew into thousands of pages. Periodically, as the government changed prosecutors or produced additional materials, the entire huge mass would have to be sorted and renumbered, a task which alone consumed weeks of tedious work. Large amounts of material coming from the Justice Department was so poorly copied and faint as to be completely illegible, and requests for other copies consumed more weeks.

One of the earliest requests for defense material was sent to the Department of State by John Regule in the fall of 1975. On October 17, Trifa learned that the Foreign Affairs Document and Reference Center had passed on his request to the appropriate departments, and he expected that his Privacy Act appeal would bear fruit.[37] Only in December did Trifa learn that he must now send a notarized statement authorizing Regule to have access to whatever was found.[38] Two weeks later, the CIA, which had received the State Department communication, outlined its own separate procedures for release of materials, and asked for its own separate notarization from the bishop, suggesting that he read Title 32, C.F.R. 1901 of the *Federal Register*.[39] Trifa forwarded the required forms on January 5, 1976, asking for a "speedy consideration" of the matter. February 25, 1976: five months since materials were first requested:

> Dear Bishop Trifa:
>
> Please be advised that no record is available to you pursuant to the Privacy Act of 1974 under 8 Code of Federal Regulations 103.22 as there is presently a United States District Court suit pending against you.

wrote the Justice Department. Trifa had 30 days in which to appeal, if he wished to travel from Michigan to Washington. The defense had requested any and all material in the government's possession bearing on Trifa. Were this a criminal case, the plaintiff would be forced to provide it. But this was a civil case, and the prosecution could share its holdings or not, as it chose. So defense requests were shuffled from one department and agency to another. The files overflow with correspondence. The CIA put up its own roadblocks, the Department of the Army pondered on the release of CIC interviews, and the FBI released its aforementioned volumes only after the defense filed and was granted a Motion to Compel Discovery. Even after the court issued such an order on April 14, 1977, officialdom took its own good time. When materials arrived from Romania in the summer of 1979, on June 28, they were sent to Woods on July 3. But at that point the trial date had been set for July 30, and the papers had only then been sent to the translators.[40] This was the first significant cache of information the prosecution had stirred itself to obtain from Romania in four years. It was not until June 1, 1979, that the CIA finally acted—three and one-half years after the initial request.[41] But on June 6, 1979, the Secret Service announced it was withholding a report in the interest of national security.[42] And what was contained in all these papers which it took the defense years to obtain? Reports from 1950 and before, showing clearly that the government had full knowledge of the so-called "Iron Guard," of the claims against it, and of Trifa's relationship to it.

But of course much of it was useful to the case, on whichever side one argued. That is why it would seem simple fairness to the defense dictated that it should have been made available in a reasonable time, to be utilized in the Motion for Summary Judgment—if indeed, truth were the objective of the courtroom process, which in most cases, under our adversarial system, it is not. Woods would claim that the material was deliberately withheld to the prejudice of the defendant, which is perhaps too strong. Even normally, government cannot act too promptly by its very nature, and there is little continuity in any Washington bureaucracy beyond a four-year period. To be sure, though, the Trifa case was an excellent example of one with many of the trappings of a criminal case, but without any of the concomitant criminal procedure legal protections guaranteed to the defendant. Trifa had to secure and pay for his own counsel; in a case involving materials and witnesses spread all over the United States, Canada, and Europe, there was no government reimbursement for travel expenses to depose witnesses or search out evidence; and the government had no obligation to turn over evidence to assist the defense. At the same time, however, somehow the man was being tried on criminal charges, not civil ones: if not in the formal complaints, then everywhere else.

Yet the very fact of being thrown on his own resources brought out one of the remarkable features of the Episcopate headed by Trifa. Never did the overwhelming majority of those in his diocese doubt throughout the years of the case that it was not simply "the bishop's case," but "the Episcopate's case." So-called simple Romanian immigrant parishioners saw the wider political ramifications and motivations behind the case. Romanian Americans, after all, had long experiences of communist-supported assaults on their American churches. So by the middle of 1976 the Episcopate Council authorized a special Seven times Seven Committee to be organized, with branches in all parishes, to engage in public relations efforts and collect a defense fund in a series of special drives, rather than financed in the regular budget.[43] The 1976 Episcopate accounts thus included $7,371 for legal fees. One year later the figure was $54,615, with an estimate for 1977 of another $35,800. The end of the fiscal year on May 31, 1978, showed another $18,733 committed to legal expenses. After two more years, i.e., by the fall of 1980, at least $115,000 was expended, and all of this had come from voluntary donations and collections from the parishes and Romanian-Americans throughout the nation. None of the money was taken from normal diocesan revenues. Each year, moreover, produced strongly worded resolutions of support both in the Episcopate Council and in the annual Church Congresses which took the issue of "the case" to a plane seldom discussed: thousands of Romanian-Americans saw what was happening not only as an assault on religious liberty, but a denial of the philosophy that innocence is presumed until guilt is proven. It is difficult to explain how Trifa's "people" throughout the whole weary business unwaveringly refused to believe any of the allegations against him. The fact that they held out to the end, however, says much in itself.

And while facing the frustration of seeking documents from the Washington files and perusing features on his "haunted past" in the newspapers, Trifa had a second trial in 1976. A campaign to remove him from the governing board of the National Council of Churches gained momentum.[44] On October 14 twenty-five members of a group calling themselves the "Concerned Jewish Youth" invaded the Riverside Drive offices of the National Council of Churches in New York City, and left only when promised that the question of Trifa's membership would be placed on the agenda of the staff meeting the following week.[45] At first the Council refused to comply with the militants' demands, noting that the constitution of the NCC contained no powers for removing board members, who were chosen by their own denominations. Only Trifa's Episcopate might remove him if it saw fit. The Orthodox Church in America also stoutly defended Trifa's right to remain on the NCC board. By the end of the month, though, the NCC Executive Committee began to fold, and decided to ask the OCA to request that Trifa "refrain from executing his duties" as a member of the body until the conclusion of the suit against him.[46] Lester Kinsolving and various Rabbis took to the columns to call this solution unsatisfactory, and Jewish protest groups turned up at every major session of the Executive Committee in the weeks that followed. In November Rabbi Avraham Weiss extended the crusade to the Holy Synod of the Orthodox Church in America, which appointed a committee to study the issue. Dr. Kremer popped up in one city after another as a speaker to Jewish Community Councils, and was extensively interviewed. He went on television and when the broadcast was shown in Southfield, Michigan, the site of Trifa's cathedral, at once the station received eighty calls of protest, a bomb threat was phoned in, and the lives of a producer and newscaster were threatened.[47] Anti-Jewish feeling had been relatively unnoticeable or at a minimum among the people of Trifa's Episcopate—and in the Romanian-American community in general—during the fifty years of its existence, but recent events tended to promote it. Finally in January, 1977, the OCA announced it was "withdrawing" the bishop from the National Council of Churches board until the case was disposed of.

Two additional factors hampered any possibility of bringing Trifa's case to trial within a reasonable time, and thus allowed for extra years of this type of spectacle: the constant changing of government prosecutors, and the uncertainty as to whether Judge Kennedy would retain the case.

In June, 1976, Ralph B. Guy, Jr., who along with Michael Gladstone had conducted the Trifa case from the beginning, was made a federal judge, and President Ford appointed Philip Van Dam the new U.S. attorney for the Eastern District of Michigan. Van Dam was a native of the Netherlands, Jewish, "who lost several relatives in Nazi concentration camps."[48] Naturally he was given time to familiarize himself with the case, and this was not a lawsuit where one could master the details in a matter of a few days or weeks. But in November, with the election of Jimmy Carter, party control in Washington changed hands. Van Dam, a Republican, ignored the long-standing tradition among U.S. attorneys of resigning when a new administration takes power, arguing that the statute at issue gave him a four-year term. What happened was that Democratic Senator Donald W. Riegle sought the post for one of his own appointees. In April, 1977, Riegle nominated liberal Detroit attorney James K. Robinson for the job. The excuse given was that Van Dam was stalling the government's foot-dragging case against Trifa. While a moot point, two months of political infighting apparently decided the issue. Attorney General Griffin Bell was no friend of Senator Riegle, who had voted against Bell's confirmation; whether Bell would put the expected pressure on Van Dam to resign was unclear. President Carter, during his campaign, had pledged to depoliticize the Justice Department, and Robert Stephenson, a spokesman for Griffin Bell, was quoted on April 22 that partisan considerations would "play no part in the decision about the U.S. attorney's job here."[49] However, one month later Van Dam was replaced by Robinson.[50] By the time Robinson was confirmed and sworn in, the summer of 1977 was over.[51] A year later there was a third federal prosecutor in charge of the case, Frederick Van Tiem, who needed time to make the transition into the office. By 1979 Eugene Thirolf, Jr. was in charge of the government's case. And while musical attorneys went on in Detroit, the special Litigation Unit came under duress.

Originally set up in July, 1977, under the INS, the special War Crime Litigation Unit had been transferred to the criminal division of the Justice Department in May, 1978. At that time Walter J. Rockler, a prosecutor at the Nuremberg trials, was made director of the office, superseding Martin Mendelsohn, who had set up and run the program since its inception.

In January, 1979, the Justice Department announced that Mendelsohn was being removed from the Special Unit office, due to a "personality conflict" with Rockler. Elizabeth Holtzman was upset. Calling the transfer "retribution for his (Mendelsohn's) cooperation with members of Congress," implying Holtzman and others, who had fought to upgrade the status of the Special Unit, she argued that it would be seen by foreign governments that the United States was not really serious about the Nazi cases.[52] But there were other opinions, notably Rockler's, who charged Mendelsohn with spending too much time on public relations.[53]

More delay was in the offing, though. Two months after this, President Carter nominated Judge Cornelia Kennedy to the Sixth U.S. Circuit Court of Appeals in Cincinnati, and the great question now was if Kennedy would keep the Trifa case, which she had handled for nearly four years, or if a new judge would be given it. For the moment, the query was academic, because Kennedy's confirmation was to take six months. And only in February, 1979, had another trial date for the Trifa case finally been set for July 30 of that year: another in a series of supposed terminal dates which somehow always seemed to deliquesce before the frustrated eyes of those who spent long days and nights preparing for them. Even so, had Judge Kennedy's nomination gone smoothly through the Senate, such a trial date might have been met. Instead Kennedy was immediately attacked as unfit for the high post in Cincinnati, by the NAACP, the Wolverine Bar Association, representing 450 black lawyers in Michigan, and the National Bar Association, a predominantly black group of 7,000 attorneys. All of these prepared to tell the Senate Judiciary Committee that Kennedy's record showed "insensitivity" and "unnecessary harshness" to the pleadings of minorities in civil rights cases. Walter Douglas, President of New Detroit, Inc., accused her of a "record of racism," while the Wolverine Bar said she had been reversed in 52% of her cases.[54]

In fact, Kennedy's record as a jurist was of the highest order, and she was only the fourth woman in the nation ever named as a federal judge. In 1977 she became the first female Chief Judge of a Federal District Court in United States history. A host of lawyers, judges, and law school savants came forth to defend her. Yet the outcry from the black community was sufficient to cause a number of senators to withhold their approval and delay the nomination, notably Howard Metzenbaum of Ohio and Senator Edward Kennedy.[55] By August 1, Senator Strom Thurmond of South Carolina objected to what he termed the "unfair delays," noting "It is a strange thing that liberal judges can get through this committee and conservatives can't." He refused to vote on any of the pending twenty-five nominees for federal judgeships in retaliation, and thus the hearings were delayed another five weeks.[56]

Even in normal times, the Federal Court in Detroit has a heavy caseload, and lacked the judicial manpower to give time to civil cases. Added to the difficulties involved in dragging on the Trifa case was the fact that under the Speedy Trial Act criminal cases legally take precedence over civil ones, and thus eighty per cent of the judges' time is tied up in criminal cases.[57] Now in addition, Kennedy had to be available for Senate committee hearings in the midst of her heavy schedule, and more than once was forced to interrupt the hearing of arguments at various stages of the Trifa case to run to the phone or dash off to a conference on her nomination. Not until September 25 was her confirmation approved by the Senate.[58] For Trifa and Woods and the defense team, this merely raised a new question: would Kennedy keep their case and finish her docket in Detroit, or hand it over to a new judge? The remainder of 1979 passed without an answer.

The previous two years were busy ones for Trifa. In the fall of 1977 he and Woods traveled to Madrid to depose witnesses, including Vasile Iasinschi, who was now so feeble he could hardly talk.[59] Again, during 1979, the pair traveled to France and Germany. It became obvious that the Justice Department intended to depose witnesses in Romania, and Woods intended to do so as well. On February 14, 1979, Woods and Sibişan traveled to the Romanian Embassy in Washington to arrange such a trip, and were assured of cooperation. When two months went by without a word, Sibişan contacted the Embassy and was told to return to Washington with additional information. Upon his arrival, rather than centering on details of a defense visit in Romania, the conversation focused on why Trifa and his Episcopate did not unify their churches with the Detroit diocese loyal to the Patriarchate; were this to be done, there would be no end of cooperation in the bishop's case. Sibişan left angrily and nothing was heard about travel arrangements again.[60] Meanwhile Eugene M. Thirolf, the new Justice Department prosecutor, traveled to Romania in May, 1979. Either on this, or on a subsequent trip, his party found that the Romanians knew exactly which witnesses Woods intended to bring to America to testify, or at least depose in Bucharest. Such knowledge preyed on Trifa's mind, especially. Romanian citizens faced no particular danger in coming forth to assist officials from the U.S. government, but it was another matter to ask them to participate for the defense in a case where the regime was clearly out to please the plaintiff. With their names known ahead of time, there was no telling the harassment to which they might be subject.

In any event, at times both the court and the Justice Department displayed an incredible naiveté regarding the workings of a communist regime, seeming to assume that it operated basically the same as a government in a free society and merely had to be called on to carry out prescribed international judicial forms. Thirolf went to Romania with no specific list of people he wished to see. As he said to Woods at one point, "We just asked for people who had knowledge of the case and they brought people to us and we talked to them."[61] In other words, the Justice Department left it up to the Romanian government who would be interviewed! At another time, when certain court-requested materials had not arrived for months, Judge Kennedy suggested the attorneys simply call the State Department to get in touch with the Romanian government, with the comment, "Well, I presume that you'll get a prompt response one way or the other."[62] They did not.

Without mentioning again the curiosity of the fact that no serious government efforts to compel Romanian cooperation on witnesses was undertaken until at least three years after the suit against Trifa was brought, the net result of such incertitude was to effectively deny Trifa access to witnesses who might help to exculpate him, for the situation did not improve later on for the defense. In the spring of 1980, plans were moving forth for another round of visits to Romania, and Woods this time fully intended to be present. On April 22 he wrote to the Romanian Embassy in Washington for visas. On July 30 he received a communication from Thirolf. "I understand from the Romanian Embassy that you have not formally made application for the trip to Romania."[63] Thirolf, however, returned to Bucharest during August, to depose three persons whom the government had talked to before. Everything this time was ready for him. The statements were taken in a Romanian courtroom, with a Romanian judge and lawyers present, everything neat and prescribed and arranged by the Romanians beforehand.

There was only one person, it seemed, who really knew how to make Bucharest cooperate. In the summer of 1979, with the Trifa trial date having been set for July 30, Elizabeth Holtzman made her statement to the House Ways and Means Subcommittee on Most Favored Nation Status for Romania. Six days later, Thirolf announced the receipt of two volumes of documentation on the Trifa case from Bucharest.[64]

Yet this, along with the drawn-out wrangling over travel to Romania, meant in each case a postponement of the trial date; it meant also more months of legal fees, of preoccupation taking Trifa away from the multifarious duties of his large and spread-out Episcopate, and more endless hours of preparation each time a new trial date was established, for the volume of material and the mass of documentation was such that no one could be expected to keep it all in his mind for long, and a lapse of six months meant going through it all again.

The longer the case was drawn out, the more the opportunity for harassment. It was irritating enough that the press carried periodic announcements of Jewish leaders and monitors being "briefed" on the Trifa case. People whom Trifa and Woods had never heard of were suddenly reported as men who had "been involved for a number of years in the quest to bring Trifa to justice."[65] When Trifa made his first lengthy deposition in January, 1977, the ADL of B'nai B'rith requested it in transcript, and only a protective order sealing it, hastily obtained by the defense, prevented its release.[66] To the credit of Michael Gladstone, who supported the order, went the statement that allowing it beyond the courtroom would probably serve only "to expand the public misinformation."[67]

Harder to bear were overt acts of misguided individuals, which ranged from posing as news reporters in Detroit and appearing at the homes of members of Trifa's St. George Cathedral asking questions about the bishop, to appearing with flagrantly vicious signs and banners in Fort Wayne or Cleveland whenever Trifa traveled there on church affairs. It was one thing for the ADL to have a counsel present in Detroit at pre-trial conferences as an *amicus curiae*, and have the case constantly "monitored" by Jewish groups. It was another when Trifa went to Florida purely on a parish visitation, for stories to appear suddenly in Hollywood urging a demonstration, along with circulars telling the local folk that Trifa was actually there to recruit more Guardist backup men from Argentina. It was one thing when the Reverend Roman Braga, who had arrived in Michigan from Brazil in 1971, was accused by certain members of the Riopelle Street Episcopate of having been one of Codreanu's chief lieutenants (which would have been when he was nine years old) and was called to talk to the FBI. It was another thing, in the winter of 1979, when an anonymous man began calling radio stations throughout the country, stating that he intended to assassinate "all the Nazis," and the head of the Jewish Defense League, happening to be in Detroit, was quoted as saying that if the man was sure of his targets he would not lift a hand to stop him. One might put up with the expected demonstration in front of the bishop's residence in Grass Lake on the anniversary of the Warsaw ghetto uprising. More grievous was the early morning of December 14, 1978. At 3:30 a.m. a firebomb was thrown through a stained glass window of St. Dumitru's Church at 50 West 89th Street in New York, producing heavy fire, smoke, and water damage. Fortunately Father Florian Gâldău, his family, and the caretaker got out safely. Moments after the attack, an anonymous caller told a receptionist at United Press International that the "Jewish Armed Resistance" had taken care of the church because it was a meeting place for the Iron Guard. In fact, of all Trifa's churches, St. Dumitru's had one of the best reputations for assisting people of all national origins and religious beliefs. Since the Second World War it was known as the "Charity Church," as thousands of refugees and fugitives from communist regimes entered the United States and were helped in their transition to a new life.[68]

While contending with such as this, there was also the sure knowledge that the actual courtroom trial, whenever it came, was going to be turned into a showpiece of emotional hysterics, demonstration, and outpouring of vindictiveness. In July, 1978, during the trial of Feodor Federenko, whom the government sought to denaturalize due to his alleged past as a Treblinka prison guard, the Jewish Defense League ran ads in newspapers offering chartered buses from Miami Beach to Fort Lauderdale on opening day. A demonstration outside the courtroom ensued with a chant: "Who do we want? Federenko. How do we want him? Dead." After the court was interrupted twice and the first three warnings were ignored by demonstrators, a leader using an amplified bullhorn was arrested. A counter-demonstration appeared in two days, producing a confrontation. Federenko's counsel was attacked by women spectators at the courtroom entrance at the trial's close. Inside the courtroom itself, deputy marshals apprehended a news reporter going through the judge's wastebasket under the bench.[69]

Moreover, the pattern of denaturalization trials focusing on alleged "Nazis" and their collaborators, has thus far been one of having witnesses emotionally relate general incidents of life in Nazi camps or tales of the brutality of the system, and describe the role of the ethnic group (Ukrainian, Romanian, Polish, or whatever) as it fit into the Nazi system of repression. What is missing, though, is specific testimony or proof that the person on trial in the courtroom in Detroit, Philadelphia, or wherever, actually shot or beat anyone. To establish guilt it is not enough merely to place the defendant at the scene or in the general geographical area and time-frame.

This method came out clearly in the September, 1980 trial of Wolodymir Osidach in Philadelphia's U.S. District Court, charged with enforcing Nazi laws relating to Jews in the Ukraine in 1942. Witnesses generalized about the role of the Ukrainian police, but few could say anything about specific acts by Osidach. Still government prosecutors played as many as 36 hours worth of videotapes of depositions by Russian citizens who lived in the region at issue during the German occupation, a procedure which outraged Ukrainian-American onlookers, who had their own tales to tell of the Soviet secret police. Meanwhile, young American-born Jews wept in the audience, Jewish activists scuffled in the street with Ukrainians, and instead of trying one man, the Ukraine during World War II was on trial.[70]

Given the close and constant "monitoring" and "briefings" to the Jewish community ever since the commencement of the suit, it was no surprise that when the latest trial date was set for October, 1980, word spread through the Romanian-American community that if one wished to attend, he had best get there early, for the seats were likely to be taken by Jewish spectators; furthermore plans to videotape the trial were discussed openly, and it is reasonable to expect that such designs were being formed, considering the central role of Trifa as a symbol of the ire of Romanian-American Jews. Even were there no substance to such rumors, there is every reason to expect that the Trifa trial would be no less a public spectacle than that of Federenko or Osidach.

False Endings

For a few months in the first half of 1979, before the extension granted to the government to process the papyraceous package from Romania, it appeared that there might actually be a trial in the offing. Understandably, with Judge Kennedy's nomination to the higher court, Woods was anxious to get a resolution lest she give up the case, or, as was always likely, a new prosecutor was assigned. The defense began to prepare an extensive Motion for Summary Judgment, but due to the new delay, and the fact that Trifa in the summer was extremely busy with the annual summer religious camps held at the Vatra, Woods was not ready until the first of August. At that point he telephoned Eugene Thirolf, and much to his consternation learned that the government's prosecutor was "out of the country," and would be gone the entire month. It did not require much thought to know where his travels had taken him. Upon Thirolf's return, Woods' motion was argued before Kennedy for two days in September. No mention was made of the trip to Romania. Only after the court appearances did a summary of the visit arrive in the mail. And the people seen in Bucharest included those on the defense list given to the Romanian Embassy by Woods and Sibişan the previous February 14. With such tactics, and given the government's apparent willingness to spend limitless amounts of the public treasury to pursue its case, without the right which would have been guaranteed the defense in a criminal case to confront the witnesses against him, Trifa was forced to argue against anonymous voices from across the seas, saw his potential witnesses cut off from him due to the revelation of their identities beforehand, and knew that the government planned to fly witnesses from Israel to Detroit. Nevertheless Woods fixed his plea squarely on the law, even if, as time went on, his motions could not but contain language indicative of his total frustration.

While it is not the intention here to parse or anatomize the strictly legal issues in Trifa's case, one or two items should be underlined, considering all that has been said. Woods' Motion for Summary Judgment, after urging that the Act of June 16, 1950, barring persons from admission into the United States under certain conditions, should be declared void both for vagueness and overbreadth, got to the heart of the issue in his third section, labeled "The delay occasioned solely by the government in bringing this action has denied the defendant due process of law" under the Fifth, Sixth, and Fourteenth Amendments. The impossibility of constructing a case dealing with events in Romania as much as half a century ago, the unavailability and death or attrition of witnesses, and the continuous investigation of Trifa for at least seven years by a host of government offices and agencies in a case that "could have been resolved better and more reliably 20 years ago," all produced this ineluctable conclusion[71]

Even were Trifa to admit certain misrepresentations in his naturalization process (which he did not) of vital importance is the question of reliance. It was absolutely necessary for the government to show that it relied on Trifa's false testimony and was therefore deceived by it into admitting him to citizenship, to the point where it did not conduct an investigation of his background which it would otherwise have pursued. Obviously this was not the case, when the facts in the record speak for themselves—countless investigations both before and after 1957. Moreover, all of the allegations in the government's

1975 complaint were known to the government in 1957, and they were investigated by the government independently of any statements made by Trifa. Indeed, throughout the five years of the case, even with its two amended complaints, the prosecution never specifically stated that there was any deception. In all of his interviews, and on his Petition for Naturalization, the bishop readily stated that he was the President of the National Union of Romanian Christian Students. In all of the interveiws he denied that such a position made him a member of the "Iron Guard," and explained why. The government implies, then, that this constituted deception? Since Trifa denied the Student Union was a member or section of the "Iron Guard" he was lying about his membership in the "Guard"? Does a legitimate disagreement as to the conclusion to be drawn from operative facts constitute fraud? Logically, it cannot; yet the government predicates its case on this premise. The government had its own multiple opportunities to find out the exact relationship between the Student Union and the "Guard" without relying on Trifa's explanation. It pursued those studies. And it concluded that no matter what Trifa had said, this was not sufficient to bar him from citizenship. Twenty years later, the government seeks a chance to make up for its bad judgment in 1957?

Finally there is a question which amidst all the furor, tidal waves of paperwork, and expenditures of uncountable sums on the part of the United States, has never been adequately addressed. Assuming that the government is successful in stripping Trifa of his citizenship, or even of deporting him elsewhere, what benefit will be gained? No person, on either side of the case, has ever argued that Trifa has been anything other than a useful, good, and law-abiding citizen of the United States for the thirty years in which he has lived here. It is apparent as well that the law over many decades recognizes the gravity and heavy responsibility of taking away a man's citizenship. In *Knauer v. United States* (328 U.S. 654, 659, 66 S.Ct. 1304, 1307 (1947) the Supreme Court ruled:

> [Denaturalization cases] are extremely serious problems. They involve not only fundamental principles of our political system designed for the protection of minorities and majorities alike. They also involve tremendously high stakes for the individual. For denaturalization, like deportation, may result in the loss "of all that makes life worth living."[72]

In light of the fact that Trifa faced the possible uprooting of the last quarter century of his life and life's work by old charges originally conceived in the struggles of the Moldovan affair, the resolution of which became an academic issue long ago in another world, one would expect some clear explication from the prosecution. We fully know the charges and allegations: but why is it so important to bring them?

It is interesting to note the policy of the Department of Justice as elaborated in 1909, at the height of the great waves of immigration with respect to the bringing of denaturalization cases:

> In the opinion of the department, as a general rule, a good cause is not shown for the institution of proceedings to cancel certificates of naturalization alleged to have been fraudulently or illegally procured unless some substantial results are to be achieved thereby in the way of the betterment of the citizenry of the country.[73]

Again, it should be asked. Is the United States going to be a better place without this man remaining one of its citizens? No one answers. The Motion for Summary Judgment was denied. The government, which was supposed to have had a "case" when it came into court, was given another year to produce one. In January, 1980, Judge Kennedy quit the case, turning it over to her colleague, Judge John Feikens. In July, Feikens became Chief District Court Judge and turned the case over to Judge Horace Gilmore. Six different prosecutors, three different judges, two amended complaints, a minimum of ten extensions, and five years of time.

> The mere filing of a proceeding for denaturalization results in serious consequences to a defendant. Even if his citizenship is not cancelled, his reputation is tarnished and his standing in the community damaged. Congress recognized this danger and provided that a person, once admitted to American citizenship, should not be subject to legal proceedings to defend his citizenship without a preliminary showing of good cause. Such a safeguard must not be lightly regarded.

noted the Supreme Court in *United States v. Zucca* (351 U.S. 91). We are still looking for the good cause.

> It must be remembered that we are here concerned not with a naturalization proceeding where a privilege is sought, but with an action to denaturalize. As such the burden lies heavily with the government to cut square corners. The Supreme Court has spoken clearly and often on the independent close scrutiny that courts should make in such proceedings.

said the Supreme Court in *Schneiderman v. United States* (1943, 320 U.S. 118, 122, 63 S.Ct. 1333, 87 LEd. 1796). Yet we find only rounded corners, in a type of case in which American legal tradition holds that the defense should be given every benefit, that the burden of proof on the government is most heavy, and recognizes the inherent prejudice caused the defendant by the mere filing of such a complaint. Yet the new decade did not seem to affect the government's insouciance nor improve its corners. One of the last pieces of correspondence received by Judge Kennedy came from the Justice Department, relative to the original copy of Trifa's manifesto of January 20, 1941, which he had personally turned over to the FBI in 1955. Several variations of the text had been floating around, and for more than a year Woods had asked for the original. On April 29, 1980, the FBI informed the judge that they had lost it.[74]

Perhaps such incidents served to convince Judge Gilmore that the prosecution deserved no more time. It may be that he simply wished to dispose of a major case which he had inherited, and get on with his own docket. Equally possible, given Gilmore's distinguished record on the bench, he may have sensed, as did scores of jurists and lawyers around the country, that not only was justice delayed, justice denied, but that no good cause would be served by any further postponement. He waited until Thirolf returned at the end of August from Romania, and then set the 28th of that month as the final date for filing motions. There would be a final pre-trial conference on September 14, and the case would go to court exactly one month later.

EPILOGUE

On Tuesday, August 26, 1980, George Woods entered the U.S. Federal District Court in Detroit and formally surrendered to Judge Gilmore Certificate of Naturalization No. 7119787, which Valerian Trifa had held for twenty-three years. Eight days later Gilmore officially revoked Trifa's United States citizenship in a court judgment which said, that Trifa "was not and is not" a U.S. citizen.[1] John J. Sibişan refused to sign the order due to this *ab initio* language, and registered a protest with the court.

In an accompanying statement, Trifa emphasized that this act was "in no way to be considered an admission of the government's allegations."[2]

It was an admission of something else. Trifa was out of money, out of energy, and, along with Woods, absolutely convinced that in the upcoming trial, sure to be an exhausting experience, all cards were stacked against him. Naturally Trifa and all four of his attorneys— Woods, Sibişan, Swor, and Regule—had discussed the matter for months, although no one else close to his church knew of it. While the impetus for such a dramatic move seems to have come primarily from Woods, in the end the decision was Trifa's alone. He couched his final judgment in terms of two major factors: his own health, and the welfare of his Romanian Orthodox Episcopate.

The time devoted to the case was inordinate and this, along with the multifarious tasks of running a religious establishment of 40,000 parishioners and churches spread from Rhode Island to Saskatchewan, from Miami to Los Angeles, told on him in sheer physical and psychological pressures. He was a phlegmatic man but the tensions of being dragged daily through the media, of anonymous phone calls and reports of swastikas painted on his churches took a heavy toll on him. In November, 1976, he suffered a minor cerebral stroke which hospitalized him in Cleveland for two weeks. His recovery was good, except for a continuing numbness in the fingers and arm on one side of the body, but this was a sign that he could not escape his 66 years.

Moreover, since 1978, his Episcopate had been moving in the direction of electing and installing an auxiliary bishop to assist Trifa, and pave the way for the next generation of the Romanian-American church. During 1980 this goal was pushed forward, and much time was consumed during the spring and summer with plans for a special Electoral Congress, nominations by the Episcopate Council, and so on. On September 20, in Cleveland, Father Nathaniel Popp of Sharon, Pennsylvania, was chosen from among three candidates to be the auxiliary bishop-elect and, presumably some day, the successor to Valerian. He was consecrated and installed in Detroit in mid-November. With all of this on the agenda, Trifa would certainly have been hard-pressed to endure a lengthy courtroom trial. And he wished his new assistant to begin with a clean slate.

The money for legal expenses had always been a constant worry to him. Making matters worse, Woods had learned that the trial was to be held only for half-day sessions, due to administrative needs of the court. This meant twice the time that one need be available in Detroit, and twice the number of days to pay attorney fees of one hundred dollars per hour. Could he go back to his long-enduring people in the parishes and tell them that he now needed another fifty thousand dollars? He knew he could not.

And so he quietly gave in. Many believed it to be a mistake, after all this time, especially when it became apparent that the major premise upon which the decision must have hinged—the expectation that this would be the end of it all—was faulty. "Trifa Faces Deportation," proclaimed the *Detroit Free Press*. "Churchman's Dropping Citizenship Doesn't Halt U.S."[3] Eugene Thirolf announced that the government expected to file a deportation resolution with the Immigration and Naturalization Service within sixty days.[4] Detroit attorney Peter Alter, a member of the National Law Commission of the Anti-Defamation League of B'nai B'rith, urged that deportation should be started "immediately."[5] Federal prosecutors said that deportation proceedings "would be based on the same charges as those aimed at stripping him of his citizenship."[6] Dr. Kremer flew to Detroit to be present at the final hearing.[7] "Any man who changes a gun for a cross has no right to go on living on the face of this earth," Kremer said.[8]

The Trifa case, then, goes on, having now raised interesting questions of constitutional and immigration law. It may be that Judge Gilmore's acceptance of Trifa's certificate, and his *ab initio* ruling, will be found invalid. There are no true precedents to go on, and the

Trifa case, as it has from the beginning, will make new law, regardless of the outcome. One wonders, indeed, if Trifa "never was" a citizen, why the United States spent five years to revoke a non-existant status. Devotees of Aquinas will find it marvelous to observe a thing taken away from him who did not possess it. Trifa, at an age when most men begin to think of retirement, finds himself still an object of contention, still telephoning, still sorting through piles of documentation, forever on trial. Surely when he set foot on the soil of New York thirty long years ago, he believed he had left the struggles of the old world behind. Student of history as he was, though, he might have known that the past is always with us. It is never even past.

AFTERWORD

The refusal of the Justice Department to desist from pressing the deportation issue, the unprecedented nature of Judge Gilmore's ruling on Trifa's surrender of citizenship, and continued pressures which automatically labeled the Bishop's action as indicative of an admission of guilt forced Trifa to take up once again the burden of defense.

A few weeks after Gilmore's ruling, George Woods removed himself from the case, which now became the responsibility of William Swor in Detroit. Swor engaged the assistance of Detroit immigration law specialist Joseph A. Gatto, and filed an appeal against Gilmore's ruling, on October 30, 1980, claiming that Trifa had been denied due process.

Late in the winter of 1981, the United States Court of Appeals, Sixth Circuit, in Cincinnati, asked for briefs to be filed on the appeal, and these were presented on March 11. The irony and endless circuitry of the case once again showed themselves, for Judge Cornelia Kennedy now sat on the Cincinnati bench. Meanwhile the front page of the *Cleveland Plain Dealer* for June 16, 1981 described an emotion-laden reunion of Holocaust survivors. And the Trifa case goes on.

APPENDIX A

STATEMENT OF THE
HONORABLE ELIZABETH HOLTZMAN (D.-N.Y.)
BEFORE THE SUBCOMMITTEE ON TRADE,
HOUSE WAYS AND MEANS COMMITTEE
June 22, 1979

Mr. Chairman, Members of the Committee, I greatly appreciate the opportunity to appear before you today to testify on the President's request for a one year extension of the freedom of emigration waiver authority under the Trade Act of 1974 with respect to permitting most-favored-nation tariff treatment for Romania.

I want to discuss briefly a matter which, while it does not fall explicitly within the ambit of the freedom of emigration requirements of Section 402 of the Trade Act, does reflect directly on the Romanian government's willingness to deal forthrightly and cooperatively with the United States on subjects of mutual concern.

It is a matter of the utmost importance to many of us in the Congress and to many of our constituents. The issue is Romania's willingness to provide judicial assistance to our government in seeking to bring alleged Nazi war criminals to justice.

One of the most infamous of the alleged war criminals living in the United States is Valerian Trifa, a leader of the Romanian Iron Guard during World War II, now a Bishop in the Romanian Orthodox Church near Detroit. In documents filed by the Justice Department in 1975, it is alleged that in January 1941 Trifa—and I quote—"rode through the Jewish sector of Bucharest... [and] ordered, participated in and observed his Iron Guards set fire to houses, stores and a synagogue. During this period, subject used his pistol, shooting with the others, and ordered his men to kill and torture the Jews."

Our government is now moving to strip Trifa of the citizenship he acquired in 1957, as a first step in deporting him back to Romania. A denaturalization proceeding, based on Trifa's allegedly illegal entry into the United States in 1950, is scheduled to begin on July 30 in federal court in Detroit. Unfortunately, until a matter of days ago, the Romanian government had provided virtually no assistance to the United States in the prosecution of this case, either in terms of identifying and making available potential witnesses with knowledge of Trifa's activities, allowing access to historical archives, or providing authentication of documents from original copies that are preserved in Romania. A recent article by David Binder in the *New*

York Times recounts the difficulties encountered by the Justice Department in its dealings with the Romanian government on this case. With your permission, I would like to submit a copy of this article for the record.

Briefly, I would like to summarize the attempts by our government to secure cooperation in the Trifa case.

The Government of Romania was initially contacted for assistance on November 9, 1976 by the American Embassy. A request was made for properly authenticated copies of any edicts, communiques or manifestos authored by Trifa, as well as the identification of any witnesses with personal knowledge of the allegations against him. On February 7, 1977, Romania provided two copies of a June 5, 1945 decision condemning Trifa to hard labor for life for his role as a leader of the Legionaire Students Corps in an abortive revolution in 1941.

On January 6, 1978, in reply to several formal requests by the American Embassy in Bucharest and informal follow-up conversations by its officers, the Romanian Ministry of Foreign Affairs officially informed the Embassy that Romania would have no further documentation to provide in the Trifa case beyond that already furnished.

Subsequently, on January 31, 1978, at the request of the Department of Justice, American Embassy officials inquired whether the Romanian government would issue a visa to a prosecutor from the Department and facilitate the search for witnesses and evidence; no reply was received to this inquiry. During July of 1978, Embassy officials once more spoke with the Foreign Ministry to determine whether Romania would provide the previously requested names of witnesses and copies of any documentation, and sanction a visit by a Department of Justice official. Romania again did not grant the requests.

In March of this year, Justice Department prosecutors, together with representatives of the State Department, met with Romanian Embassy officials in Washington to impress upon them the urgency of the problem; a final pre-trial hearing on the case was set for April 24 and trial on July 30. No response was received until April 11—less than two weeks before the pre-trial conference—when Romania informed the American Embassy that it would allow a visit by a Justice Department prosecutor.

During a trip to Romania at the beginning of May, the prosecutor met with both Foreign and Justice Ministry officials to restate the Department's requests. Again the requests were denied, for what can only be called spurious reasons: the absence of a judicial assistance treaty between the two countries, the necessity to go through formal diplomatic channels, the requirements of Romanian legal procedure, and the need to be a Romanian citizen to be granted access to the archives. On May 14, formal diplomatic notes were submitted to the Romanian Foreign Ministry, again restating the Justice Department requests.

Finally, on June 15, Romanian officials delivered to the American Embassy in Bucharest a package of documents related to the Trifa case. This occurred just two days after Chairman Vanik advised Ambassador Ionescu by letter of his concern about the Romanian government's non-cooperation in the case in the context of this Subcommittee's review of the Romanian MFN waiver and asked that the Ambassador meet with me to discuss it.

The documents only reached the Department of Justice yesterday, and, although prosecutors have advised my staff that the materials appear to be relevant to the case, they have not been translated and as of today their importance cannot be evaluated. On initial review, however, prosecutors have already determined that several of the documents were not properly certified from original copies.

Although the documents provided by the Romanian government last week may ultimately prove valuable in the prosecution of the Trifa case and the production of the materials at all represents a meaningful change in attitude on the Romanians' part, I believe that action alone is clearly inadequate. Justice Department prosecutors advised my staff last night that regardless of the content of the documents, they feel it is imperative to be able to interview available witnesses in Romania and to be given access to archival material.

While at this time I would not advocate passage of a disapproval resolution on the Romanian MFN waiver, I would urge the Subcommittee to take no action which would indicate approval of the waiver until the Romanian government has fully cooperated in the prosecution of the Trifa case. Ambassador Ionescu personally assured me in a meeting on Monday that any problems could and would be solved. Although I am certain the Ambassador was accurately representing his government's intentions in this matter, the history of delay in cooperating speaks for itself, and time is of the essence in this case. Trifa's trial is scheduled to begin at the end of July, and Justice Department prosecutors need to have all the available evidence within the next two or three weeks if they are adequately to prepare their case.

In weighing your decision on this matter, I would draw your attention to two other points. First, the record of cooperation with the United States in cases involving alleged Nazi war criminals has been far better in other Iron Curtain countries than it has in Romania. The Soviet Union, Yugoslavia and Poland—none of whom have judicial assistance treaties with the United States—all have provided government prosecutors with access to archival material and allowed investigators to interview potential witnesses. Romania alone has resisted. Second, Trifa is not the only Romanian national living in the United States alleged to have been involved in atrocities during the war. The Justice Department has numerous other cases whose out-come may depend on Romanian government cooperation. In view of this, it is critical that the United States demonstrate its commitment to obtaining all available evidence to try these cases successfully. Other countries must realize that these prosecutions are a high prior-ity of our government.

In conclusion I would say that I hope you will not view your mandate under Section 402 as limited solely to the issue of freedom of emigration and that you will take account of what I have discussed today. I firmly believe that a government's attitude with respect to cooperation on issues of mutual concern is a vital component of any decision on an MFN waiver. For certainly in determining whether a waiver will help promote the goals of the act, a country's willingness to work with the United States on other matters in which our gov-ernment has a substantial interest will be indicative of that nation's willingness to permit increased emigration.

Finally, Mr. Chairman, I would once again like to express my deep appreciation to you for inviting me to testify today and for the ef-forts you have made to bring this matter directly to the attention of the Romanian government.

APPENDIX B

STATEMENT OF BISHOP TRIFA

On August 25, 1980, my legal counsel was instructed to file a surrender of my Certificate of Naturalization with the United States District Court for the Eastern District of Michigan at Detroit, Michigan. Attached to such pleading was a memorandum or commentary, actually in book form, which in some measure attempts an analysis of the whole history of the times, places and events leading to this most unhappy day of my life.

The relinquishment of my citizenship is in no way to be considered an admission of the government allegations in any manner, form or substance. Indeed, my protests in this regard have remained unequivocal these past thirty years.

This litigation against me has actually been enlarged into something far more comprehensive—a trial of the ideological and political milieu of Romanian history in the pre-war years, nearly 50 years ago. To that obvious purpose and direction, I have been made a hostage of my own naturalization, forced to act as a vehicle in the condemnation of my country of origin; and, particularly of the Legionary Movement of those years, and of the many fine men and women who gave so much in their dedication to what was then felt as the best solution to Romania's many and complex difficulties. This I cannot and I will not permit to continue.

However much I believe in the American judicial process—and I do—it is with an equally firm conviction I feel I have been denied due process in this protracted litigation. Even if I were accorded a fair trial as such in a procedural sense, it would appear to be irrelevant when such would still render impossible any attempt to bring across the truth of the matters taking place in Romania during the critical years between the great wars.

The tremendous cost, the enormous amount of time, the heavy burdens of many years of litigation and harassment have rendered me unable to effectively defend myself and give full measure to the parishioners of my far-flung Episcopate. Of late and increasing importance, I find myself unable to act or speak freely on behalf of my Church. Even avenues of religious and political expression appear to be closed to me.

[239]

The priorities are clear. If the Romanian Orthodox Episcopate of America is to survive and remain free, outside interests and influences cannot be permitted to transform my fight to retain U. S. citizenship into a power struggle between my Church, my American government and my country of origin.

Thus, in order to preserve the integrity of my own convictions, and in the best interests of my Church and its faithful, the struggle must end!

APPENDIX C

The following is an excerpt from *The Undoing* by George E. Woods.

SUMMER, 1980 . . .

By the date of this commentary, the pursuit of Bishop Trifa in the denaturalization proceeding was over . . . for the defendant had voluntarily surrendered his Certificate of Naturalization to the United States District Court for the Eastern District of Michigan.

. . . And why did it end in this manner—why, with all of the time, all of the effort, the years of frustration and heartache. . . .

The fight for survival first began in the resistance to the pressures of the Rumanian Communist Government nearly 30 years ago in its attempts to take control of the Rumanian Orthodox Church in this country. Those in any way knowledgeable with the history[*] of the Church are keenly aware such struggle has continued to this very day— and a mere recapitulation of the effort and sacrifice over the years in order to survive in no way can demonstrate the toll taken of this man both physically and mentally.

From the very beginning there were the charges of "...war criminal... Nazi... Fascist... Communist... atrocities...." And those endless allegations, of course, initiated a continuing investigation of the defendant, one in which the government has conveniently neglected to acknowledge Trifa's cooperation whenever called upon. The first seven years of the investigation have been detailed at great length in early chapters of this book—but the regularity and intensity of it has varied but little even to the date of this writing.

Indeed, there is considerable reason to believe the Immigration and Naturalization Service will continue to "investigate" the Bishop for whatever time is left to him. After all, it would not be the first time our government has engaged in relentless pursuit after having been the cause of its own profound embarrassment. . . .

This is a man who has never denied his wholehearted support of the nationalistically-oriented Legionary Movement. At that time and in that setting he had a genuine belief it represented the ideals and the best—perhaps the last hope for the Rumanian nation and its people in those chaotic circumstances.

---

[*] Recommended reading: Bobango, *The Romanian Orthodox Episcopate of America, 1929-1979.*

Admittedly an activist for social justice in a country which admitted of little if any—and permitted far less—Trifa dedicated his time and effort to the only student organization capable of waging an incessant battle for basic human rights and an opportunity to move into the mainstream of social, political and economic responsibility. Yet in his activism, in his battle, he has always denied having committed crimes against individuals or against humanity as any means to an end.

One could hardly deny he was verbal and critical of what he and so many others felt was the undue influence of Rumanian Jews in the political and economic national fabric. Even though the Jew was the principal object of his views on *numerus clausus* and proportional representation, his views on what we might call "ethnic exclusivity", he could never have believed at the time, or now, such opinions or attitudes were or are persecutive of another in the context attributed by the denaturalization case against him. —If so, there must be a considerable number of naturalized citizens from Central and Eastern Europe, and elsewhere, who are in for a considerable shock. . . .

Nor was there ever the slightest whisper by Trifa of a race or religious hatred—and his strong belief in advocating *numerus clausus* at the time has never been a matter of any inconsistency to him, no different in fact than the proponents of affirmative action feel when they deny they are imposing "reverse discrimination" on others.

He has maintained from the beginning his position as the President of the National Union of Rumanian Christian Students made him the spokesman and leader of all of the students. Christian, Jew or otherwise—made him the representative and administrator of the rights of all Rumanian students in their problems and negotiations with the government.

However reluctantly he agreed to the assemblage, Trifa always acknowledged he was a leader of the demonstration in Bucharest on the night of January 20, 1941. And finally, after changing its mind in a succession of pleadings in the case, even the government could be seen to have arrived at a point where it tacitly admitted the evening resulted in a peaceful manifestation of a protest of what many claim was a unilateral, unlawful and arbitrary act by General Antonescu.

As for Bishop Trifa: he was not involved in the persecution of the Jews or in the torture and killing of Christian and Jewish victims of the events of January 21-24, 1941. What further or other really need be said at this point; it seems to have been said in so many ways, however inexhaustible the subject matter.

And after those tragic and horrible few days, Trifa was, as we know, given initial and then continuing sanctuary by the Germans after the fall of the National Legionary State government. Along with many Legionnaires and supporters of the movement, he was taken to Germany under armed guard and thereafter kept in a protective custody status. Most assuredly his detention was not in the manner of those many thousands of other prisoners in German concentration and extermination camps who suffered all nature of brutality and death—but he was, nevertheless, kept in prison for well over three years, albeit there were privileges enough a share of the time to insure survival.

He was released eventually, in August, 1944, found his way to Italy—after rejecting Sima's National Legionary State in Exile—and ultimately came to the United States.

For a considerable period of time prior to the writing of this epilogue, it became abundantly clear to defense counsel the defendant was "slipping away". . . . His over-all health and vigor had diminished to an extent it gave me great concern—equally alarming, he had lost his will and power to carry-on the fight. The heart, the stamina—they were faint and near-impossible of being able to go on any longer in the defense of the action brought by the government.

The 30 years of investigation and villification finally seemed to catch up and take all the heart out of him—although there was a bit more to it than that, of course. The initial Complaint had been filed against him in May, 1975—and though the government from the beginning was supposed to have "well-documented material" and evidence against him, it always seemed the government was always changing lawyers, time and again—or they were asking for additional time to get more "well-documented material". Their "do over" against him seemed endless. . . .

At one point, in October, 1977, it appeared we might be ready to try the matter and get it over and done with. . . but it didn't quite work out that way. . . .

By mid May, 1980, we had yet *another* judge assigned to try the case—completely unfamiliar with the matter and its five year litigation complexities, of course—and only a fair hope of concluding the case at the trial level by year's end. . . to be followed by the interminable time and cost of an appeal. . . .

Defendant has never had the economic means to engage in litigation with the government—a bottomless pit—or with anyone else. He has had the goodwill of his parishioners for contributions—and that is all. Already more than five years along into this complex litigation, an honest response to, "How long?"—"Well, it could take a very long time—and a bundle of money. . . ."

To the rest of you who would do combat with your sovereign state or Federal government, take note that at the date of this writing the defendant had spent well over $100,000 in an attempt to defend himself—every cent of which had come in small and individual contributions from members of the diocese. —The last we heard, the special government unit was prepared to fight with over five million of the taxpayers' money while the defendant fought with only his own, something approximating slim and none.

So there is no more money at this point—though you are probably correct to suggest he could go back to the members of his episcopate. But then, he concludes, it gets to be a matter of priorities: how long can he go to these people who not only have their own financial problems in these times of high costs and escalating inflation—but what is to be done to get the tens of thousands of dollars necessary to assure continuance of the summer camps for the youth of the Church who must have new—and expensive—dormitories? —And however legal counsel might believe he had more than a fighting chance for success in the lawsuit, how does one make too much headway in the face of these practical considerations?

It has never been easy finding witnesses and evidence these 40 years later—nor has it been inexpensive. For have you tried traveling in Europe or South America, particularly in the past two years?

When this matter could have been brought, it wasn't. —It would have been so much easier, and for both sides to this proceeding. . . .

The defendant will always be convinced—and so will others—he has been denied due process by the delay in the prosecution of this case. Nor is he persuaded he would ever be able to make anything near the presentation of his case necessary before he would get his "fighting chance". —Perhaps he's right on that one. . . .

—and Trifa's discovery he was back in the game again as a pawn to be checkmated by the Socialist Republic of Rumania over his determination to fight for the independence of his Episcopate—well, he gave up in his long and frustrating fight to free himself of being prisoner of his Certificate of Naturalization.

It has weighed heavily on his mind that he has been drained of both time and energy to minister to his far-flung parishes these past years. In the best of times, as your own leader of worship will tell you, it is a grim and constant challenge to survive. His loss of ability to express himself on behalf of his Church, his loss of over-all utility, it is believed, also contributed to the Bishop's final decision in the matter.

The media, of course, has "done a job" on him over the years—all of which has subjected him to harassment difficult for anyone else to imagine. And it has extended as well to his churches throughout the country: picketing, disturbances—firebombing—building permits being denied local parishes because their Bishop is a "Nazi", or the church is a nest of the same. . . .

Maybe, too, there might be some feeling his 30 years as a fine citizen and outstanding churchman seem to have been disregarded; his citizenship has been held hostage by the government all that time... maybe if they do not want him to have it anymore, then why is it so important to place all that much value on a certificate whose meaning has been eroded by a government he feels has made a mockery of simple fairness.

For him, it has certainly been, The Undoing. . . .

APPENDIX D

PARISH DECLARATION
OF THE
HOLY TRINITY ROMANIAN ORTHODOX CHURCH
OF YOUNGSTOWN, OHIO

[August 30, 1980]

The parishioners of the aforementioned parish have reluctantly but prudently remained silent during the litigation of the denaturalization suit against Valerian D. Trifa, Archbishop of the Romanian Orthodox Episcopate of America. But now, as his case has been removed from the jurisdiction of the U. S. Federal District Court, we now strongly remonstrate the deplorable motives and methods that many official and unofficial parties have undertaken during the five years the case has been before the court.

It is our belief that certain groups and individuals have used this case as an opportunity to spread slanderous propaganda for their own expediencies. We also believe that the reputation of Archbishop Valerian has been violated by these parties with little or no regard for the truth. These parties include television networks, newspapers, magazines, special interest groups of the Jewish community, U. S. Congressional leaders, and the Special Investigative Unit of the U.S. Department of Justice formed to prosecute the cases of "Nazi War Criminals," to name a few.

We understand the television networks, radio stations, newspapers, magazine publishers and the media at large are in the business of selling their air time and publications, but it seems obvious to us that some of these business concerns have resorted to 'Yellow Journalism' and general sensationalism in portraying the Archbishop's case for the sake of boosting ratings and increasing circulation. TELLING FRIGHTENING NAZI STORIES IS BIG BUSINESS THESE DAYS. Regardless how much or how often segments of the media allege that the Archbishop is a "Nazi war criminal," we know for a fact that nothing could be further from the truth. We are of the opinion that along with the right of freedom of the press goes a great responsibility of accurate and truthful journalism, and we protest the injustice done by them to Archbishop Valerian.

We also wish to chastise the Special Investigative Unit of the Justice Department which was responsible for the most recent investigation and prosecution of the simple denaturalization suit which was transformed into a witch hunt for an alleged Nazi war criminal. We have little faith in that bureaucracy which spent millions of our tax dollars for the primary purpose of justifying the need for additional millions. The Special Unit has been so busy justifying additional appropriations and are so busy sending lawyers all over the world that they completely disregarded the Defendant's right to due process which is a guaranteed right of all Americans. Thirty years of investigation by the F.B.I., the C.I.A., the Immigration Department and finally the Special Unit resulting in inconclusive evidence should indicate the allegations are unfounded. Furthermore, the numerous continuances requested by the prosecution lead us to doubt that the Special Unit really sought justice. We believe this department of injustice and harassment surely sought to get as many miles out of the Trifa case as it could—to create jobs, justify additional salaries and possibly to justify European vacations for its investigating employees.

In an effort to ascertain a motive for this ongoing attack by certain special interest groups of the Jewish community, we wonder if the attack is merely a means to gain sympathy for the Jewish cause. Playing on Americans' sympathy and swaying public opinion may make it easier to obtain appropriations of U. S. Foreign Aid and military aid to Israel. The gross exaggerations of the holocaust and now of the Civil War in Bucharest in 1941, lead us to believe this to be true. Could it also be possible that this attack is nothing more than Jew vs. Christian? The Jewish community cries of persecution by the Christians. We ask, "Who is persecuting whom?" One of our parishes was denied a building permit due to certain Jewish groups who claimed that our parishioners were Nazis. During December, a Jewish group was given a permit to demonstrate in front of one of our churches and the police had to be called in to protect our parishioners from the unruly crowd so they could leave the church after Sunday services. One of our parishes was firebombed by a Jewish group who publicly boasted of the atrocity. Again we ask, "Who is persecuting whom?"

We believe that the privilege of immunity of Congressional leaders has been abused—especially in the case of Congresswoman Elizabeth Holtzman in this McCarthy-type witch hunt. The Romanian government has never been sympathetic to Archbishop Valerian. Ironically, it had stated that all available documents and information about him had been supplied. The government further stated that it had no complaint against him relative to the allegations and charges. Following the release of these statements, Congresswoman Holtzman urged her Subcommittee on Trade to take no action toward approving the Trade Act with Romania "until the Romanian government has fully cooperated in the prosecution of the Trifa case." It appears Congresswoman Holtzman has been dangling the carrot of Most Favored Nation trade status with Romania in exchange for evidence that simply could not be produced and may have been inviting its manufacture.

We further believe that the Archbishop is the target of these injustices because, as a monk who serves as Bishop of a few thousand Americans of Romanian descent, he is easy prey and is no match for the vast resources of his detractors. One humble insignificant religious leader could not possibly be an obstacle for the "grand designs" of the media, bureaucrats, Congressional leaders, or the cause of Israel.

Let it be known that the members of this Parish are aware of the truth about Archbishop Valerian D. Trifa and are not influenced by the media, the Department of Justice or special interest groups, all of which are only interested in their own aggrandizement.

Let it be known that the Parish understands that the Archbishop sacrificed his American Citizenship for the well-being of his Church and its members.

Let it be further known that we continue to whole-heartedly support our Archbishop and stand with him to protect his outstanding reputation as a true man of God, as well as to protect our supposed guaranteed right of freedom of religion.

(signed)

Charles J. Chetian, Jr..   Archimandrite Roman Braga
Parish Council President   Parish Priest

Sandra Carulea   Gary N. Brott
Parish Council Secretary   Committee Chairman

APPENDIX E

RESOLUTION
OF THE CHURCH CONGRESS OF THE
ROMANIAN ORTHODOX EPISCOPATE OF AMERICA

The Congress of the Romanian Orthodox Episcopate of America, convened this 20th day of September, 1980, at Cleveland, Ohio, has resolved the following:

This Congress, the parishes and the faithful of the Romanian Orthodox Church in America cannot adequately record the shock and trauma registered in being advised that Archbishop Valerian, our Spiritual Leader, after a long and weary battle, has been forced to renounce his American citizenship.

While we found it incomprehensible that civil proceedings have been filed against the Archbishop, we always hoped that our American concept of fairness, due process and a speedy trial would have brought out the truth.

However, as the years passed by, we saw our hopes fade into uncertainty and our sense of justice outraged by the expansion of the civil suit against the Archbishop into a case bearing on the entire political and social milieu of Romanian history forty years ago, and the irresponsible coverage given by the news media to this case. A simple denaturalization case has been transformed into a national spectacle, geared to advance political interests of certain elected officials and to satisfy ambitions of specific powerful interests.

It has been with anxious and increasing shame that we have witnessed the erosion this past five years of fair play, and the deterioration of the moral fiber of our nation.

Archbishop Valerian has carried the burden of unparalleled attacks upon his background and character by those who, for upwards of 30 years, have distorted instances of fact and truth, mostly for insidious purposes.

We are fully aware that under these circumstances, it was impossible for the Archbishop to receive an impartial hearing thusly denying him a fair trial. This led to the Archbishop's decision.

[248]

This Congress, mindful of its responsibilities to the parishes of this Episcopate, to our fellow citizens one and all, of whatever faith or persuasion, categorically rejects the allegations against Archbishop Valerian as without foundation and of no material substance.

Our Congress is convinced that the Archbishop made his decision because of his continued love and dedication for his Faith, his Episcopate and his faithful. For that, this Congress expresses its unreserved appreciation; it further resolves its unrelenting and continued support of His Eminence, who has given unsparingly of himself to our Orthodox Christian Faith and our Episcopate.

THIS CONGRESS HAS JUDGED THE MAN IN HIS TIME AND ACCORDING TO HIS DEEDS; HE HAS NOT BEEN FOUND WANTING.

CHURCH CONGRESS OF THE ROMANIAN
ORTHODOX EPISCOPATE OF AMERICA

BY *(signed)* Rev. Fr. Laurence Lazar
Its Secretary

September 20, 1980
Cleveland, Ohio

NOTES

CHAPTER I

1. The Romanian Orthodox Missionary Episcopate of America vs. Ioan Trutza, *et al.*, No. 27916 District Court of the United States, Northern District of Ohio, Eastern Division, *Transcript of Evidence on Motion for Preliminary Injunction*, Vol. II, pp. 3,31,47-50.

2. *Biserica Ortodoxă Română*, LXIX, No. 3-6 (March-June, 1951), p. 238, and *Calendarul Solia* 1977 of the Romanian Orthodox Episcopate of America, p. 102.

3. *Calendarul Solia* 1977, p. 103.

4. The particular character of the first, or "pioneer" generation of Romanian immigrants has been treated widely in writings on Romanian-American history. For a recent summation see Gerald Bobango, "Romanians in America: the 'Mia și drumul' Generation, 1900-1920," forthcoming in Festschrift for Constantin Giurescu, *East European Monographs*, 1982.

5. The complexities arising from the 1929 Founding Congress, and the extensive politics surrounding the naming of Policarp Morușca are elaborated, along with the full story of the first three decades of the Romanian-American church, in Gerald J. Bobango, *The Romanian Orthodox Episcopate of America: The First Half Century, 1929-1979* (Jackson, Michigan: Romanian-American Heritage Center, 1979), chapters 3-7. (Hereafter, Bobango, ROEA.)

6. Following the 1950 schism which produced two Romanian Episcopates, this name was changed and shortened. The Episcopate headed by Bishop Valerian Trifa, which became independent from the Romanian Church, was henceforth known as the Romanian Orthodox Episcopate of America; that diocese headed by Bishop Andrei Moldovan, canonically and administratively tied to Bucharest, continued to call itself the Romanian Orthodox Missionary Episcopate of America.

7. Policarp died in Romania in 1958 and is buried in Alba Julia. To the end of his life he continued to consider himself the titular bishop of the American Episcopate founded in 1929, and the Episcopate recognized *de jure* that this was so. The election of Valerian Trifa in

1951 was the election of a co-adjutor bishop, or "stand-in" bishop, so to speak, until such time as Policarp returned to his See. In 1958, Trifa was thus formally "elevated" by the Church Congress to Policarp's place. For the complete story of Moruşca's final years and role in the Episcopate, see Bobango, *ROEA*, 1929-1979, chapters 6-8.

8. Henry L. Roberts, *Rumania: Political Problems of an Agrarian State* (New York: Archon Books Edition, 1969), pp. 263-264. Also Constantin C. Giurescu, *et al., Istoria româniei în Date* (Bucureşti: Editura Enciclopedică Română, 1971), p. 391.

9. *Calendarul Solia*, 1947, p. 61.

10. Archives of the Romanian Orthodox Episcopate of America (Hereafter, ROEA *Archives*): Policarp: Correspondence from Romania, 1939-1958, Policarp to Trutza, 8 December 1947.

11. *Telegraful Român*, Anul 115, Nr. 13-15, 1 aprilie 1967, pp. 1-2.

12. ROEA *Archives*, Protocolul Comisiei Interimare Bisericeşti a Episcopiei Ortodoxe Româna din America de Nord, 1930-1947 (Hereafter, Protocol CIB), p. 213.

13. *Calendarul Solia*, 1977, p. 93. A copy of the original is in ROEA *Archives*, Patriarhia Ortodoxă Română, Bucureşti, 1930-1950 (Hereafter, POR), for 17 February 1947.

14. Protocol CIB, p. 215.

15. POR, Western Union Telegram, 24 February 1947.

16. The complete story of the complex maneuverings between the Trutza and Moldovan factions between 1947-1953 is in Bobango, ROEA, chapter 7.

CHAPTER II

1. ROEA, File Consiliul Episcopesc şi Comisia Interimară, 1929-1951, Procese Verbale, session of 1 July 1950, p. 2 (Hereafter, PV.)

2. Photostatic copy of the original in ROEA, East State Fair Episcopate Incorporation file.

3. Cf. p. 2, *supra.*

4. ROEA Church Congress Minutes, 1941-1950, *Proces Verbal* luat in şedinţele Congresului Bisericesc. . . ţinute la 2 şi 3 Iulie 1950, in. . . Philadelphia, Pa., p. 15.

5. POR, Nr. 531/1950, 17 July 1950, and *Calendarul Solia* 1977, p. 104.

6. While the March 17 meeting in Detroit is an uncontested fact, the number of participants is not certain, and sources differ on this, attesting to the secrecy which surrounded it. There were no less than six and no more than eight present, most likely. Cf. "De ce Episcopia

Ortodoxă Română din America a fost silită să se despartă de Patriarhia Română," in ROEA Circulars, 1952, no. 2.

7. *Proces Verbal.* . . 1950, shows that Moldovan was present, with his two delegates from Akron, at the opening of the session. Those parishes which had not sent in their declarations were singled out for discussion, and Akron was not among them.

8. *Calendarul Ortodox Solia pe A.D. 1951*, pp. 64-65. This was the first of Bishop Moldovan's calendars, published until court order forbid him to use the name *Solia*. In other works I have labelled it *Calendarul Solia AM*, to distinguish it from the Solia Calendar dating from 1936 published by the Trutza-Trifa Episcopate (Bobango, *op. cit.*, p. 225).

9. Transcript, Vol. II, pp. 62-65. Cf. note 1, p. 251.

10. *Calendarul Solia*, 1977, pp. 106-107. Originals or carbons of most of the correspondence from the Patriarchate in this period are in the ROEA files POR and Romanian Patriarchate Dossier, 1950-1978, or the "Guvernul Român" Correspondence. Citation is given to the 1977 Calendar only for the sake of convenience, where the letters are published *in toto* in English.

11. *Ibid.*

12. PV, session of 16 November 1950, pp. 5-8. The general fund was shortly afterwards put at the Roumanian Savings and Loan Company in Cleveland.

13. *Calendarul Solia*, 1977, pp. 109-111.

14. ROEA, Vatra Guest Register, p. 32.

15. Transcripts, Vols. I and II.

16. *Ibid.*, Vol. II, p. 5.

17. ROEA, Morariu-Carol II file, miscellaneous; and Bobango, pp. 134, 144.

18. The Morariu file contains definite proof of two marriages, one in 1928, the other in 1950. Estimates of others are perhaps due to the fact that Morariu always seemed on the verge of proposing matrimony to someone.

19. Details of these wartime politics are in Bobango, ROEA, pp. 134-139.

20. Morariu file, miscellaneous clippings; *Detroit Free Press,* November 18, 1942, pp. 1-2; *America*, no. 135, 20 November 1942, p. 1.

21. Protocol CIB, session of January 27, 1943.

22. Policarp: Correspondence from Romania, John Bucerzan to U.S. Secretary of State, Visa Division, 28 May 1947, and to Dr. Traian Leucuţia, 5 May 1947. Martin had moved up since those days. He now operated a bar in Detroit, which presumably was the address also of his "law office."

23. I.e., that both were one inch deep, with a mouth that was a mile wide.

24. Valerian D. Trifa, *Solia: Istoria vieţii unei gazete româneşti in America* (Detroit: Romanian Orthodox Episcopate of America, 1961), pp. 21-22.

25. Protocol CIB, p. 196, and issues of *Solia* for the second half of 1945 for samples of Martin's pretentious style.

26. Policarp: Correspondence from Romania, Trutza *et al.*, to Policarp, 19 March 1946.

27. E.g., see *Ibid.*, nr. 13/1940, Policarp to Mihalţian, 10 March 1940, and ROEA Church Congress Minutes, 1929-1940, "Raport dela al 11-lea Congres Naţional al Bisericii Ortodoxe Române in America... de 1 şi 2 Septemvrie 1940 in oraşul Farrell, Pa.," p. 2 and Bobango, 129-132.

28. Protocol CIB, p. 212.

29. It is not far afield to compare Martin's pretensions with those of other self-styled delegates of tens of thousands of Romanian-Americans, who in reality represented merely themselves.

30. Policarp: Correspondence from Romania, J. Bucerzan to U.S. Secretary of State, Visa Division, 28 May 1947.

31. Church Congress Minutes, 1941-1950, *Proces Verbal* al Sedinţelor Congresului Bisericese Tinut la 4 şi 5 Iulie, 1948, la *Vatra Romaneasca . . .*, p. 5.

32. *Ibid., Proces Verbal* luat in şedinţele Congresului Bisericesc... ţinute la 2 şi 3 Iulie 1949..., p. 3.

33. PV, session of 1 July 1949, p. 1.

34. Protocol CIB, session of July 3, 1945, pp. 194-196, and 197-200, the meeting of the Spiritual Consistory.

35. *Ibid.*

36. PV, session of 9 December 1949, p. 9, and *Calendarul Solia*, 1977, pp. 99-100.

37. PV, session of 3 March 1950, pp. 2-3.

38. *Proces Verbal...* 1950, pp. 18-19.

39. See note 2, *supra*.

40. See note 6, *supra*.

41. ROEA, Vatra Guest Register, p. 32.

42. "Sachelar" was the Romanian adaptation of an archaic Greek ecclesiastical honorary title, roughly translatable as "purse-bearer," although Moga was not Moldovan's treasurer. The pretentiousness of the hierarchical awards and titles bestowed on Moldovan's priests became a matter of amusement, in some quarters.

43. Bobango, ROEA, pp. 307-315, and ROEA Circulars, 1951, 13 September 1951, Trifa to priests, parish councils, Congress.

CHAPTER III

1. PV, session of 29 September 1950, pp. 4-5.

2. ROEA Circulars, 1950. Episcopate office to parishes, undated, between 29 October and 19 November 1950.

3. Roberts, *op. cit.*, p. 329. See also *Economic Survey of Europe in 1948*, United Nations Department of Economic Affairs Publication, 1948, on the postwar Romanian economy.

4. One political prisoner who labored on this canal was Archimandrite Roman Braga, presently pastor of Holy Trinity Romanian Orthodox Church, Youngstown, Ohio. See Donald Dunham, *Zone of Violence* (New York: Belmont Books, 1962), 149.

5. *Solia*, 26 November 1950, p. 3, and 3 December 1950, p. 1.

6. *Solia*, 3 December 1950, p. 1, and following issues.

7. Transcript, Vol. I, pp. 178-220.

8. PV, session of 16 March 1951, pp. 2, 6.

9. *Solia AM*, 1 February 1951, p. 2.

10. *Ibid.*, 1 April 1951, p. 3.

11. Bobango, ROEA, 198-202.

12. *Solia*, 27 April 1952, p. 3.

13. *Raport* Presentat de Consiliul şi Biroul... Congres Bisericesc... din 1-2-3 şi 4 Iulie 1951 intrunita in oraşul Chicago..., Circulars, 1951, pp. 7ff.

14. *Solia*, 16 April 1950, p. 1, and Circulars, 5 April 1951.

15. Episcopate Council Minutes, ROEA, 1952-1960 (Hereafter, Minutes), session of 17 January 1953, p. 4.

16. Circulars, 1951, Western Union telegram, 30 June 1951, Policarp to Opreanu, also in POR.

17. *Tribuna*, January, 1952, p. 1, and monthly issues beginning September, 1951.

18. *Ibid.*, October, 1951, pp. 1-4.

19. *Ibid.*, p. 5.

20. ROEA, Walter Winchell-Drew Pearson file, Donald G. Coe to V. Hategan, 18 September, 1951; Paul F. Scheffels to Rudi Nan, 18 September 1951.

21. *Ibid.*, Paul F. Scheffels to Vasile Hategan, 18 September 1951.

22. *Solia*, 12 July 1953, pp. 1-2.

23. *Tribuna*, October, 1951, p. 7.

24. *Calendarul Credinţa* 1953, p. 77.

25. *Pe Marginea Prăpastiei*, 2 vols. (Bucureşti: Monitorul oficial şi Imprimeriile Statului, 1941), p. 224ff.

26. *Blood Bath in Rumania*, "First authentic account based upon official documents." Published by "The Record" News Bulletin,

New York, organ of the United Rumanian Jews of America, Vol. IV, Nos. 6-7, July-August, 1942, 61p.

27. *Ibid.*, see photograph section following p. 30.

28. Interview with Father Nicolae Moldovan, New Kensington, Pa., June 30, 1978. "Some priests who didn't want Trifa were passing around this book from South America that told about Trifa and the Iron Guard" (at the 1951 Chicago Church Congress).

29. Bela Vago, "Fascism in Eastern Europe," in Walter Laqueur, ed., *Fascism: A Reader's Guide* (Berkeley and Los Angeles: Univ. of California Press, 1976), p. 236.

30. Ştefan Palaghiţa, *Garda de Fer: Spre Reinvierea României* (Buenos Aires, Ave. Belgrano, publicată de autor, 1951), p. 144.

31. ROEA Circulars, 1951, Trifa to priests, parishes, Congress, 13 September 1951, p. 3ff.

32. Howard Blum, "The Hunt for an American Nazi," *Esquire*, (October, 1976), 146.

33. Interview with Archbishop Valerian Trifa, Grass Lake, Michigan, December 15, 1979.

34. ROEA Archives, Trifa Immigration File, No. 1.

35. *Calendarul Solia* 1977, p. 149.

36. ROEA Archives, "Hirotonie şi Jurisdicţie Canonică, 1951-1961, file, Western Union Telegram, 30 November 1951, Alexander Bezsmertny to Vasile Haţegan. Documents on the search for consecration are also reprinted in *Calendarul Solia* 1977, pp. 144-155.

37. ROEA Archives, Trifa Immigration file, No. 2.

38. *Calendarul Solia* 1977, p. 149. Cf. also Note 10, chapter 2.

39. Blum, *op. cit.*, p. 150.

40. *Ibid.*, p. 146.

41. *Ibid.*, p. 150ff.

42. *Ibid.* See also Bobango, ROEA History, pp. 214, 216-217, 310-313.

CHAPTER IV

1. Photostat of the original in "Hirotonie şi Jurisdicţie," *supra.*

2. Howard Blum, *Wanted! The Search for Nazis in America* (Greenwich, Conn.: Fawcett Books, 1977), 132. This is the paperback edition of Blum's hardcover edition of the same title, published in 1976 by Quadrangle Books of the New York Times Company. For convenience, citations will be to the Fawcett edition.

3. *Ibid.*

4. *Calendarul Solia* 1977, p. 155. See also *Tribuna*, May, 1952, pp. 1-2,4; *Solia*, 27 April 1952, 4 May 1952, 18 May 1952; *Calendarul Solia* 1953, pp. 67-76.

5. Blum, *op. cit.*, p. 133.

6. *Ibid.*, pp. 133-134.

7. *Tribuna*, August, 1952, p. 5, and August, 1954, p. 2. By the latter date, *Credinţa* had replaced *Tribuna*.

8. Bobango, ROEA, 218-221.

9. By contrast, during Trifa's interviews leading up to his naturalization hearing, testimony received as to the good opinion of him held by his neighbors and acquaintances in the Jackson County area was unanimous.

10. *Tribuna*, October, 1952, p. 1.

11. *Solia*, 11 January 1953, p. 1.

12. See Chapter III.

13. *Solia*, 12 July 1953, pp. 1-2.

14. Blum, pp. 134-141.

15. ROEA, Walter Winchell-Drew Pearson Campaign file, Haţegan to Frederick Brown Harris, June 7, 1955.

16. Blum, p. 141.

17. ROEA, Winchell-Pearson file, reproduction in *Detroit Jewish News*, 25 January 1974, of *New York Mirror* articles.

18. *Detroit Free Press*, 4 June 1955, 8.

19. Winchell-Pearson file, Bigg to Drew Pearson, 23 June 1955.

20. *Ibid.*, E. M. Heagerty to C. E. Bigg, 28 June 1955.

21. Interview with Bishop Valerian Trifa, December 19, 1979.

22. Blum, p. 142.

23. Blum, p. 143.

24. *Ibid.*

25. Blum, p. 146.

26. *Ibid.*

27. ROEA Archives, Trifa Immigration file, No. 2.

28. Original is in Trifa Immigration file, No. 1.

29. Interview with Bishop Valerian Trifa, December 19, 1979.

30. Trifa Immigration file, No. 2.

31. Blum, p. 158.

32. *Ibid.*

33. Bobango, ROEA, *passim.*

34. Blum, p. 148.

35. Blum, p. 149.

36. Blum, pp. 151-152. Another interesting sidelight of the Antonovici drama: in Blum's account in *Esquire* (1976, p. 156) the sculptor "ran through the cathedral and out into the street to find a telephone. On the corner of Convent Avenue he found one and called Dr. Charles Kremer." In the book *Wanted!* (1977, p. 152) the sculptor "ran through the cathedral and out into the street looking for a telephone. On the corner of Amsterdam Avenue he found a phone and called Dr. Charles Kremer." The phone booth had moved.

37. *The Michigan Journalist*, 50, no. 5 (February, 1977), p. 13ff.

38. ROEA Episcopate Council Minutes, 1952-1960, session of 27 February 1960, p. 4, and session of 1 July 1960, p. 4.

39. *Românul-American*, which preached a purely Marxist line, found itself in the difficult posture of belittling the Trifa Episcopate for taking a step which, in *Românul-American*'s necessary interpretation, meant that the Episcopate was moving closer to Moscow's way of thinking; but then, editors of such journals must be skillful in doublethink.

40. "Hirotonie şi Jurisdicţie Canonică," Leonty to Episcopate, 17 June 1960.

41. *Congressional Record*—House, March 1, 1962, p. 2844.

42. During the 1960s and 1970s it became an important goal of Romanian historiography to demonstrate the 100% anti-fascist sentiment of the entire masses of the working people and peasantry in the great anti-Hitlerist coalition in cooperation with the friendly liberating Red Army. To this end, certain elements of the Romanian army, including soldiers such as Antonescu, had to be portrayed in a more nationalistic light, since they had, after all, helped lay the ground for Romania's turnabout against Germany during August, 1944. On trends, rehabilitations and debilitations, see Michael Rura, *Reinterpretation of History As a Method of Furthering Communism in Romania* (Washington: Georgetown U. Press, 1961), 123 p.

43. See note 41, *supra*.

44. *Solia*, 27 May 1962, p. 4, and 13 May 1962, p. 2.

45. ROEA Archives, Newspaper Case File, 1962-1973, *New York Herald Tribune*, May 4, 1962, f. 1.

46. *Ibid.*, *Winnipeg Tribune*, May 4, 1962, f. 2.

47. *Ibid.*, *Le Monde*, 22-23 avril 1962, f. 10.

48. *Ibid.*, *Românul-American*, 24 martie 1962, f. 9.

49. *Ibid.*, attached notice.

50. *Ibid.*, *Jackson Citizen Patriot*, May 10, 1962, f. 8.

51. *Ibid.*, *Toronto Globe and Mail*, May 4, 1962, f. 11.

52. *Ibid.*, *Confidential Flash*, Toronto, December 7, 1963, (p. 9), f. 16.

53. See Pearson's columns in the *Detroit Free Press*, 7 June and 18 October, 1962.

54. *Philadelphia Sunday Bulletin*, 12 May 1963.

55. *Buffalo Courier Express*, 12 May 1963, 28.

56. Newspaper Case File, ROEA, 1976-1977, Extract, St. Paul-Minneapolis, February, 1977.

57. Charles R. Allen, Jr., *Nazi War Criminals Among Us* (New York: Jewish Currents Reprint No. 3, 1963), 18-22. Also see Trifa's letter to Allen, 2 October 1963 in Winchell-Pearson File. This was only one of the more egregious little publications inspired by Rabbi Rosen's trip to the West, but was the most obvious in identifying him as a major source of material. Since 1963 Romanians both in the West and in Israel have learned much more about Rosen, whose credibility is far lower today. In 1965 the publication in Jerusalem of Rabin Dr. David Safran's *Satana Român*, severely indicted Rosen, calling him one of the Romanian "men of faith who abuse the faith to advance their own interest," (p. 140) and noting that the communist party has some of its "best agents in rabbis and Sefrabins in the temples and synagogues." (p. 112) He accused Rosen of full cooperation in the intimidation of his (the author's) father in 1950, when the elder Safran was threatened with being shot for "selling state secrets to the imperialists," and he noted Rabbi Rosen's open condemnation of Israel in the Romanian Parliament as "the agent of American imperialism," and his "insults against the Zionists." Rosen far more than most, Safran states, helped to destroy Jewish liberty "without pity" in Romania. (p. 140)

Even today, one can find in Romania and in Israel numerous Jewish critics of Rosen, complete with suggestions that not only is he a compliant lackey of the Romanian government, but is not above suspicion of misappropriation of the vast sums of money which come into the country from Jews outside Romania to help friends and relatives. See *Viaţa Noastră*, 5 December 1979, letter of Moşe Maur and *Revista Mea*, no. 870, 12 December 1979, p. 5.

CHAPTER V

1. On the diplomacy of Ion I.C. Brătianu and Romanian successes in pressing her territorial claims, see Sherman David Spector, *Rumania at the Paris Peace Conference: A Study of the Diplomacy of Ion C. Brătianu* (New York: Bookman Associates, 1962), and Hugh Seton-Watson, *Eastern Europe Between the Wars, 1918-1941*, 2nd ed. (Cambridge: Cambridge University Press, 1946).

2. Roberts, *op. cit.*, 223-233.

3. Ernst Nolte, *Les mouvements fascistes* (Paris, 1969), 243,251.

4. David Mitrany, *The Land and the Peasant in Rumania: the War and Agrarian Reform (1917-1921)*, Economic and Social History of the World War, Rumanian Series, for the Carnegie Endowment for International Peace (London; New Haven: Yale University Press, 1930), and R. W. Seton-Watson, *A History of the Roumanians from the Roman Times to the Completion of Unity* (Cambridge: Cambridge University Press, 1934).

5. Zevedei Barbu, "Rumania," in S.J. Wolf, ed., *European Fascism* (London, 1968, 150.

6. Vago, *op. cit.*, p. 241.

7. Shapiro in recent years has done much to fill in one of the major gaps in interwar Romanian studies, with his well-reasoned work on the Cuza-Goga government, "Prelude to Dictatorship in Romania:The National Christian Party in Power, December 1937-February 1938," *Canadian-American Slavic Studies*, VIII, 1 (Spring 1974), 45-88.

8. Nicholas M. Nagy-Talavera, *The Green Shirts and Others: A History of Fascism in Hungary and Rumania* (Stanford: Hoover Institution Press, 1970).

9. Vago, *op. cit.*, 230.

10. Lucreţiu Pătrăşcanu, *Sub Trei Dictaturi* (Bucureşti: Editura Politică, 1970), 46. Reprint of the 1945 *Forum* edition.

11. *Ibid.*, 61.

12. *Împotriva fascismului*: Sesuinea ştiinţifica privind analiza critica şi demascarea fascismului în România. Bucureşti, 4-5 martie 1971. (Bucureşti: Editura Politica, 1971), 319p.

13. Mihai Fătu and Ion Spălăţelu, *Garda de Fier: Organizaţie Terorista de tip fascist* (Bucureşti: Editura Politică, 1971), 425p.

14. Vago, p. 235.

15. Michel Sturdza, *The Suicide of Europe* (Belmont, Mass.: Western Islands Publishers, 1968).

16. Ştefan Palaghiţa, *Garda de Fer. Spre Reinvierea României* (Buenos Aires: published by the author, 1951), 173.

17. Sturdza, pp. 107, 165.

18. The best example is D. Gazdaru, dir., *Pământul Strămoşesc*, Seria Nouă, 4 (1977-78), Volum Jubilar Semicentenarul Mişcării Legionare, 1927-1977 (Buenos Aires, 1978), 204p.

19. Vago, p. 239.

20. Stephen Fischer-Galati, "Fascism in Romania," in Peter Sugar, ed., *Native Fascism in the Successor States, 1918-1945* (Santa Barbara: ABC-Clio, Inc., 1971), 112-121, and Barbu, *op. cit.*

21. F. L. Carsten, *The Rise of Fascism* (Berkeley and Los Angeles: Univ. of California Press, 1969), 181-193.

22. Note 7, *supra*.

23. Hugh Seton-Watson, "Fascism, Right and Left," *Journal of Contemporary History*, 1 (1966), 183-197.

24. Eugene Weber, "The Men of the Archangel," *Journal of Contemporary History*, 1 (1966), 117-118.

25. Fischer-Galati, *op. cit.*, 114, 116.

26. Weber, pp. 107, 114.

27. Nagy-Talavera, *op. cit.*, pp. 357, 360-361, 374.

28. Vago, p. 240.

29. Fischer-Galati, p. 116.

30. Hans Rogger and Eugen Weber, *The European Right: A Historical Profile* (Berkeley and Los Angeles: Univ. of California Press, 1966), 554.

31. Vago, pp. 235-236.

32. Gerald Bobango, "Romania and the Balance of Power, 1877-1878," *Romanian Bulletin*, July-August, 1977, pp. 5-6.

33. Nagy-Talavera, pp. 247-248.

34. Rogger and Weber, *The European Right*, p. 515.

35. Quoted in *Ibid.*, p. 505.

36. *Romanian Encyclopedia*, III (Bucharest, 1938).

37. Vamberto Morais, *A Short History of Anti-Semitism* (New York: Norton, 1976), 300p.

38. Eugen Weber, *Varieties of Fascism: Doctrines of Revolution in the Twentieth Century* (New York: Van Nostrand Reinhold, Anvil, 1964), p. 98.

39. Vago, pp. 235-236.

40. The literature on this subject only in the past two decades is enormous, as Romanian historians have supported with their research the independent stance of their nation vis-à-vis the Soviet Eastern European power bloc. A good example of one of the most recent collections of studies is Ştefan Pascu, ed., *The Independence of Romania* (Bucureşti: Editura Academiei Republicii Socialiste România, 1977), 263p.

41. Emanuel Turczynski, "The Background of Romanian Fascism," in Peter Sugar, ed., *Native Fascism in the Successor States, 1918-1945* (Santa Barbara: ABC-Clio, 1971), p. 104.

42. For a full treatment of the generation of 1848 and the Union of the Romanian lands during the foundation years, see Gerald J. Bobango, *The Emergence of the Romanian National State* (Boulder: East European Monographs, 1979), 312p.

43. Indeed, the *Universal Jewish Encyclopedia* (p. 254) states that "the best years for the Jews" in Romania, "with the exception of those following their emancipation in 1918, were those under [Alexander Ioan] Cuza." It is a testimony not only to the prince of union, but an interesting comment about the post-1918 situation, given the coincidence of the 1920s with the supposedly harsh anti-Semitism of Professor Cuza, his LANC, and Codreanu's groups.

44. *Reminiscences of the Prince of Rumania*, Sidney Whitman, ed. (New York: Harper and Brothers, 1899), in which Carol I describes the international démarche relative to the Jewish question.

45. Turczynski, p. 105.

46. Rogger and Weber, p. 505.

47. On the Western reaction to Bolshevism and its impact on the peacemakers at Versailles, especially apt are Kent Forster, *Recent Europe: A Twentieth-Century History* (New York: The Ronald Press, 1965); Rosa Levine-Meyer, *Levine, The Life of a Revolutionary* (New York: Atheneum, 1974); Kenneth M. Setton and Henry R. Winkler, eds., *Great Problems in European Civilization*, 2nd edition (Englewood Cliffs, N.J.: Prentice-Hall, 1966); and Leslie C. Tihany, *The Baranya Dispute, 1918-1921* (Boulder, Colo.: East European Monographs, 1978).

48. Robert K. Murray, *The Red Scare: A Study in National Hysteria, 1919-1920* (New York: McGraw, 1964).

49. Must reading for anyone concerned with the ability of foreigners or embracers of "un-American" ideas to receive impartial justice in the United States is Katherine Anne Porter's *The Never-Ending Wrong* (Boston: Little, Brown, 1977), and the article by the same title by Francis Russell in the *National Review*, August 17, 1973, p. 887.

50. Rogger and Weber, p. 518.

51. *Ibid.*, p. 519.

52. Corneliu Z. Codreanu, *For My Legionaries* (Madrid: Colecţia "Omul Nou," 1975), p. 10ff.

53. Kenneth Lunn, "Political Anti-Semitism Before 1914: Fasism's Heritage?" in Kenneth Lunn and Richard C. Thurlow, eds., *British Fascism: Essays on the Radical Right in Inter-War Britain* (New York: St. Martin's Press, 1980), p. 21ff.

54. *Ibid.*, p. 21.

55. George L. Mosse, *Towards the Final Solution* (London: J.M. Dent and Sons, 1978), pp. 141, 168.

56. Lunn, p. 22.

57. See Barbara Tuchman's chapter on Dreyfus in her celebrated work, *The Proud Tower* (New York: Macmillan, 1966), as well as that labeled "The Anarchists."

58. Lunn, p. 35.

59. Lunn, p. 27.

60. Michel Sturdza, *The Suicide of Europe*, pp. 100, 191.

61. Codreanu, *For My Legionaries*, pp. 8-10.

62. *Ibid.*, p. 9.

63. Rogger and Weber, p. 519.

64. One never ceases to be amazed at how deeply ingrained became such notions among profoundly religious and "typical" rank-and-file Legionaries. Even today, one has only to mention France in the same breath with interwar Romania in the presence of Codreanu disciples or devotees, and some remark such as "yes, the Franco-Masons, they controlled everything, they ruined us. . ." and so on, comes forth like an automatic conditioned response.

65 Louise David-Ion Marii, *A Grenoble sur les traces du Capitaine* (Madrid: Editions "Dacia," 1971), p. 28.

66. *Ibid*, p. 17.

67. Eugen Weber, *Action Française: Royalism and Reaction in Twentieth-Century France* (Stanford: Stanford University Press, 1962), p. 19.

68. Cf. Rogger and Webber, pp. 522-525.

69. *Ibid*., p. 523.

70. Weber, *Action Française*, p. 13.

71. *Ibid*.

72. *Ibid*.

73. *Ibid*., p. 12.

74. Rogger and Webber, p. 520.

75. Just as "radical" student protesters in America of the 1960s indiscriminately applied the label "fascist" to anyone disagreeing with them; just as one may read today in any of the publications of the Ku Klux Klan; or, as John O'Hara once wrote, "If a man has a monogamous relationship with one woman, he's being misogynistic toward all the other women in the world. And yet you'd hardly say he was a misogynist. It's like the accusation of anti-Semitism. If a man says he loves all Jews, he's a damn fool or a liar. The Jews he doesn't like will accuse him of anti-Semitism, the ones he does like will deny it."

76. Witness the continuing popularity of West Virginia snake-handling churches, despite government efforts to outlaw such practices; or the intense emotion and psychological outpouring, accompanied by fainting or religious trances at an evangelical tent meeting where people are "healed." One of the great delusions of modern times is that the twentieth century is an age of reason which has cast aside primitivism and superstition.

77. Ion I. Moţa, *Cranii de Lemn* (München: Colecţia "Omul Nou," 1970), p. 11. A reprint of the 4th edition, Editura Mişcǎrii Legionare, Bucureşti, 1940.

CHAPTER VI

1. Nagy-Talavera, *op. cit.*, p. 346.

2. *Ibid.*

3. Shapiro, "Prelude to Dictatorship in Romania," p. 45.

4. Nagy-Talavera, p. 249.

5. Juan J. Linz suggests a number of organizations of the right which occupied intermediary positions between fascism and less extreme conservative or reactionary groups; these he terms "proto-fascist movements" and since Action Française falls into this category, so too, presumably, would the Legion of Codreanu. See his important study, "Some Notes Toward a Comparative Study of Fascism in Sociological Historical Perspective," in Walter Laqueur, ed., *Fascism: A Reader's Guide* (Berkeley: University of California Press, 1976), 3-121, the whole of which deserves careful reading for the implications to be extracted on the Romanian experience.

6. "Socialdemocratism sau poporanism," *Viaţa românească*, septembrie 1907, p. 338.

7. *Ibid.*, p. 341.

8. Vago, "Fascism in Eastern Europe," p. 249.

9. "Socialdemocratism sau poporanism," *Viaţa românească*, (aprilie 1908), pp. 60, 68.

10. Among them, Hugh Seton-Watson, Eugen Weber, Nicholas Nagy-Talavera, Stephen Fischer-Galati, all of whose works are cited elsewhere.

11. It is well to bear in mind that until very recent times, the Balkan village was an intriguing mixture of Christianity grafted onto vestiges of centuries-old paganisms combined with significant doses of medieval demonology. Both anthropologists and social psychologists are needed to enlarge upon the particular peasant religious mentality and relate it to peasant susceptibility to mass appeals couched in religious evangelism, such as Codreanu's. I have tried to explore some of this in a forthcoming article, "Religious Dualism and Romanian Animal Lore," based on the work of Iorga and Moses Gaster.

12. Nagy-Talavera, p. 250.

13. Cf. Gerald J. Bobango, "Preconditions for Nationhood in the Romanian Lands," *Romanian Sources*, III, Part 1 (1977), 24-35.

14. Vasile Marin, *Crez de Generaţie*, Ed. II-a (Bucureşti:Tip: "Bukovina" I.E. Torouţiu, 1937), p. 39.

15. Robert Lee Wolff, *The Balkans in Our Time* (New York: The Norton Library, 1967), pp. 126-127.

16. Roberts, *op. cit.*, has the most thorough treatment of this land distribution, although to be noticed is his comment that "in general, the unequal distribution of land, as a purely economic factor, was

not the primary cause for the agrarian difficulties of the interwar period;" one must look into agricultural productivity and the relations of agriculture to the whole of the Romanian economy. (p. 55)

17. Roberts, pp. 50-55. Also see David Mitrany, *The Land and the Peasant in Romania: the War and Agrarian Reform (1917-1921)* (New Haven: Yale University Press, 1930).

18. In problems of implementation, injustices, and landlord machinations to avoid giving the peasants their due, the reform of 1921 followed traditional lines, displaying similar characteristics to the first major Romanian agrarian reform under Cuza in 1864: see Bobango, *Emergence of the Romanian National State*, pp. 173-179, 259-260, and D. Berindei and N. Adaniloaie, *Reforma Agrara din 1864* (Bucureşti: Editura Academiei Republicii Socialiste Romania, 1967).

19. Wolff, p. 163.

20. The most recent and very useful work on the beginnings and evolution of Romanian political parties is Apostol Stan, *Grupări şi Curente Politice în România între Unire şi Independenţă* (Bucureşti: Editura Ştiinţifică şi Enciclopedică, 1979), 454p.

21. Rogger and Weber, pp. 514-515.

22. Roberts, p. 91.

23. Paul D. Quinlan, *Clash Over Romania: British and American Policies Toward Romania: 1938-1947* (Los Angeles: American-Romanian Academy of Arts and Sciences, 1977), 173p.

24. Rogger and Weber, p. 529.

25. *Ibid.* Cf. also The *Romanian Encyclopedia*, vol. III (Bucharest, 1938).

26. Colin Clark, *Conditions of Economic Progress* (London, 1940), p. 19. Also see C. Radulescu-Motru, *Ţărănismul, un suflet şi o politică* (Bucureşti, 1924), *passim.*

27. Charles and Barbara Jelavich, eds., *The Balkans in Transition* (Berkeley and Los Angeles: University of California Press, 1963), xiv. The essay in this volume by Leften S. Stavrianos, "The Influence of the West on the Balkans," is also worth reading.

28. Ion Mihalache, *Partidul Ţărănesc în politica ţarei* (Bucureşti, 1925), p. 27.

29. Roberts, p. 91.

30. Stephen Fischer-Galati, *Twentieth Century Romania* (New York: Columbia University Press, 1970).

31. Eric Hoffer, *The True Believer* (New York: Harper & Row, Perennial LIbrary Ed., 1966), p. 33.

32. Alexis de Tocqueville, *On the State of Society in France Before the Revolution of 1789* (London: John Murray, 1888), pp. 149-152.

33. Robert Wohl, *The Generation of 1914* (Cambridge: Harvard University Press, 1979), p. 29.

34. *Ibid.*, pp. 43, 251.

35. *Ibid.*, p. 47.

36. José Ortega y Gasset, *Obras completas*, I (Madrid, 1950), p. 286. See H. Ramsden, *The 1898 Movement in Spain* (Manchester: University Press, 1974), pp. 42-95.

37. Giovanni Papini, *Un uomo finito* (Florence, 1952), pp. 95-96.

38. See Roberts, pp. 225-226, and Titus P. Vifor, *Doctrina fascismului român, şi anteproectul de program* (Bucureşti, 1924). The most original part of the *Fascia*'s platform was to convert the clubhouses of the disbanded political parties into state-supervised brothels. One is hard-put to see how this would represent much of a change in the status quo.

39. See Roberts, p. 226, note 4.

40. Figures based on a 1924 census of minority groups taken by the state security police. These data, like all Romanian statistics, vary widely, depending on sources. We have used here those of the *Universal Jewish Encyclopedia*, p. 259, to avoid any charge of exaggeration of numbers. See also the *Encyclopaedia Judaica*, 1972 (Jerusalem: Macmillan), p. 394, and Nicolas Sylvain, "Rumania" in Peter Meyer *et al.*, eds., *The Jews in the Soviet Satellites* (Syracuse: University Press, 1953), pp. 493-499 on Jewish population and the Marzescu Law.

41. International Reference Library, eds., *Politics and Political Parties in Roumania* (London: Barron, 1936), p. 10.

42. *Ibid.*, p. 11.

43. Eugen Weber, *Varieties of Fascism*, p. 98.

44. Codreanu, *For My Legionaries*, p. 211.

45. This widely-used description of Codreanu's triumphal procession has the character of the typical Romanian stock story for returning heroes: masses of peasants line the track (or road, or street), priests bless him, he is showered with flowers, etc., and almost literal duplicates can be found for Michael the Brave, Prince Alexander Cuza's entry into Bucharest in 1862, and so on.

46. *Politics and Political Parties in Roumania*, p. 56.

47. *Ibid.*, p. 57.

48. Corneliu Z. Codreanu, *Eiserne Garde* (Berlin: Brunnen-Verlag, 1939), pp. 307-309.

49. Nagy-Talavera, p. 280.

50. Roberts, p. 165.

51. Codreanu, *Eiserne Garde*, pp. 338-348, on the Bessarabian "crusade."

52. Klaus Charlé, *Die Eiserne Garde, eine Darstellung der völkischen Erneuerungsbewegung in Rumänien* (Berlin: Deutscher Rechtsverlag, 1939), p. 23.

53. Nagy-Talavera, p. 283. This point cannot be overstressed; the proliferation of parties, movements, and groups often made it impossible to say whether this or that rightist organization or extremist squad was responsible for specific deeds: thus all were arrested or purged. Blame could be assigned later, to suit one's political needs. It is inescapable that this phenomenon operated in the aftermath of the uprisings of January, 1941.

54. Hugh Seton-Watson, *Eastern Europe Between the Wars: 1918-1941*, 3rd edition (Hamden, Conn.: Archon Books, 1962), pp. 206-207, is quite definite on this, asserting even that Carol supplied the Guard with funds through such politicians as Vaida, Inculets, and Tătărescu.

55. The testimony to Carol's political acumen and Machiavellian abilities is voluminous. See Walter Hagen, *Die Geheime Front: Organisation, Personen und Aktionen Des Deutschen Geheimdienstes* (Linz und Wien: Nibelungen-Verlag, 1950, p. 275ff.

56. See Al. L. Easterman, *King Carol, Hitler and Lupescu* (London: Victor Gollancz Ltd., 1942), 272p.

57. *Politics and Political Parties in Roumania*, p. 57, and Nagy-Talavera, pp. 282-283.

58. George N. Wilson, "The Iron Guard, 1933-1941," Unpublished M.A. Thesis, University of Chicago, 1945, p. 6.

59. Codreanu, *Eiserne Garde*, pp. 399-402.

60. Wilson, *loc. cit.*

61. *Politics and Political Parties in Roumania*, p. 58.

62. Nagy-Talavera, p. 284, and Roberts, p. 175.

63. See "Rumania's 'Strong Man' No. 2," *The Living Age*, CCCLVI (April, 1939), 140-142.

64. Codreanu, *Eiserne Garde*, p. 428.

65. The feeling was mutual; the Legion saw Titulescu and his "Russian policy" as disastrous, villainous, and evil. See Michel Sturdza, *op. cit.*

66. Walter M. Bacon, Jr., *Behind Closed Doors: Secret Papers on the Failure of Romanian-Soviet Negotiations, 1931-1932* (Stanford: Hoover Archival Documentaries, 1979).

67. Paul A. Shapiro, "Prelude to Dictatorship in Romania," p. 54.

68. Codreanu, *Eiserne Garde*, p. 434.

69. Hugh Seton-Watson, *op. cit.*, p. 199.

70. *Politics and Political Parties in Roumania*, p. 59.

71. Rogger and Weber, pp. 537-538.

72. Rogger and Weber, pp. 537-538.

73. *Ibid.*, pp. 539-540.

74. *Ibid.*

75. Codreanu, *Eiserne Garde*, pp. 434, 435, and Countess Waldeck (Rosie Goldschmidt, Countess Graefenberg), *Athene Palace* (New York: Robert McBride & Co., 1942), p. 32, who reports the most plausible story of Codreanu's whereabouts after the Duca murder, namely that he was hidden by the Jewish industrialist Auşnit, who took him to the home of a cousin of Madame Lupescu! Still the episode remains clouded.

76. Hugh Seton-Watson, p. 205.

77. Nagy-Talavera, p. 286, quoting Lebedev, *Rumy'nia vtoroy mirovoy voyny.*

78. *Politics and Political Parties in Roumania*, pp. 233-234.

79. Codreanu, *Eiserne Garde*, p. 436.

80. *Ibid.*, p. 438.

81. "Associaţia prieţenii legionarilor," in Codreanu, *Carticica şefului de cuib* (München: Traian Golea, Colecţia "Omul Nou," 1971).

82. Nagy-Talavera, p. 291.

83. Andreas Hillgruber, *Hitler, König Carol und Marschall Anton-escu: Die Deutsch-Rumänischen Beziehungen, 1938-1944* (Wiesbaden, 1954), p. 13.

84. Rogger and Weber, p. 554.

85. See the archival collection of Bernadotte E. Schmitt, *et al.*, eds., *Documents on German Foreign Policy 1918-1945*, Series D (1937-1945), especially Vol. V, *Poland; the Balkans*, etc. (Washington: Government Printing Office, 1953, Dept. of State Publication 4964), Hereafter, DGFP.

86. Rogger and Weber, p. 553.

87. *Ibid.*

88. *Ibid.*

89. *Ibid.*, p. 546.

90. Codreanu, *Eiserne Garde*, p. 436.

91. *Adevarul in procesul lui Corneliu Z. Codreanu* (Bucureşti, 1938), *passim*, in which the rumor of a Legionary "money factory" turning out counterfeit lei in Răşinari is also discounted.

92. Rogger and Weber, pp. 553-554.

93. Hugh Seton-Watson, p. 285.

94. Nagy-Talavera, p. 291.

95. *Ibid.*

96. Emanuel Turczynski, *op. cit.*, p. 116. See also DGFP, and Virgil Ionescu, "Germania Naţional-Socialista şi Mişcarea Legionara,"

Pământul Strămoşesc, 5 (1979), 90-97. Wilson, *op. cit.*, also touches on this, but glibly believes everything he finds in the *New York Times*. His only proof for German financial support for the Legion is the fact that Education Minister Costacescu, a member of Tătărescu's government which obviously had no love for the Legion, said so in a speech at Iaşi!

97. Interview with Stelian Stanicel, April 2, 1980, Detroit, Michigan. Cf. Also his "Lângă Căpitan," in *Pământul Strămoşesc*, 4 (1978), pp. 5-33.

98. On the general international situation and the options open to Carol II, see Gerald Bobango, "Besieged Dictatorship: Romania Between East and West, 1938-1940," Paper delivered to the annual conference of the New England Slavic Association, Providence, Rhode Island, April 25, 1980.

99. Roberts, p. 190.

100. Cf. Shapiro, *op. cit.*, 58-63, and on the electoral law, Roberts, 102. This was modelled on Mussolini's Acerbo legislation. The party gaining a plurality and at least 40% of the popular vote automatically received half the seats in the Chamber, plus a number of remaining seats according to its percentage of the total vote. Therefore any plurality party gaining 40% of the vote was guaranteed at least 70% of the seats in parliament, the remainder being divided among the other parties which had gotten 2% or more of the popular vote.

101. Shapiro, p. 58; Roberts, p. 191 on voter turnout. An astute analysis of the 1937 elections is C. Enescu, "Semnificaţia alegerilor din decemvrie 1937 in evoluţia politică a neamului românesc," *Sociologie Românească*, 2, Nr. 11-12 (November-December, 1937), 512-526. Also indispensable is Eugen Weber, "The Men of the Archangel," in Walter Laqueur and George Mosse, eds., *International Fascism, 1920-1945* (New York: Harper and Row, 1966), 101-126, for a study of the sources of support for the Legion and the LANC, and their contrasting geographic and socio-economic appeal.

102. Approximately one-fourth of the country's Jewish population of 757,000 (1930 census) might have been expelled under the PNC program. On illegal Jewish immigration into Romania see also Hector Bolitho, *Roumania Under King Carol* (New York: Longmans, Green, 1940), pp. 42-47.

103. *Politics and Political Parties in Roumania*, pp. 174-177 describes the PNC platform at length.

104. Shapiro, p. 51, and note 33.

105. *Ibid.*

106. *Ibid.*, p. 53.

107. *Ibid.*

108. *Ibid.*, p. 54.

109. Nagy-Talavera, p. 295.

110. *Time Magazine*, January 24, 1938, p. 16.

111. Corneliu Zelea Codreanu, *Circulări şi Manifeste* (Madrid: Colecţia "Omul Nou," 1951), and his *Circulări, scrisori, sfaturi, ganduri*, p. 82. Cf. also Hillgruber, *op. cit.*, p. 15, where Goga specifically asks the Germans not to support the Legion. For detailed discussion of this period by one who was at the center of events, valuable is Virgil Ionescu, "Pregatirea dictaturii regale," *Pământul Strămoşesc*, 5 (1979), 79-85.

112. Nagy-Talavera, p. 296.

113. *Almanahul Cuvantul 1941: Ziar al Mişcării Legionare*, p. 44.

114. Codreanu, *Eiserne Garde* (Appendix), p. 455.

115. Forty-two years later, we still have no absolutely reliable account about what happened at this meeting between Carol and Hitler. Compare Waldeck, *Athene Palace*, p. 28, with the more plausible Hillgruber, pp. 26-29. It is also enlightening to note Wilson's description (*op. cit.*, pp. 47-48) of the death of Codreanu and his comrades. The *Chicago Daily News* on December 1, 1938, basing its story on information from M. Fodor, special correspondent in Bucharest, had it all wrong. So did the *New York Times* on November 30, 1938. The result of such immediate acceptance of "official reports" is that even today one finds the erroneous *New York Times* version repeated in what purport to be serious articles or studies on Codreanu, forty years later. It is hard to forbear mentioning once again how little short of ridiculous appears the use of contemporary partisan *Romanian* newspapers from this intensely volatile decade as proofs in an American federal court that so-and-so was this or that.

CHAPTER VII

1. Macinica M. Trifa died on January 1, 1960 in Coiara, south of Brăila, where she and her husband and daughter had been sent into exile by the Romanian communist regime eight years earlier. She never again saw her home region in Transylvania, hundreds of miles away. Dionisie Trifa lives today near Câmpeni. While it hardly seems necessary to document Viorel Trifa's birth as occurring in 1914, on June 28, innumerable writings about him in the mass media today so consistently have his age wrong, one wonders as to their arithmetic ability. Also interesting are stories which all but place Trifa as a founding father of Codreanu's movement, putting him in Moldavia in the 1920s, etc., or marching into Bessarabia in 1930, when he was merely 15 years old.

2. A good example of the militance of the Transylvanian clergy is provided by the pastorate of Policarp Moruşca, first bishop of the Romanian Orthodox Missionary Episcopate of America from 1935-1939. See Bobango, *ROEA History*, 90-120, 200-201, and *passim*.

3. Hugh Seton-Watson, *op. cit.*, pp. 307-308, discusses the differences of mentality between Transylvanian Romanians and those of the Old Kingdom, differences which heightened at times the traditional inter-provincial rivalries in Romania. "The combination of Turco-Byzantine practice and French theory which characterizes the intellectuals of the Old Kingdom is alien to... Transylvanian Roumanians. . . . The centralising tendencies of Bucharest were bitterly resented in Transylvania...." and so on. One finds little of this overtly in Trifa's personality, although one of his strongest objections was the servility of the Romanian regime to Paris. Nevertheless Trifa himself was well versed in French culture as a result of his university studies. His own opinion on regionalism in Romania is that the system of university scholarships opened to young men throughout the country after World War I, and not limited to specific schools which one must attend depending on residence, helped to diminish provincialism.

4. "Faculty" in the Romanian sense is the same as "College" in America, i.e., Trifa attended the College or School of Theology of Iaşi University.

5. One of Trifa's most memorable professors at Chişinău was the renowned Petre Constantinescu-Iaşi, whom he had for Byzantine Church art history.

6. Trifa's licentiate thesis dealt with "The Christian Attitude in the Philosophy of Nicolas Malebranche," the 17th century Cartesian mathematician-philosopher. At the University of Bucharest, had he been able to complete his doctorate, he was preparing a thesis on "Orthodox Lay Missionaryism."

7. His Certificate No. 2308 from the University Theological School, Chişinău, issued on his 21st birthday, June 28, 1935, is in Trifa's possession today.

8. Hugh Seton-Watson, p. 336.

9. Nagy-Talavera, p. 281.

10. Hugh Seton-Watson, pp. 336-337.

11. Roberts, *op. cit.*, pp. 117-118.

12. *Ibid.*, p. 35.

13. Nagy-Talavera, pp. 258-259.

14. Trifa would certainly also have known of Moţa's father even before this, for Ion Moţa *père*, priest in Oraştie, was as well known for his writing and reforming work in Transylvania as was Iosif Trifa.

NOTES

15. Nor is there any central membership list for the Legion containing Trifa's name, for such a list was not kept, in a time when close police surveillance and harrassment of the movement was always at hand. Only after the Legion came to share power with Antonescu in September, 1940, were such lists compiled, and Trifa's name is not to be found, nor is he listed on any of the thousands of membership lists for individual "nests." Many there are who could testify to the relationship of Trifa to the Legion as we have described it, among them Stelian Stanicel, private secretary to Codreanu during this period, and the engineer Nicolae Horodniceanu, today living in San Juan, Argentina, who was Codreanu's Office Manager at No. 3 Str. Gutenberg between 1935-1938.

16. This system, observed superficially by would-be Justice Department historians, may have been the basis for the theories which have circulated over the years that the Legion had special connections with the "Siguranţa," or secret police in the Dept. of the Interior.

17. Interview with John J. Sibişan, Cleveland, Ohio, January 17, 1980.

18. *Cronologie Legionară* (Madrid: Colecţia "Omul Nou," 1953, pp. 122-123, lists the Braşov process for May 17, 1937, though some dates in this listing are in error.

19. Palaghiţa, p. 109.

20. *Cronologie Legionară*, p. 178.

21. Horia Sima, *Sfârşitul Unei Domnii Sângeroase* (Madrid: Editura Mişcării Legionare, 1977), p. 21.

22. In Trifa's possession is his *Studienbuch*, Reichs Nr. A/11282, from Friedrich-Wilhelms-Universität zu Berlin, showing his attendance from 15 January 1940 to 11 September 1940.

23. Interview with Valerian D. Trifa, Grass Lake, Michigan, April 4, 1980.

24. Waldeck, *op. cit.*, p. 13.

25. Nagy-Talavera, p. 299.

26. If this is too strong a word, at the very least it must be admitted that even today there is an identifiable Sima-group and non-Sima group in the Legionary exile community, stemming in part from the divisions of philosophy which followed Codreanu's death and the tactics adopted by Sima during the critical 1939-1941 period. Cf. as an example Ion Fleşeriu, *Amintiri* (Madrid: Colecţia Generaţia 1922, 1977), p. 174 and *passim*.

27. Nagy-Talavera, pp. 297-298.

28. Rogger and Weber, p. 552.

29. Interview with Stelian Stanicel, April 2, 1980, Detroit, Michigan.

30. Rogger and Weber, p. 555.

31. *Ibid*, p. 556.

32. D. Gazdaru, "Note Marginale la Memoriile Lui Virgil Ionescu," *Pământul Strămoşesc*, 5 (1979), pp. 200-201.

33. *Ibid.*, and see Stanicel, *op. cit.*, and the *New York Times*, 5 December 1938, which identified the attorney Ion Victor Voziu as the Legion's "new leader." Once again the *Times* was wrong: it was Ion Victor Vojen.

34. Nagy-Talavera, p. 299.

35. Palaghiţa, p. 109, suggests this, while Virgil Ionescu, *Pământul Strămoşesc*, 5 (1979), pp. 189-190 says it plainly, that Sima was working with (if not for) Carol's secret police.

36. *Cronologie Legionară*, pp. 178-179.

37. Constantin Papanace, "Evoluţia Mişcării Legionare După Arestarea Şi Asasinarea Căpitanului: Cazul Horia Sima," *Pământul Strămoşesc*, 4 (1977), p. 15.

38. See DGFP, XI, No. 360, Neubacher to Minister Clodius from Bucharest, November 19, 1940, relating that "From within the Guard there was a romantic and amateurish attempt at a Putsch by the old Codreanu and a few persons got accidentally killed," while referring to the incompleteness of Sima's authority, he suggests that Sima must "risk a split with his extremists" (p. 628).

39. Corneliu Codreanu's concern for at least two years before his death was that the green shirt was being prostituted, was able to be obtained by just about anyone, and that nests were not being strict as to whom they admitted to membership. Various circulars restricted the wearing of the shirt to special ceremonies and holidays and urged a tightening up of screening for potential members . Cf. *Circulari şi Manifeste* (Madrid: Colecţia "Omul Nou," 1951), Circular 41, 20 September 1936, as an example. He also established a new commission for admissions on November 1, 1936 to combat this tendency.

40. The best testimony for the existence of a "new Legion" around Sima is that of Sima himself, who writes at large of those who "defected" from the group in Berlin during the first exile. In *Sfârşitul*, p. 58, he again lists Trifa as one who lived apart from the Legionary community, and on p. 40 plainly states "Trifa was a traitor." What can this mean, except that many who had supported Codreanu refused to cooperate with Sima, or believed that his strategems for the movement portended disaster? In the end they were right.

41. Codreanu in *Circulari şi Manifeste*, No. 76, had written sarcastically, "I have the impression that these Gentlemen (i.e., the regime, the camarilla) will come one fine day and send us, also, a head of the party," referring to Carol's long-used tactic of playing off party leaders against one another through the back door, by bringing a man to the palace, offering him money, offices, position, then sending him to lead his group, ostensibly as a free agent, but actually to serve the court's interests. Cf. DGFP, V, Wohlthat to Göring, No. 155, 14 December 1937 for one German official's analysis of Carlist technique.

42. Nagy-Talavera, p. 302.

43. *New York Times*, 7 March 1939.

44. Wilson, *op. cit.*, pp. 51-53, for a profile of Călinescu. The Premier had for some time expected assassination, and knew that protection was impossible. Most interestingly, he called the Legion "instruments of maneuver by the politicians," in his diary for May 25, 1936, suggesting that even though he was sworn to crush them, he understood one of the realities of the day. The Legion was a convenient scapegoat to cover the crimes (or policy errors) of whomever was in power. At one point in 1938 the King told Călinescu to use even gas against the Legion, if need be. See Al. Gh. Savu, "Armand Călinescu: Insemnari Politice (I)," *Magazin istoric*, XI, nr. 4 (aprilie 1977), 54-61.

45. Nicolae Minei, "Corespondenţă diplomatică Bucureşti-Bruxelles, Garda de Fier in Solda Germaniei Naziste," *Magazin istoric*, XIII, nr. 9 (septembrie 1979), 34-38; *New York Times*, 22 September 1939; *Chicago Daily News*, 22 September 1939.

46. Nagy-Talavera, p. 304, and Constantin Papanace, *Martiri Legionari* (Rome: Ed. "Armatolii," 1952), pp. 19,21-22, and his "Orientări Pentru Legionari," Newsletters (Erding/Bavaria) beginning with Vol. III, No. 34 (July 1960), p. 10.

47. Hillgruber, p. 66.

48. Easterman, p. 14.

49. *Cronologie Legionară*, pp. 185-187, and Editura Mişcării Legionare, *Legiunea în Imagini* (Madrid, 1977), p. 57.

50. *Time Magazine*, July 1, 1940, p. 25.

51. *Cronologie Legionară*, p. 197.

52. Sturdza, p. 159.

53. *Cronologia Legionară*, p. 189.

54. *Ibid.*, p. 193.

55. *Studienbuch*, n. 22, *supra*.

56. *Cronologie Legionara*, p. 197.

57. Sima goes to some length in *Sfârşitul*, pp. 253-254 and *passim* to show how he had approached Codreanu's father, sought his advice on vital matters, and obtained his approval for his, Sima's, plans.

58. Interview with Valerian D. Trifa, Grass Lake, Michigan, July 30, 1980.

59. *Libertatea*, December 25, 1940, p. 1.

60. *Libertatea*, October 13, 1940, p. 1. That same year Hector Bolitho, in his *Roumania Under King Carol* (New York: Longmans, Green, 1940) was writing, "Roumania was forced into making her unhappy agreement with Germany because, after 20 years of pleading, she realised that British help was uncertain." (p. 59). Speaking

of the diplomatic realignment at the end of 1940, C.A. Macartney and A.W. Palmer note that Russia's policy toward southeastern Europe was the same as always—expansionistic—but "What was new was that France and Britain had temporarily dropped out of the common front which the West had for so long traditionally opposed to Russian expansion towards the Straits. . . the British government had virtually invited Russia to make herself the patroness of the Balkans." Macartney and Palmer, *Independent Eastern Europe: A History* (London: Macmillan & Co., 1962), 427-428.

61. *Ibid.*, and issue of December 15, 1940, p. 1. Churchill put it well when he stated that the Munich Agreement deprived Europe of any system of security and shattered the bonds between East and West. "It must now be accepted that all the countries of Central and Eastern Europe will make the best terms they can with the triumphant Nazi Power. . . . There was always an enormous popular movement in Poland, Roumania, Bulgaria and Yugoslavia which looked to the Western democracies. . . and hoped that a stand would be made. All that has gone by the board." *Roumania at the Peace Conference* (Paris, 1946), p. 10.

62. *Libertatea*, October 20, 1940, p. 1.

63. George E. Woods, "The Undoing," Unpublished MS on the Case of the United States vs. Valerian D. Trifa, Detroit, Michigan, XI, 15-16.

64. *Cronologie Legionară*, p. 203, notes this decree, but the actual legislation appeared in the *Monitorul oficial* for 15 October 1940, pp. 5898-5899, signed by Minister of Education Traian Brăileanu.

65. Woods, MS, XI, 12-13.

66. Easterman, pp. 14-15.

67. *Ibid.*, p. 15.

68. Nagy-Talavera, pp. 318-320.

69. Rogger and Weber, p. 562.

70. Constantin Papanace, *Orientări Pentru Legionari*, p. 10. Also cf. note 39, *supra*. In his famous Circular No. 41, Codreanu clearly foresaw this, and tried to prevent it. The fact that the Captain could not do so makes it the more obvious that neither could Sima. Codreanu wrote even in 1936, "A great danger threatens the Legionary Movement. The admission into the framework of the organization of a large number of weak, even bad, elements. It is well known that whenever a strong current appears in favor of an organization, an entire series of inferior elements invade it—bums, vagabonds, crooks, scoundrels, and so on. Another type is. . . political travelers. . . [Now we are seeing] minor bums, chaff of the villages and the cities, men with no stability."

Clearly also, thousands of those in Green Shirts were hardly representative of Legionarism. Codreanu went on, "the abuse of the green shirt is becoming worse. On every street corner you see the green shirt on one or another body which does not always do it honor, or in dubious places such as saloons, clubs, cafes. Any panderer can enroll in the Legion and the next day be seen on the streets or in a saloon with a green shirt. You county chiefs, are you not disgusted at such a sight? Be attentive! The Green Shirts are our vestments." Cf. Also Rogger and Webber, p. 561.

71. Nagy-Talavera, p. 311.

72. Rogger and Weber, p. 562.

73. Nagy-Talavera, p. 311.

74. *Ibid.*, p. 317.

75. DGFP, XI, Memorandum Foreign Ministry Staff, September 10, 1940, pp. 53-54.

76. Woods, MS, XIII, 15-16.

77. Petre Ilie and Nicolae Aureliu, "În Culisele Conflictului Dintre Horia Sima şi Ion Antonescu," *Magazin Istoric*, I, nr. 4 (iulie 1967), p. 25.

78. DGFP, XI, Legation in Romania to German Foreign Ministry, no. 151, October, 1940, p. 261, and no. 167, Ambassador Ritter to Embassy in Italy, October 9, 1940, p. 277.

79. DGFP, XI, Wehrmacht High Command to Foreign Ministry, no. 84, September 21, 1940, p. 144.

80. DGFP, XI, Neubacher to Clodius, no. 360, November 19, 1940, p. 629.

81. Woods, MS, X, 1-6.

82. Gheorghe Barbul, *Memorial Antonesco, le IIIe homme de l'axe* (Paris, 1950), pp. 73-76, and *passim*; Hillgruber, pp. 117-119.

83. Ilie and Aureliu, *op. cit.*, p. 26.

84. Barbul, p. 94. Nagy-Talavera, p. 324, has the wrong date for the Antonescu-Hitler meeting. For the complete report, DGFP, XI, no. 652, Memorandum by an Official of the Foreign Minister's Secretariat, January 16, 1941, pp. 1087-1091.

85. Even communist historiography has accepted this British connection, as in Mihai Fatu and Ion Spălăţelu, *Garde de Fier: Organizaţie teroristă de Tip Fascist* (Bucureşti: Editura Politică, 1971), pp. 347-348. Trifa's reference to this in his speech of January 20, 1941, was more than just a guess. Nagy-Talavera also calls the assassin, "apparently a British agent" (p. 325).

86. DGFP, XI, no. 631, Fabricius to Foreign Minister, January 9, 1941, p. 1060.

87. Woods, MS, XIII, 15-16. Fatu and Spălăţelu, pp, 344-345 provide the citations from the Arhivele Statului, Bucureşti, fond Preşidenţia Consiliului de Miniştri, Cabinet militar, *inter alia*. The critical documents are Orders 536 and 352, dated January 21, 1941.

88. Woods, MS, XIII, 15-16 and *Pe Marginea Prapastiei* (Bucureşti, Imprimeriile Statului, 1941), esp. Vol. II.

89. Rogger and Weber, p. 566.

90. DGFP, XI, no. 691, Ribbentrop to the Legation in Romania, January 22, 1941 (sent January 23—3:00 a.m.), pp. 1169-1170.

91. *Ibid.*, p. 1169, note 2.

92. Rogger and Weber, p. 566.

93. Matatias Carp, *Cartea Neagra: Suferinţele Evreilor din Romania, 1940-1944*, Vol. I (Bucureşti: Atelierele Grafice SOCEC & Co.S.A.R., 1946), pp. 370-373.

94. Woods, MS, VIII, 9.

95. Rogger and Weber, p. 566.

96. Woods, MS, VIII, 18.

97. The Romanian Jewish community itself accepts Carp's research as the most accurate, which makes it all the more incomprehensible why Dr. Kremer and the Jewish press continue to repeat outrageous figures linking Trifa and the Legion to anywhere from 10,000 to 40,000 deaths: one must conclude that this is merely sensationalist exaggeration for the purpose of gaining attention to their claims. In the *Revista Cultului Mozaic*, January 15, 1975, the official magazine of Romanian Jewry published in Bucharest, is an article describing the commemoration by Chief Rabbi Rosen of the 34th anniversary of the uprising of 1941, noting how the people prayed "with deep piety for the 123 brothers and sisters fallen" in this event. The January 15, 1976 issue contains the same kind of story, but the number of dead is now changed to 120. Yet the Rabbi himself on his American visits has not been innocent of gross distortion of the proportions of the affair.

98. "The possessions of the Jews will in large part be expropriated in exchange for some indemnification. The Jews who came to Romania after 1913,...will be set aside as soon as possible, even if they have become Romanian citizens.... Jews may live here, but may not be the beneficiaries of the resources and riches of this country. In Romania, Romanians must be taken into consideration first of all.... (From an interview given by Marshal Antonescu to the Italian newspaper *Stampa*, reprinted in Romania on September 30, 1940).

99. F. Brunea-Fox, *Oraşul Măcelului: Jurnalul Rebeliunei şi Crimelor Legionare* (Bucureşti, 1944), pp. 21-22.

100. *Curentul*, January 14, 1941. For the text of Trifa's speech (Borobaru's manifesto), *Pe Marginea Prǎpastiei*, II, p. 290.

101. Marin Preda, *Delirul* (Bucureşti, Cartea Româneascǎ, 1975), pp. 256-257. This is the 2nd edition. Since all writing and research on the Legionary Movement in Romania was prohibited by the present regime for more than 25 years, the appearance of this work hit the Romanian reading public like a bolt of lightning; the first edition sold out of the bookstores completely in a matter of weeks. The author owes his possession of a copy to the work of Vasile Bobango.

102. Fatu and Spǎlǎţelu, p. 350.

103. Palaghiţa, pp. 143-144, after describing the Sima-Trifa meeting on January 20, and the dispersal of the demonstration, concludes, "From this date, Trifa gave not one further order and played no role in events which followed."

104. Brunea-Fox, p. 16ff.

CHAPTER VIII

1.The documents are now a matter of record, in Civil Case No. 570924, United States District Court, Eastern District of Michigan, Southern Division, as well as in the files of George Woods, Esq., and those of Trifa himself.

2. See the volumes of the DGFP, and Walter Schellenberg, *Hitler's Secret Service*, pp. 205, 320, 327, and *passim*.

3. See Walter Hagen, *Die Geheime Front* (Linz und Wien: Nibelungen-Verlag, 1950), p. 292, on Sima's flight. Even before this, Hagen notes, "Ribbentrop warned them that, if they will not abide by that rule [no contact whatsoever with Romania], they would be turned over to Antonescu," which reaffirms the hostage conditions. Cf. also Schellenberg, and Sima's own works on his effort to solicit Mussolini's intervention with Hitler on behalf of the Legionaries: an attempt which failed, since the *Fuehrer* by late 1941 had little use for these Romanian meddlers.

4. *Cronologie Legionarǎ*, p. 218.

5. *Ibid.*, p. 219.

6. Kogon's work, translated by Heinz Norden, appeared in English in March, 1958, under the title, *The Theory and Practice of Hell* (New York: Berkley Publishing Corp.). In the 9th edition of February, 1980, the Buchenwald map is on pp. vi-vii.

7. Paul Berben, *Dachau: 1933-1945; the Official History* (London: Comité International de Dachau, 1975), pp. 11, 226.

8. Interview with Valerian D. Trifa, Grass Lake, Michigan, April 4, 1980. Niemöller's incarceration at Dachau is also, of course, a matter of record. The most recent references to the pastor's opposition to the Nazi regime are in David Irving, *War Path: Hitler's Germany, 1933-1945* (New York: Viking Press, 1978), pp. 220-223.

9. Berben, p. 57.

10. Berben, p. 49.

11. Berben, pp. 50-51.

12. Berben, p. 165.

13. Berben, p. 98.

14. Berben, p. 49.

15. Palaghiţa, p. 306.

16. See "Defendant's Answers to Interrogatories," U.S. District Court, Eastern District of Michigan, Case No. (7)570924, 30 August 1978, p. 5, and *passim*.

17. Transcript of Proceedings in U.S. District Court, Eastern District of Michigan, 12 September 1979, p. 7.

CHAPTER IX

1. *Philadelphia Inquirer*, Section B, November 1976, Romanian-American Heritage Center, Trifa Case File (hereafter RAHC file).

2. Susan Morse, "Bishop Trifa Delays Reaction," *Detroit Free Press*, 2 November 1976, RAHC file.

3. *Detroit Free Press Magazine Section*, 26 October 1975, p. 14.

4. *The Miami Herald*, 1 February 1977, 8Aff.

5. On Trutza's life, cf. Bobango, *ROEA History*, *passim*.

6. Columbia Journalism Review (Gloria Cooper, compiler), *Squad helps dog bite victim* (New York: Dolphin Books, 1980), unpaginated. *Milwaukee Sentinel* 10/31/77.

7. *Ibid.*, The *Journal*, The *Citizen*, and *Today* (Ottawa), 10/28/77.

8. *Ibid.*, UPI photo wire, 6/6/75.

9. *Ibid.*, *Milwaukee Journal*, 7/16/76.

10. *Ibid.*, *Peoria Journal Star*, 6/14/70.

11. *Ibid.*, *Milwaukee Journal* 10/26/76.

12. *Ibid.*, *Ann Arbor News*, 11/7/77.

13. *Ibid.*, *St. Paul Pioneer Press*, July 7, '67, *Seattle Times*, 1/1/68, *Contra Costa Times*, 5/31/77.

14. *Ibid.*, *Alamogordo Daily News*, 8/13/75.

15. *Ibid.*, *Tarrytown Daily News*, 8/16/75, and *passim*.

16. *Ibid.*, and see *Time Magazine*, March 10, 1967.

17. *Ibid.*, The *Washington Post*, 8/19/75.

18. *Ibid.*, 11/11/76.

19. *Ibid.*, The *Mountain Echo*, 5/15/75.

20. Godfrey Hodgson, *America in Our Time* (Garden City, N.Y.: Doubleday & Company, 1976), p. 5.

21. See Roland Bauman, "The Party Press in Philadelphia, 1790-1800," Unpublished Ph.D. thesis, The Pennsylvania State University, 1971.

22. This statement, and the series of newspaper headlines, compiled from the MS, "The Incredible Case of Archbishop Trifa," in the RAHC files, the work of the Reverend Eugen Lazar, pp. 1-14.

23. *Ibid.*, p. 14.

24. Charles R. Wright, *Mass Communications: A Sociological Perspective* (Los Angeles: University of California, 1959), p. 110. The absence of antidotal propaganda and its effects are more fully treated in Robert K. Merton, *et al.*, *Mass Persuasion* (New York: Harper and Brothers, 1946).

25. Herbert I. Schiller, "Mind Management: Mass Media in the Advanced Industrial State," in Alan Wells, ed., *Mass Media and Society* (Palo Alto: National Press Books, 1972), 283-295.

26. Gerhart D. Wiebe, "Two Psychological Factors in Media Audience Behavior," *Public Opinion Quarterly* (Winter, 1969-70), p. 523.

27. Schiller, *op. cit.*, p. 292.

28. A vitally important piece of research is C. Hovland and W. Weiss, "Source Credibility and Communication Effectiveness," in *Public Opinion Quarterly* (Winter, 1951-52), pp. 635-650. The experiments on mass communications undertaken by Carl Hovland and his colleagues at Yale showed clearly that changes in source-consciousness and awareness affected source-trustworthiness and thus levels of belief.

29. In his widely-read books, *The Defense Never Rests* (1971) and *For the Defense* (1975).

30. Carolyn Jaffe, "Fair Trials and the Press," in Wells, *op. cit.*, p. 337.

31. *Ibid.*, p. 338.

32. *Ibid.*, p. 339.

33. *Ibid.*, p. 341.

34. Joseph T. Klapper and Charles Y. Glock, "Trial by Newspaper," in Daniel Katz, *et al.*, eds., *Public Opinion and Propaganda* (New York: The Dryden Press, 1954), p. 112.

35. Martin Millspaugh, "Trial by Mass Media?" in Daniel Katz, *op. cit.*, pp. 113-114.

36. Richard B. Morris, *Fair Trial* (New York: Harper Torchbooks, 1967), p. ix.

37. Parish Declaration, Holy Trinity Romanian Orthodox Church, August 30, 1980 (Youngstown, Ohio), p. 1, RAHC file.

38. The shift in American public priorities is well discussed in Hodgson, *supra*, chs. 1-2.

39. Harold King, *Closing Ceremonies* (New York: Pocket Books, 1980, back cover.

40. Wright, p. 91.

41. I. Janis and S. Feshbach, "Effects of Fear-Arousing Communications," *Journal of Abnormal and Social Psychology*, Vol. 48 (1953), pp. 78-92.

42. Leon Festinger, "Behavioral Support for Opinion Change," in Wells, *op. cit.*, pp. 218-226.

43. Henry Feingold, "Four Days in April: A Review of NBC's Dramatization of The Holocaust," *Shoah: A Review of Holocaust Studies and Commemorations*, Vol. 1, No. 1 (1978), p. 15.

44. Feingold, pp. 15-16.

45. As early as 1976 special Holocaust lectures and courses were being offered at Temple University, Elie Wesel lectured at the Pennsylvania State University in State College, Pennsylvania, and at the Williamsport Area Community College: this from personal experience. As we write these words, this morning's edition of the *Detroit News* advertises a number to call for a "Holocaust Education Project" at Mercy College (27 September 1980, p. 13A), the film version of "The Boys from Brazil" is being shown on Channel 4, Detroit, and the three-hour Vanessa Redgrave film about Auschwitz is being announced for two days hence. As George M. Kren, author of the recently published *The Holocaust and the Crisis of Human Behavior* remarked in conversation at Kansas State University, "Thousands *lost* their lives in the Holocaust, and today thousands *make* a living off it."

46. *Shoah, op. cit.*, pp. 1, 14.

47. Abraham Cooper, "Justice, Unlimited," *Jewish Living*, September/October, 1979, p. 63.

48. One must bear in mind also that such mass circulation papers are generally bought and read by far more people than buy the serious *New York Times* or the *Wall Street Journal*, given the general literacy level and tastes of the American public. This writer was speaking to a church group in Los Angeles about media distortion of the Trifa case on the very day this issue of the *Star* appeared, and someone produced it from the audience.

49. Al Dempsey and Robin Moore, *The Red Falcons* (Los Angeles: Pinnacle Books, 1980), p. i.

50. Radio TV Reports, Inc., Broadcast Excerpt, December 6, 1979, New York City, p. 1, RAHC file.

51. *Ibid.*

52. Arthur L. Ginsburg, Chief, Complaints and Compliance Division, Broadcast Bureau of Federal Communications Commission, to V.E. Martin, 18 July, 1979, RAHC file.

53. *Ibid.*

54. Gerald J. Bobango, "Context and Fact in the Case of Archbishop Valerian Trifa," Printed Resolution of the ROEA Ohio and Western Pennsylvania Deanery, adopted by the Church Congress July 4, 1980, (RAHC file), p. 3.

55. *Akron Beacon Journal*, 13 January 1980, p. 2.

56. *Ibid.*, p. 25.

CHAPTER X

1. RAHC, Trifa Case file, Kremer to Guy, 10 March 1973 (Kremer does not have the attorney's name, uses "Dear Sir").

2. *Ibid.*, Salturelli to Guy, 16 April 1973, Detroit.

3. *Ibid.*, Greene to Kremer, 2 March 1973.

4. *Ibid.*, Salturelli to Horowitz, 5 April 1973, and Greene to Kremer, 11 February 1972.

5. *Ibid.*, Gordon to Kremer, 20 November 1973.

6. *Ibid.*, Greene to Javits, 3 July 1973.

7. *Ibid.*, Kremer to Richardson, 14 July 1973.

8. *Ibid.*, Horowitz to Salturelli, 12 June 1973.

9. The *Michigan Journalist*, 50, no. 5 (February 1977), p. 13.

10. Romanian Orthodox Episcopate of America, Church Congress Reports, 1979, "Resumé of the Bishop's Case," p. 2.

11. For Trifa's twenty-year standoff with the Romanian church and government, see Bobango, ROEA, chapters 8-10.

12. ROEA, file Romanian Patriarchate, 1950-1978, "Report on a Visit to Romania," John Meyendorff to Metropolitan Ireney, 1974.

13. *Ibid.*, Patriarchate, Trifa to Archbishop Sylvester, 29 July 1974, and Trifa to Meyendorff, 15 July 1974.

14. *Ibid.*, Trifa to Sylvester.

15. For the story of Mihail Iancu, see Bobango, ROEA, pp. 301-303, and G. Bobango, R. Braga, J. Toconita, *Historical Anniversary Album, 1929-1979* (Jackson, Michigan: ROEA, 1979), St. Simeon entry.

16. ROEA, Episcopate Council Minutes, 1970-1980, session of 30 March 1974, p. 4.

17. ROEA, file Patriarchate, *Scrisoare Deschisă Domnului Anthanase Joja, Preşedintele Asociaţiei "România,"* 1972.

18. *Ibid.*, Metropolitan of Banat to Trifa, 1 December 1972.

19. *Ibid.*, Trifa to Metropolitan Nicolae, 12 December 1972.

20. A postcard in the RAHC, Trifa case file. Sent on 23 December 1967 by Kremer to Rev. Florian Galdau in New York City; not only shows Kremer with Patriarch Justinian, but the dentist is receiving a decoration from the Romanian Orthodox Church, which means from the Romanian state. One must ask exactly what a Jewish-American had done to merit such consideration. The answer may lie in a piece of FBI correspondence accompanying the postcard, which Trifa received at the time, to the effect that the FBI was advised through its own sources that Kremer while in Romania was contacted by the Romanian Intelligence Service, or *Securitate*; he was instructed to attack Trifa as a former fascist in order to destroy his position. While such things may be hearsay, the postcard, Rosen's visits to New York, conferences between Kremer, Horowitz, and representatives of the Romanian Embassy in the United States, and the treatment accorded to Kremer whenever in Romania speak for themselves. In addition, Antonovici, who always seemed to be lacking for money, was able to make a trip to Romania after his various statements about Trifa, where he did not travel tourist class. See also issues of the *United Israeli Bulletin* (New York) for November, 1971, pp. 1,4; June, 1972, p. 3; Summer, 1973, pp. 6,7; Winter, 1973, p. 4. The *Bulletin* took full credit as the source of Blumenthal's *New York Times* article of December 26, 1973, which helped to set off the case once more. In the Spring, 1974 issue, p. 4, it was noted that Blumenthal "based much of his data on exposes that appeared in the. . . Bulletin and on material received from Dr. Charles Kremer and the ADL of B'nai B'rith."

21. Transcript, *Motion to Dismiss*, United States District Court, Eastern District of Michigan, Southern Division, United States of America vs. Valerian D. Trifa, No. 570924, December 11, 1975, p. 4.

22. *Newsweek*, September 8, 1980, p. 27.

23. *New York Times*, 9 January 1980, B1, B5.

24. *Hollywood Sun-Tattler*, 19 March 1979, p. 2A.

25. RAHC, Trifa case file, Misc. Correspondence, July-August, 1980, response to Congress' Memorandum.

26. *Ibid.*, Transcript, "Statement of the Honorable Elizabeth Holtzman (D-N.Y.) Before the Subcommittee on Trade, House Ways and Means Committee, June 22, 1979," 6p.

27. *Ibid.*, Transcript, "Statement of the Honorable Elizabeth Holtzman (D-N.Y.) Before the Subcommittee on Trade, House Ways and Means Committee, June 10, 1980," 3p.

28. RAHC, Trifa case file, Doc. R 201932z Jan 78 FM SecState WashDC to AmEmbassy Bucharest, 2p

29. Transcript, United States District Court, Eastern District of Michigan, Southern Division, United States of America v. Valerian D. Trifa, No. 570924, Summons and Complaint, May 16, 1975, with attached Affidavit of Cause, February 14, 1975, RAHC file.

30. *Ibid.*, Answer to Complaint, October 21, 1975, 2p.

31. *Ibid.*, Motion to Dismiss, December 11, 1975, p. 3.

32. *Ibid.*, p. 6.

33. *Ibid.*, p. 12.

34. Woods, MS, III, 42.

35. Interview with John H. Sibişan, Cleveland, Ohio, January 17, 1980.

36. Interviews with William W. Swor, and George E. Woods, Detroit, Michigan, December 5, 1979.

37. Woods, MS, II, John S. Pruden to Trifa, 17 October 1975.

38. *Ibid.*, John S. Pruden to Trifa, 8 December 1975.

39. *Ibid.*, Gene F. Wilson to Trifa, 22 December 1975.

40. *Ibid.*, and Trifa to Gene F. Wilson, Central Intelligence Agency, 5 January 1976 and A.J. Salturelli to Trifa, 25 February 1976.

41. *Ibid.*, Thomas F. Conley to Trifa, 1 June 1979.

42. *Ibid.*, William J. Bacherman to Trifa, 6 June 1979.

43. On this and the following expenses, consult the ROEA Annual Reports to the Church Congress, under *Raport Anual prezentat la Congresul Episcopiei ţinut.* . . 1976, 1977, and 1978, as well as ROEA, Episcopate Council Minutes, 1970-1980, session of 5 July 1974, pp. 4-5, session of 5 July 1975, pp. 6-7.

44. See *Jackson Citizen Patriot*, 11 October 1976, RAHC file.

45. *New York Times*, 15 October 1976, RAHC file.

46. National Council of Churches News Release, 30 October 1976, RAHC file.

47. *Southfield Eccentric*, 23 December 1976, *et al.*, RAHC case file.

48. *The Detroit News*, 28 June 1976, 5-B, and 11 June 1977, 19-A.

49. *Detroit Free Press*, 22 April 1977, 1A, 6A.

50. *Ibid.*, 26 May 1977, 1A, 12A.

51. *The Detroit News*, 30 July 1977, RAHC file.

52. *New York Times*, 6 January 1979, pp. 1, 18.

53. *Ibid.*

54. *The Detroit News*, 7 September 1979, 3-B; 26 September 1979, 18-A, and cf. Pete Waldmeir column, "Judge Kennedy: Bum Rap," Detroit, September, 1979, RAHC case file.

55. *Ibid.*, 7 September 1979, 1-B, 3-B, 26 September 1979, 1A, 18-A, 14 October 1979, 1A, 14A.

56. *Ibid.*, 26 September 1979, 1A, 18A, and *Jackson Citizen Patriot*, 26 September 1979, D-1, RAHC file. On the Thurmond move, issue of 1 August 1979.

57.*Sunday News*, Detroit, 11 December 1977, Cornelia Kennedy Interview, 3A, 10B.

58. *The Detroit News*, 26 September 1979, 1A, 18A.

59. Others included Professor George Uscatescu, the Reverend Basile Boldeanu in Paris, and former Foreign Minister of Romania Michel Sturdza and his son Ilie Sturdza.

60 Interview with John J. Sibişan, Cleveland, Ohio, January 17, 1980.

61. Transcript of Proceedings of Pre-trial Conference, United States District Court, Eastern District of Michigan, Room 744, November 20, 1979, p. 63ff.

62. *Ibid.*

63. Interview with George E. Woods, Detroit, July 31, 1980.

64. Woods, MS, II, 26.

65. *Detroit Jewish News*, 13 July 1979, p. 12.

66. "The Incredible Case of Archbishop Trifa," MS, RAHC file, p. 48, and Transcript of Motion for Protective Order Adjourning the Taking of Defendant's Deposition, January 6, 1978, Attached Opinion and Order, RAHC file.

67. *Ibid.*

68. *Solia*, January, 1979, pp. 7-8.

69.Transcript, *United States of America vs. Feodor Federenko*, United States District Court, Southern District of Florida, No. 77-2668-Civ-NCR, July 25, 1978, p. 9. RAHC file.

70. *Philadelphia Inquirer*, 21 September 1980, 1B, 7B.

71. Transcript, U.S. vs. Trifa, United States District Court, Eastern District of Michigan, June 1, 1979, *passim*, for this and following material drawn from Motion for Summary Judgment and Memorandum of Law, RAHC file. Cf. also Swor's Motion to Dismiss, note 21, *supra*.

72. Cited in Federenko, *op. cit.*, p. 7.

73. Department of Justice Circular Letter No. 107, September 20, 1909, reprinted in *Immigration and Naturalization Service Handbook*, 6508, 08.1.

74. Woods, MS, II, William H. Webster to Cornelia Kennedy, 29 April 1979.

EPILOGUE

1. *Detroit News*, 1 September 1980, p. 2B.

2. "Statement of Bishop Trifa," accompanying the surrender of his naturalization certificate, August 25, 1980, RAHC file. See also *Time Magazine*, September 8, 1980, p. 55, and "Note Informative pentru uzul Românilor din lumea largă," filed with statement.

3. *Detroit Free Press*, 27 August 1980, pp. 1, 5A.

4. *Jackson Citizen Patriot*, 4 September 1980, pp. 1-2A.

5. *Detroit Jewish News*, 5 September 1980, p. 19.

6. *Detroit Free Press*, 27 August 1980, p. 1.

7. *Detroit News*, 1 September 1980, p. 2B.

8. *Jackson Citizen Patriot*, 4 September 1980, p. 2A.

INDEX

Action Française, 78-80
Acţiunea Românească, 81
Akron Beacon Journal, 206,282
Allen, Charles R., 58,259
Alliance Antisémitique Universelle, 74
Amalienhof, 146-147
America, 6,22,186
Anania, Bartolomeu, 210
Anderson, Jack, 205-206
Andrei, Vasile, 163,174
Anti-Defamation League of B'Nai B'rith (ADL), 208,224,232,283
Antonescu, Ion, 25,28,33,41,45, 53,57,66,68,120,224,232,283 160,162-173,176-178,179-181, 184,242,258,276,277
Antonovici, Constantin, 50,209, 212,257,283
Argeşanu, Gheorghe, 154
Asociaţia România, 209,211

Bagnoli, 186
Bailey, F. Lee, 195,280
Balan, Metropolitan Nicolae, 7,48
Balea, Moise, 3,50
Banea, Ion, 152,154
Barbu, Zevedei, 63,66,260
Barbul, Gheorghe, 168,276
Bell, Griffin, 220
Belloc, Hillaire, 76
Berben, Paul, 183,278-279
Berkenbrueck, 181-182,183
Bessarabia, 75,107,132-136,156, 162,270
Bigg, Clayton E., 42
Blood Bath in Rumania, 28,255
Blue Shirts, see League of National Christian Defense

Blum, Howard, 31,34-35,39,40, 41,50,192,199,256,257
Bolintineanu, Petrica, 139,145-146,159
Borobaru, Traian, 174
Braga, Roman, 224,247,255,282
Braşov, 138,143,145,158
Brăileanu, Traian, 162,178,275
Brătianu, Constantin, 158
Brătianu, Gheorghe, 118,122
Brătianu, Ion I. C., 94,102,259
Brott, Gary N., 247
Buchenwald, 179,182
Buna Vestire, 44

Calendarul Ortodox Solia...1951, 253
Calendarul Solia, 251,252,253, 254,256
Câmpeni, 129-130, 270
Carol II, King of Romania, 15, 66,106,108-109,118,119,120, 121-124,126-128,136,144,149-158,164,267,269,270,273,274
Carp, Matatias, 172-173,277
Carsten, F.L., 66,260
Cartea Neagră, 172-173,277
Carter, Jimmy, 206,220,221
Carulea, Sandra, 247
Călinescu, Armand,110-111,127-128,149,152-154,274
Central Intelligence Agency (CIA), 216-217,246
Cernăuţi, 4,135,144,146,162
Chetian, Charles J., 247
Chişinau, 31,132-133,138,162
Christopher, Warren, 214
Church Congress: of 1929, 4,7; of 1947, 10; of 1948, 17;